THE MURRAY METHOD

JOHN T. MURRAY, SR.

Cover: John T. Murray, Jr., at age 29 months

A golf swing
is not made from separate movements of the body,
  it is a continual motion.
It is not a state of mind,
  but a physical act.
It must be kept simple to feel,
  it happens in less than two seconds.

In playing the game,
each swing is a separate action;
don't try to do more than you can do.
Seek improvement, be as good as you can be.

My wife, Marilyn, deserves special recognition for, among other things, listening to and reading every line of this book several times over.

I dedicate this book to her.

ACKNOWLEDGMENTS

I would like to acknowledge with gratitude the support I received from the late Dr. Ward Wick, a member of Bodega Harbour Golf Links who inspired me to write this book.

In addition, I give special thanks to Jerry Richardson for all his help and suggestions; Anita Gillespie and David Sweet for their fine job of editing; Alfred Franger for his illustrations; Ivan Spane of Studio A for the photographs; Merrill Shields from Octagon Graphics; and Bob Craft from Craft Press.

I also thank Dr. Pete Zidnak, who provided special assistance in editing and organizing this book. I appreciate his invaluable advice and enthusiasm for The Murray Method and this book.

Dr. Zidnak is an emeritus professor of the School of Business at San Jose State University, an honorary member of the Northern California Section of the Professional Golfers' Association, and 1992 recipient of the California Golf Writers Association Golden State Award for service to golf.

About the author

John T. Murray, Sr., a native of Northern California, was introduced to golf at a young age by his uncle, PGA of America golf professional George Twitchell. He started playing golf competitively at age 10 and entered the PGA apprentice program at age 19. In high school he earned letters in golf, football, basketball, and baseball and was offered scholarships in three of these sports.

John received his PGA credentials working full time at the Bennett Valley Golf Course and the Oakmont Golf Club in Santa Rosa while also attending the California State University, Sonoma, where he earned his B.A. in business management. He then played tour golf for three years. He started his head professional career at Bodega Harbour Golf Links in Bodega Bay, as one of the youngest PGA Class "A" head professionals in California.

Currently the Class "A" PGA head golf professional at the Presidio Golf Club in San Francisco, John has been one of the leading golf instructors in Northern California for over 20 years. He and his wife, Marilyn, have two children, John, Jr., and Melinda.

CONTENTS

Introduction

A golf swing can be easily learned.

In learning anything, it is important that the process be as simple and as complete as possible. Learning a golf swing should be no exception, but until recently, simple and complete did not coexist in the learning process.

Too many people believe that their golf swing is successful only if they can precisely coordinate a number of different body movements during the swing motion. But this mechanical approach is complicated and difficult to repeat and is frustrating for most golfers. A golf swing must be kept simple enough so that it can be executed, in its entirety, in the less than two seconds it takes to swing a club.

Unfortunately, over the last 30 years or so, teaching the golf swing has evolved from a simple procedure to one that involves literally hundreds of movements or checkpoints requiring constant attention. We live in a complex, technical world, and evidently, golfers feel a need for the complex and the technical in their golf game.

Golfers have been on a lifelong quest for the perfect swing, the secret move, the *key*. The golf business has been more than willing to accommodate those hungry souls with videos that can freeze a swing 30 frames per second, and with articles, magazines, books, and tapes on how the professionals play.

Let us look more closely at those professionals. One very important fact is frequently forgotten. When the pros were kids, they learned to swing by mimicking the swings of other golfers. They were not interested in sophisticated techniques and complex mechanics, nor did they need them to become good players.

However, once these professionals became successful, many people wanted to know their swing "secrets." So the pros wrote books on key swing techniques, key moves, key thoughts. Analyzing everything piece by piece, these authors emphasized different aspects of the same old mechanical swing. But it is important to understand that their swing keys worked best for them, at their level of play, not yours. The point is that you must learn to play *your* own game, with *your* abilities, *your* strengths, and *your* weaknesses, and seek improvement when desired.

The so-called New Age of enlightened awareness has created yet another approach to golf: the mental approach, which emphasizes imagery, positive thinking, visualization, inner calm, zone finding, and so on. But your ability to control your mind, block out negative thoughts, visualize successful shots, and play a round of inner golf does not necessarily guarantee a successful golf swing. Why?

There is a very strong force within everyone that prevents the human body from physically performing perfectly at command. This force is our nervous system. Most golfers have little problem with practice swings or meaningless shots. But swing with an audience, an obstacle to hit over, or greater importance on the shot, and it is only natural for their bodies to react accordingly—muscles work, twitch, and contract. A swing that was free flowing moments ago has transformed into a spasm. You may have all the intentions in the world to swing correctly, but your nervous system is just too strong and easily overwhelms any effort to swing effectively, even when you try to visualize a good shot or think positively.

Another factor affecting the mental approach is the nature of the golf swing motion. Sports such as baseball, tennis, or basketball involve spontaneous motions that happen quickly while hitting, catching, or throwing a ball. Players must depend mostly on their natural talent and coordination to play the game. In tennis and baseball, the swing plane varies according to the location of the ball. But golf is different. The ball does not move, the player does not run up to it, and the target is stationary. Also, a golf shot is not spontaneous because there is time that passes between positioning yourself over the ball and starting the swing.

Golfers have been led to believe that if they stand over the ball and *concentrate* on everything they are supposed to do, they will do it successfully. This may stun some readers, but the golf swing is not really a product of concentration. There are, of course, some mental processes involved, but they are all done *before* the swing is initiated. Too often, golfers assume that because they are thinking of what they want to do, they will do it. This is simply not the case. A golf swing cannot be locked up in the mind, for if it were, it would stay there. You *concentrate* when you play chess; you *feel* a golf swing.

Generally, the golf swing has been taught in a way that no sport is played: conscious placement of body parts to create a swing. The only problem is, those assembled movements lack effectiveness and consistency, and the harder you try, the worse you get. It is impossible to make a fluid motion by consciously controlling precise physical movements in any sport.

In a Chinese fable written over 2,200 years ago, a walrus asks a centipede, "How do you manage all those legs you have?" The centipede replies, "I don't manage them, my natural mechanism moves without my knowing how I do it." And a snake points out that "one's natural mechanism is not a thing to be changed." *

For 20 years I have been teaching a method of swinging that is different from the conventional approach of mechanics/counter mechanics, of conscious placement of body parts to create a swing. The success of my approach has been remarkable. Beginners hit quality shots consistently, *even in their first lesson,* and find the game enjoyable immediately. Intermediate students learn how easy it is to be more consistent and improve rapidly. Advanced players learn how to produce successful shots when the pressure is really on.

Now let me present The Murray Method to help you more easily develop a golf swing you can trust and enjoy.**

* "The Walrus and the Centipede," from *The Importance of Understanding* by Lin Yutang (Cleveland, Ohio: World Publishing Company, 1960)

** For the sake of simplicity, instructions are written with the right-handed player in mind. Left-handed players reverse the directions.

CHAPTER 1
The Murray Method

The Murray Method blends intellectual understanding of the golf swing with practical guidelines on how to execute it. You will learn a method of swinging a golf club that is both simple and doable in the brief time span you have to swing. A golf swing happens; it is not manufactured or assembled piece by piece. It is not a deliberate, thought-out, sequential action. Remember, a golf swing lasts less than two seconds.

There are very few golf swing principles. The picture below illustrates how basic a complete golf swing is.

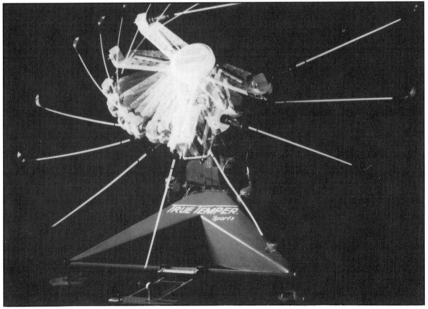

courtesy of True Temper

Notice that the swing machine has a solid base, no lower body drive. All it does is swing the club around in a full circle and hinge where the club attaches. This machine is capable of hitting a ball farther than a human can.

The Murray Method is based on the same principles. You feel and pay attention throughout the entire swing to only three things, which do not change throughout the entire game. They are the basic principles of a golf swing:
1. The swing must stay on a constant swing path,
2. The arc of the swing must return to the same extension that it had at setup, and
3. The swing must be tension free and have speed.

How to swing on a constant swing path, how to maintain a nice full arc, and how to develop speed are the essence of The Murray Method. You will learn to *feel* these things *as you swing* when you follow my method.

It sounds simple enough. The only problem is that these three things will never be automatic, particularly if your impulse is to:
1. *Hit* the ball,
2. Give the swing as much *power* as you can, and
3. *Control* the direction of the shot.

One of the problems with this game (and also one of the joys) is that you can occasionally swing well and astound yourself with a good shot. Unfortunately, you usually have no idea how you did it, so you go back to your old ways and do whatever it takes to survive the round.

If you truly want to learn this game or improve, you must make a very important decision. *Are you just going to try to hit the ball or do you want to learn to swing a golf club properly?*

"OK," you say, "I'll swing the golf club. But where's my guarantee that I'll make good contact if I'm swinging the club so freely? I need that guarantee or my 'hit' tendencies will take over just to make sure I hit that ball. If I swing and miss a baseball or tennis ball, that's OK, it's all part of the game. But nothing is more embarrassing than to miss a ball that is just sitting there. Furthermore, I need to know where power comes from or I'm going to try to kill that ball every time. And I need to know how I'm going to hit a ball straight or how I'm going to try to steer the clubface to the ball and the ball toward the target."

The Murray Method clarifies these issues.

The reason the clubhead comes back to the point from where it started at address is simply that you are *swinging the club on one continual swing plane.*

It is very easy to swing the club on the proper swing plane; however, it will never be automatic, and you need to *feel it as it happens.* To get the club into your proper plane in your backswing, simply use . . .

The Murray Method
SWING COMPONENT #1:
Feel the left hand PUSH the grip and arms straight back into your backswing slot or swing plane.

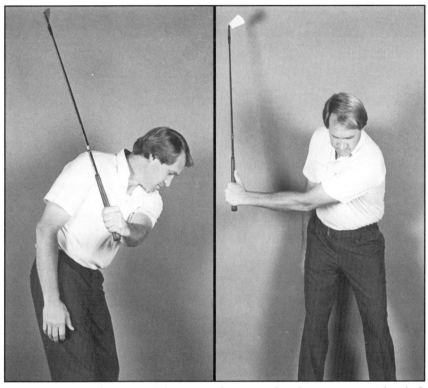

Because of your address and upper-body position, the left hand pushes the grip and the arms in only one direction, straight back. Straight back is *your* proper backswing swing plane.* When you feel your left hand push back, the club will not abruptly lift up or wander outside or inside the proper swing plane as it does so easily when you manipulate a shoulder or back turn. To establish the feel of this motion, grip the club with only the left hand. Push the grip straight back. Notice how the arm travels across the upper body and into one single swing slot with every backswing.

*Technically, the golf swing is on a tilted inside plane. This is of no consequence because all you have to do is feel the left hand push *your* arm straight back. Your posture, skeleton, and push back take care of what plane the arms, hands, and club swing on unless you deliberately manipulate it otherwise.

3

However, your backswing plane can vary if you grip the club with only your right hand and pull the club back. Notice how the club can easily wander outside or inside or travel up instead of back. Why is this?

When the right hand pulls the club back, your right shoulder joint is open, free to move all over the place. Pulling the club back with the right side can also be quick and snappy, which can result in erratic backswings.

The problem with the left-hand push back is that it will never be automatic; you need to pay attention to feeling it on every swing. If you do not, the right side is more than willing to take the club back, and you will automatically engage your hand-eye linkage (the "see-it-and-hit-it" syndrome). All you can do at this point is to try to hit at the ball with the clubhead—and the swing is gone.

Just as an aside, isn't it funny how we call it a backswing and then end up changing it to a "takeaway," maneuvering it back instead of swinging it back. You must *feel* push back and swing and not assume it will happen just because you think it.

The importance of the left-hand push back is proven by demonstrating my one-arm-looking-away shot. I set up for a golf shot, look up directly at the student, and *feel* my left hand push the grip and arm straight back, not up.

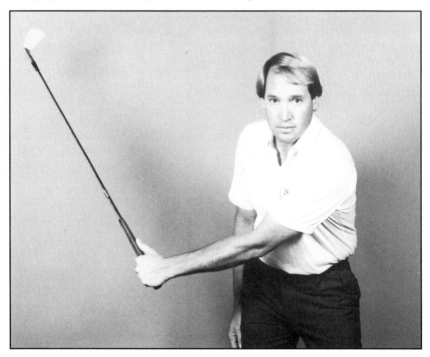

Then I let the arm swing freely to the other side in the proper plane. The shots are always successful when ball contact is trusted to the swing plane.

I have beginning students close their eyes or look up from the ball and feel the right hand take the club back. They clearly feel the arm and the club wander into their backswing and then find that the swing path rarely brings the clubhead back to the ball. I then have them push the grip straight back with the left hand, and they are amazed at how consistently the clubhead comes back to the ball.

Once you fit your hands, arms, and grip into the proper backswing slot, you must neutralize—that is, you must not pull down, push down, transfer weight, drive legs, turn shoulders, shift hips, or perform any of the other downswing movements that are commonly suggested. Use . . .

The Murray Method
SWING COMPONENT #2:
Let the arms, hands, and grip simply swing to the other side, TENSION FREE.

As you swing to the other side, your arms, hands, and grip *will* return on the same path. Swing your golf club around yourself as you would a baseball bat. Notice that you simply swing the club around, with no particular body part initiating the swing. The arms swing around, and the motion of the swing pulls the rest of the body through. In The Murray Method, instead of body movements creating the swing,

THE MOTION OF THE SWING CREATES ALL THE NECESSARY BODY MOVEMENTS.

You do not want to apply force from your arms or hands or create movement from your legs, hips, or shoulders to interfere with this very simple motion. It is at this point that so many golfers make a critical mistake. Because they fear making a bad shot or missing the ball, their free-flowing swing vanishes and their control tendencies take over. Their eyes see the ball, and their mind understands that the ball needs to be hit and engages the muscles to do so. The moment their arms *bring* the club down, any swing they may have had is gone. *Swing, do not bring!* Trust that your clubhead returns to the ball because your club is on a constant swing plane. Your see-it-and-hit-it tendencies must never restrict your free-flowing swing.

Furthermore, *never stiffen any part of the body during the swing.* Body parts do not work properly when locked; if they are, injuries are likely. The arms and the rest of the body have very specific roles in the golf swing, but one thing they do not do is *work*. The arms serve the same purpose as the shaft of your club— they maintain the extension of the arc. Not by stiffening or bringing, but by swinging freely, back and forth, tension free. Remember, your clubhead *will* return to the ball because you are on a constant swing plane.

↦ CHAPTER 2 ↤
Grip and Stance

Before you learn to swing, you must have a proper foundation of grip and stance. Never tamper with your grip and stance when problems crop up. Only when executing short shots or specialty shots (see Chapters 5 and 8) may you adjust your grip or stance.

Just as you are trying to repeat the same swing throughout the game, you also want to set up precisely the same way every time. The setup consists of two parts: the grip and the stance.

Type of Grip

The grip connects your hands to the club. Once you learn the proper grip *for you,* do not mess with it. Too many golfers adjust their fingers and hands when shots go wild or, in their nervousness, they milk the grip and move their fingers and hands without even noticing. Learn to grip the club and then *leave the grip alone!*

Place your left hand on the grip as illustrated below, the thumb stretched down the middle and the top of the heel pad level with the end of the grip. Make sure the grip is in the base of the fingers and not in the palm of the hand.

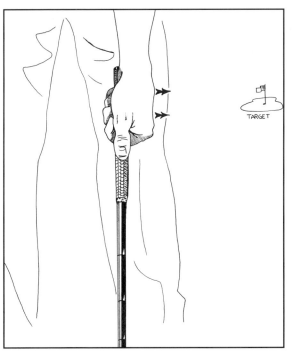

There are three ways to place the right hand on the grip. One is the full-finger grip in which all five fingers of the right hand are placed on the grip. However, in this grip the hands tend to work independently of each other, which is something you want to avoid.

Another grip is the interlock in which the index finger of the left hand and the little finger of the right hand intertwine. The problem with this grip is that you might as well break off your left index finger, for it is completely useless when it is not resting on the club. Right-handed golfers using the interlock find that the already strong right hand is now even stronger than the left.

I believe the third grip, called the overlap, is the best. Like the interlock, the overlap keeps the hands working together as a unit; however, unlike the interlock, this grip utilizes your strongest finger, the left index finger.

To overlap, place your left hand solidly on the grip. Lift up the little finger of your right hand and slide your right hand up until your right ring finger reaches your left index finger. Then lay your right little finger on top of your left index finger or in between the middle and index fingers.

To check the proper position of your hands on the grip, the back of your left hand and the palm of your right hand should point toward the direction of your shot as shown below.

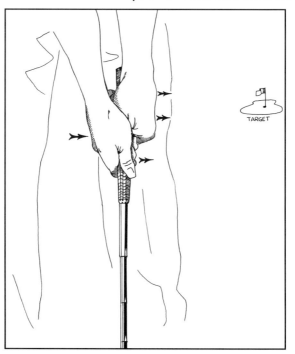

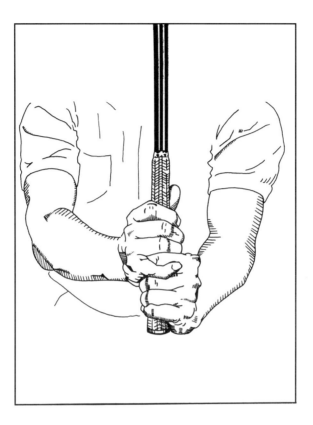

The illustration above shows how your grip should look from underneath. The right little finger overlaps the left index finger. The right thumb extends down and slightly to the left side of the grip. Notice the butt of the grip is level with the pad of your left hand.

Grip Pressure

The hands and wrists play a vital role in sports. The proper grip pressure in golf involves all fingers grasping the club firmly enough so that the club will not slip in your hands or let go and create gaps between your fingers and the club, but supple enough so that the wrists can waggle the club back and forth. There are *no* particular pressure points; all the fingers work together as one unit.

The Murray Method
SWING COMPONENT #3:
The wrists must remain supple throughout the entire motion so that RELEASE is possible.

To test for proper suppleness, hold the grip with your left hand and grab and twist the clubhead with your right hand. You should feel your left fingers holding firmly onto the grip, but your wrist should be supple, not rigid or stiff. Now put your right hand on the grip with the same amount of pressure and waggle the clubhead around, flexing at the wrists. If you have ever watched the pros on TV, you have seen many of them do this as they prepare to swing. Why? They are making darn sure, even though there is a lot of tension and adrenaline flowing through them, that their wrists will remain supple. In fact, you see some version of this waggling in almost every sport when the player is in lag time.

What Is Release?

Release is what the hands and wrists naturally do in all sports motion as long as the wrists remain supple. What exactly do the hands and wrists do when releasing in the golf swing? *They do what your skeleton wants them to do as the arms swing into your backswing and back over to your follow-through.*

Stand straight with your arms at your sides. Now put your arms straight out as illustrated below. Notice how your palms are facing straight out. Now swing your left arm down and up to the right.

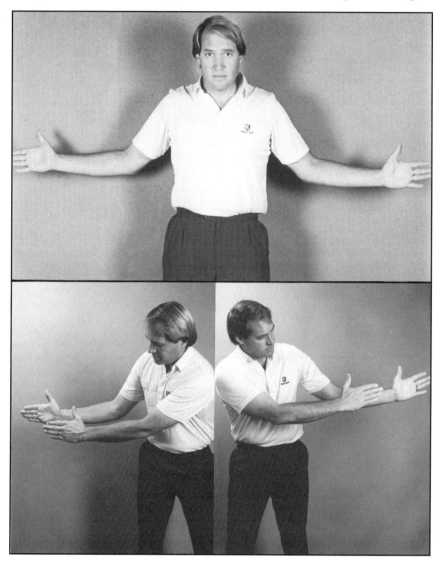

As the left hand and arm swing up to the right, the palm goes from facing outward to facing inward. Notice that the palm of your left hand is now facing you.

Now swing both arms to the other side and observe that your palms have turned over. Why has this happened? Because that is the way the human skeleton works!

Now for the important wrist action of golf. Grip your club. With supple wrists, feel your left hand push the grip straight back. Notice how flat the left wrist is in the backswing.

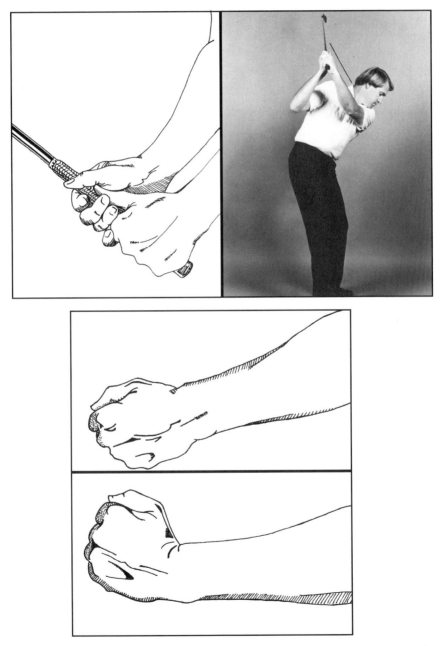

The wrists hinge up and down as when you hammer a nail.

Let's look at some other wrist movements. The wrists can hinge back and forth, concave and bent. The right hand desperately wants to pull back or pick up the club into the backswing. When the right hand pulls back, the left wrist bends. When the right hand picks up, the left wrist becomes concave.

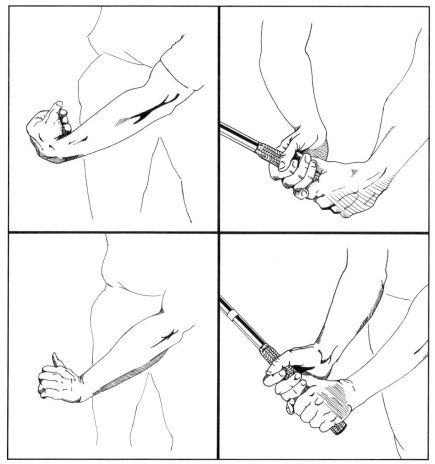

At this point not only do your hands *feel* floppy and out of control, they *are!* When the wrists hinge properly, they never lose their squareness throughout the swing, and you are in perfect control, *without deliberately controlling your hands!*

For a free-swinging action, you should *never tell your hands what to do.* You pay attention only to proper pressure throughout the swing so the hands and wrists can do whatever they want to do *according to your skeleton, not your mind.* When you deliberately try to control or manipulate the hands and wrists you add a destructive, tension-building factor to your golf swing.

The Stance

Your stance positions your body to the ball and involves proper posture, ball placement, and desired alignment for the direction of the shot. Your stance remains the same with every full-swing shot in golf. Just like your grip, don't tamper with it. Get it set and leave it alone!

Your stance should never feel uncomfortable. Too many golfers get themselves into twisted positions and feel strained in their setup. This makes it impossible to have any semblance of a swing and also opens the door to injury. A stance should be very easy to assume.

1. **Stand straight.**
2. **Position your feet shoulder-width apart.**
3. **Roll your knees inward so that your weight shifts to the insides of your feet.**

Your weight is not on your toes or back on your heels but evenly distributed along the insides of your feet. Don't press the knees tightly, just roll them inward lightly, keeping tension out. *Do not bend your knees or allow them to stiffen.*

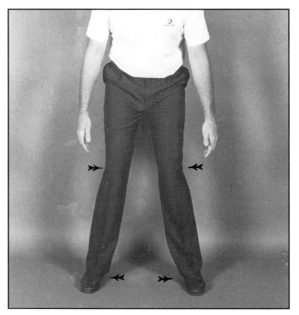

If I told you to bend at your knees, how much would you bend? You would bounce in the knees until you thought it was about right, or I would say bend more, not too much, and so on. You see the problem; bending varies. And there is no room for variation in the setup.

4. Push your buttocks out.

Make sure your lower back is flat. If you feel strain in your lower back, you are pushing out too much. You also do not want to feel the weight of your upper body lean over to the point where you feel your stomach, thigh, or back muscles strain.

5. Let your left arm hang straight down.

Do not stiffen your arm. It is unfortunate that golfers are often told to keep the left arm stiff to prevent arc collapse. That's the last thing you want to do. Stiffening the arm tightens the shoulders, which restricts your backswing, stiffens the hands and wrists, and prohibits release. Remember, at no time, in any other sport, do you ever stiffen any part of your body. Just let your arm hang straight down. Now grip the club. Where your arm is hanging is where your skeleton naturally wants to go. This posture is vital if you are going to truly swing, for *every swing in golf.*

Many golfers make the mistake of reaching the arms out to set up to the ball, especially when using the longer clubs. This causes a strain in the lower back from bending over, but more important, it flattens out your arc, which creates all kinds of erratic shots to the left and right.

You are determining exactly how far you are from the golf ball when you ground your club (placing the clubhead on the ground behind the ball), letting your left arm hang straight down. In addition, grounding the club helps release tension that would otherwise exist if you held the clubhead above the ball at address.

Also, if you are in any position other than where your skeleton wants to hang your arm down, you must engage hand-eye coordination and *bring* the club back out to, or in to, the ball. The swinging ceases and the "hitting at" begins.

Ball Placement

If all your clubs were the same length, you would be free to play the ball from one location in your stance. They are, however, all completely different in length. A set of clubs consists of three groups, each requiring the ball to be played differently in your stance.

Group 1, short irons, 7-, 8-, and 9-irons, pitching wedge, and sand wedge: The ball is played in the center of your stance.

Group 2, mid irons, the 4-, 5-, and 6-irons: The ball is played slightly to the left of center to accommodate the slight increase in length of the club.

Group 3, all other long clubs: The ball is played off the inside left heel.

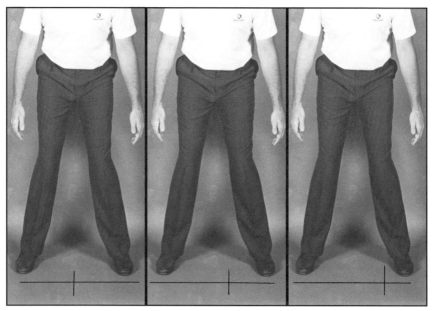

Once your setup is complete, which means club selection has determined the desired distance of your shot, and stance has determined the direction in which you intend the ball to go, you must change gears and forget the shot. Now you must be a swing maker and *feel* your swing!

16

⇒ CHAPTER 3 ⇐
The Half Swing

To learn anything, you must start out slowly and develop one stage before going on to the next. Learning the golf swing is no exception to that rule.

This is the reason for the half-swing exercise—to learn to swing by developing good-quality, consistent ball contact with little swings first, building your confidence, and going on to the full swing from there. The half swing is not an *easy* swing; it's just a smaller, scaled-down swing.

Some instructors teach you to swing as hard as you can and worry about consistency later. The problem with this advice is that it is not in keeping with what is important in playing the game. To score well in golf, it is important to hit good shots consistently, not an occasional super shot mixed with mostly bad ones. Beginning tennis players, for example, try not to slam one-hundred-mile-an-hour shots at each other; they just try to rally. If you are an ice skater, remember the first time you were on the ice. Did you start skating with big, flowing strides? Of course not. You took little steps, careful not to fall on the hard ice. As you became more familiar with the ice, your strides got bigger and you actually started to skate.

You should use the half swing to start a practice session or to fall back on when you are not satisfied with your full swings. Practicing the half swing develops your ability to contact the ball squarely and consistently. This accomplishment breeds confidence, and confidence helps you develop a freer swing with more speed and consistency when you move on to the full swing. Distance in golf comes not overnight but gradually, from sustained practice.

Take your grip and stance. *Feel* your left hand, and with supple wrists, push the grip and your arms straight back to about waist-high.

Notice that there is not a lot of movement going on in your body when you push back to waist-high. This isn't because your body is locked or rigid; it's simply because not much is going on at this point. *Your body does whatever that particular size swing asks it to do.*

When you push your hands and arms to your proper backswing point, which I will call "A," neutralize and let the arms, hands, and club swing to the same position on the other side, or point "B."

This is a critical point in your swing. You are performing this exercise to convince a part of your brain that it is not necessary to engage your hand-eye linkage and deliberately *bring* the clubhead down to *hit at* the ball. When you push back and then let the arms swing freely to the other side, the arms and the club stay on the same path they went back on; the ball is simply in the way of the club swinging back and forth. Supple push to "A" and free flow back to "B." This motion is similar to that of a pendulum swinging back and forth, continual and uninterrupted from one point to the other.

Most golfers have no problem pushing the club to "A"; it's swinging to the point on the other side that causes problems. In most cases, "B" is greater than "A," because of the energy burst from the arms trying to rip the cover off the ball. Instincts are very strong here, and the arms are not content with the passive role of merely swinging. They want to be strong and to work hard. Practice this swing a great deal. Remember, let the arms swing freely to "B" without letting your muscles work!

Sometimes golfers let "B" be smaller than "A"; in other words, their follow-through is shorter than the backswing. Their impulse is to engage their hit-at-the-ball tendency instead of swinging, thereby creating a stopping action just after impact with the ball. Decelerating at the ball is quite common when the golfer becomes overly concerned about making contact with the ball with the clubhead. The golfer is not swinging from "A" to "B" but from "A" to ball.

Success with half-swing shots should help eliminate the hit impulse and convince you that the club *does* return to the ball while you swing freely. Keep in mind, however, that there is no power in the half-swing shot, not because you are swinging easy, but because the size of the swing arc is small.

Your backswing is always a deliberate motion. If there is any time your muscles work, it is in moving the club back. From that point, neutralize your hands and arms and freely swing the club to the other side. Otherwise, do not consciously work any other muscles throughout the remainder of the swing! Arm flow does not mean arms swinging easy or hard. It simply means swinging freely from "A" to "B."

The best clubs to use for the half-swing exercise are the 5-, 6-, 7-, and 8-irons. The difference in distance between clubs in the half swing is not too significant. In other words, your 5-iron may not go any farther than your 8-iron. Why? Because the dynamics of the longer clubs are not in effect with a half swing. There is very little additional clubhead speed from and an 8-iron to a 5-iron. Do not expect relative difference in distance or you will be sure to give the shot an energy burst from the arms, trying to add power with the longer clubs.

CHAPTER 4
The Full Swing

Once you are satisfied that your half swings are consistent and of good quality, you may now proceed to the full swing.

It is very important to understand that a bigger swing is just a bigger arc. But what does common sense tell us to do when we swing bigger or, for that matter, have a club in our hand that is supposed to hit the ball farther? Well, to swing harder, of course. And what swings harder? The arms and the shoulders swing harder, and the legs and the hips start to drive harder. *Do not let this happen!* A bigger swing or longer club is just that, a bigger arc, and the object at the end of the arc, the clubhead, is moving faster, following a simple principle of physics. All bad swings and poor shots are a result of muscles working incorrectly. Muscles at work create tension. And tension is the root of most bad swings and poor shots.

How full is a full backswing? Everyone has a particular maximum backswing point. Your maximum backswing point, to full-body torque, is achieved by continued pushing of the grip back until you run out of *flex in your left shoulder joint,* as illustrated below.

You must always feel that full stretch on every full swing. If you don't, you may have done one of the following:

Not pushed back to full-shoulder stretch. If you cut your backswing short, the mind has to make a quick decision. You have eliminated centrifugal force with this shortened backswing, so your mind calls upon your strong arm, shoulder, back, leg, or hip muscles to lunge or push into the ball to play catch-up and apply some force to the shot.

Common sense tells you that if you are not hitting good shots with a full backswing, you should cut the backswing down to keep the swing compact so that the clubhead meets the ball. If the intention is to have a full-distance shot, where is the power going to come from? Certainly not from centrifugal force with this shortened backswing. So what is left? Nothing else but a body lunge or an energy burst from the strong muscles, especially from the right side. Bad shots will follow, I assure you.

Turned your shoulders or back excessively. The golfer who has little or no body turn often tries to correct the problem by consciously turning the shoulders or back. Unfortunately, this is the wrong remedy. The lack of upper-body turn is caused by a rigid lower body or right-hand pickup.

When you push back to full stretch, your shoulders turn properly without your making a conscious effort to turn your shoulders or back. As the left hand pushes, the left arm travels back, and as the arm goes back, the shoulders turn.

To see how much you can throw your swing off its plane, try this simple test. With the club in your hands, push back to full-shoulder stretch.

Now consciously turn your shoulders. When you are told to turn your shoulders or back, you only flatten out your arc, spinning your body around similar to that of a baseball swing instead of back and forth on a more upright plane. Once the golf swing is off its track or swing plane, all sorts of errant shots can follow.

Collapsed your arc. This often occurs when you allow the right side to pick up the club on the backswing rather than feel the left hand push the club back. This more than likely will create a snappy backswing, causing arms, fingers, and wrists to break down the arc at the top of the backswing. Golfers with fast backswings are told to slow them down. But all this does is create an unbalanced swing. If you take the club back slow, will you have a slow downswing? The backswing and the downswing would have different tempos, and that type of movement is not true swing rhythm. As long as your left hand pushes the club and arms back into your backswing, it is physically *impossible to have too fast a backswing.*

It is common for golfers to try to "get the club to parallel," or parallel to the ground, at the top of the backswing. The only problem is that most of us are not that flexible to properly reach so big of a stretch. In an attempt to reach that position, golfers hinge at the elbows. A common correction to hinging elbows is to keep the left arm stiff. But once you stiffen your arm, everything tightens. Your left shoulder joint loses its flexibility and your wrists loose their suppleness. There is also the possibility of hitting the ground too hard, jarring your body, which will irritate tendons and joints as well as the wrists, elbows, shoulders, neck, and back bones.

Another arc-collapser is loose fingers, a common over-correction to a tight grip. Once this happens, your fingers let go of the grip at the top of the backswing, or the club slips in your hands at impact with the ball or on the follow-through. Remember, fingers should be firm enough on the grip so that there is no slippage, but the wrists should remain supple!

Center movement. Your swing arc can be detrimentally affected by excessive movement from your center. Golfers commonly sway or lift in their backswings, trying to create their biggest possible backswing.

An arc is part of a circle. For any circle to be perfectly round, the center of the circle must not move about. A good golf swing is one in which the arc swings around the body while the body remains on a center axis. The center of your swing is your sternum. If you had a giant compass, this point would be found in your lower chest and the pencil would start at the clubhead, making a perfect circle.

It is difficult sometimes to feel the difference between a good push to stretch and a sway or lift. But you can observe your own movement. Imagine a beam between your eyes and ball at setup. Take a backswing and sway to your right side.

Notice that the beam between your eyes and the ball is now at an angle instead of straight down as it was at setup. Your center has moved to the right. Instead of a circle, your swing arc has taken on more of an oblong shape.

It is common for golfers to believe that shifting their weight from side to side will somehow give power to their swing. As we have discussed in previous chapters, power is clubhead speed, but this shifting of weight from right to left is hardly a fast movement. What this does to your swing is decrease your chances for consistent ball contact. Once you move off center, you had better move back. On occasion you can return to center and hit a good shot, but it is very difficult to establish consistent ball contact when your arc center moves about during your swing.

Swinging to the Other Side

This is where you can make or break your golf swing. In a full swing, because the clubhead is so far from the ball at the top of the backswing, golfers often attempt to *bring* the clubhead down at the ball just to make sure they hit the ball. At that moment, any semblance of a swing has vanished, and you are simply hammering at the ball. You must swing to the other side!

Swing or flow to the other side *as fast as you can swing tension free.* Now hold your club like a baseball bat. Swing freely around yourself and notice that your arms are not *bringing* the club around, but are merely swinging around, freely and uninterrupted. The extension of your arms is maintained not by stiffness but by continual motion and elastic arms. Try to imagine the tachometer in a car. The engine runs at top efficiency when the needle runs right up to the red line but not in the red area. If the needle goes into the red, the engine is straining and working too hard. Your swing should never enter the red.

Your arms are elastic like bungee cords, swinging with free centrifugal force around you but not to a point where you are straining any muscles or red lining your swing. However, arms do not like this passive role; they want to be the strong parts of your body and hit the ball hard. The hands also do not like the passive role of just being fast. They want to be strong, delivering a force into the grip, down the shaft and firmly into the ball. Trick shot artists demonstrate this is not the case regarding the deliverance of power to a golf ball. Using a driver with a rubber hose for a shaft, they swing away, and, to everyone's surprise, their ball flies as far as any drive with a steel shaft.

Practice hundreds of swings without a ball, experimenting to find out just how fast your arms can freely flow *without letting your muscles "work" anywhere throughout the entire swing.*

The feel of power can be very deceptive. When you hit with your maximum clubhead speed, your most powerful swing, there is a part of you that says, "Wow, I know I can swing harder than that!" I have seen, time after time, a student hit a career shot only to flub the next one with a harder swing. Remember that your most powerful and efficient swing is not your hardest swing; it is your fastest swing.

Swinging too easy is just as damaging as swinging too hard. You never want to run your engine too slow, because when the engine lags, efficiency is poor. It takes working muscles to slow down your swing from its natural free rhythm, just as muscles work to swing hard. Unfortunately, when golfers swing too hard, their immediate response is to over-correct and swing easy, slow, relaxed, or loose. *Never swing easy, slow, relaxed, or loose!* Swing your golf club again like a baseball bat. Let it swing freely around and hear the wind whistle. You are not swinging easy, not swinging hard; you are just swinging around with good centrifugal force. The golf swing is similar, only on one constant swing plane. It is vitally important that you *feel a supple push to "A," maintain center, and let the arms flow, tension free, to "B."*

The Role of the Body

There has been a tremendous emphasis placed on leg drive, hip turn, and weight shift to power a golf shot. But do these movements really give you that much power? Let's take a closer look.

It is very important to understand power in golf. Is power an act of hitting a ball as hard as you can with strong muscles? Imagine the strongest man in the world with a sledgehammer in his hands. In one sense, he is very powerful and could easily knock down a stone wall. But have him hit a golf ball with that sledgehammer and the ball would go nowhere.

What about the source of power in other sports? Do the legs deliver the power? When a pitcher throws a ball, there is certainly a lot of body motion. But is that the source of his power? Let's take one little part of the pitcher's body—his wrist—and tape it up so there is no mobility, no release. Let that pitcher drive, shift, thrust his body as hard as he can and guess where the ball will go. It may not even reach home plate! Swing a baseball bat with tight wrists and see how awkward the motion seems. Try shooting a basketball with no wrist release. It just doesn't work.

What most golfers don't realize is that the pros are not swinging out of their shoes on every shot. Only on a need-be basis do they stretch out their swings and call on every part of their body to kick in 100 percent. Even then they fully understand that they are putting quality and control at risk. Also, keep in mind that the

27

professionals practice and play many hours a day most days of the week throughout the year and that they are very familiar with the intricacies of their swing.

Remember, the woods are full of long ball hitters. The possibility of adding a slight distance to your drive can hardly be justified when control is sacrificed. An attempt to incorporate legs and hips as independent movements is surely the amateur golfer's biggest misconception of the golf swing—if not done just right, these movements can result in horrifying shots and tremendous frustration.

Where Does Power Come From?

Power in golf is clubhead speed. The large parts of your body—legs, hips, shoulders, back, and arms—do not move fast; they are powerful but not when we define power in golf. The parts of your body that move fast are the smaller parts, the hands and wrists.

Power in golf comes from the continual, free-flowing motion of the arms swinging tension free around yourself, fast enough to build centrifugal force so that supple wrists release.

Finishing the Swing

What and where is the finish of your swing? The finish of your swing is where *your* swing finishes. There is no one position that all golfers can achieve, and watching the tour professionals attests to that. There are just too many different body shapes and sizes and types of swings to expect a standard swing finish. *Your* finish is where *your* free-flowing swing to the other side puts *you.* Here's an important swing fact: Whatever motion your body makes on the backswing, the same motion should occur on the follow-through. In a full swing, when you push to full shoulder stretch, you have indeed made a body turn without making a conscious effort to turn anything. When you freely swing to the other side, the motion of the swing will pull to the left side whatever body parts that need to move, without any concentrated effort on your part to shift, slide, or drive over to the left side! Your hands and arms will naturally flow to where they will finish unless you somehow manipulate and try to put them someplace else. Swing freely and be done with it!

Learning how to execute a full swing is just one phase in the process of learning to play golf. Golf also requires swings that are less than full, and they are an important part of playing the game. Let's look at these now.

CHAPTER 5
Short Shots

The short game involves any shot that is not a full swing. Your shortest club, either the pitching wedge or the sand wedge, can hit the ball a particular distance with a full swing. But your short game starts when your distance falls inside that full-swing distance and includes putting, chipping, pitching, and sanding.

In the long game, you have the luxury of choosing from a whole bag of clubs to determine distance, and you pay attention to only one swing. But in the short game you have only one club, and you pay attention to only the *size* of your swing, nothing else.

What becomes most important in the short game is to develop a *feel* for what size swing you must make for the desired distance. You swing the club from one point on the backswing to the opposite point on the follow-through. Use no extra force or in any way *bring* the club to or *hit at* the ball, but swing as a pendulum swings, from one point to the other. Let the weight of the clubhead and the size of the swing be the only contributing force to the shot. Stay the heck out of the way of a very simple process! Do not let your muscles engage. Never hit the longer shots *harder* or shorter shots *easier.* Many golfers ease up on the shorter shots. But how easy are you going to hit the ball? A little tap, maybe a little harder? Who knows? If your shot needs to go farther, how hard do you hit it . . . a little harder . . . not so hard, harder yet? Who knows?

By letting the size of swing determine distance, practicing certain size swings, and seeing how far the ball goes with that swing, you will develop your feel for the short game. As you did with the half swing (see Chapter 3), call your backswing point "A" and your follow-through point "B." Whatever size swing you wish to apply, you *feel*
A SUPPLE PUSH TO "A" AND A FREE FLOW TO "B."

Setup Adjustments

When you are scaling the swing down for a short shot, you must make sure certain body movements do not interfere with this simple motion. There is a tendency to do more with the body than whatever that certain size swing asks it to do. With a full-swing short iron, you are playing the ball in the middle of your stance, and the body naturally moves to the left. In the short game, golfers tend to hit and jab at the ball and stop the swing just after contact with the ball. Because they are instructed to follow through, they will often exaggerate the follow-through movement. This exaggerated movement is totally unnecessary and, in fact, only gets in the way of a very simple motion. Many good golfers have hit short shots "straight right" because they attempted to incorporate body motion into this scaled-down swing. To eliminate this excess, interfering body motion, you must play the ball off the *inside left foot and favor your weight on the left foot.*

There are two other setup adjustments in the short game that differ from the standard setup:

Keep feet closer together. Because the swing is scaled down, the feet no longer need to be shoulder-width apart. Let the feet gradually get closer together as the swing becomes smaller. You must be the judge on how wide apart they should be on different shots.

Open stance slightly. Instead of the line along your toes pointing toward your target, you must open your stance slightly. In other words, the line along your toes should now point to the left of your target. Why not just leave your stance square to the target? In the long game, distance is determined by club selection only. In the short game, distance is determined by the size of the swing. In order to gauge the distance of your shot, your ability to judge distance, or depth of field, is critical.

When you look at the target with a square stance, as shown in the illustration on the next page, left, your eyes have a difficult time seeing proper depth of field. Now, as in the illustration on the right, open your stance and notice a completely different picture, one in which your view of the shot has considerably improved.

Furthermore, because the swing is so scaled down, direction is no longer determined by body alignment. *Direction in the short game is determined by clubface alignment and hands, arms, and club swinging on the proper swing plane.*

Problems in the Short Shots

It is common to let the hands, specifically the right hand for right-handed people and the left for left-handed people, become too involved in this mini-motion, this delicate short shot. During your entire life, you have called on your right hand/arm/side (or left, if you're left handed) to do most of the work for strength and precision movements. It was trained to be dominant. It naturally wants to take over, even in golf.

In the long game, the dominant side wants to get involved for power; in the short game, it wants to get involved for control. The hands become so active they overpower the arm swing. Typically, both arms move on the backswing but seem to have trouble swinging past the left thigh on the follow-through. Because of the importance of the shot, the precision of it all, the subconscious mind calls upon the more dominant, controlling hand to involve itself. This hand picks the club up on the backswing, then flips the clubhead at the ball. This movement is deceptive in that it sometimes works; however, when it does not, the result is a disastrous shot. *Let the hands do what they want to do according to the size swing you are applying.*

The hands will do what they are supposed to do when you maintain suppleness in the wrists and swing your arms from point "A" to point "B." The over-involved dominant hand can be discouraged from taking control by feeling proper grip pressure. As in the full swing, the scaled-down swing must have the supple push back and the flow of the arms, tension free, to the other side, letting the hands and the rest of the body do whatever they want to do for that given size swing.

Common problems in the short-game swing are:

1. Floppy wrists or hands—caused by hands, specifically the dominant hand, working instead of staying supple. A common correction is to stiffen up the hands, but this only makes things worse. Push and flow the arms with supple wrists, not working hands.

2. Arms not following through, stopping at the ball—caused also by hands working. Again the dominant hand is pushing and not letting the arms flow to "B." A common fix is to maintain a triangle with the arms by stiffening the elbows. This rigidity can cause all kinds of problems.

3. Tendency to steer clubface and ball—caused by a last-second desire to "help out" the direction and not to trust the predetermined alignment.

4. Tendency to lift the shot—caused by the desire to help the ball up instead of allowing the clubface loft to do the necessary lifting.

5. Acceleration—caused by not developing feel for distance by size of swing. Usually the backswing is not big enough, and the mind commands the body to give the swing a last-second energy burst.

6. Deceleration—again no feel for distance. This is caused by using too large a backswing, and the mind at the last moment telling the muscles to slow down because the backswing is too big.

7. Mental hang-ups—making more out of the short game than there really is.

Putting

Rolling a ball into the hole should be less difficult than many people try to make it. If you use The Murray Method, it will be.

As we discussed earlier, the only two factors involved in all golf shots are distance and direction. Direction is determined by proper clubface alignment and swing path, and distance is determined by the size of the swing. Stay the heck out of the way of a very simple process!

The only way you can get a true perspective of direction is from behind the target line as when you play pool or shoot a rifle. Unfortunately in golf, you stand next to and over your line. Proper alignment, therefore, is difficult. To make sure your clubface is square, do one quick check. Set the putter head behind the ball and align the clubface in the proper direction. Hold the top of the putter with the fingertips of your left hand, step around directly behind the ball, and look from behind at your alignment of the clubface toward the target.

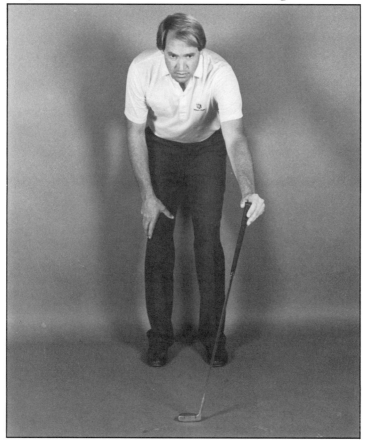

Practice this and see how proper alignment looks while you are addressing the ball. It may not look correct when you assume your stance, but that is because your perspective for alignment is off. You knew it was correct when you were behind the ball. It won't take long before your perspective will adjust to proper alignment. Do nothing in your swing to "help out" in direction, or you will only foul up the very simple swing process. Now that your direction is taken care of, *trust it.*

Take a couple of practice swings and try to decide what size swing feels correct for your desired distance. Feel that swing, maintain supple hands and wrists, feel the push back, and swing the arms, hands, and grip through to the other side. Let only the weight of the putter head and the size of the swing contribute to the roll of the ball.

To help you understand just how much you can stay out of the way of the clubhead as it swings through, hold your putter with your right thumb and index finger. Stand next to the ball and line up the clubface behind the ball in your desired direction. Using the index finger of your left hand, push the putter back to any particular backswing point and let it swing forward like a pendulum. Let only the weight of the putter head and the size of the swing propel the ball. You will be amazed just how far the ball goes with only that motion. So again, push back to desired backswing "A" and stay out of the way of the clubhead's natural swing to "B."

With the exception of making sure your eyes are directly over the ball at setup, you can stand and hold the club any way you want. Since direction no longer depends on your body alignment, stand any way that feels comfortable. Hold the club as you must to make the best possible swing, straight back and straight through. If you have no special preference, stay with your standard golf grip as discussed in Chapter 2.

Chipping

The chip-and-run shot is one of the big stroke savers in the game. The swing of the chip and run is very similar to putting, the difference being that the ball flies over the long grass and then onto the green. Grip the club with your standard full-swing grip and the standard short shot setup; it is not necessary to have your eyes over the ball. Now, with supple wrists, push the grip and arms to "A" and flow to "B." Make the stroke, do not punch at the ball, or flip the hands at it. Do not try to steer the ball toward the target; trust your alignment for direction.

The standard chip-and-run situation is a relatively level green of average speed. Any variation of this requires different club selections. A 6-iron is your best chip-and-run club for the standard situation.

Under the standard conditions of a flat shot with average speed greens, when you chip the shot, the ball will fly about one-third the distance and run or roll the other two-thirds.

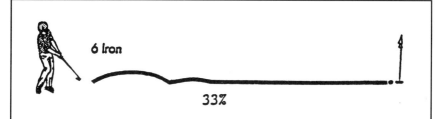

6 Iron

33%

One prerequisite for the chip-and-run shot is that the first one-third landing spot should be on the green. So the shot depends entirely on how much green you have to work with, which means you may be some distance off the green and still chip and run. The speed of the green, fast or slow, and whether you are going uphill or downhill also must be factored in when calculating your distance ratios. So experiment, remembering, one-third flight and two-thirds roll is a general "rule of thumb" when conditions are standard or you know little about the greens.

Also, aim toward the landing spot, not the flagstick. Of course, you want the ball to end up by or in the hole, but you have no idea where your landing spot is when you focus on the hole. Establish your line, find your landing spot, focus your eyes on *that* spot, and apply whatever size swing you need to get the ball to that spot. When you plan properly and make a good swing, your shot will be a success.

Pitching

Pitching is the shot you resort to when you cannot chip and run. When there is not enough depth in the green to run your shot, or when you must go over a mound or obstacle, consider the pitch. Your ball will pitch up into the air because of the clubface loft, not because you "help" lift the ball up. All it takes is a simple sweeping of the grass, and the ball will lift nicely.

Like the other short-game swings, pitching is a supple push of the hands and arms to "A" and flow to "B." Practice to find what size swing you need to take to achieve your desired distance. Avoid all the natural tendencies in the short game: hitting, flipping the hands, and steering the clubface to guide the ball to the target.

Your setup is the standard short-game setup. If the situation warrants a higher shot, you simply adjust your setup (to be discussed in Chapter 8).

Sanding

This is clearly the most feared shot in golf for the average golfer. Why? Fear of the unknown. Sand is different from grass, and in most cases, the ratio of practice shots off grass to shots out of sand is a hundredfold, so rarely do golfers develop sufficient confidence in their sand play. Ironically, the sand shot is quite simple. The difference between a pitch shot and a sand shot is infinitesimal. It is simply a matter of knowing how to deal with the sand.

With a typical sand shot, you never hit the ball—*you look at and slice out a layer of sand 1/2 to 4 inches behind the ball.*

Because you are never making contact with the ball, and because sand has more resistance than grass, your swing is a little bigger than your swing off grass. How much bigger depends on the distance of the shot.

Many golfers make a common mistake at this point; they just whack at the sand. Remember, you must still swing from "A" to "B" with a strong emphasis on "B." It is not the impact of the club hitting the sand that gets the ball out of the sand. Impact just moves the ball a little, and most likely not out of the bunker. *It is the slicing of the sand out of the bunker that gets the ball out; the ball travels along with the sand.*

The setup for a normal sand shot is the standard short-game setup. Assume an open stance, and also open your clubface. When the clubface is open, the leading edge becomes the hosel side of the clubface. This makes it much easier to slice through sand.

Let's take a look at what is actually happening when you're sanding. If you were to replace a golf ball with a small rock in a bunker and slice out a layer of sand, you would notice one very interesting thing . . . the sand flairs out a few feet, but the rock carries out farther. Why? Because it is heavier. That's how you must approach your sand shots . . . *think of the ball as just a big piece of sand.* Your job is to decide the size swing, focus your eyes on a spot 1/2 to 4 inches behind the ball, and slice out a layer of sand swinging from "A" to "B." Nothing more, nothing less.

Understanding Your Most Lofted Clubs

Your pitching wedge and sand wedge have lofts greater than 45 degrees, which means the clubface is busier hitting the ball higher rather than farther. This means you must be *generous* with your backswing. The drawback to this is that in most cases you are using your pitching wedge for more delicate shots close to the green, and you know that if you catch the ball a little thin, it is going to fly across the green into who knows what. Because of that, golfers are a little hesitant on this shot and invariably shorten up their backswing. Ironically, it is because of this shortened backswing that you catch the ball a little thin to begin with. Remember, from a shortened backswing, the mind tells the body there will not be sufficient centrifugal force and calls on the arms to energy-burst through to play catch-up. Muscles tighten, up comes the club, and topped goes the shot. Instead, trust your swing, and with the lofted clubs be generous rather than stingy when you take your backswing.

☜ CHAPTER 6 ☞
Playing the Game

This chapter would not be as necessary if golf were played in a controlled environment with one piece of equipment as in tennis or bowling. But this is not the case. You have as many as 14 different clubs in your bag and never the same shot twice on a golf course. And as players of this game know, hitting balls in practice and playing on the course are as different as night and day.

Don't confuse or intermingle the many different aspects of golf. Learning the swing and playing the game are two different phases of the sport. You have preswing routines to prepare for swing action. Here are just a few factors to consider in your preshot decision making. What kind of a lie is the ball in? Good or bad? Uphill or downhill? What are the conditions of the turf? Deep rough, hard pan, fluff lie? Is there room for your backswing and forward swing? Where do you want the ball to go? On what path or trajectory? Under, over, or around trees and obstacles? Will you chip or will you pitch?

These all require preshot deliberations and must be considered when playing the game. I've talked about physical interference. Now I must give some space to mental interference in golf.

Interfering Impulses

The interfering impulses in the golf swing mainly involve the instinctive tendencies to hit at, power, and control the ball and to think in terms of inappropriate end results.

These tendencies only magnify themselves when the shot has a greater importance or when a lack of self-confidence sets in. That's why many golfers *choke* when the "chips are on the line."

Pay attention to the job at hand. Do not let your mind wander! Your first priority is to *feel* the swing components of The Murray Method as you swing to eliminate your physical tendency to hit, power, and control.

To prepare for a shot, stand next to your bag and decide which club you will need for this particular shot. Once you select the club, your concern for distance is over. Do not set up to the ball thinking, I have a driver and I have to hit this ball far, or I have a 5-iron and I have to hit it onto the green. If you let thoughts such as these enter the process, you automatically give your nervous system another reason to react.

Remember:
>**Direction** is set in your preshot setup routine only.
>**Distance** is taken care of with club selection (or in the
>short game, with the size of swing).

Focusing on the Results

In golf, a low score is usually the desired goal; however, a low score is not attained by just thinking about it. It is achieved by making one single effective swing, again and again and again. This brings us to . . .

The Murray Method
PLAYING COMPONENT "A":
Treat each swing as a separate action.

Disconnect your shots. Each shot is an individual experience. It has no past . . . it has no future. It doesn't matter if you just had five good shots or five bad shots; the next one has no connection to them. It doesn't matter if you are about to shoot a score of 150 or the course record, you must still put your best swing into the next shot. It doesn't matter if this is the most important putt in the world or the least important. Whether it is for a birdie or a double bogey. This is one singular, unconnected putt, counting one stroke! If you have just made three 10-footers in a row, does that mean your chances are less that you can make the fourth? If you flip a coin three times and it comes up heads three times in a row, what are the odds of it coming up heads a fourth time? Always 50-50. Every flip is individual and unconnected to other flips. That means if you just parred four holes in a row, the fifth is next and should not be thought of as any more difficult. In fact, you should think the opposite. If you can par one, you have the physical capability to par them all. Only your lack of belief in yourself prevents you from doing it. Sometimes students need convincing that they *are* getting better. These good shots are not accidents. Get used to them.

Furthermore, don't let your score, high or low, interfere with swing making while you play the game. Golfers many times get unduly frustrated when swinging, playing, or scoring poorly.

They also get elated and excited when swinging and playing or scoring well. Ironically, the body responds to a good shot the same way it responds to a bad shot. The muscles contract in similar fashion under both conditions. You must try to stay on an even keel, not get excited about the good shots or frustrated with the bad shots. Don't let these emotions affect your approach to the task you face—making the necessary swing for this shot, the one at hand.

Powering the Ball

What is supposed to happen as the golf club gets longer? Why, of course, the ball is supposed to go farther. What does common sense tell you to do? Well, of course, you try to apply more power and you swing *harder!* But as we know, when you swing harder, muscles tighten.

As the club gets longer, the mental problems are compounded. When the driver is in your hands, changes occur. Your breathing becomes irregular, your muscles start to pump up, your jaw is so tightly clenched your teeth crack, and your eyes water staring at the ball. Exaggeration? Yes, but doesn't it sound familiar? Don't worry; if this hits home you are more the norm than not. It is not the longer club that creates these changes, it is how the mind interprets the longer club to be used. Suddenly the driver is an impossible club to hit. The irony of the tee shot is that it is the only shot in golf in which you control the spot from where you hit and the height of the ball off the ground. Instead of being the most feared club in the bag, the driver should be your favorite.

It's important to keep in mind that the golf club manufacturer has gone to great lengths to design each club in your bag as a tool for a particular distance. That means the equipment changes, not your swing. You should concern yourself only with one swing, regardless of the club in your hands. Do not allow yourself to switch gears and direct attention to what the equipment in your hands is supposed to do.

Stand your clubs up along a wall in numerical order. Notice how the length of each club gets longer as the number of each club gets smaller. The longer the shaft, the longer the arc. More centrifugal force is generated as the arc becomes longer and the clubhead at the end of the arc moves faster.

In addition to trying to power the longer clubs, your "hit at" impulse can take over because the clubhead is so far away from the ball at the top of your backswing that you feel a need to control the clubhead down to meet the ball. The best way to work through this fear is through the half-swing exercise.

Your doubting subconscious mind must first see good consistent contact with whatever club you are using, especially a troublesome club. You can achieve this by practicing with that club using the half swing. Once you have established consistent contact and shots, you can stretch out into your full swing.

Controlling the Ball

Just as there is often the temptation to power and hit with the longer clubs, there is also a tendency to try to control the direction of the ball as your desired line becomes more precise. I know players who are quite comfortable hitting 270-yard drives down the tightest of fairways, but when that pitching wedge is put in their hands, they have trouble hitting the green. Why is this so?

As the target gets closer, our expectations increase, and our control tendencies increase. We expect to hit the green with an 8-iron but not necessarily with a 3-wood. We expect to get close to the pin with a pitching wedge but not necessarily with a 5-iron. Whenever your expectation for accuracy increases, your subconscious mind naturally reacts to increase control tendencies.

The Murray Method
PLAYING COMPONENT "B":
Be a swing maker, not a shot maker.

Once you stop swinging and start steering or trying to power the ball, you're in trouble because the motions that should happen won't—specifically, the arms swinging tension free on a swing plane with supple wrists releasing. You must *trust* your swing and direction to proper setup, swinging your arms and club on your proper swing plane and letting your hands, wrists, and arms take care of themselves! Always remember, you must *be a swing maker* and let the shot follow.

⟶ CHAPTER 7 ⟵
More on the Short Game

Putting

If greens were perfectly flat, there would be no need to discuss break in putting. However, seldom will you find a flat green—there is usually some kind of slope that you must consider when planning your line of putt.

Playing for the break in the green means allowing for slope and choosing the speed of the role that will put the ball into the cup. For even the finest putters, determining break allowance is always, at best, an educated guess.

The distance of your putt is your most important consideration. Preferably, you never want to go much farther than a foot beyond the cup. Remember one important fact about break: The ball "takes the break" only when it starts to slow down at the end of its journey. You can hit through the break by using too large of a swing and zipping by the hole before the ball has a chance to break at all.

Take a look at the green as you are approaching it from 10 to 30 yards out. Do you see any slope? When you get to the green, look at your line of putt from various angles. See any slope? If you do, imagine holding a bucket of water and pouring it out along your line of putt. Which way would the water run off the green? You just discovered your slope.

What size swing are you going to apply while allowing for the slope and also not letting the ball roll past the cup more than one foot? There is only one answer—practice. To really develop feel for a green, practice putting to the hole from various angles and to various locations. Trial and error is your true teacher on the golf course. Sometimes you think there is a break and there isn't. Sometimes you see no break at all, and the ball will break a mile. Many times I have executed a putt perfectly only to have the ball miss the hole because I erred in planning my speed and/or break. At other times I made a poor stroke and missed my intended direction, but the ball went in anyway. That's golf!

Putting a ball into a relatively small hole calls for precision; however, *perfection is not obtainable*. Studies have shown that even a "perfect pendulum putting machine" will not make all putts of 6-foot length and only about 88 percent of the 10-footers. Top professionals make only about 60 percent of the 6-footers and only about 30 percent of the 10-footers.

There are just too many physical variables on the green, and some are not always visible, such as inconsistent grass growth or mowing, footprints, and spike marks. Each blade of grass is in constant motion. Moreover, studies have shown that golf balls are somewhat imbalanced. Most golf balls will not roll in a perfect line on a perfectly flat surface. So cut yourself some slack; there are a lot of variables working against you. All you can do is line up and make your best stroke. Unfortunately, even that may not be enough to keep the ball on line to and into the hole.

Practice your putting stroke hundreds if not thousands of times, with or without a ball. Remember, you are practicing a stroke, and a stroke it will always be, whether or not a ball is there, or whether the stroke means everything or nothing.

Club Selection for Chipping

For short shots off the green, you should try to favor the chip-and-run shot whenever possible. The lower you keep the ball to the ground:

1. **The simpler the shot,**
2. **The more room there is for error than with a lofted shot,**
3. **The less vulnerable the shot is to spin,**
4. **The less vulnerable the shot is to landing either on a downslope on the green where the ball would pick up speed or on an upslope where the ball's motion would die when it lands, and**
5. **The less vulnerable your shot is to soft or firm greens.**

The reason you always use a putter to roll the ball on the green, regardless of the length of the putt, is to retain maximum feel for control and to minimize the variables. It never ceases to amaze me how often I see golfers pull out a pitching wedge or, worse yet, a sand wedge when they are in more effective and easier chip-and-run territory. You may choose from a 4-iron to a 9-iron to chip and run with, depending on the speed, firmness, or softness of the green, or if your shot is uphill or downhill.

In a standard situation with relatively level and average speed greens, use the 6-iron. Practice with the 4- to 9-irons and observe what trajectory and roll the balls take. At times there will be enough green to work with, but because of either a hazard or a high slope, the trajectory of the 6-iron will not take the ball over the obstacle. It is at this time you must know, through practice, what type of trajectory each club makes. Take whatever club is necessary to get the ball to the green on the fly, but still roll as much as possible.

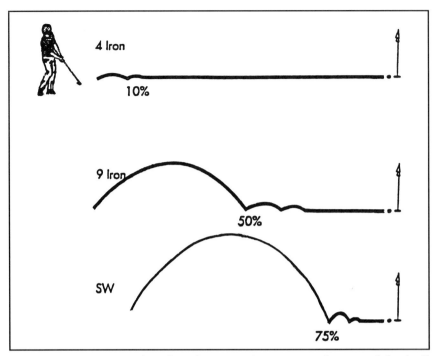

4 Iron

10%

9 Iron

50%

SW

75%

Some greens are hard or the grass is cut very short and the ball can role very fast. A 6-iron's trajectory may keep the ball too low so that when the ball lands on the green, it will roll more than your desired two-thirds. Experiment to find which club is best suited for the particular course you are playing. You should also expect the results of this shot to be as good as if you were putting from the same distance. If you sink 15-footers on the green 10 to 20 percent of the time, expect the same percentages from your chip-and-run shots. Practicing this shot can be a real stroke saver on the course.

Pitching

Your pitching wedge is the most versatile club in your bag. Its range can be anywhere from a few feet to over 100 yards for some players with a full swing. I tell my students to look at their pitching wedge with full swings as they would a 10-iron. Once inside the full-swing distance, the wedge becomes a tool for pitching the ball. Pitch whenever you cannot chip and run. Avoid pulling out the sand wedge to pitch with. Your sand wedge is most effective out of sand by design. It is the heaviest club in your bag. It has a big sole to slice through sand, a rounded head, and a leading edge that is usually not flush to the ground. Why use the heaviest and most awkward club in the bag for the most delicate shot in golf? Sometimes sand wedges are very close in design to the pitching wedge. The trade-off is that such sand wedges are more effective off grass lies, but less effective out of sand.

Don't let an obstacle such as a bunker or water hazard between you and your target become an issue. Approach it as though it does not exist. The golf course architect put the obstacle there for only one purpose: to make you think of it, thus affecting your swing. You have only one job to do, and that is to make a certain size swing. Getting the ball over that obstacle will be the result of that swing.

Sanding

Many golfers believe that because they are in sand instead of grass everything has to change. They will attempt to blast the ball out of the bunker or change the swing entirely by doing things like taking the club outside or inside or more upright and so on. These actions are not necessary. You may run into a variety of bunker conditions: wet sand, buried ball, fairway bunkers, and extremely difficult lies. Although you approach each condition differently, keep in mind that the swing does not change.

Wet Sand: When your ball lies in wet sand or hard-packed sand, forget that you're in a sand bunker. Play it as a pitch off hardpan, using a pitching wedge. The clubface of a sand wedge will not enter wet sand easily or consistently. If you attempt your normal sand shot, the sand wedge will not enter the sand but will bounce off the hard lie, and, most likely, you will blade the ball.

Buried Ball or Fried Egg Lie: Do not fret over this shot. What is at hand here? The ball is lying deeper into the sand, which simply means you will have to move more sand, not by swinging harder but by swinging *bigger!*

Because you now have to dig into the sand instead of slicing out a layer from under the ball, there is a recommended setup adjustment. For the typical sand shot you are open-stanced, which opens the clubface, making the hosel side of the face slice through the sand first. But for an embedded lie, close the clubface slightly, toe inward, making *it* the leading edge as illustrated on the following page.

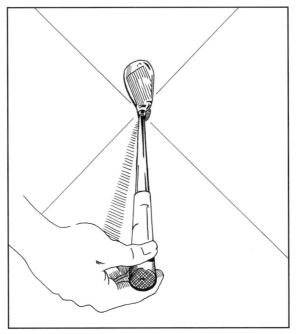

The toe enters the sand first and digs down quickly. Furthermore, the resistance of more sand and the force pulling on the hosel side of the clubface will automatically open the clubface, so the clubface aimed to the left when you set up will square to the target when the club is moving through the sand.

Fairway Bunkers: In most cases, when your ball is in a fairway bunker, it has probably rolled in and is not buried as it would be if it landed in a greenside bunker from a high shot. If your ball has a nice lie and the bunker has little lip, use whatever club you need for that particular distance. Treat the shot the same as if your ball is on a thin lie. If these conditions do not exist, just get the heck out of the sand with your sand wedge. Do not attempt a low percentage shot, hoping for a miracle.

Extremely Difficult Lies: There will be times when it is impossible to make a shot in a bunker or, for that matter, in many other places on the course. If your ball is under a lip of a bunker or buried too deep, forget it. Take your unplayable stroke penalty and drop according to *The Rules of Golf*. Too many times golfers find out too late (after a couple of swipes at the ball) that the shot was impossible to begin with, and that the penalty drop would have been the smarter play.

⚛ CHAPTER 8 ⚛
Different and Abnormal Lies and Specialty Shots

It would be ideal if all golf courses were like the range tee—flat. Many times, the only level lie on the course is the teeing area. Often, uneven lies go unnoticed, and your shot is unsuccessful not from poor swing execution but from lack of preparation in setup. You must pay close attention to any slope in your shot. Is the ball below or above your stance or on an uphill or downhill incline? If you do notice an uneven lie in your stance, remember to make adjustments in your *setup,* not in your *swing.*

The Presidio Golf Club is one of the oldest golf courses west of the Mississippi River; it is called a native golf course. It was built like those courses in Scotland and Ireland, long before golf course builders graded and sculpted fairways. As one club member says, "Every shot at the Presidio is a science project." This is because the subtle, uneven lies of the course require the golfer to pay constant attention to every shot.

This chapter discusses how to adjust for different and abnormal lies and specialty shots. Keep in mind that any change is always in setup, *never in the swing.*

Ball Placement
Where the ball is placed in your stance for the following shots varies according to the severity of the slope. There are no hard and fast rules. The practice swing is the key to all shots on the golf course, especially for abnormal situations. Start with what you believe to be the proper readjusted setup and proceed to take practice swings. Where the clubhead tends to cut through the grass is precisely where your natural swing makes contact with the ground, and you must adjust to the ball according to that particular slope.

Uphill Shots
When your shot is going uphill, you must play the ball and favor your weight more toward your uphill foot (for right-handed players this means the left foot; for left-handed players, the right foot).

On uphill shots, your ball trajectory increases as the slope of your shot increases. Taking this into consideration, you may choose to take a longer hitting club, depending on the severity of the slope.

Because your ball is toward the left side, your clubhead actually arrives later to the ball than normal. This usually causes the clubface to be slightly rolled over at impact. The shots have the tendency to go left, so you must adjust your stance to the right accordingly.

Downhill Shots

You must play the ball and favor your weight toward your uphill foot, which for the right-handed golfer is now the right side and for the left-handed golfers, the left side. Anytime you play the ball to the right of its original position in your stance, you are decreasing loft from your club. Taking this into consideration, you will find a low-lofted club such as your 3-wood becomes extremely difficult to get airborne, so you are better off switching to a 5-wood or perhaps an iron, depending on the severity of the slope.

When your shot is downhill, the ball travels farther, so you generally need less club. And since moving the ball back in your stance causes a lower shot trajectory, when the ball lands it will roll considerably more. Whereas the uphill shot moves left, the downhill shot tends to go right, so adjust accordingly.

Ball Above Your Feet

Take a practice swing or two. Notice how flat your swing becomes, how your arc swings around you more because the ball is so much closer to you. What happens when your swing is flat? Your swing is almost baseballish, more roundhouse, with a tendency to hook and pull shots to the left because of the slope. There is nothing you can do to prevent this flat swing, but you can make an adjustment to hit the ball straight. Slightly open the face of the club. How much open depends on the severity of the slope. It doesn't have to be much, so experiment when you practice.

Because the ball is so much closer to you, you may have to choke up on the club (put your hands farther down the grip). Be sure to take into consideration that you are shortening your arc when you choke up on the club, as this may affect your club selection. For example, if you are at 7-iron distance but choke up an inch, you are using less of your club. You may be better off switching to a 6-iron. Ball placement does not change from your standard placement.

Ball Below Your Feet

This is one of golf's most awkward shots. In order to reach the ground with your clubhead at address, you must bend over at the lower back or hunch your shoulders in order to reach down to the ball. It is very common for golfers to lift up from this bent-over position going into their backswing. Do not let this happen—maintain your center throughout the swing. Therefore, your swing for this shot is relatively restricted, so you may need a longer club to make up for this restricted swing. If you are a 7-iron away and the ball is below your feet by a few inches or more, consider a 6- or a 5-iron.

High Shots

There will be occasions when you have to go over an obstacle on the course, but have little green to work with. If you would like your shot to land softly with only a little roll, select your pitching wedge and use a double opener. *Open the clubface* to the desired loft and keep *opening your stance* until the clubface is square again toward the target.

Remember, be very generous with your swing because the lofted clubface hits the ball up more than out. If you wish to hit a higher shot with a less lofted club, play the ball farther out toward the left side of your stance. With this setup, you will make contact with the ball slightly in the upswing of your swing arc, which will, in turn, raise the trajectory of the shot.

Low Shots

The occasion may arise when you need to hit a lower shot, such as into the wind or under tree limbs. For a lower trajectory, de-loft the clubface angle by playing the ball farther back in your stance toward your right foot. When hitting into the wind, select a less lofted club and scale down your swing. Many players make the mistake of attempting to knock the ball down into the wind. Highly volatile, the knock-down shot is executed by pushing a downward blow to the ball with the right side. But when the right side pushes the downward blow it can also put a hook spin on the ball, and into wind, this action can create a drastic hook. Also, when the right side pushes down, it puts greater backspin on the ball. It is the backspin of the ball that creates lift, something you are trying to avoid when you are hitting into the wind.

Long Grass

Even when you are using The Murray Method, there may be a time or two when you end up in a less than desirable place such as long grass. But long grass should not be a score killer. Play it smart. If you are in really long grass, say four inches or more, just get the heck out of there and back into the fairway with your sand wedge. If the grass isn't that long, take a club (up to a 5-iron) and swing fast through the grass. Don't think you have to swing hard with strong muscles through the longer grass, for you will only slow down your clubhead. Just make a fast swing. A less lofted club than a 5-iron will more than likely not get the ball airborne. Don't try for the miracle shot and hit a wood or long iron unless you have a utility wood with grooves or rails on the sole made specifically for trouble lies.

Hardpan

Playing a shot off bare ground is not as difficult as many golfers make it. What you want to avoid is hitting the ground with the clubhead as this might cause the club to bounce off the ground and scull the ball. You want to catch the ball thin, picking the ball off the ground. This can be done by making one of two setup adjustments:

1. **Play the ball farther left in your stance, hitting the ball slightly on the upswing, or**
2. **Stand a little more upright in your stance, so that you can raise your arc slightly off the ground.**

◆━◇ CHAPTER 9 ◇━◆
Error Prevention and Troubleshooting with The Murray Method

The golf swing lasts less than two seconds, and it is impossible to pay attention to more than a few things during that brief time span. The essence of The Murray Method is to keep it simple enough so that you can feel swinging on a swing plane, as fast as you can, tension free.

But suppose you are not satisfied with your shots or the consistency of them. What to do? Well, let's look at some possible swing problems and how you can correct them.

Golf is not a matter of perfect conditions, lies, and/or breaks. You can get good or bad breaks, and make some good or bad swings. If things go awry, don't fret or sweat, there is a simple answer. Most bad swings are related to *tension*. For those who like specifics, the following is for you. They refer to the right-handed player.

Topped Shots
The topped shot (in which the clubhead grazes the top of the ball causing it to roll along the ground) is unquestionably the most commonly missed shot for the beginning golfer. For whatever reason, you allowed your muscles to work and simply were not swinging tension free. The culprit could be the muscles in your forearms, shoulders, hands, back, or legs. Once muscles work they tighten, shorten, and pull the club up off the ground. The famous caddy cure-alls, "Keep your head down" and "Keep your eye on the ball," do not help you eliminate muscle glitch. In fact, keeping your head down only restricts the swing motion. As we discussed earlier, golf is not a game of "see-it-and-hit-it," or keeping your eyes on the ball. Trust ball contact to the swing plane and swing tension free from "A" to "B."

Sliced and Pushed Shots

The sliced and pushed shot (in which the ball either spins off to the right or is right of the target line from the onset) is another commonly missed shot for amateur golfers. All golfers open the clubface on the backswing; it's how your skeleton wants to work. You would have to do something very awkward to avoid opening the clubface as you push back.

The reason for most slices is that the wrists are so tight at impact that the release is locked out and the hands stay open. Maintain supple wrists so that the hands are allowed to do what they are supposed to do—release.

Another cause for a slice is excessive lower-body movement, which results from trying to get power from the legs, hips, or transfer of weight. This manufactured movement can cause a block out, which occurs when the lower body moves ahead of the arm flow, keeping the clubface open at impact. This is a sure invitation to disaster.

Fat Shots

The fat shot (in which the clubhead has hit too far behind the ball or too deep into the ground) is caused by a drop of the clubhead down from the original swing plane arc. This downward movement results from the mind reacting to the ball's presence and commanding the right side to assist in "making sure" the clubhead hits the ball. The right hand, arm, and/or shoulder is more than willing to accommodate.

There is *no* automatic adjustment that will eliminate the right side's desire to help out with striking, powering, and controlling. The right hand is in such a strong position at every point of the swing that it is very easy for it to engage and push the club at the ball. On the backswing, it is much easier for the right hand to pick up or pull back the grip than it is for the left hand to push and swing it back. At the top of the backswing, it is much easier and more instinctive for the right side to push the hand, arm, and shoulder down at the ball. At impact, the hands, specifically the right hand, want terribly to exert control.

At this point, we are dealing with very strong human reactions and impulses, and it is imperative that you *feel and maintain proper suppleness in your wrists and a tension-free swing throughout the entire motion.* If you do not, your hands will automatically tighten, and when they do, the right side becomes dominant. You can be sure that the right hand will try to hit, power, and control.

Hooked and Pulled Shots

The hooked and pulled shot (in which the ball spins left or is to the left of target line from the onset) is in the same family as the fat shot, but instead of a derailment of the club off the swing plane downward, the hands, arms, and clubhead take the club offtrack by picking up and pushing the club around you. Remember, when your left hand pushes the grip straight back and you swing to the other side, the club stays on the proper swing path. However, if you allow the stronger, more controlling right hand to engage, you can do one of two things. First you can take the club offtrack by picking the club up outside the proper swing plane. Once your arms and club travel outside, they can only travel back inside on the follow-through; in other words, your entire swing plane has shifted. This swing plane will pull the ball to the left. The term "pulled shot," as you can see, is a deceptive one. You have not pulled the shot to the left from pulling with the left side; you have actually pushed the ball to the left with the pushing right side.

Second, if you allow the right side to pull the club back, it can pull the arc inside the proper swing plane, and hook shots can result from this flatter arc.

Most bad shots are varying degrees of topped, sliced, fat, hooked, or pulled shots, and all are caused by muscles working as they should not. Muscles are working because the nervous system is responding to added stimulus caused by that important upcoming shot. There is nothing you can do to eliminate the nervousness that you may feel, but you can deal with the tension that comes from the nervousness. Two of the three Murray Method swing components deal directly with tension: (1) feeling the suppleness of the wrists and (2) feeling the tension-free flow of the arms.

Trouble with Alignment

If you have trouble lining yourself up in the proper direction, there is an easy way to check your alignment. Follow the same procedure we discussed in Chapter 5. Square the clubface by standing behind the ball and hold the grip with your left hand. With irons, the track lines of your clubface (the lines vertical to the score lines) should point toward your target. With woods, either the name or some design on the top of the wood is always square to your clubface and should point toward the target. Without moving your clubface, move into your setup position and square your stance off the club. *Do not change the clubface alignment once you are in your address position, even if it looks off.*

⇒ CHAPTER 10 ⇐
Practice

Learning and improving in the game of golf is directly related to practice. Practice is important because it instills the *feel* of the proper swing that the golf shot requires.

Golf is unique. Unlike any other sport or game, it does not matter how good an athlete you are or how good your hand-eye coordination is. As I have shown earlier, your ability to play golf well depends first and foremost on your ability to make a swing that is tension free and on a single swing plane.

Professional golfers must be in fairly good shape to withstand the grueling physical and mental pressures of the game. However, many are not very good athletes. This is good news for those amateur golfers who want to play golf but have never been particularly adept at other sports. *Golf skills are acquired skills, not God-given ones.* Without exception, all golfers who play the game well have had to work at it.

What made Jack Nicklaus great? Was it his teacher? Was it his equipment? It was Jack Nicklaus. It was his dedication to hard work and his competitive drive. It is the same thing that makes all great golfers what they are. There has never been nor will there ever be an exception to that fact. No one ever simply decides to play golf and go out and instantly play well overnight.

Unfortunately, when most golfers do take the time to practice, they rarely practice properly. They usually grab a club and a bucket of balls and start whacking away, judging success by how many good shots they hit way out to the trees. However, great shots on the practice range are meaningless if the golfer paid no attention to the feel of the swing.

The objective of practice is to swing properly. Be attentive to the feel of the swing, and practice that swing over and over again. Your goal is consistently good shots, not erratically great ones. Johnny Miller once said, "You know you are swinging pretty good when your misses are still pretty good." In other words, you can still score well in this game when your shot is perhaps a little thin, or slightly short or long, left or right. The swing does not have to be perfect every time; in fact, don't expect that. There has never been an athlete nor will there *ever* be an athlete who repeats perfect motion at will.

Too many golfers expect too much of themselves, getting frustrated if each shot is not perfect. *Golf is not a game of how many perfect shots you hit; it is a game of how good are your misses.*

Ben Hogan once set a course record and said he was truly satisfied with only four shots. From everyone else's perspective, it was a perfect round; from his, it was just four good shots.

In many a round, I have made shots unlike anything I had planned, yet they ended up great. I looked like a hero! In other rounds, I executed shots perfectly, but they turned out to be disasters. I looked like a bum!

There are just too many variables in golf to ever get it "just right" all the time.

Taking Shots from Practice to Play

The practice range is entirely different from the golf course. The pressures are not there on the range. No one is keeping score. You don't have to find the ball and hit it again. There are no problems to avoid.

On the practice range, repetition is a factor and you can be fooled when you are practicing with a stack of balls in front of you or when taking a lesson. But unfortunately, on the golf course we don't have the advantage of repetition. Rarely do you have the same shot twice. On the range, you can easily fall into a groove without having to focus on the feel of the swing, simply repeating it from short-term memory. But on the course, it may be 5 or 10 minutes, perhaps even more between full swings. To be successful on the course you need to:

1. *Know* what to do and
2. **Pay attention to the feel of your swing and practice to build confidence *to be a swing maker,* not a shot maker, under any circumstances.**

This means you can accomplish a lot from just swinging a club. Even beginners can feel the difference between a good swing and a bad swing without having to strike the ball.

To Practice Swing or Not to Practice Swing

On the course, all you have between your desire to swing well and the actual shot is your practice swing. When you have an idea of what your swing is supposed to be like and feel like, you will not fear the golf shot. You will have full confidence that you will perform the swing because you know what to do and what it feels like. This does not guarantee a successful shot; however, it does give you a little edge of confidence rather than just hope for a good shot. If you are concerned about the speed of play, make up time by picking up your walking pace. Never rush your golf shot routine.

How to Practice on the Range

You should start every practice session and warm-up session with half swings. Keep in mind that the impulse to hit will always be ready to rear its ugly head. The half swing is what will get you on the track of swinging and not hitting. It never ceases to amaze me how often I see golfers who start out a practice session by pulling out their driver and start whacking out balls as far as they can hit them.

You will never see good players start out practicing with full swings or long clubs. They start with a short or mid iron. On the practice tee, your initial objective is to make good, consistent, quality contact with proper trajectory on the shots. As always, distance is not a factor in the half swing.

When you are satisfied with a dozen or so quality contact shots and consistent swings, you are ready to expand into a fuller arc. Simply extend out your swing. At this point you are free to use any club. If you make two unsatisfactory shots, don't continue swinging the same swing; instead, scale it back down. The half swing is an important tool, so feel free to return to it at any time.

⊷⟹ **CHAPTER 11** ⟸⊷
More About the Game and You

You can learn a lot about yourself in a round of golf. The game reveals parts of your character that even you may know little about: your competitiveness, your need to be powerful or in control, your ability to deal with success and failure, or how you perform under pressure.

In *The Murray Method,* you have learned that in golf all you need is but one swing for all shots. The only exception is in the short game, where the same swing is applied on a scaled-down basis. But learning to play the game of golf will be never-ending. During a round of golf, you never hit the same shot twice. You must make decisions regarding club selection and strategy of play on every shot because conditions such as wind, terrain, and slope vary.

Too often, golfers do not pay enough attention to their swing. They make some halfhearted swing, hoping that automatic reflex action will suffice. Out goes the swing that was practiced so rigorously and in come the instincts to hit, power, and control. The results can be disastrous. Then golfers wake up only too late and wonder how they could have hit such a bad shot.

This is what makes golf both the fascinating and the frustrating game that it is—just when you think you've got it mastered and try to make it automatic, you lose it. Learn to have patience even if you don't, or the game will drive you nuts.

Setting Goals

Setting reasonable yet challenging goals is important in golf. The better the golfer, the smaller the improvement target. In other words, someone who shoots 120 might set a goal at 110, an improvement of ten strokes. Someone who shoots 75 might set a much tougher goal and try for 72.

It never ceases to amaze me how well some students hit the ball only to find that they score poorly on the course. The simple fact is that bogey golf is not an unrealistic goal for most golfers, even beginners. Look at it this way: To shoot bogey golf all you have to do is get on every par 3 in two, every par 4 in three, and every par 5 in four, and you get two putts on every green! You might sink a putt here and there, chip one up close, or hit a green in regulation once or twice. Bogey golf is very possible when you trust your swing and believe in yourself.

If you are a better golfer, you should chart your round and see what areas of your game need specific work. Improvement is slow and gradual, so do not expect your scores to come down in big chunks. Approach your long game as the part of your game that puts you in good enough position to score with your short game. In other words, if your long game keeps you out of trouble and on or around the green, then with a decent short game, par is achievable. Hit a shot close or sink a long putt, and birdies and pars will be recorded.

Whether you are a high-handicap or a low-handicap golfer, be patient while striving to reach your goal. Anything is easy when you work at it. Respect the game. Don't expect to play like a golf professional just because you worked on your game for a week. Remember, golf professionals have dedicated their lives to this game and have played it for a lifetime. I have had students comment, "How come I can't hit like that?" My answer is, "I've been doing this every day for the last 30 years. When you work at it that much, you will hit a shot like that."

Responding to Bad Shots

You must understand one very important fact about golf. Even the best golfers miss shots. They hit shots out of bounds, into the woods, into the lake, and along the ground, just like you. Don't put too much pressure on yourself. The game will bury the perfectionist. Keep it in perspective. If you are a professional trying to earn a living to feed your family and work hard on your game, you have all the right to get upset if your shots are not to your liking. If you are not a professional, don't get mad if you are not playing as well as you think you should. It amazes me how some golfers get so piping mad, throwing clubs and tantrums and making themselves look quite ridiculous. If you are guilty of that type of behavior, you are taking the game too seriously and need to work on your sense of humor; after all, golf is just a game.

The game is good to the steady player. It is not necessary to hit all your shots great. What is it that makes Joe Montana a great quarterback? Does he have a great cannon arm? No. Is he a fast runner? No. He is great because, among other things, his level of play does not change from practice to the final seconds to win a Super Bowl!

Play the game aggressively, but do not swing aggressively. In other words, your shot selection, club selection, and course strategy should be positive and sometimes aggressive. Too many times golfers mix aggressive play into their swing, and then free-flowing motion and suppleness turn to work and tension.

Too many times, golfers look at golf from a negative point of view. They miss a shot, panic, and say, "Oh no, I'm losing it. What am I doing wrong?"

If at first you don't succeed, be prepared for a lot of advice. In fact, even if you are succeeding, advice may be forthcoming. My experience has led me to believe that almost anybody is willing to give someone else a golf tip. However, remember that those tips are most likely mechanical corrections—an approach you no longer have a need for.

Do not accept one or two bad shots as the norm for the rest of the day. When I missed a three-foot putt on the first hole one time, my playing partner said, "Looks like you're missing those short ones today!" If I had agreed with my partner, I would have accepted failure. Never accept failure; learn from it and move on.

Approach the game from the positive side. If the shot was not to your liking, don't try to correct anything. You simply didn't do what you were supposed to do, *so try again!*

Golf: A Game of Honor

Golf can be either a social event or a tournament competition. In either case, it is a game of honor. In fact, Section I of *The Rules of Golf* is devoted to the etiquette of the game and emphasizes courtesy on the course and care of the course. Consideration for other players is an integral part of the game.

The rules are promulgated to assure, as much as possible, that all players fairly play the same game. A true competitor is satisfied with victory only when it has been a fair match.

Golf Can Be Fickle; Don't You Be

Golf can be unpredictable. One day you may experience a good long game only to have your short game go sour, or a bad long game but feel happy because your short game was good enough to make up for it. Why is it so hard to put it all together? Most golfers have a certain scoring range in which they feel comfortable. This scoring range becomes their comfort level and makes it difficult for them to believe they are capable of pulling off anything better. When some golfers find themselves in a position to score better, more often than not they will find a way to foul it up.

Because we react so strongly, and there is such a natural tendency to want to hit, power, and control, these impulsive reactions can easily change a free-flowing swing motion into a glitching spasm that hardly can be called a swing. A meaningless 50-yard shot is easy, but put a lake between you and the hole and suddenly everything changes. Now you feel you have to *help* the ball over the lake. There is no mechanical correction or adjustment that will eliminate interfering movements the body makes when instinctive reaction engages. You must make a decision from the very onset—are you going to "make" the shot or are you going to *feel* the swing? You must be a swing maker and feel a supple push to "A" and free flow to "B."

There is simply nothing you can do to aid in distance or direction *as* you swing the club. Check off distance and direction once you have set up to the ball.

Feel your swing, not the pressure.

There has never been a golfer and there will never be a golfer who does not feel the pressure of a shot at one time or another. The pros may stroll down the fairway looking so cool and collected, but their adrenaline is flowing like crazy. The difference between the golfer who can perform under these conditions and the one who cannot is how one deals with pressure without letting muscles react. You cannot let what is happening become so important that the results are more important than what must prevail . . . *feel your swing!* Let the shot happen because of a proper stance, proper club selection, and a good swing. That's all you can do, and if you do, you will be astounded at how good you really can be when you use The Murray Method.

Conclusion

The Murray Method promotes the development of a natural, nonmechanical golf swing that, because of its very short duration, precludes focusing on a great number of checkpoints. The primary goal is to help the player develop a swing that is as simple as breathing. We don't think about each breath we take, nor should golfers try to check head, toes, elbows, or whatever during each millisecond they swing at a golf ball.

For the nonexpert golfer, The Murray Method is quite simple to grasp, and success can be yours quickly. But like anything in life, changing habits is not so simple. What is most important to the golfer who is looking for help is that help has arrived! But you must have patience. Work on the drills such as the half swing if success is evading you. Some amateurs believe a simple swing is fine for starters, but once they "get into golf," they need something more complex. Nothing could be further from the truth; in fact, the opposite is true.

Four years ago, someone recommended an elderly women to me for lessons. She explained that at one time she was quite an accomplished golfer, but the last few years had been so frustrating that even though she still loved the game, she would not continue playing if she had to play so poorly. She had taken numerous lessons, read books, and attended several golf schools. I was her last hope for golf. After we discussed The Murray Method, she started hitting shots better than she had in years and kept exclaiming, "It can't be this easy!" I replied, "I'm sorry, but it is."

Golf, indeed, is in many ways a puzzling, perplexing, and an all-encompassing game whose subtleties may best be described by the following definition written by David R. Forgan:

It is a science—the study of a lifetime, in which you may exhaust yourself but never your subject.

It is a contest, a duel, or a melee, calling for courage, skill, strategy, and self-control.

It is a test of temper, a trial of honor, a revealer of character.

It affords the chance to play the man, and act the gentleman.

It means going into God's out-of-doors, getting close to nature, fresh air, exercise, a sweeping away of the mental cobwebs, genuine recreation of the tired tissues.

It is a cure for a care—an antidote to worry.

It includes companionship with friends, social intercourse, opportunity for courtesy, kindliness and generosity to an opponent.

It promotes not only physical health but moral force.

THE MURRAY METHOD

A golf swing that makes sense and one you can trust.

HAVE FUN!

Study Guide to Accompany Brealey and My[...]
Principles of
Corporate Finance

Study Guide to Accompany Brealey and Myers

Principles of Corporate Finance

Charles A. D'Ambrosio
University of Washington

Stewart D. Hodges
London Graduate School of Business Studies

McGraw-Hill Book Company
New York   St. Louis   San Francisco   Auckland   Bogotá   Hamburg
Johannesburg   London   Madrid   Mexico   Montreal   New Delhi   Panama
Paris   São Paulo   Singapore   Sydney   Tokyo   Toronto

Study Guide to Accompany Brealey and Myers
PRINCIPLES OF CORPORATE FINANCE

ISBN 0-07-007381-3

567890 DODO 898765432

This book was set in Times Roman by Better Graphics. The editors were Bonnie E. Lieberman, Michael Elia, and James B. Armstrong; the design was done by Caliber Design Planning; the production supervisor was Charles Hess. The drawings were done by VIP Graphics. The cover was designed by Ben Kann.
R. R. Donnelley & Sons Company was printer and binder.

Contents

Preface

This Study Guide to *Principles of Corporate Finance* by Brealey and Myers will help you learn about finance as quickly and as easily as possible. The purpose of the Study Guide is to make you more proficient in the science and art of financial decision making. It helps you achieve this end in three ways.

1. *As an aid to reading the text.* The Study Guide sets the scene for each chapter by telling you how it relates to other chapters and what the key ideas are that you should look for. Additional explanations and worked examples are provided to help deepen your understanding of particular points in the text.

2. *As a source of additional exercises.* The Study Guide provides both questions and answers.

3. *As an aid to reviewing for exams.* The summaries of each chapter and the lists of terms will help you to remember the main points. The summaries will help you to review what you have learned, either after you have studied a chapter or when you are preparing for an examination. As you study both the text and the Study Guide, always assume that you are the financial manager, keeping in mind his or her goals, perspective, and rationale for doing what he or she does.

Structure of the Study Guide

Each chapter of the Study Guide refers to the corresponding chapter of the Brealey and Myers text. Except for Chapter 33, each chapter contains the following sections:

- *Introduction.* The short introduction gives a concise guide to what the chapter is about. It will help you to both determine the chapter's main thrust and see how it fits in with any neighboring chapters that relate to it.

- *What to Look For.* The second section, which is entitled "What to Look For in Chapter ____," will help you find your way through the detail of the corresponding chapter in the text. Special attention is paid to explaining the points which students most often find difficult.

You will probably want to read these first two sections of the Study Guide before studying the corresponding chapter of the text.

- *Worked Examples.* Worked examples are provided depending on the nature of the chapter. They enhance the explanations presented earlier and give you a guide to the sorts of calculations you should be able to make after you have studied the chapter.

- *Summary.* The summary provides a concise synopsis of the chapter. Whereas you might read this before studying the chapter, it is wiser to use it to review what you have learned, either after reading the chapter or when preparing for an examination.

- *List of Terms*. This section provides a list of the most important *new* terms that you will have encountered in reading the chapter. It is a good idea to check this list *immediately* after you finish reading a chapter. If you find that you have forgotten the meaning of a term, check it in the Glossary at the back of the text, or if necessary go back to the place in the chapter where it was introduced.

- *Exercises*. The exercises take three main forms. The first set of exercises in each chapter are fill-in ones, which provide you with a further check to determine whether you know what the new terms mean and how they are used. By filling in these exercises you will provide yourself with a chapter-by-chapter glossary of the most important terms. The second set of exercises consist of problems. These correspond broadly to the types of problems given as worked examples. Finally, a number of suggested essay questions are presented. Even if you don't actually write any essays, these questions are worth reading because they indicate the kinds of issues that you should be able to discuss after you have studied the chapter.

- *Answers*. Where it is possible to do so, we have provided answers to all the exercises other than the essay questions. In many cases fairly complete solutions are given. Nevertheless, we urge you to make sure that you complete your answer before you succumb to the temptation to look at ours!

One point about our answers is in order. Many of the mathematical solutions were calculated either with a hand-held calculator or by computer. Consequently, some of your answers may differ from some of ours because the tables in the text's Appendix are rounded to three significant digits, whereas most hand-held calculators carry eight digits and computers carry more than that. The differences should not be great, however.

Starred Sections

Some parts of the summary and some problems are indicated by a star, or asterisk. As in the text, these are of unusual difficulty, and many students will want to omit them on a first reading. We hope that some of the starred problems will provide an interesting challenge even to more advanced students.

Some Tips

You should realize that authors of books work from outlines. The subject matter is broken down into very small parts, but never so small as to become burdensome. The first way in which to break down the subject matter is by chapters. So before studying the subject of corporate finance, look over the chapter headings in order to locate yourself in the milieu called financial decision making. You should know at the outset, for example, that firms make decisions on what investments to make and how to finance them. By perusing the chapter headings, the topics of financial decision making will be placed in perspective.

When you first tackle a chapter, employ the same process you used with respect to the entire book: examine the headings of each section and subsection of the chapter and simply page through the chapter. By so doing you will have a preview of events to come, and, as you study one section of the chapter, you will doubtlessly recall some of the other headings so that the one currently being studied will be placed in perspective relative to earlier ones.

Then study the chapter, section by section. After you have done that, go over the summary several times. Then go back over each of the headings and subheadings, stopping for a moment to recall what each contained. Finally, close the text and sit back and tell yourself, aloud if possible, the major points of the chapter.

This approach will reap you large benefits and enhance your understanding of the process of financial decision making; the rewards will be far in excess of the costs.

The same approach should be taken as you study the Study Guide, keeping in mind that the Study Guide *summarizes* most of the chapters of the text. As noted above, the format of the Study Guide is straightforward.

Bon Voyage

Not all students will use the Study Guide in exactly the same way. However you use it, we trust you will find it helpful. And we know you will get as much knowledge and enjoyment from the Brealey and Myers text as we have. Good luck!

Charles A. D'Ambrosio
Stewart D. Hodges

Study Guide to Accompany Brealey and Myers

Principles of
Corporate Finance

1 *Why finance matters*

Introduction

This chapter, like the first chapter of many other large textbooks, is a brief introduction to the book. It is important because it sets the scene for what is to follow. The chapter answers the following three questions:

1. What kinds of problems occur in finance, and why are they interesting?
2. Who do we really mean when we talk about "the financial manager"?
3. What topics does the book cover and in what order?

What to Look For in Chapter 1

Chapter 1 has three short sections corresponding to the three questions described above and an even shorter concluding section. The full meaning of Sections 1.1 and 1.3 will become apparent only as you progress through the whole book. In the meantime, look out for the following three major sets of problems faced by financial managers. First, in order to carry on business, companies spend money to purchase various *real assets* such as factories, plants, and machinery. Decisions regarding which specific assets to purchase (or invest in) are the company's *investment* decisions. Chapters 2 to 12 are concerned with investment decisions.

The second set of problems centers on ways to obtain money or credit. After all when a company wants to make an investment, it may first have to obtain cash in order to be able to do so. Financial managers raise money in various ways. For example, they may borrow money by signing a loan agreement with a bank or by selling debentures (long-term bonds). Alternatively, they may decide to raise additional money by issuing new shares of stock for cash. In both cases the company sells pieces of paper (called *financial assets*) whose value is based on its claims to the profitability of real assets. Decisions about how cash should be raised are *financing* decisions. Financing is dealt with in Chapters 13 to 24.

The remaining chapters (25 to 33) are concerned with the third set of problems, a variety that involves *both* investment *and* financing decisions. These include the management of various forms of short-term borrowing and lending, financial planning, mergers, and international operations. The book concludes with a summary of what is known and what is still unknown in finance.

In sum the financial manager's tasks are compartmentalized into investment decisions, financing decisions, and a combination of investment and financing decisions.

The Challenge of Financial Management　We have just sketched a few of the wide range of decisions that financial managers have to make. But what criterion is to be applied to select the best decisions? Remember, legally the shareholders are the ultimate owners of the firm and the role of the manager is that of an agent acting on behalf of the owners. Therefore, the financial manager's duty is to make decisions that will benefit shareholders, that is, will increase the value of their stake in the firm. Of course, although the financial manager's main duty is to the shareholders, there are also obligations to creditors, employees, and society.

Because the prime concern is to try to increase shareholder value, it is hardly surprising that the theory and implications of how financial assets are valued play a key role in the text. They represent an exciting challenge to students and practitioners alike.

The text also stresses the importance of understanding how capital markets work. Capital markets are important to a financial manager for two main reasons. First, a financial manager cannot understand how the values of financial assets are determined without knowing something about the markets in which they are traded. Second, a financial manager is often a direct participant in the capital markets.

Both the text and the study guide provide the solid foundation of concepts and information on which sound financial decisions are based. You will build on this foundation with your own experience, talents, judgment, creativity, and initiative.

The Financial Manager   So far we have begged the question of precisely who we mean by the "financial manager." Section 1.2 of the chapter deals with that issue. Naturally a large number of managers in a firm may be involved in contributing to financial decisions. Any of these may justifiably be called a financial manager. Of course, some managers specialize in finance. Look out for the special role of the treasurer. In large companies there may be a controller as well as a treasurer. Look out for how their roles differ. Finally, bear in mind the importance of the board of directors. Directors are elected by shareholders (the ultimate owners of the company) and act as their representatives. The final decisions on dividend payments, public issues of securities, and the approval of major investment projects are made by the board of directors.

Summary

Financial Decisions   Companies make *investment* decisions about which real assets to purchase.

They make *financing* decisions about how to raise cash.

The usual criterion for success is value. The shareholders are the ultimate owners of the firm, and managers act as their agents. The financial manager should make decisions that will *increase the value of the shareholders' stake in the firm*. (At the same time there is clearly a further duty to honor the firm's obligations to its creditors, its work force, and society at large.)

Four Aspects of the Financial Manager's Job   The financial manager's job cannot be learned just by reading a textbook. The text is no substitute for experience, although it supplies the conceptual foundation on which good financial decisions are based. Here are four challenges of the financial manager's job:

1. *Understanding capital markets*   The financial manager acts as an intermediary between the firm's operations and the capital markets in which the firm's securities are traded. Correct investment and financing decisions require an understanding of how capital markets work.

2. *Understanding value* We can't expect to make financial decisions that will consistently increase the wealth of shareholders unless we understand how financial assets are valued. A large part of the text is devoted to explaining the theory of financial value and its implications.

3. *Understanding the effects of time and uncertainty* Most investments do not repay themselves for some years, and their outcomes are often very uncertain. The financial manager must understand how the timing and uncertainty of future earnings affect the value of a prospective investment.

4. *Understanding people* The financial manager needs the opinions and the cooperation of many people. Understanding how people tick is essential if damaging misunderstandings or conflicts of interest are to be avoided.

The Financial Manager No one person is responsible for all the financial decisions described in the book. The term *financial manager* is used to refer to anyone responsible for a significant financial decision of a company.

The *treasurer* of a company is its principal financial manager. The treasurer is responsible for obtaining financing, managing relations with banks, making sure the company meets its obligations to its security holders, and generally managing the company's capital.

Large corporations may have a *controller* as well as a treasurer. The controller manages budgeting, accounting, and auditing, functions which involve inspecting to see that money is used efficiently. In the largest companies the treasurer and controller may both report to a financial vice-president who acts as chief financial officer.

The power for ultimate financial decisions often rests with the board of directors, although the authority for approving small- or medium-sized investments is commonly delegated. Moreover, only the board has the legal power to declare a dividend or sanction a public issue of securities.

Topics Covered in the Book

The following outline provides a key to the main sections of the book and to the main topics covered within each section.

Main sections	Part	Chapters	Topics covered
Introduction	1	1	Why finance matters
The investment decision	2	2– 6	How to value assets
	3	7– 9	The link between risk and value
	4	10–12	Managing the investment process
The financing decision	5	13	Can securities be issued at a fair price?
		14–15	How are securities issued?
	6	16–19	Dividend policy and debt policy
	7	20–24	Valuing different kinds of debt
Interactions of investment and financing	8	25–28	Managing short-term assets and liabilities
	9	29–31	Issues in financial planning
	10	32	Pension plans
Conclusion	11	33	What we do know and do not know about finance

You will find it useful to refer back to this outline as you progress through the book.

List of Terms

Capital market
Controller
Financial assets
Financing
Intangible assets
Investment
Real assets
Tangible assets
Treasurer

Exercises

Fill-in Questions

1. A company's _____ consist of the tangible and intangible assets that it uses to carry on its business.

2. _____ assets consist of physical assets such as factories, offices, plant, machinery, and equipment.

3. Trademarks, patents, and technical expertise are examples of _____ _____ assets.

4. Stocks and bonds are pieces of paper that represent claims on real assets. They are called _____ assets.

5. The firm's _____ decisions are concerned with what assets it should purchase.

6. The firm's _____ decisions are concerned with how cash should be raised.

7. The markets in which financial assets are traded are called _____ markets.

8. The _____ is the principal financial manager of the firm.

9. Large corporations may have a further financial executive, called a _____, who is responsible for budgeting, accounting, and auditing.

Problems

1. Which of the following are investment decisions and which are financing ones:
   a. Issuing common stock

b. Developing a new product
c. Buying a factory
d. Paying a dividend to stockholders
e. Borrowing from a bank
f. Selling a warehouse
g. Purchasing shares of another company

2. Which of the following are real assets and which are financial assets:
   a. A patent
   b. An office building leased by the company
   c. A debenture
   d. Raw materials inventory
   e. A lease
   f. A bank loan

Essay Questions

1. Describe the differences between each of the following:
   a. A tangible asset and an intangible asset
   b. Investment and financing
   c. The treasurer and the controller
2. Explain what capital markets are and why financial managers need to understand them.

Answers to Exercises

Fill-in Questions

1. real assets	**4.** financial	**7.** capital
2. tangible	**5.** investment	**8.** treasurer
3. intangible	**6.** financing	**9.** controller

Problems

1. a, d, and e are financing decisions; b, c, f, and g are investment decisions.
2. a, b, and d are real assets; c, e, and f are financial assets.

2

The concept of net present value

Introduction

This chapter introduces the single most important idea in finance: *present value*. Most investments produce revenues at some later date, and the time value of money, expressed as *present value,* tells us how much the prospect of future income is worth today. *Net present value* measures how much an investment will add to the value of the company because it is the amount by which the investment's present value exceeds its cost. By accepting positive net present value projects and rejecting negative net present value projects, financial managers will increase the value of the company. Such increases always serve the best interests of shareholders as long as they can buy and sell shares and other financial claims in an efficient capital market such as we have in the United States.

What to Look For in Chapter 2

The value of an asset stems from the future cash flows it produces. *Present value* is the method we use to determine how much the prospect of a future cash flow is worth today.

Present Value Present value is worth spending some time on because it is important; it tells us how much an investment is worth today, given its expected cash flows. Suppose you have an investment which is expected to pay $100 in 1 year. How much is it worth to you today? Well, it all depends. On what? On the return you expect to make on other investments of comparable risk. If comparable-risk investments offer a return of 10 percent, an investment of $90.91 ($100/1.1) today also is expected to produce $100 in 1 year. Your original investment has a *present value* of $90.91. If it costs only $80, it has a *net present value* of $10.91 ($90.91 − $80.00), and it makes you better off by $10.91 relative to the alternative investments. Make sure you understand the meaning of return, present value, and net present value and that you can calculate each of them.

The Separation of Ownership and Management Present value has important implications. How can the managers of a large company make decisions that will win the approval of *all* their stockholders (who may number thousands)? The answer is by using present value. When managers make an investment with a positive net present value, they can be certain that they are making every stockholder better off. The *capital market* makes it possible for individuals to postpone their consumption or bring it forward. Companies can obtain capital at the *capital market rate*. Investments with a return which is higher than the capital market rate make the stockholders better off. Investments with a lower return are inferior to investing directly in the capital market. The existence of the capital market makes it easy for management to be separated from ownership. Managers don't have to keep asking owners, "Would you like me to do this?" Instead they can ask themselves, "Does this investment offer more than the capital market rate?"

Finally, if you want to go deeper into the theory and the detailed assumptions which underlie these principles, you should study Section 2-2 of the chapter. This section is summarized in section 4 of our Summary.

Worked Example

The following numerical example illustrates how to calculate a present value and why ownership and management can be separated.

Problem

A company has $20,000 to invest in a project which will pay back $23,000 in 1 year's time.
1. What return does the investment offer?
2. What are its PV and NPV if the capital market rate is 20 percent?
3. What are they if the capital market rate is 10 percent?
4. What difference does it make if the company has no cash currently available for this investment?
5. What difference does it make if some shareholders would prefer to consume more this year and less next year?

Solution

1. $\text{Return} = \dfrac{\text{profit}}{\text{investment}} = \dfrac{\$23,000 - \$20,000}{\$20,000} = 15$ percent.

2. $\text{Present value} = \dfrac{\$23,000}{1.2} = \$19,167.$

   Net present value $= \$19,167 - \$20,000 = -\$833.$
   The investment would make stockholders worse off. The company should either invest the $20,000 in the capital market to earn 20 percent or return the money to the stockholders for them to consume or reinvest.

3. $\text{Present value} = \dfrac{\$23,000}{1.1} = \$20,909.$

   Net present value $= \$20,909 - \$20,000 = \$909.$
   The investment will make the stockholders better off by $909.
4. It should make no difference to the investment decision. The company can borrow or issue more shares to raise the necessary capital.
5. It should make no difference to the company. Shareholders are free to sell some of their shares to increase their immediate consumption.

Summary

1. Why we need a theory of value
   a. The aim of investment: to find assets which are worth more than they cost.
   b. When there is a good market, value = market price, *but* we still need to know *how* asset values are reached.

c. The market for many kinds of assets is very thin.

2. Present value

  a. Calculation:

$$PV = \frac{1}{1 + r}C_1$$

NPV = PV − cost of investment

$$= C_0 + \frac{1}{1 + r}C_1$$

where C_0 = cash flow at time 0 (usually negative)

     C_1 = cash flow at time 1

     r = discount rate (= return offered by comparable investment alternatives)

  b. Why we discount:

A dollar today is worth more than a dollar tomorrow.

$1 invested now is worth $1(1 + r)$ in a year's time.

To get $1 after a year I must invest $1/(1 + r)$ today.

C_1 in a year's time is worth $C_1/(1 + r)$ today.

  c. Rates of return:

Return = profit/investment. Investments with positive NPVs are ones which offer a return which is higher than the discount rate. We may either (1) accept investments with positive NPVs or (2) accept investments with a return greater than their opportunity cost of capital.

3. Separation of ownership and management

  a. *Shareholders* want

to increase their wealth

to choose when they consume

to choose what risks they take

  b. An efficient *capital market* provides

choice of when you consume

choice of what risks you take

  c. *Financial managers*

should accept all investments with positive NPVs

because this adds to shareholder wealth.

  d. Irving Fisher (1930) discovered this fundamental principle.

  e. Other criteria: PV is also relevant where the interest of shareholder wealth has to be balanced against other, wider interests.

 *4. The underlying theory (Section *2-2)

  a. The argument:

The *capital market* enables people to lend or borrow.

Lending postpones consumption, *borrowing* brings it forward.

Investments giving less than the market rate are never worthwhile: it's better to lend.

Investments giving more than the market rate should *always* be made: I can borrow (or sell securities) to leave my current consumption unchanged.

b. The assumptions:
Market rates can be used when the following conditions for a *perfect market* are satisfied:
(1) No individual can influence prices.
(2) Access to the market is free. Trading is costless.
(3) Information about securities is freely available.
A market is called *imperfect* when these assumptions fail.
Shareholders may disagree about what discount rate the manager should use in an imperfect market.

List of Terms

Discount factor
Net present value (NPV)
Opportunity cost of capital
Present value (PV)
Return

Exercises

Fill-in Questions

1. The current (discounted) value of a future cash flow is called its

   _____.

2. A _____ is the present value of a single dollar received at some future date.

3. _____ is the profit from an investment expressed as a proportion of the initial outlay.

4. A future cash flow is multiplied by a _____ to give its present value.

5. The existence of a capital market facilitates the _____ of ownership and management.

6. The expected return from a comparable investment in bonds or shares represents the _____.

7. The _____ of an asset is the difference between its present value and its cost.

8. A risky dollar is worth _____ than a safe one, and it is discounted at a _____ rate of return.

9. Financial managers will benefit the firm's stockholders if they maximize _____.

Problems

1. If a 1-year bill (which pays $1000 after 1 year) costs $920, what is (a) the 1-year rate of return, (b) the 1-year discount factor (DF)?
2. Calculate the 1-year discount factors for discount rates of (a) 5 percent, (b) 15 percent, (c) 0 percent.
3. I get a 1-year student loan of $5000 at 3 percent interest instead of the 12 percent rate my bank would charge me. (a) How much money does that save me next year? (b) How much is that saving worth today?
4. A. Miser, Sr., has $2000 to invest. He is considering two projects. Project A requires $1000 and will pay $1100 after a year. Project B also requires $1000 but will pay only $1070 after a year. What should he do if interest rates are (a) 6 percent, (b) 9 percent, (c) 12 percent?
5. S. Prodigal, Jr., has just $50 to his name. He is interested in spending as much money as possible as quickly as possible. He is interested in investment only as a way of increasing his disposable income. Faced with the same opportunities as Miser, Sr., in question 4, what should S. Prodigal, Jr., do? (Assume he can borrow to invest, but not to consume.)
6. I see in the *Wall Street Journal* that I can buy No. 2 cotton at 59.2 cents per pound for immediate delivery, and that I can simultaneously contract to sell it at 65.8 cents in 12 months. (a) What return does this represent? (b) I also notice that I can get a return of 9½ percent by investing in safe 1-year bonds. What do you think is the *least* I would have to pay for storage at the end of a year if I decided to buy and store the cotton?
7. Imagine an economy in which there are just three individuals A, B, and C. Each has money to invest and a number of possible investment projects, each of which would require $1000. A has $2000 to invest and has two projects that offer a return of 11 percent and one that offers 8 percent. B has $1000 to invest and has projects yielding 8 percent and 7 percent. C has $1000 to invest and has projects offering 15 and 12 percent. (a) What projects will be undertaken if there is no borrowing or lending? (b) If they do lend and borrow to each other, what projects will be undertaken and what will the interest rate be?

Essay Questions

1. Explain the meaning of net present value and why it is relevant to the financial manager.
2. ''Many of our shareholders are retired and cannot afford to lose any of the value of their savings. That is why we demand a higher rate of return on our new investments than do many other companies.'' Discuss.
3. Explain how the existence of a financial market can benefit both consumers and businesspeople.

Answers to Exercises

Fill-in Questions

1. present value	4. discount factor	7. net present value
2. discount factor	5. separation	8. less, higher
3. return	6. opportunity cost of capital	9. net present value

Problems

1. (a) 8.70 percent; (b) 0.9200
2. (a) 0.9524; (b) 0.8696; (c) 1.0000
3. (a) $450; (b) $401.79
4. The return on project A is 10 percent; on project B it is 7 percent. As long as the return exceeds the cost, accept the project. Project A may be accepted as long as the opportunity cost of capital is 6 and 9 percent. Project B may be accepted only when the opportunity cost of capital is 6 percent.
5. Invest in project A because it has the greater rate of return.
6. (a) 11.15 percent; (b) 89 cents per pound per year.
7. (a) Always take those projects with the highest returns, all else the same. So A takes two 11 percent projects, B takes an 8 percent project, and C takes a 15 percent project. (b) C's 12 percent project will be undertaken instead of one of the 8 percent projects. The interest rate will be 8 percent.

3

How to calculate present values

Introduction

It is essential to master the techniques for calculating present values described here. The present value of a single cash flow which will occur after a number of years is the basic building block. It enables us to work out the value of any stream of cash flows by adding together the present values of all the separate cash flows. We can often save a lot of time in these calculations by knowing the present values of three special types of cash-flow streams:

1. Perpetuity: a fixed payment each year forever.
2. Constant growth: payment increasing at a constant rate each year forever.
3. Annuity: a fixed payment each year for a limited number of years.

The chapter also explains the difference between compound interest and simple interest, and the effect of different compounding intervals.

What to Look For in Chapter 3

The emphasis in this chapter is on numerical problems. The best way to learn how to calculate present values is to practice. You can save time on the calculations by using a calculator, by using the tables in the appendixes at the end of the text, or by using both.

Invested at an interest rate of r per year, $1 will grow to $\$(1 + r)^t$ at the end of n years. Appendix Table 2 gives values of $(1 + r)^t$, the future value of $1. The amount of money which must be invested today to produce $1 in n years' time is $\$[1/(1 + r)]^t$. Appendix Table 1 gives values of this, the present value of $1.

Appendix Table 1 makes it easy to calculate the net present value of any stream of cash flows. We often need to evaluate situations such as the following:

"An investment of $100 will produce $60 in 1 year's time, a further $50 after 2 years, and a final $40 in 3 years. What is the net present value of this investment if a return of 10 percent is required?"

The calculation (shown below) is done in four steps:

1. Write down the column showing cash flows in each year.
2. Write down next to it the discount factors (from Appendix Table 1).
3. Multiply across.
4. Add up to get the net present value.

Net present value calculation	Year	Cash flow	Discount factors (10%)	Present value
	0	−100	1.000	−100.00
	1	60	0.909	54.54
	2	50	0.826	41.30
	3	40	0.751	30.04
			NPV =	25.88

Provided the calculations are set out neatly, it's hard to go wrong. Be careful, though, not to confuse the interest rate with the number of years when you look up the discount factors. Notice that in this example we assumed the same discount rate (10 percent) for each year. Although the text allows for the possibility of different discount rates for different time periods (i.e., r_1 different from r_2), in practice we almost always use a single rate throughout our calculations.

The formulas for the three special types of cash-flow streams are quite important. Here are some tips on how to remember them:

Perpetuity   The text describes the rate of return on a perpetuity as equal to the interest rate (so $C/PV = r$). Alternatively, some students prefer to remember that the annual payment is just the principal value times the interest rate ($C = PV \times r$). Thought of this way, it is clear that we must wait until the *end* of the first year for the first payment. Either way, it is easy to rearrange to get $PV = C/r$.

Constant Growth   The constant-growth formula must simplify to $PV = C/r$ when $g = 0$. Since positive g must obviously *increase* PV, it is easy to remember that $PV = C/(r - g)$. (If you're not convinced, see problem 18 for a further exercise on this.)

Annuity   Think of an n-year annuity as a perpetuity *minus* another perpetuity which starts n years later. This makes it easy to write down the formula $PV = C/r - C/r \, [1/(1 + r)^t]$ and impress your friends. Annuities are particularly useful and crop up in many situations and in different disguises. Students often find it difficult at first to recognize annuities or solve annuity problems. It is worthwhile spending a little extra time to master them. Problems 13 to 16 provide a range of exercises involving annuities, and Appendix Table 3 in the text provides a table of annuity present values.

Present Values on a Calculator   With a calculator, the following method of discounting a stream of cash flows is much quicker than the one described above and in the text. Instead of writing down a column of discount factors, we simply start with the last cash flow and discount back 1 year at a time, adding cash flows as we go. The calculation (shown below) is done in the following steps:

1. Write down the cash flows.
2. Enter the value in the last year as the last cash flow.
3. Divide by $(1 + r)$ to discount back 1 year and add (across) the corresponding cash flow.
4. Repeat step 3 *up* the table until it is complete.

NPV on a calculator	Year	Cash flow	Value in each year		
	0	−100	25.92	(4)	(= 138.51/1.1 − 100)
	1	60	138.51	↑	(= 86.36/1.1 − 60)
	2	50	86.36		(= 40/1.1 + 50)
	3	40	40	(2)	

This shows that the net present value of the investment (its value in year 0) is $25.92. This calculation is actually more accurate than the previous one (which gave $25.88) because there is no rounding of discount factors. Before you start the calculation, put 1.1 (or in general, $1 + r$) into the memory of your calculator, if it has one, to save having to enter it each time.

Worked Examples

Finally, before you start on the numerical exercises, you may find it helpful to work through the following examples.

Problem 1

I invest $200 in a savings account where it earns interest at 6 percent. How much will my investment be worth **(1)** after 5 years, and **(2)** after 10 years?

Solution

After 1 year I will have $200 \times (1.06)$; after 2 years I will have $200 \times (1.06)^2$; and so on. Appendix Table 2 tabulates *future values* for various interest rates and time periods. I therefore have

1. After 5 years, future value $= \$200 \times (1.06)^5 = \$200 \times 1.338$
   $= \$267.60.$
2. After 10 years, future value $= \$200 \times (1.06)^{10} = \$200 \times 1.791$
   $= \$358.20.$

[Notice that because the interest is compound (rather than simple) I received more interest in the second 5 years ($90.60) than in the first 5 years ($67.60).]

Problem 2

My rich uncle wishes to make an endowment of $2000 a year to his alma mater but proposes that the first payment should not be made until 4 years' time. If he can invest at 8 percent, how much must he invest to do this?

Solution

The endowment is a *perpetuity*. We know that if the first payment was in 1 year's time, the value of the perpetuity would be

$$PV = \frac{\$2000}{0.08} = \$25,000.$$

Since the perpetuity starts 3 years later, its value is

$$PV = \$25,000 \times \frac{1}{1.08^3} \quad \text{(Use Appendix Table 1 to find the value of this discount factor)}$$

$$= \$25,000 \times 0.794$$

$$= \$19,850.$$

Problem 3

I borrow $1000 at 10 percent interest. The capital and interest are to be repaid in four equal installments. Work out the size of my annual payments, and calculate the outstanding balance of my loan at the end of each year.

Solution

My payments represent a 4-year annuity. The amount I borrow is the *present value* of this annuity. From Appendix Table 3, I know that I can borrow $3.170 if I pay $1 each year. To borrow $1000 I must therefore pay $1 × (1000/3.17) = $315.46 each year. We can now work out the loan balance year by year as follows:

Year	Opening balance +	Interest at 10% −	Annual payment =	Closing balance
1	1000.00	100.00	315.47	784.53
2	784.53	78.45	315.47	547.51
3	547.51	54.75	315.47	286.79
4	286.79	28.68	315.47	0.00

Note that the closing balance in year 4 comes to exactly zero, as it should.

Summary

1. Present value
   a. Future values:
      $1 invested at an annual rate r will grow to $1(1 + r)$ at the end of 1 year, $1(1 + r)^2$ at the end of 2 years, and $1(1 + r)^t$ at the end of t years. Appendix Table 2 provides a table of values.
      The interest is *reinvested* each year: this is *compound interest*.
      Under *simple interest* (seldom used in finance) interest is not reinvested; so I get $1(1 + r)$, $1(1 + 2r)$, $\cdots$, $1(1 + tr)$.
   b. Discount factors:
      To get $1 after t years I must invest $1[1/(1 + r)]^t$ today.
      $DF_t = 1/(1 + r)^t$ is the discount factor for year t cash flows.
      Appendix Table 1 provides a table of discount factors.
   c. Present values:
      PV of a cash flow C_t at the end of year $t = C_t/(1 + r)^t$.
      PVs can be *added*, just like the cost of items at a supermarket checkout. So, for an extended stream of cash flows,

$$PV = \frac{C_1}{(1 + r)} + \frac{C_2}{(1 + r)^2} + \cdots + \frac{C_t}{(1 + r)^t}$$

   NPV = PV of cash flows from investment − cost of investment.
*2. Term structure of interest rates
   Sometimes we apply different interest rates to different time periods: $DF_1 = 1/(1 + r_1)$, $DF_2 = 1/(1 + r_2)^2$, etc. $1 in year 2 must always be cheaper than $1 in year 1. That is, DF_2 is less than DF_1, for if DF_2 is greater I have a money machine. I could *borrow* DF_2 and lend DF_1 to cover the repayment. The remainder (DF_2–DF_1) could be used to buy beer. Similarly, $DF_{t+1} \leq DF_t$ for any t.
3. Shortcuts
   a. Perpetuity:
      A perpetuity pays an amount C at the end of each year, forever.

$$PV = \frac{C}{1+r} + \frac{C}{(1+r)^2} + \frac{C}{(1+r)^3} + \cdots$$

$$= \frac{C}{r}$$

(Remember: $r = C/PV$; so $C = r \times PV$ and $PV = C/r$.)

b. Constant-growth perpetuity:

$$PV = \frac{C_1}{1+r} + \frac{C_1(1+g)}{(1+r)^2} + \frac{C_1(1+g)^2}{(1+r)^3} + \cdots$$

$$= \frac{C_1}{r-g}$$

c. Annuity

An annuity makes t equal payments C, at the end of years $1, 2, \ldots, t$.

$$PV = \frac{C}{1+r} + \frac{C}{(1+r)^2} + \frac{C}{(1+r)^3} + \cdots + \frac{C}{(1+r)^t}$$

$$= C\left[\frac{1}{r} - \frac{1}{r}\frac{1}{(1+r)^t}\right]$$

(Remember: this is a perpetuity *minus* a second perpetuity which starts t years after the first.)

Appendix Table 3 gives a PV of $1 annuity $= 1/r - \{[1/r][1/(1+r)^t]\}$.

Future value: $1 received at the end of years $1, 2, \ldots, t$ has present value $1/r[1 - 1/(1+r)^t]$. Reinvested at interest rate r, it is worth $(1+r)^t$ times as much by the end of year t. That is, it is worth $1/r[(1+r)^t - 1]$.

*4. The compounding interval

Compounding twice a year gives $(1+r/2)^2$ after 1 year.

Compounding m times a year gives $(1+r/m)^m$ after 1 year.

As m approaches infinity, $(1+r/m)^m$ approaches $(2.718)^r$, which is e^r.

$1 invested at a continuously compounded rate of r grows to $\$e^r$ in 1 year, and to $\$e^{rt}$ in t years.

Appendix Table 4 gives values of e^{rt}.

5. Summary of Tables in Appendixes

Appendix Table 1. Present value of $1 (discount factors) $= 1/(1+r)^t$

Appendix Table 2. Future value of $1 $= (1+r)^t$

Appendix Table 3. Present value of an annuity $= 1/r - [1/r(1+r)^t]$
($1 at the end of each year for t years)

Appendix Table 4. Future values with continuous compounding $= e^{rt}$

Appendix Table 5. Present value of an annuity received as a continuous stream $= 1/r[1 - (1/e^{rt})]$.

List of Terms

Annuity

Compound interest

*Continuously compounded rate of interest

Discounted-cash-flow (DCF) formula

17

HOW TO
CALCULATE
PRESENT VALUES

Perpetuity
Simple interest
*****Term structure of interest rates**

Exercises

Fill-in Questions

1. _____ interest is calculated on the accumulated amount of the investment, with interest reinvested.

2. The formula for present value is also called the _____ formula.

3. The present value of a future cash flow is calculated by multiplying it by the appropriate _____.

4. _____ interest is calculated on the initial investment only, without reinvestment of interest.

5. The present value of a future cash flow _____ when the interest rate rises.

6. An asset that pays a fixed number of dollars a year for a limited number of years is called _____.

7. The _____ of interest rates explains why bonds which pay off in different years offer different returns.

8. An asset which pays a fixed number of dollars a year forever is called _____.

Problems

1. How much does $1 grow to after (a) 8 years at 6 percent interest, (b) 6 years at 8 percent interest?

2. I invest $50 at 7 percent interest. How much will my investment be worth (a) after 5 years, (b) after 10 years?

3. What is the value of $200 after 5 years invested at (a) 12 percent per year, (b) 3 percent per quarter, (c) 1 percent per month?

4. How long will it take $1 to double when it is invested at (a) 3 percent, (b) 5 percent, (c) 10 percent, (d) 12 percent, (e) 15 percent?

5. How much should I be prepared to pay for (a) $1 in 10 years' time at an interest rate of 10 percent, (b) $1 in 5 years' time at an interest rate of 21 percent?

6. At an interest rate of 9 percent, which is more valuable: a payment of $100 in 4 years' time or one of $130 in 7 years' time?

7. An investment costing $2000 will produce cash flows of $700 in year 1, $700 in year 2, and $900 in year 3. Calculate its net present value at a (a) zero, (b) 5 percent, (c) 10 percent, (d) 15 percent discount rate.

8. I have savings amounting to $1200 and I expect to save an additional $600 next year. I need my savings to pay for school fees of $800 in 2 years' time and $900 in 3 years' time. How much can I afford to spend now on a stereo set if my savings will earn (a) 5 percent, (b) 7 percent, (c) 9 percent?

9. I will receive from my late uncle's estate $40 in 1 year's time and annually thereafter in perpetuity. What is the value of this perpetuity at an interest rate of (a) 8 percent, (b) 10 percent?

10. How much is the previous perpetuity worth if it begins in 5 years' time instead of 1?

11. I now discover that my uncle's will provides that I shall receive $40 in 1 year's time and that this amount is to be increased annually at a rate of 6 percent. What is the present value of this growing stream of income at an interest rate of (a) 8 percent, (b) 10 percent?

12. IBM's dividend is expected to be $3 next year. If the shareholders require a return of 15 percent and the current share price is $80, what rate of dividend growth must they be expecting?

13. At an 8 percent rate how much would the $40 a year income of problem 9 be worth if it lasts for only (a) 20 years, (b) 10 years?

14. My bank will lend me money at 12 percent interest. How much should they lend me if (a) I promise to make five annual payments of $300 starting in 1 year's time or (b) I make the first of five annual payments of $300 immediately?

15. I am saving for the deposit to buy a house. I have just invested $1500 and I expect to save a further $1500 at the end of each future year. If I invest my savings at 6 percent interest, how much will I have after (a) 3 years, (b) 5 years?

16. A store offers the following credit terms on a color television set "slashed" to a price of only $320: only $20 down and 18 monthly payments of $20. (a) Is this an attractive proposition if I can borrow at 1 percent per month? (b) What monthly interest rate is being charged? (c) What annual rate is being charged?

17. How much does $1 grow to at continuously compounded interest when invested for (a) 8 years at 6 percent, (b) 6 years at 8 percent? Compare your answer with that in problem 1.

*18. Use the perpetuity formula $PV = C/r$ to derive the constant-growth formula

$$\frac{C_1}{1+r} + \frac{C_1(1+g)}{(1+r)^2} + \frac{C_1(1+g)^2}{(1+r)^3} + \cdots = \frac{C_1}{r-g}$$

Answers to Exercises

Fill-in Questions

1. compound
2. discounted-cash-flow
3. discount factor
4. simple

5. falls
6. an annuity
7. term structure
8. a perpetuity

Problems

1. (a) $1.59; (b) $1.59

2. (a) $70.13; (b) $98.36

3. (a) $352.47; (b) $361.22; (c) $363.34

4. (a) 23.45; (b) 14.21; (c) 7.27; (d) 6.12; (e) 4.96 years

5. (a) $0.39; (b) $0.39 as before

6. Payments are worth $70.84 and $71.11. The $130 is more valuable.

7. (a) $300.0; (b) $79.04; (c) −$108.94; (d) −$270.24

8. I can spend the present value of my savings *minus* the present value of my school fees: (a) $268.35; (b) $327.33; (c) $382.15

9. (a) $500; (b) $400

10. (a) $367.52; (b) $273.20

11. (a) $2000; (b) $1000

12. $80 = 3/(0.15 − g)$, which gives $g = 11.25$ percent

13. (a) $392.73; (b) $268.40

14. (a) $1081.43; (b) $1211.20

15. (a) $6561.92; (b) $10,462.98

16. (a) Present value cost is $347.97, unattractive; (b) The monthly interest rate is that rate which gives the 18-period annuity of $20 a present value of $300. That is, which gives an 18-period annuity of $1 a present value of $15. From Appendix Table 3 we find that this is just under 2 percent per month. More exactly, it is 1.99 percent. (c) This is equivalent to an annual rate of $(1.01994)^{12} = 26.73$ percent.

17. (a) $1.62; (b) $1.62 as before

***18.** We may regard the series

$$\frac{C_1}{1 + r} + \frac{C_1(1 + g)}{(1 + r)^2} + \frac{C_1(1 + g)^2}{(1 + r)^3} + \cdots$$

as consisting of a *constant* stream of payments which are discounted at the discount rate $(1 + r)/(1 + g) - 1$.

The annual payment is equal to $C_1/(1 + g)$.

The PV of the series is therefore

$$\frac{[C_1/(1 + g)]}{[(1 + r)/(1 + g) - 1]}$$

which rearranges to give $C_1/(r - g)$.

4 *Present value of bonds and stocks*

Introduction

The present-value techniques developed in Chapters 2 and 3 enable us to understand the market prices of bonds and common stocks. In each case the value of the security is equal to the expected stream of cash payments discounted at the rate of return expected by investors.

If we know the market price of a bond or a stock, we can estimate the rate of return investors require. Financial managers need to know about these rates in order to make correct investment and financing decisions. Regulatory agencies also need to know about them in order to set prices for regulated monopolies such as AT&T so that their shareholders can expect a "fair rate of return."

Some companies reinvest a large proportion of their earnings in order to achieve rapid expansion. Others pay out most of their earnings as dividends and grow at a slower rate. A company's share price reflects the market's assessment of its opportunities for profitable growth. A company which is expected to make a lot of investments with positive NPVs can command a high market price relative to its current level of earnings. It will have a high price-earnings ratio (P/E ratio).

What to Look For in Chapter 4

Our knowledge of present value doesn't mean that we can expect to make our fortunes speculating in stocks and bonds. However, it does help us to understand why various securities are priced as they are.

Bonds The chapter starts by looking at the prices of bonds. Bonds are especially simple because everyone knows what cash flows they promise to pay. A bond pays a regular stream of coupon payments until the date of its *maturity,* when it also pays off its *face value*. The price of a bond is simply the present value of the cash flows expected from it, discounted at the rate of return required by investors. Notice that the coupons form a constant annuity stream and the face value is a single future payment.

Example: Price of a Bond What is the price of a 15-year 8 percent coupon bond with a $1000 face value if investors require a 12 percent return?

Solution Price = ($80 × PV annuity 15 years, 12%) + ($1000 × PV 15 years, 12%)

= ($80 × 6.811) + ($1000 × 0.1827)

= 727.58

How can we tell what return investors require from bonds? By looking at the prices they pay for them. The present value of a bond's cash flow depends on what discount rate we use. The discount rate that makes the present value of the bond exactly equal to its price is called its *yield to maturity*. When we want to work out how much a bond is worth, it is usually helpful to calculate the yields to maturity of other similar bonds. To calculate the yield to maturity of a bond, we must try different discount rates until, by trial and error, we get the right one. Alternatively, special tables and calculators are available which give the yield directly.

Don't worry too much about the further complication of annual versus semiannual compounding. Most bonds make two coupon payments a year (i.e., a 6 percent coupon bond pays $30 every 6 months rather than a single payment of $60 every 12 months). Because of this, yields to maturity are usually quoted as an annual rate which is compounded semiannually. In other words for a 2-year 6 percent coupon bond with a yield to maturity of 8 percent (i.e., 4 percent every 6 months):

$$\text{Bond price} = \frac{30}{1.04} + \frac{30}{1.04^2} + \frac{30}{1.04^3} + \frac{1030}{1.04^4}$$

The true *annually compounded* rate is given by $1.04^2 - 1 = 8.16$ percent.

Stocks   The chapter describes three equivalent ways of viewing the price of a stock. These are

1. The present value of future dividends.
2. The present value of free cash flow.
3. The present value of current activities *plus* the present value of growth opportunities.

As before with bonds, we sometimes want to use the capitalization rate to calculate the value of the security, and we sometimes want to infer the capitalization rate from the price of the security.

Dividends and Free Cash Flow   The central idea here is that the price of a stock is its future dividends D_t discounted at the market capitalization rate r:

$$P = \sum_{t=1}^{\infty} \frac{D_t}{(1 + r)^t}$$

Make sure you understand why this doesn't ignore the value of capital gains. Dividends are hard to forecast, as they depend on whatever dividend policy the company adopts. Instead, we may prefer to forecast the flow of cash that the activities of the company are likely to produce. (We add depreciation back to the earnings figure, and subtract any additional investment and increases in working capital.) The company can distribute this so-called *free cash flow* to the shareholders as dividends, and we can discount them to work out the value of the stock. In some situations we may expect dividends to increase at a constant rate g, and in this case we may use the constant-growth formula $P = D_1/(r - g)$.

Present Value of Growth Opportunities (PVGO)   If the current level of earnings can be maintained without any new investment having to be made (and that is what earnings means), the price of the stock must be at least E_1/r. The price is exactly equal to E_1/r if all new investments have a zero net present value. Finally if there *are* growth opportunities with a positive NPV, this must be added, giving

$$P = \frac{E_1}{r} + \text{PVGO}$$

This relationship immediately implies that stocks with good prospects for profitable growth (large PVGO) have high P/E ratios. We must be careful to remember that PVGO represents more than just growth: it represents the net present value of future growth opportunities. Growth by itself is easy to achieve. By plowing back earnings a company will grow at the rate

$$g = \text{plowback ratio} \times \text{ROE}$$

where ROE is the average return on equity of its new investments. But these investments will not have a positive NPV and will not give the company a positive PVGO unless their return is greater than the market capitalization rate.

Finally, here is another numerical example, a bit like Fledgling Electronics, which illustrates the different viewpoints.

Worked Example

Problem

Next year Penn, Inc., will have earnings per share of $4. The company is expected to continue to plow back 60 percent of its earnings into new investment projects with an average ROE of 20 percent. Its capitalization rate is estimated to be 16 percent. Calculate

1. The stock price.
2. The P/E ratio.
3. The PVGO.
4. Show directly the amounts of investment which produce PVGO.

Solution

1. Next year's dividend $= 0.4 \times \$4 = \$1.60$
Growth of dividends $= \text{plowback ratio} \times \text{ROE}$
$= 0.6 \times 20\% = 12\%$

$$\text{Price} = \frac{D_1}{r - g} = \frac{\$1.60}{0.04} = \$40$$

2. $P/E_1 = 10$; so $P/E_0 = 11.2$, since earnings grow at 12 percent
3. $\text{PVGO} = P - (E_1/r) = \$40 - (\$4/0.16) = \$15$
4. Plowback in year 1 amounts to $0.6 \times \$4 = \$2.40$. This earns 20 percent, i.e., $0.48 a year in perpetuity, which is worth $\$0.48/0.16 = \$3.00$. The NPV of this investment is $0.60. Further plowback leads to new NPVs increasing at 12 percent. $\text{PVGO} = \$0.60/(0.16 - 0.12) = \$15$ as before.

Summary

1. **Bonds**

   If we know the return required from a bond, we can work out its price. For example, if a 10 percent return is required on a 3-year 6 percent coupon bond with a face value of $1000, its price is given by PV $= 60/1.1 + 60/1.1^2 + 1060/1.1^3 = \$900.53$. Conversely, if we know the price we can work out the return (by trial and error). So if the bond has a market price of $877.81, then since $877.81 = 60/1.11 + 60/1.11^2 + 1060/1.11^3$, it promises a return of 11 percent. This is its *yield to maturity*.

2. **The value of common stocks**

   The price of a stock today is the discounted value of the dividends expected in the next year plus its forecast price 1 year hence. That is,

   $$P_0 = \frac{DIV_1 + P_1}{1 + r}$$

   The expected return r is often called the *market capitalization rate*.

   All securities in the same risk class are priced to offer the same expected return. (If one stock offered a higher return, everyone would rush to buy it, pushing its price up and the expected return down.)

   The price expected next year depends on dividends and price the year after:

   $$P_1 = \frac{DIV_2 + P_2}{1 + r}$$

   Substituting this into the previous equation for P_0 gives

   $$P_0 = \frac{DIV_1}{1 + r} + \frac{DIV_2 + P_2}{(1 + r)^2}$$

   and repeating the process:

   $$P_0 = \frac{DIV_1}{1 + r} + \frac{DIV_2}{(1 + r)^2} + \frac{DIV_3}{(1 + r)^3} + \cdots = \sum_{t=1}^{\infty} \frac{DIV_t}{(1 + r)^t}$$

   The value of a company's stock is therefore equal to the discounted stream of *all future dividends* paid on that existing stock. Future dividends expected on stock not yet issued are not included. Dividends are cash produced by the company and not reinvested, i.e., revenue minus costs and investment. Another word for this is free cash flow.

3. **The constant-growth model**

   If dividends are expected to grow at a constant rate g, then, as we saw in Chapter 3:

   $$P_0 = \frac{DIV_1}{r - g} \qquad \text{(provided } g < r\text{)}$$

   Conversely, the market capitalization rate r is the dividend yield plus the rate of dividend growth:

   $$r = \frac{DIV_1}{P_0} + g$$

Companies can use this to estimate the return expected by their shareholders. The tricky part is to estimate g. One useful approach is to use

g = plowback ratio × return on equity

4. Setting electricity prices

   The Federal Energy Regulatory Commission (FERC) sets prices for interstate sales of electric power. The price is supposed to provide a "fair" rate of return on the equity invested. The market capitalization rate r *is* this fair rate of return. So the FERC has to estimate r and then set prices to enable r to be achieved.

5. Pitfalls for the unwary

   a. Estimates of r may be inaccurate for a single stock. An average of estimates from a large sample of companies is usually better.

   b. High growth rates are usually short-lived; so the constant-growth model is inappropriate. Instead, work out the dividends expected during the period of high growth and use the constant-growth model to predict the price at the end of that period.

   c. No easy money. If you think that the market price of a stock is too high or too low, it is probably because *you* have used poor dividend forecasts.

6. The relation between stock price and earnings

   Three cases are considered:

   a. All earnings are distributed as dividends which remain constant through time. The earnings-price ratio equals the capitalization rate as

   $$r = \frac{DIV_1}{P_0} = \frac{EPS_1}{P_0} \qquad (\text{EPS} = \text{earnings per share})$$

   b. Some earnings are plowed back into new projects, but these have zero NPVs. Although DIV_1 is reduced, P_0 is unchanged, and in the short run earnings are unchanged. That is,

   $$r = \frac{EPS_1}{P_0} > \frac{DIV_1}{P_0}$$

   so the earnings-price ratio still equals the capitalization rate. In both these cases $P_0 = EPS_1/r$.

   c. It is more usual for a company to have some growth opportunities with positive NPVs. P_0 is increased by the present value of future growth opportunities PVGO; so

   $$P_0 = \frac{EPS_1}{r} + \text{PVGO}$$

   Rearranging gives

   $$\frac{EPS_1}{P_0} = r \left(1 - \frac{\text{PVGO}}{P_0} \right)$$

   so the earnings-price ratio is *less* than the capitalization rate.
   (PVGO is rarely negative, since firms can usually reject projects with negative NPVs.)

7. Meaning of the P/E ratio

a. *Price-earnings ratios* are published along with stock price quotations in the newspaper. They do not give P_0/EPS_1 but are based on the most recent earnings announcements.

b. A high P/E ratio indicates that earnings are expected to rise—but it may just mean they are currently very low.

c. The P/E ratio provides a useful yardstick for valuing companies whose stock is not traded publicly.

d. A high P/E *does not* indicate a low capitalization rate.

e. The EPS figure depends on the company's choice of accounting procedures and is unlikely to reflect the amount of money which could be paid out without affecting its capital value. The P/E ratio can therefore be very misleading, even for comparisons between similar companies.

List of Terms

Coupon rate	Maturity date
Dividend yield	Payout ratio
Face value	P/E ratio
Free cash flow	Plowback ratio (retention ratio)
Growth stock	Return on equity (ROE)
Income stock	Yield to maturity
Market capitalization rate	(internal rate of return)

Exercises

Fill-in Questions

1. The _____ value of a bond is the amount of money that is repaid when the bond matures (usually $1000).

2. A bond's _____ is its interest payment, usually expressed as an annual percentage rate.

3. A bond must be repaid on its _____.

4. The _____ of a bond is the rate of return it offers if held to maturity.

5. The _____ is the return that investors require from investment in a stock or bond.

6. Annual dividend per share/Share price = _____.

7. The proportion of earnings paid out as dividends is called the _____.

8. The proportion of earnings kept in the business is called the _____.

9. The _____ is the net profit of a company expressed as a proportion of the book value of the equity.

10. _____ stocks are held primarily for future capital gains.

11. _____ stocks are held primarily because they provide a regular income.

12. Cash which is generated by a company and not retained in the business is often known as _____.

13. A firm with good growth opportunities will usually have a high-_____ ratio.

Problems

1. You are asked to put a value on a bond which promises eight annual coupon payments of $50 and will repay its face value of $1000 at the end of 8 years. You observe that other similar bonds have yields to maturity of 9 percent. How much is this bond worth?

2. You are offered the bond of problem 1 for a price of $755.50. What yield to maturity does this represent?

3. Your company has an issue of 7 percent debentures outstanding which mature in 17 years. They are currently being traded at a price of $829.10. **(a)** What is their yield to maturity? **(b)** What price would you expect to get for a new issue of 8½ percent coupon 20-year debentures?

4. Company X is expected to pay dividends of $5.50 a share in 1 year's time and $5.80 a share in 2 years' time, after which its stock is expected to sell at $91. If the market capitalization rate is 10 percent, what is the current stock price?

5. You forecast that ITT will pay a dividend of $2.40 next year and that dividends will in future grow at a rate of 9 percent a year. What price would you expect to see for ITT stock if the market capitalization rate is 15 percent?

6. If the price of ITT is $30, what market capitalization rate is implied by your forecasts of problem 5?

7. The current earnings of B & S Video are $2 a share, and it has just paid an annual dividend of 40¢. You forecast that the company will continue to plow back 80 percent of its earnings for the next 5 years and that both earnings and dividends will grow at 25 percent a year over that period. From year 5 on, you expect the payout ratio to be increased to 50 percent and that this will reduce the subsequent growth rate to 8 percent. If the capitalization rate for this stock is 15 percent, calculate **(a)** its price, **(b)** its price-earnings ratio, **(c)** the present value of its growth opportunities.

*8. If the current price of B & S Video in Problem 7 is $35, **(a)** what capitalization rate does this imply; **(b)** what is the present value of growth opportunities?

9. The price of UPP shares is $30 and next year's earnings are expected to be $3 a share. The current level of earnings can be maintained indefinitely with no new investment. What is the present value of growth opportunities if investors require a return of (a) 12 percent, or (b) 15 percent?

10. Company A retains 80 percent of its earnings and invests them at an average return on equity (ROE) of 10 percent. Company B retains only 20 percent of its earnings but invests them at an average ROE of 25 percent. Which company has the higher P/E ratio? (Hint: Assume each company has current earnings of $1, and work out its price for a number of values of the market capitalization rate.)

11. Look up Hewlett Packard's current stock price, earnings, and dividend payment. (a) If the capitalization rate is 9 percent above the 3-month Treasury bill rate, what (constant) rate of growth does this imply? (b) At the current retention rate what ROE would produce this rate of growth? (c) What is the present value of growth opportunities?

*12. The calculations for Hewlett Packard in problem 11 took no account of inflation. (a) If the capitalization rate is 9 percent in real terms, what rate of *real* growth does this imply? (b) What *real* ROE does this imply if current earnings can be sustained in *real* terms with no plowback? (c) What is the present value of growth opportunities?

*13. Derive the formula

$$\frac{P}{E_1} = \frac{1}{r - \dfrac{\text{plowback ratio}}{\text{payout ratio}}(\text{ROE} - r)}$$

from the constant-growth formula and the equation $g = \text{ROE} \times \text{plowback ratio}$, where ROE is the average return on equity on new investments and r is the capitalization rate.

Essay Questions

1. What does the P/E ratio mean? Explain how it is possible for a low P/E stock to be expected to grow faster than a high P/E stock.

2. A company's earnings figure represents money which may in principle be distributed to shareholders. Explain why the stock price represents the present value of dividends rather than earnings.

3. "Some companies have a policy of retaining all earnings and never paying a dividend. Doesn't this invalidate the principle that the stock price equals the present value of future dividends?" Discuss.

4. What can you say about the effect of an increase in interest rates on the prices of (a) bonds, (b) stocks?

Answers to Exercises

Fill-in Questions

1. face
2. coupon
3. maturity date
4. yield to maturity
5. market capitalization rate

6. dividend yield
7. payout ratio
8. plowback ratio
9. return on equity
10. growth

11. income
12. free cash flow
13. price-earnings

1. $778.61
2. 9.50 percent
3. (a) 9.00 percent; (b) $954.36
4. $85
5. $40
6. 17 percent
7. Earnings and dividends over the next 6 years are as follows:

Year:	0	1	2	3	4	5	6
Earnings	$2.0	$2.5	$3.125	$3.906	$4.883	$6.104	$6.592
Dividend	$0.40	$0.50	$0.626	$0.781	$0.977	$3.052	$3.296

In year 5 it will be worth $3.296/.07 = \$47.09$, so discounting this and each year's dividends at 15 percent, we get (a) the current price is $26.91, (b) P/E = 13.46, (c) $EPS_1/r = (\$2.5/.15) = \$16.67$; so PVGO = $10.24.

8. (a) the capitalization rate r must satisfy:

$$35 = \frac{0.50}{(1 + r)} + \frac{0.626}{(1 + r)^2} + \frac{0.781}{(1 + r)^3} + \frac{0.977}{(1 + r)^4} + \frac{3.052 + 3.296/(r - 0.08)}{(1 + r)^5}$$

This gives $r = 13.57$ percent.

(b) $\dfrac{EPS_1}{r} = \dfrac{\$2.50}{.1357} = \$18.42$, so PVGO = $16.58.

9. (a) $5; (b) $10
10. Company B unless the capitalization rate is below about 9 percent.

5

Why net present value leads to better investment decisions than other criteria

Introduction

Chapters 2 and 3 introduced the net present value (NPV) method for making capital budgeting decisions. In practice, companies often use other measures for evaluating investment projects. Four of the most commonly used are:

1. Payback.
2. Average return on book value.
3. Internal rate of return (IRR).
4. Benefit-cost ratio (or profitability index)

Chapter 5 describes these methods and explains why they do not always give correct or even consistent decisions. These methods continue to be used despite the superiority of NPV; so *you need to know:*

1. How to calculate each measure.
2. Its major weaknesses.

This should equip you to argue convincingly against their use, or if you have to use them, you will at least be able to avoid their most dangerous pitfalls.

What to Look For in Chapter 5

Review of NPV The first section gives a straightforward review of the net present value method. Always remember that present values represent market values. The NPV of a project measures the amount by which it will increase the value of the company to its stockholders. Accepting a project with a positive NPV will make the stockholders better off by the amount of its NPV. With the NPV method fresh in your mind, you can compare the other methods against it. Any rule which can give different decisions from the NPV rule will not serve the best interests of the stockholders.

The Time Value of Money Net present value takes account of the time value of money: that is, I am better off if I receive $1 today than if I have to wait a year to receive it. Look out for methods of investment appraisal which do not take account of the time value of money.

Mutually Exclusive Projects Some methods appear to be similar to NPV in the sense that they use discounting and generally lead to the same accept-reject decisions as NPV. The internal rate of return and benefit-cost ratios are examples of such methods. The problem with these methods is that they can easily give an incorrect ranking of projects and result in an incorrect choice from alternative projects. For example, project A may have a higher NPV than project B, and hence may be a better project. At the same time it may have a lower internal rate of return and so appear to be inferior under that criterion. If we can accept both projects, this may not matter. Unfortunately, projects are often mutually exclusive. That is, only one can be accepted because, for example, they would be built on the same site or compete for the same market. In this case it is not enough to know that they are both desirable projects; we must know which is better. Few of the alternatives to NPV are good at handling this situation.

Incremental Analysis Unless we are using NPV, which always provides the correct answer, the only way to compare two such projects is as follows. If we accept project A, we will have to forgo the cash flow from project B. We therefore calculate the incremental cash-flow stream of project A's cash flow *minus* project B's cash flow. We thus analyze the effect of accepting project A rather than project B, or "project (A − B)" for short. If (A − B) appears worthwhile, A should be chosen in preference to B. If (A − B) is not worthwhile, then B should be chosen rather than A. Provided this method of incremental analysis is used, both the IRR and the profitability index methods generally give a correct comparison of mutually exclusive projects.

The Effect of Combining Projects The use of this method of incremental analysis [evaluating (A − B)] avoids another common problem you should look out for. Capital budgeting methods other than NPV can lead to inconsistent decisions. Let us suppose that a decision is being taken as to whether to build factory A or factory B, and that there is also a proposal to build warehouse C, irrespective of which factory is built. In present value terms, if the NPV of factory A is greater than that of factory B, the factory-warehouse combination A + C will also have a higher NPV than the alternative of B + C. However, under some of the other criteria (such as payback and IRR) it is possible for the combination of factory A and the warehouse C to appear *worse* than B + C, even though by itself A appears better than B. In this case the ranking of A and B is changed by "packaging" the proposals with the proposal for warehouse C. The incremental approach avoids this inconsistency: when we calculate the cash flows of (A + C) minus those of (B + C), the C cash flows cancel out and the comparison is therefore exactly the same as we would make between A and B directly.

The following worked example illustrates how the different evaluation measures are calculated.

Worked Example

Problem

The Multicash Corporation is considering an investment in new equipment costing $500,000. The equipment will be depreciated on a straight-line basis over 5 years, and it will have a zero salvage value at the end of that period. The equipment will produce annual cash operating revenues of $180,000 for 5 years. Multicash has a required rate of return for this project of 10 percent after taxes and its tax rate is 50 percent. Calculate **(1)** average return on book, **(2)** payback, **(3)** NPV, **(4)** IRR, and **(5)** profitability index for the project.

Solution

First, calculate the annual after-tax earnings and cash flows (figures in $1000s):

Operating revenues	180
Less depreciation	100
Profit before tax	80
Less tax at 50 percent	40
Profit after tax	40
Operating revenues	180
Less tax (calculated above)	40
Cash flow	140

1. Average profit after tax $= \$40,000$
Average book value of investment $= \$250,000$
Average return on book $= 40/250 = 16$ percent
2. Payback: the first 3 years generate cash flows amounting to 420, which is 80 short of payback. Payback is $3 + 80/140 = 3.6$ years. Or $500/140 = 3.6$ years.
3. Net present value:

	Amount	Discount factor	PV
Year 0: initial investment	−500	1.000	−500.0
Years 1–5: after-tax cash flows	140	3.791	530.7
Net present value =			30.7

4. First calculate NPV at various discount rates:

NPV at 10 percent = 30.7

NPV at 11 percent = 17.4

NPV at 12 percent = 4.7

NPV at 13 percent = −7.6

Next, interpolating between 12 and 13 percent,

$$\text{IRR} = 12 \text{ percent} + \frac{4.7}{4.7 + 7.6} = 12.4 \text{ percent}$$

Note: This shows the general trial-and-error method. In this example the IRR can be obtained more easily as the rate which gives a 5-year annuity factor of $500/140 = 3.57$.
5. Profitability index $= 530.7/500 = 1.061$

Summary

1. Review of net present value
   a. Calculation:
      Forecast the incremental cash flows generated by the project.
      Determine the discount rate; this represents the opportunity cost of capital.
      Calculate the present value (PV) of the cash flows, by adding their discounted values.
      Calculate the NPV of the project, by subtracting the investment's initial cost, i.e., NPV = PV − initial investment.
   b. Decision rule:
      Accept projects with NPV greater than zero.
   c. Interpretation:
      The NPV indicates how much the value of the company (to its stockholders) will be changed if the project is accepted.
      The *discount* rate should be the market rate of return which stockholders can expect to earn by holding other securities with equivalent risk.
   d. Advantages:
      Correctly accounts for the time value of money.
      The NPV of a project is not affected by "packaging" it with another project.

2. Payback period
   a. Calculation:
      Number of years required for the sum of the cash flows to equal the initial investment.
   b. Decision rule:
      Accept projects with payback less than some specified period.
   c. Interpretation:
      Number of years required for the original cash investment to be returned (but without interest).
      Do not be misled into thinking that all cash flows after payback represent profit.
   d. Advantages:
      Simple to calculate.
   e. Disadvantages:
      Does not allow for the time value of money, since it gives equal weight to cash flows before the cutoff date. Ignores cash flows after the cutoff date.
      Can be inconsistent: the ranking of projects may be changed by "packaging" with other projects.
      To give the same decisions as NPV, different cutoff periods should be used for different projects, depending on the project life, the pattern of cash flows, and the risk of the project.

3. Average return on book value [return on investment (ROI)]
   a. Calculation:

$$\text{ROI} = \frac{\text{average profit after depreciation and tax}}{\text{average book value of the asset}}$$

   b. Decision rule:
      Accept project with ROI greater than the return on book value of the firm, or some external yardstick.

33

WHY NET
PRESENT VALUE
LEADS TO BETTER
INVESTMENT
DECISIONS THAN
OTHER CRITERIA

c. Interpretation:

Uses the company's average return on book value or other external yardstick as the sole criterion of profitability. This is extremely unlikely to maximize the returns to stockholders.

d. Advantage:

Fits in with accounting procedures used by firms.

e. Disadvantages:

Makes no allowance for the time value of money; gives too much weight to distant earnings.

Uses accounting earnings rather than cash flows. It therefore depends on the choice of depreciation method and on other accounting conventions.

Can give inconsistent ranking of projects; rankings may be altered by "packaging."

Bears no relationship to the IRR or to the required rate of return in the market.

4. Internal rate of return (DCF rate of return)

a. Calculation:

IRR is the discount rate which makes NPV = 0.

It is calculated by trial and error: calculate NPV for two or three discount rates and plot them on a graph. Use the graph to decide which discount rate to try next. Continue until sufficient accuracy has been obtained with the NPV close to zero.

b. Decision rule:

Accept projects with IRR greater than the opportunity cost of capital.

c. Advantages:

Gives the same accept-reject decisons as NPV for most projects other than mutually exclusive ones.

d. Disadvantages:

Can rank projects incorrectly, and the rankings may be changed by the "packaging" of the projects.

But mutually exclusive projects can be compared correctly by calculating the IRR on the differences between their cash flows.

Some projects give cash inflows followed by outflows, which amounts to borrowing. These should be accepted if their IRR is *less than* the hurdle rate.

For projects whose cash flows change sign more than once: (1) it may not be obvious whether a high IRR is good or bad; (2) there may be several IRRs; and (3) there may be no IRRs.

Does not allow different discount rates to be used for different time periods; i.e., no account can be taken of the term structure of interest rates.

5. Profitability index (or benefit cost ratio)

a. Calculation:

$$\text{Profitability index} = \frac{\text{present value of net cash inflows}}{\text{present value of net cash outflows}}$$

$$= \frac{PV}{I} = 1 + \frac{NPV}{I}$$

where   I = investment

PV = present value

NPV = net present value

   b. Decision rule:
   Accept projects with profitability index greater than 1.
   c. Advantages:
   Gives the same accept-reject decision as NPV for all projects other than mutually exclusive ones.
   Provides a method for ranking projects under capital rationing.
   d. Disadvantages:
   Can rank projects incorrectly, and the ranking may be changed by "packaging" projects together
   But, mutually exclusive projects can be compared correctly using the differences between their cash flows.

6. Other points
   These methods are used by companies: if you *have* to use them, make sure you use them in the best possible way. For example, always compare mutually exclusive projects on the basis of the difference between their cash flows.
   Remember that it is the cash flows which determine the value of a project. Inadequate forecasts of the cash flows can be far more disastrous than using the wrong appraisal technique. Cash-flow forecasts can be expensive and difficult to make. It is silly to waste them by using an inferior method of appraisal.

List of Terms

Average return on book (or book rate of return)
Benefit cost ratio
Discounted-cash-flow rate of return
Internal rate of return
Mutually exclusive projects
Payback period
Profitability index

Exercises

Fill-in Questions

1. The _____ is the length of time it takes an investment to repay its initial cost but without providing any return.

2. Average profit/Average depreciated value of investment = _____ .

3. The discount rate which gives a project a NPV of zero is called its _____ .

4. When it is possible to accept only one of a number of competing projects, they are said to be _____ .

35

WHY NET
PRESENT VALUE
LEADS TO BETTER
INVESTMENT
DECISIONS THAN
OTHER CRITERIA

5. The _____ rate of return is an alternative name for the internal rate of return.

6. The present value of a project divided by its initial cost is called its _____ or its _____ ratio.

7. When the cash flows from a project change sign more than once, the IRR may give _____ rates of return.

Multiple Choice

Indicate which one (if any) of the five measures of investment worth applies: net present value (NPV), payback (P), average return on book (ROI), internal rate of return (IRR), or profitability index (PI):

	NPV	P	ROI	IRR	PI
1. Puts too much weight on distant cash flows.					
2. Depends on the scale of the project.					
3. May have several values.					
4. Gives the same accept-reject decisions as NPV on single projects.					
5. Does not depend on the method of depreciation used for tax purposes.					
6. Puts too little weight on distant cash flows.					
7. Can use different required returns for different time periods.					
8. Is the most complicated to calculate.					

Problems

1. The Pratt Piston Company is considering an investment in a new plant which will entail an immediate capital expenditure of 2000 ($1000s). The plant is to be depreciated on a straight-line basis over 10 years and there will be no salvage value. Annual operating revenues (before depreciation and taxes) are expected to be 550 for the first 5 years of the plant and to be 400 for the following 5 years. Assuming that the company has a required return of 12 percent after taxes for such an investment and that its marginal tax rate is 40 percent, calculate (a) average return on book, (b) the payback period, (c) NPV, (d) IRR, (e) the profitability index.

2. For each of the following four projects calculate the IRR, NPV, and profitability index at a 10 percent discount rate. Note how the rankings differ for each method.

Cash flows	Time period			
	0	1	2	3
Project A	−100			145
Project B	−100	115		
Project C	−100	230	−120	
Project D	−45	20	20	20

3. Under some circumstances the average return on book value is approximately equal to the internal rate of return. Show that an investment which produces a level stream of cash revenues (i.e., with no accruals) for T years will have an annual return on book exceeding the rate r if

Annual cash flow $\geq$ depreciation + average investment $\times$ r

and that its IRR will exceed r if

$$\text{Annual cash flow} \geq \frac{\text{cost of investment}}{\text{PV annuity}_{T \text{ years, } r\%}}$$

Compare these required cash flows under straight-line depreciation for an investment costing \$100, with $r = 8$ and 16 percent and $T = 5$ and 10 years. Which of the two methods is the more conservative, and why?

4. Thanet House Investments has an opportunity cost of capital of 13 percent. Which of the following projects should Thanet accept?

	Cash flows (\$1000s)				
Project	C_0	C_1	C_2	C_3	IRR, %
A	−112	40	50	60	15
B	45	60	−70	−70	16
C	−100	−26	80	80	11
D	146	−70	−60	−50	12
E	−100	425	−576	252	20

5. Thanet House Investments is considering the following mutually exclusive investments:

	Cash flows (\$1000s)			
Project	C_0	C_1	C_2	C_3
A	−400	220	310	
B	−400	130	190	260

Thanet's opportunity cost of capital is 13 percent. Calculate the NPV, IRR, and payback of the two projects. Why do the methods give different rankings? Which project should be chosen?

6. Thanet House Investments' opportunity cost of capital is still 13 percent. Thanet is now considering the following mutually exclusive investments:

	Cash flows (\$1000s)			
Project	C_0	C_1	C_2	C_3
B	−400	130	190	260
C	−800	360	360	360

37

WHY NET
PRESENT VALUE
LEADS TO BETTER
INVESTMENT
DECISIONS THAN
OTHER CRITERIA

Calculate the NPV, IRR, and profitability index of the two investments.

7. Beanstalk Enterprises expects to generate cash flows of $100,000 in year 1 and $200,000 in year 2. If they make an immediate investment of $35,000, they can expect to receive $190,000 in year 1 and $150,000 in year 2 instead. Beanstalk's opportunity cost of capital is 12 percent. Calculate the NPV and IRR of the proposed project. Why is the IRR a poor measure of the project's profitability?

8. Beanstalk Enterprises in problem 7 now finds that the cost of their proposed investment has risen from $35,000 to $42,000. Recalculate the NPV and IRR of the project. Why is the IRR a poor measure of the project's profitability?

Essay Questions

1. Describe four common methods of appraising capital investments. Discuss the advantages and disadvantages of each.
2. Describe carefully under what circumstances the IRR and NPV methods may imply different investment decisions.
3. Explain why comparing the IRRs of two mutually exclusive projects may lead to an incorrect decision. Describe the correct way to compare such projects using the IRR method.
*4. Explain how return on book differs from the DFC rate of return. Under what circumstances do they produce similar values?

Answers to Exercises

Fill-in Questions

1. payback period
2. average return on book
3. internal rate of return
4. mutually exclusive
5. discounted-cash-flow
6. profitability index; benefit cost
7. multiple

Multiple Choice

1. AROB
2. NPV
3. IRR
4. PI
5. none
6. P
7. NPV and PI
8. IRR

Problems

1. (a) 16.5 percent; (b) 4.88 years; (c) $132,500; (d) 13.7 percent; (e) 1.066
2.

Project	NPV	IRR,%	PI
A	$8.94	13.18	1.089
B	4.55	15.00	1.045
C	9.91	−20.00; +50.00	1.099
D	4.74	15.89	1.105

3.

| Required cash | T = 5 years | | T = 10 years | |
flows under	r = 8%	r = 16%	r = 8%	r = 16%
Return on book	$24.00	$28.00	$14.00	$18.00
IRR	$25.00	$30.50	$14.90	$20.40

IRR is more conservative because it takes account of the need to earn compound interest rather than simple interest.

4.

Project	NPV
A	4.14
B	−5.24
C	−4.91
D	2.41
E	−0.34

Accept projects which have positive net present values, namely, A and D.

5.

Project	NPV	IRR, %	Payback, years
A	37.47	19.73	1.58
B	44.04	18.68	2.31

Take the project which produces the higher net present value, Project B.

6.

Project	NPV	IRR, %	PI
B	44.04	18.68	1.11
C	50.01	16.65	1.06

7. NPV = $5497; IRR = −18.81 percent and 75.95 percent. The two values provide totally different impressions of the project's profitability.

8. NPV = −$1503. The IRR does not exist; there is now no discount rate that will give this project a positive NPV.

6 Making investment decisions with the net present value rule

Introduction

Anyone making capital budgeting decisions will want to be familiar with the issues that are discussed here. The chapter considers the following three problems.

1. How to decide which items should be included in the cash-flow analysis.
2. How to evaluate investments which affect other activities or decisions of the firm. Sometimes, for example, we are forced to choose among alternative projects with different lives. It is pointless to compare the capital cost of a machine which lasts 10 years against that of one which lasts only 5 years. We can, however, compare them in terms of the annual rental (paid over the life of the machine), which has the same present value as the capital cost. This annual rental is called the equivalent annual cost.
3. How to choose investments so as to make the best use of limited capital, management time, or other scarce resources.

What to Look For in Chapter 6

What to Discount   Sections 6-1 and 6-2 explain how to work out the incremental cash flows from a project and discount them. Notice that cash flow can be *very* different from the earnings figure that an accountant would calculate. First, while the accounting earnings for a period do relate to that period, they need not have been received in cash. For example, if I buy 100 grommets for $1 (cash) each, and I sell 40 of them at $1.50 each, I have a profit of $20 (= 40 × 50 cents). However, in cash terms I am still $40 out of pocket [= 100 − (40 × $1.50)]; and if I sold the grommets on credit, I am $100 out of pocket. A second, and even more important difference, is in the way capital items are treated in the accounts as separate and different from income. For example, suppose that I invest $100 in a machine which produces $60 a year for 2 years and then falls apart. Accountants will regard $50 a year as a return which is necessary if I am to recover my investment over the life of the machine. They will deduct this $50 (as depreciation) to arrive at the earnings figure of $10 a year. Nevertheless my cash flows are still −$100, +$60, +$60, and it is these cash flows that I should discount to evaluate the investment.

It is often quite tricky to work out exactly which costs and benefits depend on a project's being accepted (are incremental) and which do not. The best way to tell is to consider what will happen *with* the project and what will happen *without* the project. Whatever changes between the two cases is incremental to the decision.

Look out too for the correct way to treat inflation. The easiest way is to project cash flows in (nominal) future dollars (i.e., grossed up for inflation) and to discount them at a nominal (dollar) rate which is sufficiently high to offer a reasonable return above the inflation rate. If you prefer, you can discount real cash flows (in constant-base-year prices) at a real rate (which is the nominal rate deflated by the expected rate of inflation).

Finally, make sure that you understand the three different methods of depreciation and the way in which depreciation tax shields affect cash flow (although depreciation in itself does not). The first worked example below shows three different ways of looking at the relationship among taxes, depreciation, and cash flow.

Project Interactions   Most capital budgeting investments affect other activities. For example, they may compete for land, factory space, the time of key managers, or the market for existing products of the company. Often, when one investment proposal is accepted, it means that other alternative proposals must be rejected, as, for example, when alternative sizes and locations are considered for a new plant. In making decisions of these kinds, it is essential to take a sufficiently broad view of net present value and to remember that the goal is to maximize the present value of the whole company.

Look out for decisions where there is a choice of project timing, location, or size. Look out too for the equivalent annual cost (EAC) technique. This technique is particularly useful for deciding among similar facilities (such as machines) with different lives, and for deciding on when an existing facility should be replaced. The second worked example illustrates the use of the EAC method.

Resource Limitations   Section 6-4 is rather less important than the earlier sections. There are two key ideas. First, when only a limited amount of funds is available for investment, we must get as much present value as possible for each dollar we invest. The way to do this is to pick the top-ranking projects in terms of their ratio of present value to investment. This ratio is our old friend (from Chapter 5) the profitability index. Second, where resource limitations are more complicated, we can often use a technique called linear programming (LP) to choose the combination of projects which gives the biggest NPV. Finally, bear in mind that most companies can raise large sums of money on fair terms if they want to. Budget constraints are often imposed to curb overoptimistic managers, or because of the problems which might be created by very rapid corporate growth.

Worked Example

Problem 1   Depreciation and Cash Flow

A company has:
  Net cash revenues of $300 (R)
  Annual depreciation of $100 (D)
  So taxable earnings are $200 (R − D)
  It pays tax at a tax rate of 40 percent (T)
Calculate its cash flow (CF).

Solution

1. Cash flow = revenue − tax

   CF = $300 − 0.4($300 − $100)   [R − T(R − D)]
   = $300 − $80 = $220

2. Cash flow = revenue after tax + depreciation tax shield

   CF = $300(1 − 0.4) + 0.4 × $100   [R(1 − T) + TD]
   = $180 + $40 = $220

3. Cash flow = earnings after tax + depreciation

   CF = ($300 − $100)(1 − 0.4) + $100   [(R − D)(1 − T) + D]
   = $120 + $100 = $220

The second of the methods in this example is usually the easiest one for capital budgeting. You just take off tax on the whole of the revenues and then add back the depreciation tax shield. Financial analysts often arrive at cash flow by the third method: they add back depreciation to after-tax earnings. Changes in working capital, etc., necessitate further adjustments.

Problem 2   Equivalent Annual Cost Method

Homemaker, Inc., wishes to acquire a new retail outlet. The leases on two similar shops are up for sale. Shop A has a 7-year lease involving lease rental payments of $15,000 a year payable in advance. The lease can be acquired for $70,000. The lease on shop B has only 4 years to run. It can be acquired for $55,000, and it involves lease rentals of $10,000 a year payable in advance. Which of these shops is financially the more attractive if the opportunity cost of capital is 10 percent?

Solution

Shop A involves an immediate payment of $85,000 followed by six annual payments of $15,000. Its present value (in $1000s) is therefore

$$85 + 15 \times PV \text{ annuity}_{6 \text{ years, } 10\%} = 85 + 15 \times 4.355 = \$150,300$$

Similarly the present value cost of shop B (in $1000s) is

$$65 + 10 \times PV \text{ annuity}_{3 \text{ years, } 10\%} = 65 + 10 \times 2.487 = \$89,900$$

We cannot compare these present values, though, for shop A provides a facility over a longer period of time than does shop B. We must translate the cost of each shop into an annual rental over the period of the lease. We can then compare the annual rentals.

What annual equivalent rental (EAC) on shop A (paid at the end of each year for 7 years) would have a present value cost of $150,300?

$$EAC \text{ (shop A)} \times PV \text{ annuity}_{7 \text{ years, } 10\%} = \$150,300$$

$$\text{Clearly, } EAC \text{ (shop A)} = \frac{\$150,300}{PV \text{ annuity}_{7 \text{ years, } 10\%}} = \frac{\$150,300}{4.868}$$

$$= \$30,900$$

Similarly, for shop B

$$\text{EAC (shop B)} = \frac{\$89,900}{\text{PV annuity}_{4 \text{ years, } 10\%}} = \frac{\$89,900}{3.170}$$

$$= \$28,400$$

That is, the total cost of shop B is equivalent to payments of $28,400 at the end of each year for 4 years. This cost is cheaper than the corresponding annual cost of $30,900 for shop A.

Summary

1. **What to discount**
   a. Only cash flow matters

   Calculate cash flows on an after-tax basis.

   The cash flows represent dividends which *could* be paid if the project were financed entirely with equity; so ignore any projected dividend or interest payments.

   Depreciation is *not* a cash flow, but it does affect tax payments.

   Include investment tax credits.

   b. Discount incremental cash flows

   With or without principal: incremental cash flows are the difference between the cash flows if the project is accepted and if it is not.

   Distinguish between average and incremental. A division which is very profitable may include some (marginal) projects which are unprofitable.

   Include incidental effects, such as benefits from the disposal of waste.

   Include working capital requirements.

   Sunk costs are irrelevant.

   Include opportunity costs.

   Beware of allocated costs and overhead.

   c. Treatment of inflation

   Discount rates are usually quoted in *nominal* terms.

   It is easiest to discount *nominal* (money) cash flows at a *nominal* discount rate.

   Instead, some companies prefer to project cash flows in *real* terms and discount them at a *real* rate of interest. If r_N is the nominal rate, r_I is inflation, and r_R is the real rate, then $1 + r_N = (1 + r_I)(1 + r_R)$; so the real rate is given by

   $$r_R = \frac{1 + r_N}{1 + r_I} - 1$$

   Never discount real cash flows at a nominal rate.

2. **Methods of depreciation**

   Depreciation is important only because it reduces taxable income. Each year the tax saving is the depreciation allowance times the marginal tax rate.

   If we call the depreciable life T, the three methods depreciate the following amounts in each year:

   a. Straight-line:

$$\text{Annual depreciation} = \frac{1}{T} \times \text{depreciable value}$$

$$\text{Depreciable value} = \text{initial cost} - \text{salvage value}$$

b. Sum-of-the-years'-digits:

$$\text{Annual depreciation} = \frac{\text{remaining life}}{\text{sum of } T \text{ years}} \times \text{depreciable value}$$

$$\text{Depreciable value} = \text{initial cost} - \text{salvage value}$$

c. Double-declining-balance:

$$\text{Annual depreciation} = \frac{2}{T} \times \text{depreciable value}$$

$$\text{Depreciable value} = \text{initial cost} - \text{depreciation to date}$$
Asset cannot be depreciated below its salvage value.

Example   Asset with cost of $440 and salvage value of $40 after 4-year life:

Year	Straight-line	Sum-of-the-years'-digits $(1 + 2 + 3 + 4 = 10)$	Double-declining balance Depreciable value	Depreciation
1	$\frac{1}{4} \times \$400 = \$100$	$\frac{4}{10} \times \$400 = \$160$	\$440	$\frac{2}{4} \times \$440 = \$220$
2	$\frac{1}{4} \times 400 = 100$	$\frac{3}{10} \times 400 = 120$	220	$\frac{2}{4} \times 220 = 110$
3	$\frac{1}{4} \times 400 = 100$	$\frac{2}{10} \times 400 = 80$	110	$\frac{2}{4} \times 110 = 55$
4	$\frac{1}{4} \times 400 = 100$	$\frac{1}{10} \times 400 = 40$	55	$55 - 40 = 15$
Totals	$\overline{\$400}$	$\overline{\$400}$		$\overline{\$400}$

3. Project interactions

   Most capital expenditure decisions involve choices of the kind: "either A or B but not both." The chapter gives five examples of how to maximize NPV subject to interactions of this kind.

   a. Optimal timing of investment

      The fact that a project has a positive NPV does not mean that it is best undertaken now; it may be even more valuable if undertaken at a later date. We must choose the date which gives the highest present value.

      For example, if we can harvest a tract of timber immediately with a NPV of $10 million or in 5 years with a NPV then of $20 million, we must compare $10 million with $20 million$/(1 + r)^5$ and choose whichever is greater.

      More generally we must maximize (net future value at t)$/(1 + r)^t$.

   b. Projects with different lives

Mutually exclusive projects with different lives cannot be simply compared on the basis of NPV. To do so would ignore the value of a likely replacement project.

One method is to construct chains of projects and compare the NPVs of chains extending over equal periods.

A neater method is to restate each project's NPV as equivalent to a constant stream of cash which occurs over the life of the project.

For example, machine X costing $2000 with a 4-year life and machine Y costing $3000 with a 7-year life are compared as follows, assuming a 10 percent interest rate: $1 a year for 4 years is worth $3.170, and $1 a year for 7 years is worth $4.868 (from the PV of an annuity table or formula). The capital cost of X is equivalent to $2000/$3.170 = $631 a year. The capital cost of Y is equivalent to $3000/4.868 = $616 a year. Therefore, machine Y is preferred because it is cheaper.

c. The replacement decision

The capital cost of a new machine can be restated as an equivalent annual cost (EAC). Its optimal life is the one which minimizes its EAC.

We can decide whether to replace an existing machine by comparing its cost for the next year (including the loss of salvage value over the year) against the EAC of the new machine; i.e., replace if $EAC < C_1 + S_1 - (1 + r) S_0$.

Remember that these comparisons are based on simplistic assumptions. We can take account of inflation by doing the analysis in real terms. This still ignores other important considerations such as technical change.

d. The cost of excess capacity

Increased utilization of a facility (such as a computer or a warehouse) may bring forward the dates of further expenditures. These changes should be included either with or without principal. If possible, their cost should be compared against appropriate commercial rates.

e. Fluctuating load factors

Consider different sizes of investment and choose the size which has the highest (positive) NPV. A new project may affect the value of other investments: sometimes we must work out detailed scenarios to unravel these effects.

4. Limited resources

a. Capital rationing:

With limited cash for investment the greatest NPV comes from accepting projects with the highest NPV per dollar of initial cost.

$$\text{Profitability index} = \frac{\text{present value}}{\text{investment}}$$

provides an equivalent method of ranking. Positive NPV projects have a profitability index greater than 1.

b. Drawbacks:

This method may waste resources if the capital budget is not exactly satisfied.

When more than one resource is rationed, a more complicated (linear programming) analysis is needed.

The profitability index cannot cope with mutually exclusive projects or where one project is contingent on another.

Capital constraints are often self-imposed to force divisions to focus on priorities and to weed out projects which stem from overoptimism.

List of Terms

Accelerated depreciation
Capital rationing
Double-declining-balance
  depreciation
Equivalent annual cost
Investment tax credit
Linear programming

Net working capital
Nominal interest rate
Real interest rate
Straight-line depreciation
Sum-of-the-years'-digits
  depreciation
Sunk costs

Exercises

Fill-in Questions

1. Costs that have occurred in the past and are irrecoverable are called

   _____.

2. Current assets minus current liabilities equals _____.

3. An interest rate expressed in dollars with no adjustment for inflation is called

   a _____ rate.

4. An interest rate adjusted for inflation so that it represents an increase in purchasing power is called a _____ interest rate.

5. Under _____ depreciation the deduction for depreciation is the same amount each year.

6. Under _____ depreciation the annual depreciation is proportional to the remaining life of the asset.

7. Under _____ depreciation the annual deduction is twice the depreciable value of asset divided by the life of the asset.

8. _____ depreciation is the general term for any depreciation method that provides larger deductions in the early years of the asset's life.

9. The _____ is a special tax allowance which enables a proportion of the asset's cost to be offset against tax in the first year of its life.

10. The _____ of a piece of equipment is the constant annual

charge which over the life of the equipment has the same present value cost as the equipment.

11. _____ refers to a situation in which a company has only limited funds available for investment.

12. We can sometimes find the most profitable combination of activities subject to a number of budget constraints (or other kinds of constraints) by using a technique called _____.

Problems

1. Galactic Engineering is considering an investment of $40 million in plant and machinery. This is expected to produce sales of $8 million in year 1, $16 million in year 2, and $24 million in year 3. Subsequent sales will increase at the expected inflation rate of 10 percent. The plant is expected to be scrapped after 8 years with a salvage value of $8 million, but the tax authorities will allow the investment to be depreciated to a salvage value of $4 million. Operating costs are expected to be $7 million in year 1 and $12 million in year 2, and to increase at 10 percent for the remaining 6 years. Working capital requirements are negligible. Galactic Engineering pays tax at 46 percent. Calculate the expected cash flows in each year and the NPV of this investment when the required rate of return is 21 percent. (Use the sum-of-the-years'-digits method of depreciation.)

2. Repeat the calculation of problem 1 doing the analysis in *real* instead of nominal terms. (Discount at the real rate of 10 percent.)

3. In problem 1, would Galactic Engineering have been better off if they had elected to use double-declining-balance depreciation instead of sum-of-the-years'-digits? Calculate the depreciation in each year and the present value of the depreciation tax shield under both methods to decide. Use a discount rate of 21 percent. Is your conclusion the same if the discount rate is 12 percent instead?

4. A machine costs $3600 and has a depreciable life of 8 years with no salvage value. Calculate the depreciation in each year, and the present value of the depreciation tax shield at an interest rate of 12 percent under (a) straight-line depreciation, (b) sum-of-the-years'-digits depreciation, and (c) double-declining-balance depreciation.

   The corporate tax rate is 46 percent.

5. What difference does it make to your calculations in problem 4 if the asset can be written off over 5 years instead of 8?

6. An investment of $200,000 in a computer is expected to reduce costs by $40,000 a year in perpetuity. However, the prices of computers are predicted to fall at 10 percent a year for the next 5 years. When should the computer be purchased if the cost of capital is 13 percent?

7. The Sundowner Company must choose between two machines which perform exactly the same operations but have different lives. The two machines have the following costs:

Year	Machine A	Machine B
0	$30,000	$40,000
1	$5,000	$7,000
2	$5,000 + replace	$7,000
3		$7,000 + replace

Which is cheaper if the discount rate is 10 percent?

8. A machine costs $100,000. At the end of the first year $5000 must be spent on maintenance. Each year the cost of maintenance rises by 15 percent. How long should the machine be kept before it is scrapped if the opportunity cost of capital is 10 percent? (Assume the machine has a zero salvage value.)

9. XYZ Company is considering whether to replace an existing machine or to spend money on overhauling it. The replacement machine would cost $18,000 and would require maintenance of $1500 at the end of every year. At the end of 10 years it would have a scrap value of $2000 and would not be maintained. The existing machine requires increasing amounts of maintenance each year, and its salvage value is falling as shown below:

Year	Maintenance cost	Salvage value
0	$2000	$2500
1	$3000	$2000
2	$4000	$1500
3	$5000	$1000
4	$5000	none

If XYZ faces an opportunity cost of capital of 15 percent, when should it replace the machine?

10. The acceptance of a particular capital budgeting proposal will mean that a new computer costing $200,000 will be purchased in 1 year's time instead of in 3 years' time. This also implies that an extra computer programmer costing $30,000 a year must be hired in year 1 instead of year 3. Work out the present value cost of these two items when the opportunity cost of capital is 14 percent.

11. Unimagic is planning a new plant to make a consumer packaged good called Unibubble. The latest proposal is as follows: A plant with the capacity to produce 10 million units of Unibubble a year is to be constructed at a cost of $17 million. Sales of this amount will produce revenues of $15 million a year for 10 years, and the direct manufacturing costs are expected to run at $9 million a year. Unimagic pays corporate tax at 46 percent. They would depreciate the plant on a straight-line basis over 10 years, and it would have no salvage value at the end of that period. No investment tax credit would be received.

   Mr. Johnson, the financial director, has figures that indicate that the investment offers an internal rate of return of about 20 percent. Since Unimagic's required rate of return for a project of this kind is 12 percent, he is strongly in favor of the proposal. Mr. Jackson, the production manager, agrees that the project is viable, but he would like to see the company build an even bigger plant. He points out that there are significant economies of scale in the costs of building a bigger plant. Within the capacity range of 7 to 13 million units per year, each additional 1 million units of capacity costs only $0.80 million, as against the average cost of $1.70 million per million units for the proposed plant. The operating costs would remain at $0.90 per unit. Mr. Smith, the marketing manager, also likes this idea. He reports that demand for Unibubble is very elastic, and he is sure that he can sell an extra 1 million units with only a very modest decrease in price from $1.50 to $1.45. Conversely, if they reduced the capacity and output of the proposed plant by 1 million units, they would still be able to increase the selling price only to $1.55. On the basis of these figures, what size of plant should Unimagic build?

12. Rank the following projects in order of desirability when the funds available for investment are limited. Which projects should be accepted when the company considering them has imposed a budget limit of $800,000?

Project	Investment ($1000s)	NPV ($1000s)	IRR, %
1	100	8	13.9
2	400	43	14.4
3	300	25	16.0
4	200	23	14.1
5	200	21	16.1
6	200	19	15.7

*13. In 1980, sinking an oil well in the North Sea offered a real return of about 20 percent. The income accrues over a 10-year period in a level stream. Some critics have argued that for a well of this kind it would be better to leave the oil under the sea a little longer. Suppose that the real price of oil is expected to increase continuously at a rate of 4 percent a year and investors require a real rate of return of 8 percent, when would be the best date to sink the well?

Essay Questions

1. Describe carefully how you would decide what cash flows to include as incremental in a capital budgeting appraisal situation. Give a list of items which are commonly treated incorrectly and say how they should be treated.
2. "We always allocate a proportion of company overhead to a new project in relation to its payroll requirements. After all, in the long run there's no difference between average and marginal cost." Discuss.
3. Describe how to work out the economic life of a piece of machinery and how to decide when to replace an existing machine which performs the same function.
4. Explain how linear programming can be used to select capital investments under a variety of capital rationing and other kinds of constraints. Show how

the profitability index provides the solution to one particular problem of this kind.

*5. Timber is a renewable resource; oil and other mineral reserves are not. Both the value of a tract of timber and the value of a known oil reserve increase with time. The costs of "harvesting" each stay relatively constant in real terms. Discuss how the problem of when to log a tract of timber (renewable resource) differs from the problem of when to exploit a known reserve of oil (nonrenewable resource) so as to maximize its value.

Answers to Exercises

Fill-in Questions

1. sunk costs
2. net working capital
3. nominal
4. real
5. straight-line
6. sum-of-the-years'-digits

7. double-declining-balance
8. accelerated
9. investment tax credit
10. equivalent annual cost
11. capital rationing
12. linear programming

Problems

1. The expected cash flows and their present values look as follows (in $ millions):

Year	Cash flow	Present value factor	Present value
0	−40	1.000	−40.000
1	4.220	.826	3.486
2	5.380	.683	3.675
3	8.592	.564	4.846
4	8.715	.467	4.070
5	8.897	.386	3.434
6	9.142	.319	2.916
7	9.459	.263	2.488
8	16.012	.218	3.491
			NPV = −11.592

2. Provides the same result as problem 1, with a NPV of −$11.6 million.
3. The two depreciation schedules are as follows:

Year	Depreciation method	
	S-O-Y-D	D.D. balance
1	8	10.000
2	7	7.500
3	6	5.625
4	5	4.219
5	4	3.164
6	3	2.373
7	2	1.780
8	1	1.335

At 21 percent the PVs of the tax shields are $9.363 million and $9.783 million, respectively, so the double-declining-balance method is preferred.

At 12 percent they become $11.624 million and $11.931, so the double-declining-balance method is still preferred.

4.

Year	Depreciation method		
	Straight line	S-O-Y-D	D.D. balance
1	$450	$800	$900.0
2	450	700	675.0
3	450	600	506.3
4	450	500	379.7
5	450	400	284.8
6	450	300	213.6
7	450	200	160.2
8	450	100	480.4
PV of tax shield	$1028.3	$1162.4	$1140.6

5.

Year	Depreciation method		
	Straight line	S-O-Y-D	D.D. balance
1	$720	$1200	$1440.0
2	720	960	864.0
3	720	720	518.4
4	720	480	311.0
5	720	240	466.6
PV of tax shield	$1193.9	$1283.6	$1290.7

6. The computer should be purchased in 3 years' time.

7. Equivalent annual costs are $22,286 for machine A and $23,085 for machine B, so A is cheaper.

8. The equivalent annual cost (EAC) for various lives is given below:

Years	EAC
5	$32,280
10	$25,480
11	$25,310
12	$25,320
15	$26,200

The machine should be kept for 11 years.

9. The equivalent annual cost of the new machine is $4914.2. The costs of each year's operation of the old machine (adjusted to the end of each year) are given below:

Years	Cost of operation
1	$3175
2	$4250
3	$5325
4	$6900

The machine should be replaced after 2 years.

10. Present value cost of change in computer timing = $40,444. Present value cost of extra programmer = $49,400.

11. (a) Net present value at various plant sizes is as follows:

Capacity (million units)	8	9	10	11
NPV ($ million)	5.689	5.859	5.725	5.286

The capacity of 9 million units has the highest NPV.

12. The ranking of projects according to their profitability index is: 4, 2, 5, 6, 3, 1. With a budget limit of $800,000, projects 2, 4, and 5 should be accepted.

13. To give a real return of 20 percent, an investment of $100 must produce 10 years' real income of $23.85 per year. At an eight percent real rate this has a present value of $160.05 and an NPV OF $60.05 If we decide to defer the investment to year t, its NPV is:

$$[160.05 \times (1.04)^t - 100]/(1.08)^t$$

This has a maximum value of $64.60 when the investment is made in 6 years' time.

7 *Introduction to risk in capital budgeting*

Introduction

Most people agree that risk is a bad thing and that a safe dollar is worth more than a risky one. Investors expect a higher rate of return from a risky investment than they do from a safe investment. This basic principle was introduced back in Chapter 2, but it was not developed in any detail there. Chapters 7, 8, and 9 form a single unit which deals with what we mean by risk, and how it affects the opportunity cost of capital for a project.

Chapter 7 is mostly about how we measure risk. When I buy a 6-month Treasury bill, I know exactly what return I will get over the next 6 months: it is riskless. On the other hand, if I hold a portfolio of common stocks, such as Standard and Poor's Composite Index of 500 stocks, my return is quite unpredictable. To compensate me for this risk, I can expect to earn a higher return, on average, than from holding Treasury bills. The variation of past returns on Standard and Poor's Index gives some idea of just how unpredictable they are. We can use statistical measures (like the standard deviation) to describe this variability.

Individual stocks are even more risky than Standard and Poor's Index. Diversification (holding a lot of different stocks) provides a way of reducing risk. Unfortunately there is some risk that you can never diversify away. This undiversifiable risk stems from economy-wide perils that threaten all businesses; it is called *market risk*. The risk a security adds to a well-diversified portfolio depends on its market risk, which we measure by its *beta*. As long as investors can diversify on their own account, they have no reason to pay companies to do it for them. This principle ensures that values can be added: the value of a project does not depend on whether or not it adds to the diversification of the company which undertakes it.

With these concepts of risk established, Chapters 8 and 9 are about how to choose the discount rate so that it takes proper account of the risk of the project. Chapter 8 describes the relationship between risk and expected return in the stock market. Chapter 9 applies this knowledge to the practical needs of capital budgeting.

What to Look For in Chapter 7

This chapter develops the concept of risk in a precise way. It is mostly concerned with the risks faced by individual investors holding portfolios of securities. This builds toward Chapter 9, which describes how corporate financial managers should take account of risk when they make capital budgeting decisions. Managers of corporations act on behalf of their stockholders. They want to see the price of their company's shares as high as possible: this will make the stockholders as well off as possible. It is logical to begin by examining risk from the stockholder's point of view, and then to move on to the implications for companies.

There are three key ideas that you should find in this chapter. The first is that Treasury bills and the market portfolio of common stocks provide two useful benchmarks of risk and return. We will often refer to these benchmarks when we assess the risk and expected return of an investment. The second idea concerns the effects of diversification. Shareholders can, and do, reduce their risk very significantly by diversification. The risk that matters to them is therefore the market risk that each security adds to a diversified portfolio. We measure this market risk as the security's beta. Beta measures the sensitivity of the return on the security to the return on the market. The third and final idea is that of value additivity. The value of a project does not depend on how well its returns mesh with the returns on other activities of the company. This is because the shareholders can diversify directly to obtain whatever benefits of diversification are available. They are unlikely to accept lower returns in order to have a corporate manager diversify for them.

Statistics. You will find this chapter quite easy if you already know some elementary statistics. The text gives all the necessary definitions, but you may want to refresh your memory from a statistics textbook. It will help if you are familiar with the terms variance, standard deviation, and covariance, and if you have already met a normal distribution.

Risk. The idea of risk is a familiar one. It means that there are a number of possible outcomes (which are not equally desirable), and we cannot be certain which one will occur. The return on a portfolio of common stocks cannot be predicted with any accuracy. It is risky. The use of statistics helps us to analyze this type of risk in a precise way. The spread of past returns gives a good indication of the range of uncertainty about future returns. This spread is best measured by the standard deviation or the variance.

The standard deviation of the annual returns on Standard and Poor's Index is about 20 percent. That's quite a lot of risk. It accounts for why (over the last 50 years) common stocks have on average earned about 9 percent more than Treasury bills (which are virtually riskless). These two numbers (20 and 9 percent) are useful ones to remember.

Diversification. The standard deviation of an individual stock is generally much higher than for the market as a whole. In fact it is usually about double (35 to 40 percent). The risk in a diversified portfolio is lower than for a single security because the prices of different stocks do not move perfectly together. Diversification is an important concept with powerful implications. When we hold many stocks, the risks which are *unique* to each one tend to cancel each other out, as they are largely unconnected. Some risks, though, stem from uncertainty about factors which affect the whole of the market. This *market* risk cannot be eliminated by diversification: it must be borne by investors, and the investors can expect to earn a higher return for bearing it.

The calculation of the variance of a portfolio is rather involved, and that is why it is in a starred section of the chapter. The following rule of thumb provides a useful guide to the benefits of diversification. The variance of a portfolio consisting of equal holdings of N stocks is equal to

$$\text{Average covariance between stocks} + \frac{1}{N} (\text{average variance} - \text{average covariance between stocks})$$

Typically, the average variance of annual returns is about 1500, and the average covariance between stocks is about 400. As N becomes large, the variance of the portfolio returns comes down toward the average covariance of 400. The standard deviation of the returns from a portfolio is simply the square root of their variance. If you want to go into the calculations in greater detail, work through the worked example given below. If you don't, skip it.

Beta. The contribution a security makes to the risk of a well-diversified portfolio depends on how sensitive it is to market movements. The average stock will tend to move up 5 percent when the market moves up 5 percent. Of course, sometimes it will go up more than the market and sometimes it will go up less than the market. On average, though, it goes up (and down) one for one with the market. This means its beta is 1. A stock which is more sensitive to market movements might tend to move twice as far (10 percent) in response to a market rise of 5 percent. Conversely, it would tend to fall 10 percent if the market fell 5 percent. This stock is twice as sensitive as the average and its beta is 2.

The beta of a portfolio is just an average of the betas of the stocks included in it (weighted according to their value in the portfolio). In other words, if a portfolio consists 60 percent of stocks with betas of 0.8 and 40 percent of stocks with betas of 1.2, the beta of the portfolio is $0.6 \times 0.8 + 0.4 \times 1.2 = 0.96$. When a portfolio is well diversified, the amount of unique risk it contains is negligible. In this case the standard deviation of the portfolio is just its beta multiplied by the standard deviation of the return on the market portfolio. This makes beta an important number. Beta measures how much a stock contributes to the risk of a well-diversified portfolio. And we haven't finished with beta yet. In Chapter 8 we'll see how the returns expected from stocks depend on their betas.

Worked Example

Problem

Calculate the standard deviation and expected return for the portfolio given below:

| Stock | Percentage held | Expected return, % | Standard deviation | Correlations between stocks | | |
				Stock 1	Stock 2	Stock 3
Stock 1	50	10	20	1.0	0.5	0.3
Stock 2	30	15	30	0.5	1.0	0.1
Stock 3	20	20	40	0.3	0.1	1.0

Solution

To work out the standard deviation of a portfolio we need information on the covariances between stocks. In this example we are given the *correlations* between stocks. We can work out the covariances σ_{ij} from the standard deviations σ_i and the correlations ρ_{ij} as $\sigma_{ij} = \sigma_i \; \sigma_j \; \rho_{ij}$. This gives the following table of covariances:

Stock	Stock 1	Stock 2	Stock 3		S 1	S 2	S 3
Stock 1	20 × 20 × 1.0	20 × 30 × 0.5	20 × 40 × 0.3	=	400	300	240
Stock 2	30 × 20 × 0.5	30 × 30 × 1.0	30 × 40 × 0.1	=	300	900	120
Stock 3	40 × 20 × 0.3	40 × 30 × 0.1	40 × 40 × 1.0	=	240	120	1600

Notice that this table is symmetric about the diagonal (that is, $\sigma_{12} = \sigma_{21}, \sigma_{13} = \sigma_{31}$, etc.). This symmetry is also preserved when we calculate the variance of portfolio returns using a similar table:

Portfolio
variance =
$$
\begin{aligned}
&0.5 \times 0.5 \times 400 + 0.5 \times 0.3 \times 300 + 0.5 \times 0.2 \times 240 &= \quad 100 \; + 45 \; + 24 \\
&+ 0.3 \times 0.5 \times 300 + 0.3 \times 0.3 \times 900 + 0.3 \times 0.2 \times 120 &\quad +45 + 81 \; + 7.2 \\
&+ 0.2 \times 0.5 \times 240 + 0.2 \times 0.3 \times 120 + 0.2 \times 0.2 \times 1600 &\quad +24 + 7.2 + 64
\end{aligned}
$$

= 397.4

Since the variance of the portfolio's returns is 397.4, its standard deviation is just the square root of this, which is 19.9 percent.

The expected return on the portfolio is the weighted average:

$0.5 \times 10 + 0.3 \times 15 + 0.2 \times 20 = 13.5$ percent

Summary

Measurement of Portfolio Risk A *risky* portfolio is one in which a *variety* of different returns is possible. We can measure the past variation in returns by their *variance*, the expected value of $(\tilde{r} - r)^2$, where $\tilde{r}$ = actual return and r = expected return, and which in turn equals $[1/(N - 1)] \times$ sum of squared deviations from average. Risk is also measured by the *standard deviation*, the square root of the variance.

Note that the variance is easier to calculate, but the standard deviation is easier to interpret.

Note also that for a normal distribution 68 percent of returns are within 1 standard deviation of the average, and 95 percent of returns are within 2 standard deviations of the average.

The variation of past returns is a good guide to the uncertainty of future returns. Historical risk and average return from various securities were:

	Average annual return, %		Standard
	Nominal	Real	deviation, %
Common stocks (Standard and Poor's 500)	11.3	8.7	22.4
Long-term corporate bonds	4.2	1.8	5.7
Long-term government bonds	3.5	1.1	5.7
Treasury bills	2.5	0.2	2.1

Note that returns include cash payments and capital gains; the figures refer to the period 1926–1977 (Ibbotson and Sinquefield); Treasury bills give a very low real return (0.2%); the average nominal risk premium on common stocks was 8.8 percent; and the standard deviation of Standard and Poor's 500 was higher than average in 1926–1945, lower than average in 1946–1975.

The standard deviation of the returns on a single stock is usually much higher than for the market portfolio (for example, 43.5 percent for Kaiser Steel). Diversification reduces variability; it can roughly halve the standard deviation of portfolio returns.

Unique risk stems from perils unique to an individual company. It can be eliminated by diversification. *Market risk* stems from economy-wide perils that threaten many companies. It cannot be eliminated by diversification.

How to Calculate the Expected Return and Risk The *expected return* from holding a portfolio of stocks is a weighted average of the expected returns on the individual stocks. Expected portfolio return $r_p = x_1 r_1 + x_2 r_2 + \ldots + x_N r_N$, where x_1 = proportion of portfolio in stock 1, r_1 = expected return on stock 1, etc.

We *cannot* calculate the standard deviation of portfolio returns as a weighted average of the individual standard deviations (unless they are perfectly correlated). Rather

$$\text{Portfolio variance} = \quad x_1^2 \sigma_1^2 + x_1 x_2 \sigma_{12} + \cdots + x_1 x_N \sigma_{1N},$$
$$+ \; x_2 x_1 \sigma_{21} + x_2^2 \sigma_2^2 + \cdots + x_2 x_N \sigma_{2N}$$
$$\vdots \qquad\qquad \vdots \qquad\qquad\qquad \vdots$$
$$+ \; x_N x_1 \sigma_{N1} + x_N x_2 \sigma_{N2} + \cdots + x_N^2 \sigma_N^2$$

Where σ_1^2 = variance of stock 1 (σ_1 is its standard deviation)
σ_{12} = covariance between stock 1 and stock 2
$\quad\; = \sigma_1 \sigma_2 \rho_{12}$, where ρ_{12} is the correlation between stock 1 and stock 2

When there are N equal-sized holdings (so $x_i = 1/N$),

$$\text{Portfolio variance} = \left(\frac{1}{N}\right)^2 [N \times \text{average variance} + (N^2 - N) \times \text{average covariance}]$$

$$= \frac{\text{average}}{\text{covariance}} + \frac{1}{N} \times [\text{average variance} - \text{covariance}]$$

The Effect of Individual Stocks on Portfolio Risk The risk of a well-diversified portfolio depends on the *market risk* of the securities included in the portfolio. *Beta* (β) measures the market risk of a stock as its sensitivity to market movements. Stocks with beta greater than 1 are unusually sensitive to market movements. Stocks with beta less than 1 are unusually insensitive to market movements.

The beta of a portfolio is the weighted average of the beta of the securities included in it. That is, $\beta_p = x_1 \beta_1 + x_2 \beta_2 + \ldots + x_N \beta_N$. The standard deviation of a well-diversified portfolio is its beta times the standard deviation of the market portfolio.

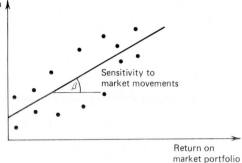

Remember the relationship between diversification and value additivity. Because investors can diversify by holding a variety of stocks, they have no reason to pay more for the stocks of companies which are already diversified, nor should they pay less. Also, the value of a project does not depend on how its returns mesh with the returns from other activities of the company which undertakes it. If the capital market establishes a value PV(A) for asset A, and PV(B) for asset B, the market value of a firm that holds only these two assets is

$$PV(AB) = PV(A) + PV(B)$$

This is the *value-additivity principle*.

List of Terms

Beta (β)	**Normal risk premium**
Correlation	**Risk-free rate of return r_f**
Covariance	**Standard deviation (σ)**
Diversification	**Unique risk**
Market portfolio	**Value additivity**
Market return r_m	**Variability**
Market risk	**Variance (σ^2)**

Exercises

Fill-in Questions

1. Standard and Poor's Composite Index is often regarded as the _____ portfolio.

2. The average annual _____ between 1926 and 1977 was 11.3 percent.

3. Diversification cannot eliminate risk entirely because stocks have _____.

4. Diversification reduces _____.

5. The difference between the expected return on the market and the risk-free rate is called the normal _____.

6. The risks of investing in common stocks can be reduced by _____.

7. Projects with the same risk as Standard and Poor's 500 Index should be evaluated with a discount rate equal to the _____ plus the normal risk premium for the market portfolio.

8. Over the last 50 years the average annual _____ of the return on the market portfolio has been about 20 percent.

9. The _____ of the market as a whole is 1.0.

10. The _____ is the square of the standard deviation.

11. _____ measures the risk a stock adds to a well-diversified portfolio.

12. The principle of _____ means that PV(AB) = PV(A) + PV(B). It implies that firms cannot expect to increase their value by just diversifying.

*13. The variability of a well-diversified portfolio depends almost entirely on the average _____ between individual stocks.

*14. The covariance between two stocks is the product of their standard deviations and the _____ coefficient between them.

Problems

1. A firm is considering a new machine which costs $24,000 and which will directly save a net cash amount of $10,000 each year for 3 years. The firm has no other projects to consider. The funds would be obtained by selling Treasury bills, currently yielding 9 percent, which are owned by the firm. Assuming that the risk of this project is the same as that of the market portfolio, should the firm purchase the machine?

2. A portfolio of stocks has risk similar to a portfolio consisting 30 percent of Treasury bills and 70 percent of Standard and Poor's 500 Index. The Treasury bill rate is 10 percent, and you expect a normal risk premium of 9 percent on Standard and Poor's Index. What return would you expect from the portfolio of stocks?

3. Your investment will give a return of either −10 or +30 percent. (a) Calculate the expected return and the standard deviation of return if these outcomes are equally likely. (b) Calculate them if there is a 0.6 probability of the −10 percent return and a 0.4 probability of the +30 percent return.

4. A portfolio consists of the following stocks:

Stock	Percentage of portfolio	Expected return, %	Beta
Stock A	10	18	0.9
Stock B	30	22	1.3
Stock C	25	24	1.5
Stock D	20	17	0.8
Stock E	15	21	1.2

Calculate the expected return and the beta of this portfolio.

5. The diagram below shows the effect of diversification. Fill in the appropriate words for the labels at A, B, C, and D.

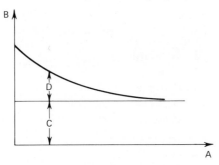

6. What are the betas of the following stocks?

Stock	Expected return, %, if market return is −10%	Expected return, %, if market return is 20%
A	−15	18
B	−7	17
C	−6	24
D	−17	25

*7. The average variance of the annual returns from a typical stock is about 1500 and its average covariance with other stocks is about 400. Work out what this implies for the standard deviation of returns from: (a) a fully diversified portfolio, (b) a portfolio of 64 stocks, (c) a portfolio of 16 stocks, (d) a portfolio of 4 stocks. Assume equal-sized holdings of each stock.

*8. You hold a portfolio of 16 stocks, each of which has a variance of 1500 and a covariance of 400 with the other stocks. One stock comprises 25 percent of your portfolio, and the other stocks are held in equal amounts of 5 percent each. (a) What is the standard deviation of your portfolio? (b) How many stocks held in equal amounts would give approximately the same standard deviation?

*9. Two stocks have standard deviations of 10 and 30 percent. A portfolio consisting of these stocks held in equal proportions has a standard deviation of 16 percent. (a) Guess how correlated the two stocks are, and (b) calculate the coefficient of correlation between them.

Essay Questions

1. Describe how diversification can reduce the risk in an investment portfolio. Why can risk only be reduced and not eliminated in this way?
2. Describe what is meant by the beta of a stock. Why is a stock's beta more important than its standard deviation?
3. Describe what sort of characteristics are likely to be possessed by a company with a high standard deviation but a low beta.
4. Stockholders of publicly quoted companies do not benefit from corporate diversification, since they can diversify for themselves. Discuss under what conditions (if any) this principle extends to the case of a privately held company which is 100 percent owned by a single individual.

Answers to Exercises

Fill-in Questions

1. market	8. standard deviation
2. market return	9. beta
3. market risk	10. variance
4. unique risk	11. beta
5. risk premium	12. value additivity
6. diversification	13. covariance
7. risk-free rate	14. correlation

Problems

1. Discount rate = risk-free rate + risk premium

   = 9 percent + 8.8 percent

   = 17.8 percent

   Net present value = $2187.42; reject the project
2. 16.3 percent
3. (a) Expected return: 10 percent; standard deviation of expected return: 20 percent; (b) expected return: 6 percent; standard deviation of expected return: 19.6 percent
4. Expected return: 20.95 percent; beta: 1.195
5. A: number of securities; B: portfolio standard deviation; C: market risk; D: unique risk
6. A: 1.1; B: 0.8; C: 1.0; D: 1.4
7. (a) 20.05 percent, using 500 stocks; (b) 20.42 percent; (c) 21.65 percent; (d) 25.98 percent
8. (a) 22.583 percent; (b) 10
9. (b) 0.04

8 *Risk and return*

Introduction

This chapter describes the relationship between the risk of a security and the return investors expect from it. This builds on the measures of risk developed in Chapter 7. The central result of Chapter 8 is that there is a straight-line relationship between expected return and market risk (measured in terms of beta). This relationship is called the *capital asset pricing model* (CAPM).

The concept of the CAPM is as follows. The risk premium offered by a security (above and beyond the risk-free rate) must compensate for the risk that the security adds to a well-diversified portfolio. As we saw in Chapter 7, the amount of risk added by a security is proportional to its beta. It follows that the risk premium must also be proportional to beta. While this argument is entirely theoretical, the empirical data broadly confirm the predictions of the CAPM.

What to Look For in Chapter 8

This chapter builds on the ideas about risk that were introduced in Chapter 7. Make sure you remember what standard deviations and betas are before you start on Chapter 8. The capital asset pricing model is developed in three stages.

Efficient Portfolios   The first stage is the idea of efficient portfolios. This is quite an easy concept to grasp. Most investors like high expected return and prefer a low standard deviation of return. Portfolios which give the highest possible return for a given standard deviation are called *efficient*. Investors need only consider efficient portfolios, for all other portfolios give them a poor deal.

You may wonder if it's reasonable to assume that an investor can choose between portfolios solely on the basis of their expected returns and standard deviations. The answer to this is that it usually *is* a reasonable assumption. Every portfolio has a different probability distribution of possible future returns, and the investor has to choose between them. In most cases the investor can reasonably regard the future return from any portfolio as coming from a normal distribution. This means that the whole distribution of possible returns is completely defined by the expected return and the standard deviation; so they are the *only* two measures which the investor need consider.

The Opportunity Set   The second stage in the argument is to introduce the possibility of lending or borrowing at a single risk-free rate, r_f. The effect of this is to present the investor with investment opportunities whose expected returns and standard deviations plot along a straight line. The portfolios along this line represent combinations of lending or borrowing with investment in a single risky portfolio S. The investor's job can be *separated* into two parts: first to choose the best (risky) portfolio of stocks S, and second to combine it with the right amount of lending or borrowing to adjust its risk. In a competitive market there is no reason to concentrate portfolios in particular stocks, and we can identify S as the *market portfolio*.

The Capital Asset Pricing Model In the final stage of the argument, the standard deviation is replaced by beta in a relationship for expected return which holds for all stocks. Remember that the *characteristic line* of a stock shows how it responds to market movements. The slope of this line is the stock's beta. The *market line* shows how expected return depends on beta (under the CAPM). The proof in the text shows that the characteristic line of every stock must correspond exactly to that for a combination of holding the market portfolio plus lending or borrowing. This means that a stock with a given β must have an expected risk premium of exactly $\beta(r_m - r_f)$, and therefore its expected return lies on the market line.

Alternatively, we can argue in terms of the market line itself. No stock can lie below the market line if it is to be as attractive as a combination of the market portfolio plus lending or borrowing. When any two stocks (such as P and Q below) are combined, the portfolio they form is on the straight line between them (e.g., at R). The combination of all stocks together has to be the market portfolio, and not some point above it. The only way in which this can happen is if *all* the stocks individually lie on the market line.

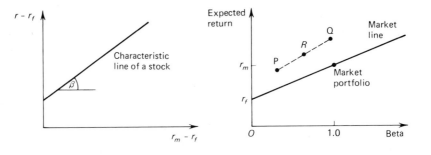

Worked Examples

Problem 1

Why does the possibility of lending or borrowing make the investment opportunities lie on a straight line? Assume an investor, Mr. Richards, can lend or borrow risk-free at 6 percent interest. He can also invest in a risky portfolio S of equities which has an expected return of 14 percent and a standard deviation of 20 percent. Show how he can construct a portfolio with standard deviations of (a) 10 percent or (b) 30 percent, and work out the expected returns on these portfolios. Show that these four investment opportunities lie on a straight line.

Solution

To halve the standard deviation of the risky investment, S, Mr. Richards must halve the amount he puts into it. Instead of investing $100 in S, he would have to invest $50 in S and the remaining $50 at the risk-free rate. Similarly, to increase the standard deviation from 20 to 30 percent, he must increase his investment in S

from $100 to $150 by borrowing $50 at 6 percent interest. The expected returns and standard deviations from these portfolios are given in the table below. The table also shows the returns that will be obtained one standard deviation above or below the expected value; this is a useful check that the standard deviations are correct.

Investment	Expected return	Standard deviation	Expected return *plus* one standard deviation	Expected return *minus* one standard deviation
S: $100 in S	$14	$20	$34	−$ 6
r_f: $100 in r_f	6		6	6
a: $50 in S	7	10	17	− 3
+ 50 in r_f	3		3	3
$100 total	$10	$10	$20	$ 0
b: $150 in S	$21	$30	$51	−$ 9
− 50 in r_f	− 3		− 3	− 3
$100 total	$18	$30	$48	−$12

It is now clear that each additional 10 percent standard deviation earns an additional expected return of 4 percent. The investment opportunities plot on the straight line shown below:

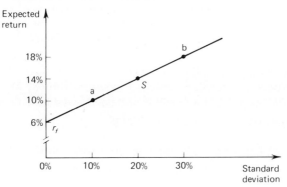

Problem 2

The Treasury bill rate is 7 percent and the expected return on the market portfolio is 15 percent.

1. What is the risk premium on the market?
2. What is the required rate of return on an investment with a beta of 1.25?
3. If the market expects a return of 11 percent from XTC Leisure, Inc., what is its beta?
4. If an investment with a beta of 1.5 offers an expected return of 20 percent, does it have a positive NPV?

Solution

1. The risk premium on the market is the difference between the expected return on the market portfolio and the Treasury bill rate. In this example it is 15 percent − 7 percent = 8 percent.

2. The expected return on *any* investment is given by expected return = risk-free rate + (beta × market risk premium). For a beta of 1.25 this gives

$$\text{Expected return} = 7 + (1.25 \times 8)$$

$$= 7 + 10$$

$$= 17 \text{ percent}$$

3. An expected return of 11 percent represents a risk premium of 4 percent. Since this premium is beta times the market premium of 8 percent, beta must be 0.5. In general, beta = risk premium on stock/risk premium on market.

4. An investment with a beta of 1.5 has a required rate of return of $7 + (1.5 \times 8) = 19$ percent. This investment has an expected return of 20 percent; so its NPV is positive.

Summary

Portfolio Theory

Expected Returns and Standard Deviation   The returns on stocks over short periods of time conform closely to the bell-shaped normal distribution. A normal distribution is completely defined by two numbers: its expected value and its standard deviation. It is therefore reasonable to assume that investors will choose between portfolios on the basis of their expected return, and the standard deviation of return. This much we know: *all* investors want high expected returns; and *all* investors who dislike uncertainty want a low standard deviation.

Efficient Portfolios   Portfolios which give the lowest possible standard deviation for a given expected return are called *efficient portfolios*. Markowitz introduced the idea of efficient portfolios in 1952, and he showed how they can be calculated by a method called *quadratic programming*.

Borrowing and Lending   We suppose investors can borrow or lend at a single riskless rate r_f such that the following graph emerges:

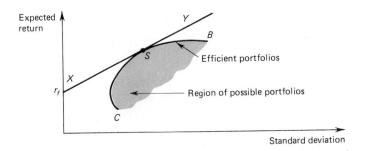

And these concepts emerge:

1. Combinations of portfolio S and lending (along XS), and of portfolio S and borrowing (along SY) are now preferred to other efficient portfolios (along CSB).

2. The composition of the portfolio S of common stocks does not depend on the investor's attitude toward risk.
3. Investors who are the most willing to bear risk invest farthest to the right along the line XY.
4. In a competitive market there is no reason for anybody to hold a different portfolio of common stocks from anybody else.
5. In this case S is the market portfolio.

Capital Asset Pricing Model

Summary of CAPM   Now let's turn to the *capital asset pricing model (CAPM)*. In a competitive market the CAPM says that the expected risk premium for every security is proportional to its beta: all assets must lie on the *market line*. The figure below depicts the relationship. In other words, the expected excess return for any stock can be calculated from its *beta* value and the two benchmarks of the *Treasury bill rate* and the expected *risk premium on the market*:

Expected risk premium = beta × (expected risk premium on the market)

$$r - r_f = \beta \times (r_m - r_f)$$

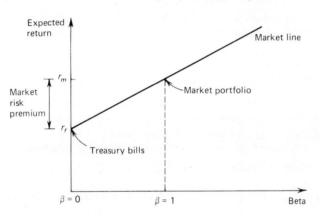

Proof of CAPM   The proof of the logic of the CAPM runs this way:

1. An investor can construct a portfolio with any given beta and no unique risk by investing a proportion β in the market portfolio and $(1 - \beta)$ in Treasury bills. This portfolio has expected return

$$r = r_m\beta + (1 - \beta)r_f$$
$$= r_f + \beta(r_m - r_f)$$

Its expected risk premium is

$$r - r_f = \beta(r_m - r_f)$$

2. A stock with this beta value must also offer an expected risk premium of *at least* $\beta(r_m - r_f)$ to be attractive. The stock's characteristic line must not lie below the combination of the market portfolio and Treasury bills, as shown below.

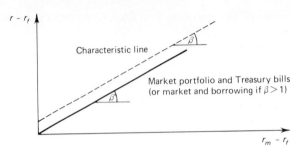

3. Adding all stocks together gives the market portfolio. No stock can have a risk premium *greater* than $\beta(r_m - r_f)$, for this would make the market risk premium greater than $(r_m - r_f)$.
4. The above argument shows that the risk premium for any stock must be at least $\beta(r_m - r_f)$, but no greater. That is,

$$r - r_f = \beta(r_m - r_f) \qquad \textit{for every stock}$$

Limitations of the CAPM   As with any model, the CAPM is a simplified statement of reality. Most people agree that: (1) investors require some extra return for taking on risk, and (2) investors are principally concerned with risk they cannot eliminate by diversification.

Assumptions of the CAPM   The CAPM captures these ideas in a conveniently simple way. But there are four important assumptions behind the CAPM.

1. Investors are only interested in the expected return and standard deviation of their investments. This implies that they will be content to invest in a mixture of Treasury bills and the market portfolio.
2. The return from Treasury bills is assumed to be risk-free. This ignores the risk of uncertain inflation.
3. Borrowing costs are the same as lending costs.
4. Generality of the CAPM: as long as investors are content to hold a limited number of benchmark portfolios, the expected return on any stock can be expressed in terms of the expected returns on these benchmarks.

Empirical Tests of the CAPM   As with all models, the CAPM has been tested for its correspondence with reality. Remember, however, the CAPM is a theory about *expected* returns. We can only measure *actual* returns. This makes it difficult to test. Nonetheless, Fama and Macbeth grouped all New York Stock Exchange stocks into 20 portfolios with different betas. The estimated betas of these portfolios gave a partial explanation of their average returns over a subsequent 5-year period. This evidence is broadly consistent with the CAPM. But one major pitfall remains: the market portfolio should include all risky investments; most market indexes are only a sample of common stocks.

List of Terms

Capital asset pricing model
Characteristic line

Efficient portfolios
Expected return
Expected risk premium
Market line
Market risk premium
Normal distribution
Quadratic programming

Exercises

Fill-in Questions

1. When measured over fairly short time periods, the rates of return on almost any stock conform closely to a _____ distribution.

2. A portfolio which gives the highest expected return for a given standard deviation is called an _____.

3. _____ programming can be used to calculate efficient portfolios.

4. The capital asset pricing model implies that the risk premium for any stock is equal to its beta multiplied by the _____.

5. A normal distribution is completely defined by the _____ and the _____.

6. The model which relates expected return to risk (measured in terms of beta) is called the _____.

7. The difference between the expected return on a stock and the risk-free rate is its _____.

8. According to the CAPM, the expected returns from all investments must plot along the _____ line.

9. The _____ line of a stock shows how its expected return is affected by the return on the market portfolio.

Problems

1. Which one of each of the following pairs of portfolios would an investor be most likely to choose:
   a. Portfolio A: expected return 14 percent, variance 400.
      Portfolio B: expected return 13 percent, variance 441.
   b. Portfolio J: expected return 20 percent, variance 529.
      Portfolio K: expected return 20 percent, variance 400.
   c. Portfolio R: expected return 8 percent, variance 225.

Portfolio S: expected return 9 percent, variance 225.

d. Portfolio X: expected return 12 percent, variance 380.

Portfolio Y: expected return 15 percent, variance 460.

2. Label the important features (A to G) of this diagram:

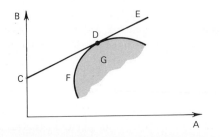

3. Calculate the expected returns on stocks with the following betas: (a) 0.5, (b) 1.0, (c) 2.0. Take the risk-free rate to be 9 percent and the expected return on the market portfolio to be 18 percent.

4. If stock Z has a beta of 0.8 and an expected return of 16 percent, and stock Y has a beta of 1.5 and an expected return of 23 percent, what must be (a) the expected return on the market; and (b) the risk-free rate of return, to be consistent with the capital asset pricing model?

5. Your broker is urging you to invest in one of three portfolios on which the returns are expected to be: Portfolio A: 12 percent, portfolio B: 15½ percent, portfolio C: 20 percent. You believe these estimates, but you also have sufficient data to calculate the betas of the portfolios with confidence. You find the betas are 0.5 for A, 1.1 for B, and 2.0 for C. Which portfolio is best and why?

6. What do you estimate are the expected returns investors require today for stocks with (a) betas of 0.5, and (b) betas of 1.5?

7. The following diagram shows several characteristic lines. Name the line that goes with each of the investments listed. (a) Standard and Poor's Index, (b) short-term government securities, (c) a high-beta stock, (d) a stock which is negatively correlated with the market, and (e) a mutual fund whose performance is not sufficiently good to recoup all the costs of its transactions.

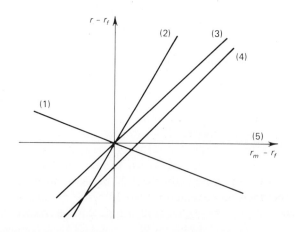

8. Can a security have a negative expected rate of return and still be correctly priced? What sort of beta would it have?

9. The capital asset pricing model is often stated in the alternative form:

$$r = \alpha + \beta r_m$$

where r is the expected return on a stock and r_m is the expected return on the market. (a) If α is zero, what must beta be? (b) What must α be if beta equals 2? (c) What must α be if beta equals zero? (d) Give a general expression for α.

***10.** Stock A has an expected return of 15 percent and a standard deviation of 30 percent. Stock B has an expected return of 17½ percent and a standard deviation of 35 percent. The correlation between them is 0.3. (a) Calculate the expected return and the standard deviation of the following four portfolios:

Portfolio	Percentage in A	Percentage in B
1	20	80
2	40	60
3	60	40
4	80	20

(b) If the risk-free rate is 8 percent, which one of these four portfolios is the best?

Essay Questions

1. Describe the concept of efficient portfolios. What assumptions does it rest on?

2. Some investors are prepared to take bigger risks than others. Explain why they still may all be content to invest in the same portfolio of common stocks.

3. Explain the difference between a stock's characteristic line and the market line.

4. Explain why the expected return on any security depends solely on its sensitivity to market movements and is unaffected by its unique risk.

Answers to Exercises

Fill-in Questions

1. normal
2. efficient portfolio
3. quadratic
4. market risk premium
5. expected return; standard deviation
6. capital asset pricing model
7. expected risk premium
8. market
9. characteristic

Problems

1. (a) A; (b) K; (c) S; (d) One cannot tell unless the investor's utility function—how she feels about the trade-off between risk and expected return—is known.

2. A is the standard deviation of expected returns; B is expected returns; C is the risk-free rate of return; D is the market portfolio; E is the capital market line; F is the set of efficient portfolios; and G is the feasible set of portfolios.

3. (a) 13.5 percent; (b) 18 percent; (c) 27.0 percent

4. (a) 18 percent; (b) 8 percent

5. Portfolio B seems to offer the best value. If we combine 60 percent of A with 40 percent of C, we obtain a portfolio with the same beta as B, but with an expected return of only 15.2 percent.

6. No pat answer may be given, but investors should expect a return equal to the sum of the returns on the risk-free asset and the historical risk premium on equities, adjusted for the risk of each portfolio.

7. (a) 3; (b) 5; (c) 2; (d) 1; (e) 4

8. Yes, provided its marginal contribution to the portfolio is overall positive. How can that be? By having a negative beta, of all things. Negative betas are to be prized because the stocks that have them are negatively correlated with the market and almost all other stocks. Negatively correlated stocks tend to reduce portfolio risk considerably. If stocks with negative betas also have negative expected returns, chances are the reduction in portfolio risk is expected to be greater than the reduction in portfolio expected return, thereby rendering them attractive investments.

9. (a) 1; (b) minus the risk-free rate; (c) the risk-free rate; (d) $(1 - \beta)r_f$, where r_f is the risk-free rate.

10. (a)

Portfolio	Expected return, %	Standard deviation, %	Excess return per unit of risk
1	17.0	30.34	0.2966
2	16.5	27.13	0.3133
3	16.0	25.91	0.3088
4	15.5	26.94	0.2784

(b) Portfolio 2, because the excess return per unit of risk is greatest. The numbers are derived in this way: $(r_p - r_f)/\sigma_p$, where r_p is the expected return on the portfolio, r_f is the risk-free rate of return; and σ_p is the standard deviation of the portfolio.

9 *Capital budgeting and the capital asset pricing model*

Introduction

Chapter 9 applies the theory of risk and return, developed in Chapters 7 and 8, to the practical problem of measuring the opportunity cost of capital for an investment project. The return required on a project depends on the nature of the project, rather than on which company undertakes it. Nevertheless, we may still want to know what return is expected from the securities of a company: from this we can work out what return is required from projects whose risks are similar to those of the company's existing business. Riskier projects should have a higher cutoff rate, and safer projects a lower cutoff rate.

To work out the expected return on a company's stock, we estimate its beta. It is often best to calculate the beta for a group of similar companies instead of for a single company. To get the required rate of return on the investment in an average project, we must take into account any borrowings of the company: these will have increased the beta of the company's stock. Finally, the general nature of a new project is sufficient to tell us something about its probable riskiness. The projects which are most likely to have high betas and high required rates of return are the ones whose earnings are cyclical (depend on the state of the business cycle) or which have high fixed costs.

What to Look For in Chapter 9

The Cost of Capital The first section of Chapter 9 describes an apparent paradox. Many companies estimate the rate of return required by investors in their securities and use this "company cost of capital" as the discount rate for evaluating new projects. Different companies have different costs of capital and would therefore use different discount rates even for identical projects. However, we also know that as long as the cash flows from a project don't depend on which company owns it, then neither does its value. A given project is worth the same amount to all firms, and all firms should apply the same required rate of return in appraising it. The correct discount rate for a capital investment project depends solely on the risks associated with that project and not on which company happens to undertake it.

Why then do we describe how to estimate the cost of capital *of a company* if the cost of capital for a project is something different? The answer to this is that *we don't have* a way to estimate the required return on a project directly, and so we have to make do with a second best approach. Once we know what return security holders require a company to earn on its total assets, this tells us what return is required on a typical investment by the company. Clearly a higher return will be required from projects with higher systematic risk (beta) than is typical. Conversely, a lower return will be required on less risky projects.

Estimating Beta for a Project We saw in the last two chapters that the required rate of return for a project depends on its systematic risk, and that this is measured by its beta. The problem of choosing a suitable discount rate for a project therefore amounts to working out what sort of beta it has. We cannot do this directly (as individual investment projects don't have prices quoted daily on the New York Stock Exchange); so we must do the best we can by looking at the betas of companies.

The beta of a company's stock measures how its price responds to market movements. You could estimate this beta by plotting monthly returns on the stock against monthly returns on the market index, and fitting a line through the scatter of points. The slope of this line gives you the beta of the stock. Alternatively you can just go to a published "beta book" and look up someone else's estimate. "Beta books" are published regularly by a number of brokerage and advisory services. The Merrill Lynch one described in the chapter is fairly typical of the sort of information you can get from such services.

The beta book gives an estimate of the beta of every stock that has traded regularly, and it gives some other information as well. The most useful of this additional information is probably the column giving the standard error of beta. We can never know exactly what the "true" beta of a stock is. We can only estimate what it appears to be from its price behavior in the past. Our estimates could never be perfect even if betas never changed through time (which they do). The standard error tells us how much confidence we can put in a particular estimate. For example, the estimated beta of Walt Disney Productions is 1.87 and its standard error is 0.22. This means that if the true beta really is 1.87, then two-thirds of the time we should have expected to have estimated a beta within plus or minus 0.22 of this, i.e., between 1.65 and 2.09. Similarly 95 percent of the time we should have estimated beta within plus or minus two standard errors, i.e., between 1.43 and 2.31. We can at least be pretty confident that Walt Disney's beta is greater than 1!

As you see, the standard error of the beta of a single company can be uncomfortably high. This is because a lot of its price movements are unrelated to the movements of the market as a whole. There is a broad scatter of points around the line we have to fit to estimate beta, and so we cannot be very confident as to exactly what the slope of this line ought to be. Fortunately, we can estimate the beta of an entire industry with much more precision than we can estimate the beta of an individual stock. The errors in our estimates for individual companies tend to cancel themselves out. If we average the betas of N stocks to get the beta of a particular industry sector, then as a rule of thumb we will have to multiply the standard error by a factor of about $1/\sqrt{N}$. For example, if we took 50 stocks with standard errors of their betas of 0.21, the standard error of the average beta would be only about $0.21/\sqrt{50} = 0.03$. In most cases, then, a beta calculated for an industry group will provide a more accurate yardstick for the beta of a project than could be obtained by looking at a single company.

One further problem remains. The betas we have described so far measure the risk of company's shares. However, what we want to measure is the risk of their assets, which may be financed by debt as well as by equity (shares). In other words, since the value of the company's assets must equal that of its liabilities, we can write (in terms of market values)

Value of assets = value of equity + value of debt

If the value of the assets is divided between shareholders and debtholders, the risk of the assets must also be divided between them. Remember that betas can be averaged in a very simple way. If I invest two-thirds of my portfolio in a stock with a beta of 1.2 and I invest the other third in a stock with a beta of 0.3, the beta of my portfolio is

$$\left(\frac{2}{3} \times 1.2\right) + \left(\frac{1}{3} \times 0.3\right) = 0.9$$

We can regard the beta of the company's assets in a similar way. The assets are partly equity and partly debt, and the beta of the assets is an average of the beta of the equity and the beta of the debt (weighted according to their market values). Thus:

$$\beta_{asset} = \beta_{equity} \times \frac{equity}{debt + equity} + \beta_{debt} \times \frac{debt}{debt + equity}$$

The beta of debt is usually very close to zero; so a company with high-beta shares may have low-beta assets (and a low cost of capital) if it has a lot of debt. It is therefore quite important to be able to make this adjustment when working out required rates of return. The worked example provides a further illustration of the procedure.

Determinants of Beta   The third section of the chapter discusses what determines whether a particular asset has a high or a low beta. Remember here to distinguish between systematic and unique risk. The question is not simply what makes an asset's future earnings uncertain. What matters is the extent to which abnormally low earnings are likely to coincide with low earnings in the economy as a whole. For example, the returns from the shares of gold mines are very risky, but they tend to fair remarkably well when everything else is doing badly, a fact born out by the classic market report on the radio newscast: "Gold drifted lower today, because of the absence of bad news." Gold stocks have low betas. On the other hand, companies with cyclical earnings, which are strongly dependent on the state of the business cycle, tend to have high betas. When a company has a high beta, this usually means that its earnings are very variable. This is often the case with companies which have high fixed costs. The high level of fixed costs produces a leverage effect which make profits particularly vulnerable: a small percentage change in revenues will produce a much larger percentage change in profits. Companies with high fixed costs (often called high operating leverage) tend to have high betas.

Another Look at Discounted Cash Flow   The earlier parts of the chapter have concentrated on how we may estimate the beta of a project. Once we know this beta, we normally use it to calculate the project's opportunity cost of capital by means of our capital asset pricing model formula:

$$r = r_f + \beta(r_m - r_f)$$

The expected cash flows C_t are then discounted at this rate to give the project's net present value:

$$\text{NPV} = \sum_{t=0}^{T} \frac{C_t}{(1 + r)^t}$$

This final section of the chapter reveals an alternative method of taking the risk of a project into account in evaluating it. Instead of adding a risk premium to the risk-free rate, as long as we make appropriate adjustments to the cash flows, we may discount at the risk-free rate. Given any uncertain cash flow C_t, there must be some fixed cash flow which investors find equally attractive. This is called a certainty-equivalent cash flow CEQ_t. If we replace expected cash flows by the corresponding certainty equivalents, we can discount at the risk-free rate. The Appendix shows how this approach can also be derived from the capital asset pricing model.

Comparison of the two methods reveals that the earlier procedure implies risk increases at a constant rate as you look further out into the future: a constant r is consistent with your more distant forecasts being less certain than your near ones. A constant r is therefore *not* appropriate when much more uncertainty will be encountered in some periods than in others.

Worked Example

Problem

You want to know the cost of capital of your construction company. You find that the average beta of a group of similar construction companies is 1.32 and that their average debt-equity ratio is 0.20. Your company has a debt-equity ratio of 0.30. If the risk-free rate is 12 percent and the expected risk premium on the market portfolio is 9 percent, what is:
1. The required return on the assets of the company?
2. The required return on the shares of the company?

Solution

1. The average beta of the shares of the other construction companies is 1.32 but, because of their financial leverage (debt), this overstates the beta of their assets. We know that

$$\beta_{\text{assets}} = \beta_{\text{equity}} \times \frac{\text{equity}}{\text{debt} + \text{equity}} + \beta_{\text{debt}} \times \frac{\text{debt}}{\text{debt} + \text{equity}}$$

so if $\beta_{\text{debt}} = 0$ (which is likely, at least as an approximation), then

$$\beta_{\text{assets}} = 1.32 \times \frac{1}{1.2} = 1.10$$

The required rate of return on the *assets* (i.e., the cost of capital of the firm) is therefore 12 percent + (1.1 × 9 percent) = 21.9 percent.

2. Rearranging the earlier equation and making use of the fact that $\beta_{debt} = 0$, we have

$$\beta_{equity} = \beta_{assets} \times \frac{debt + equity}{equity}$$

For your construction company this gives

$$\beta_{equity} = 1.1 \times 1.3 = 1.43$$

The required rate of return on the *shares* of your company is therefore

12 percent + (1.43 × 9 percent) = 24.87 percent

Summary

The Company Cost of Capital   Many companies discount cash flows at the company's cost of capital, that is, at the rate of return required by investors on its securities. The true cost of capital depends on the use to which the capital is put. The discount rate should depend on the beta of the project and is determined by $r = r_f + \beta(r_m - r_f)$. The use of a single discount rate for all projects means that too many high-risk projects (and too few low-risk ones) will be accepted. We need to be able to estimate the betas of individual projects. This is a difficult problem, but one that won't go away.

Measuring Beta   The beta of a stock can be estimated by fitting a line through its (monthly) rates of return plotted against the corresponding returns on the market index. The slope of the line is the stock's beta. The line may be fitted by least-squares regression analysis.

Betas estimated in one period, however, are imperfect guides to the future, because the actual beta may change through time and there is an estimation error. Beta estimates are not exact; so fine distinctions between stocks are not possible. The errors tend to cancel out when you estimate the beta of a portfolio: the betas of portfolios can be estimated much more accurately than the betas of individual stocks.

Some brokerage and advisory services publish estimates of beta, and other statistical information. For example, the Merrill Lynch "beta book" provides:

1. Beta: the regression-analysis estimate of beta.
2. Alpha: the intercept of the fitted regression line.
3. *R* squared: the proportion of the variance of price changes explained by market movements.
4. Residual standard deviation: the standard deviation of the unique risk of the stock.
5. Standard errors of beta and alpha: measures of the probable accuracy of these estimates.
6. Adjusted beta: the earlier estimate adjusted to take account of the effect of estimation errors.

The beta of a portfolio of stocks drawn from a single *industry* is easier to estimate than the beta of a single company. This *industry beta* can provide a useful estimate of the cost of capital for a *division* of a company. The beta of a company is an average of the betas of its various divisions, weighted by their importance.

Adjustment for Financial Leverage   Financial leverage (company borrowing) increases the risk of the common stock. It also increases its expected return. Consequently, the beta of a company's assets is a weighted average of the betas of its securities:

$$\beta_{asset} = \beta_{debt} \frac{debt}{debt + equity} + \beta_{equity} \frac{equity}{debt + equity}$$

It is the asset beta that is relevant to assessing the risk of a capital investment project. The beta of debt is usually very close to zero, which means that:

$$\beta_{asset} = \frac{equity}{debt + equity} \beta_{equity}$$

$$\beta_{equity} = \frac{debt + equity}{equity} \beta_{asset}$$

What Determines Beta?   As fate would have it, no completely satisfactory explanatory theory of betas exists. In some cases betas may be estimated directly. Even at that, stock or industry betas provide only a rough guide to the typical risk in various businesses. Both earnings cyclicity and high operating leverage tend to produce high betas.

Cyclical firms, whose earnings are strongly dependent on the state of the business cycle, tend to have high betas. Variability of earnings can be due to unique risk. A strong relationship between a firm's earnings and aggregate earnings means high market risk. The *accounting beta* or the *cash-flow beta* can be used to measure this.

The cash flow of a company with high fixed costs is very sensitive to changes in revenues, and the company is said to have high *operating leverage*. With financial leverage the fixed costs of debt increase the risk of shareholders' returns and make the equity beta higher. With *operating leverage* the fixed operating costs increase the risk of the operating cash flows and make the asset beta higher:

$$\beta_{asset} = \beta_{revenue} \frac{PV(asset) + PV(fixed\ costs)}{PV(asset)}$$

Certainty Equivalent Cash Flows   We usually evaluate projects by calculating the NPV of their expected cash flows, which are discounted at a *risk-adjusted rate* derived from the capital asset pricing model. That is,

$$NPV = \sum_{t=0}^{T} \frac{C_t}{(1 + r)^t}$$

where $r = r_f + \beta(r_m - r_f)$

This procedure would be incorrect for a project whose beta is expected to vary through time.

The certain cash flow CEQ_t is the *certainty equivalent* of an uncertain cash flow C_t (which occurs on the same date) if investors are indifferent as to which they receive. Since CEQ_t is certain, it can be discounted at the appropriate risk-free rate; so

$$NPV = \sum_{t=0}^{T} \frac{CEQ_t}{(1 + r_f)^t}$$

The certainty equivalent CEQ_t is some fraction a_t of the expected cash flow C_t. The two methods must give the same present value; so

$$NPV = \sum_{t=0}^{T} \frac{CEQ_t}{(1 + r_f)^t} = \sum_{t=0}^{T} \frac{C_t}{(1 + r)^t}$$

$$= \sum_{t=0}^{T} \frac{C_t}{(1 + r_f)^t} \frac{(1 + r_f)^t}{(1 + r)^t}$$

so $CEQ_t = a_t C_t$

with $\quad a_t = \left(\frac{1 + r_f}{1 + r}\right)^t$

By using a constant risk-adjusted discount rate, the manager is assuming that the risk borne per period will be constant. This is appropriate when risk is re-solved at a steady rate through time. It implies a larger deduction for risk from late cash flows than from early ones.

It is incorrect to use a constant risk-adjusted discount rate when most of the project's risk is resolved *either* very *early* in the project, *or* very *late* in the project. Take the Vegetron example in which most of the information arrives *during the first year*. The investment of $125,000 will be worth $0 or $1.5 million at the end of a year. Return over the first year will be -100 or $+1200$ percent. In subsequent years the risk is "normal." Discounting at a constant risk-adjusted rate would have made this project look unattractive. And in the shipowner example, the investment of $100,000 is expected to be worth $138,000 in 2 years' time, which represents an annual compound return of 17½ percent for 2 years. But all the risk is resolved *at the end of the 2 years;* so the investment earns only 5 percent ($= r_f$) over the first year. At the end of the first year the investment is worth $105,000; so its expected return over the sec-ond year is 31.4 percent.

List of Terms

Accounting beta	Financial leverage
Alpha	Financial risk
Business risk	Operating leverage
Certainty equivalent	Project beta
Company cost of capital	Residual standard deviation
Cyclical	

Exercises

Fill-in Questions

1. The use of the company _____ as a discount rate ignores differences in the risk of projects.

2. The discount rate for evaluating a capital budgeting proposal should be derived from the _____ beta.

3. _____ measures the average rate of price appreciation on a stock in the past, when investors in the market as a whole earned nothing.

4. The _____ of a stock is a measure of its unique risk.

5. When a company raises debt finance, it increases the _____ risk borne by its shareholders.

6. The cost of capital depends on the _____ risk of the firm's investments.

7. Financial risk is produced by _____.

8. Companies with high fixed costs have high _____.

9. A firm whose revenues and earnings are strongly dependent on the state of the business cycle is said to be a _____ firm.

10. The sensitivity of a firm's book earnings to the aggregate book earnings in the economy is called its _____ beta.

11. Instead of discounting the expected value of a cash flow at a risk-adjusted discount rate, we may discount its _____ at the risk-free rate.

Problems

1. A firm is considering the following projects:

Project	Beta	Expected return,%
A	0.5	12
B	0.8	13
C	1.2	18
D	1.6	19

(a) Which projects have a higher expected return than the firm's 15 percent cost of capital? (b) Which projects should be accepted? (c) Which projects would be accepted or rejected incorrectly on the basis of the cost of capital as a hurdle rate? The Treasury bill rate is 8 percent and the expected market premium is 7 percent.

2. **Walt Disney Productions has the following characteristics:**

Adjusted beta	1.58
Alpha	0.59% per month
R squared	0.55
Residual standard deviation	8.49% per month

(a) How much did Disney tend to go up in a month in an unchanged market? (b) How much did Disney tend to go up in a month when the market went up 10 percent? (c) How likely would it be for the price of Disney to fall in a month in which the market went up 10 percent? (d) What economic reasons can you give to explain why Disney's beta is so high and its residual standard deviation is so low?

3. The following table shows the returns on a mutual fund against the corresponding returns on the market portfolio in successive quarters:

	Quarter 1	2	3	4	5	6	7	8	9
Return on mutual fund	8.9	−3.3	−4.4	7.3	2.1	−6.4	4.9	8.7	1.4
market	10.1	−4.3	−5.6	8.2	2.1	−7.9	5.4	9.8	1.2

Plot a graph of these returns and estimate alpha and beta for the fund.

4. Acetate, Inc., has common stock with a market value of $20 million and debt of $10 million. The current Treasury bill rate is 10 percent and the expected market risk premium is also 10 percent. A plot of the returns on the stock against the market returns shows a scatter of points through which a line can be fitted with a slope of 45°. (a) What is Acetate's financial leverage? (b) What is the beta of Acetate's stock? (c) What is the beta of Acetate's assets?

5. Acetate, Inc., of problem 4 now decides to invest in $10 million of additional assets which are similar to its existing assets. It decides to finance this investment by borrowing a further $10 million of debt. (a) What is the beta of the additional assets? (b) What discount rate should be used for these additional assets? (c) What is the beta of Acetate's stock after the debt issue?

6. The market value of the shares of Astrofab Corp. is currently $24 million and their beta is 1.4. Astrofab has a nominal $6 million of 8 percent coupon debentures outstanding which mature in 7 years. These debentures have a beta of 0.1, and they currently yield 10 percent. What is the beta of Astrofab's assets?

7. Other things being equal, which company (from each of the following pairs) do you think should be using the higher discount rate in its capital budgeting: (a) **(1)** a steel company, **(2)** a brewing company; (b) **(1)** a manufacturer of recreational vehicles, **(2)** a mining company; (c) **(1)** a company with high operating leverage, **(2)** a company with high financial leverage; (d) **(1)** a manufacturer of office equipment, **(2)** an electric utility company.

8. A project is expected to generate net cash flows of $1000 in each of years 1 and 2. Its beta will be 1.5 throughout its life. The risk-free interest rate is 10

percent and the expected return on the market is 18 percent. Calculate (a) the present value of the cash flows, (b) the certainty equivalents of the cash flows, and (c) the ratios of the certainty equivalents to the expected cash flows (i.e., a_1 and a_2).

*9. Business Aids, Ltd., is investing $2 million in equipment and promotion to launch a new product. Virtually all the uncertainty about the success of this product will be resolved by the end of the first year. Its success depends critically on the climate for business as a whole. The Dow Jones Industrial Average (DJI) stands at 945 as the investment is about to be made, and Business Aids predicts that its net cash flow in year 1 from this product will be $600,000 less than the level of the index in 12 months' time. They expect this income to amount to $500,000, and whatever income they get in year 1 will continue unchanged for the following 4 years (making 5 years in all). Assuming that the risk-free rates to all maturities are 10 percent, what is the net present value of this project? What is its expected return over the first year? (Ignore the effects of dividends on the return of the DJI.)

Essay Questions

1. Write a short memorandum describing why you think companies can benefit from using the capital asset pricing model to set cutoff criteria for new investment projects.

2. Your company uses the DCF rate of return to appraise new investment projects in the following way:
   Projects with payback less than 3 years are accepted if their DCF rate of return exceeds 12 percent.
   Projects with payback longer than 3 years are accepted if their DCF rate of return exceeds 16 percent.
   Discuss the advantages and disadvantages of this rule.

3. Describe how you would calculate the cost of capital of a company by estimating its beta.

4. Describe some of the characteristics that tend to be associated with companies whose shares have high betas.

5. Explain the difference between the use of risk-adjusted discount rates and certainty-equivalent cash flows. Give an example of a situation where you think the certainty-equivalent method is preferable.

Answers to Exercises

Fill-in Questions

1. cost of capital
2. project
3. alpha
4. residual standard deviation
5. financial
6. business
7. financial leverage
8. operating leverage
9. cyclical
10. accounting
11. certainty equivalent

Problems

1. (a) C, D; (b) A, C; (c) A incorrectly rejected; D incorrectly accepted
2. (a) 0.59 percent; (b) $r = 0.59$ percent $+ (10$ percent $\times 1.58) = 16.38$ percent; (c) About 2½ chances in 100, because a zero return corresponds to two residual standard deviations below the mean predicted return. The chances of getting a return *lower* than two standard deviations are only 2½ percent. (d) Chances are its earnings are highly cyclical. The residual standard deviation is low because the rates of return on Disney track closely the rates of return on the market (R squared $= 55$ percent).
3. The actual alpha is 0.34 and the beta is 0.85, which is roughly what the "eyeballed" graph (Figure 9-1) tells us. The correlation in rates of return is almost perfectly positive, as is obvious from the fit of the scatter to the line. The computed correlation coefficient is 0.999989.

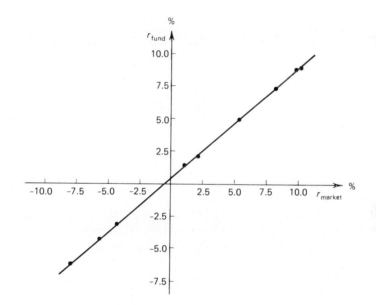

4. (a) 1/3; (b) 1; (c) 0.67, assuming beta of debt is zero
5. (a) 0.67; (b) 16.7 percent; (c) 1.33
6. Value of debt: market price per bond $\times$ 6000 bonds $= \$902.63 \times 6000 = \$5,415,790$
   Value of equity: $24 million
   Total market value of firm = value of debt + value of equity
   $$= \$5,415,790 + \$24,000,000$$
   $$= \$29,415,790$$

$$\beta_{assets} = \beta_{debt} \frac{debt}{debt + equity} + \beta_{equity} \frac{debt}{debt + equity}$$

$$= 0.1 \frac{\$5,415,790}{\$29,415,790} + 1.4 \frac{\$24,000,000}{\$29,415,790}$$

$$= 1.1607$$

7. (a) 1; (b) 1; (c) 1; (d) 1

8. (a) Using $r = 10$ percent $+ (18$ percent $- 10$ percent$)1.5 = 22$ percent, PV $=$ 1491.53; (b) Certainty equivalent cash flows are 901.64 and 812.95; (c) $a_1 =$ $1.1/1.22 = 0.9016$ and $a_2 = 0.8130$.

9. The cash flow in year 1 equals the DJI minus $600,000. Such a cash flow could have been obtained by investing $945,000 in the DJI and by borrowing the present value of $600,000 (i.e., $600,000/1.1) in order to create the $600,000 deduction. The overall investment necessary to do this is $945,000 $-$ ($600,000/1.1) = $399,545, which represents the present value of the first cash flow. Because the interest rate is 10 percent, the certainty equivalent cash flow is $1.1 \times $399,545 = $439,500. This certainty equivalent cash flow applies in all 5 years, so discounting the $439,500 annuity at 10 percent results in a present value of the cash inflows of $439,500 $\times$ 3.791 $=$ $1,666,145 and an NPV of $1,666,145 $-$ $2,000,000 $=$ $-$333,856.

10 *A project is not a black box*

Introduction

Chapters 2 to 6 described how to calculate net present values and how to use them to make capital budgeting decisions. Chapters 7 to 9 explained how the risk of a project affects the discount rate that should be used to evaluate it. You might expect that this gives us everything we need to enable us to make capital budgeting decisions. Unfortunately it is not quite as simple as that. There are a number of practical issues that must still be considered, and these are the subjects of Chapters 10, 11, and 12. These three chapters are concerned with the difficult problems of how to analyze capital investment projects, how to ensure that cash-flow forecasts are realistic, and how to organize and control capital expenditures.

Chapter 10 describes three techniques of project analysis which can help the financial manager to think clearly about what might go wrong with a project. These techniques are called sensitivity analysis (which includes break-even analysis as a special case), Monte Carlo simulation, and decision trees.

What to Look For in Chapter 10

The general theme of this chapter is given (surprise!) by its title: "A project is not a black box." If projects *were* black boxes (so we couldn't find out what went on inside them), we would be quite happy to hear our financial manager say: "Well, I put this money in here, and wait a bit, and then if I'm lucky I get so much more out at the other end." Of course, the world isn't like that: we *can* find out what will determine a project's success or failure, and it is part of the financial manager's job to know. The financial manager doesn't simply take a set of cash-flow forecasts out of a convenient file, choose a discount rate, and crank out a net present value. He or she must think about where those cash flows came from, and what can go wrong with them. This chapter describes three important techniques for getting to grips with the key factors that determine the success of a project. Of these, by far the most important is the first one: sensitivity analysis.

Sensitivity Analysis   The idea of sensitivity analysis is an easy one. The NPV of a project was arrived at by combining a number of different forecasts to arrive at after-tax cash flows. The forecasts might include such things as the size of the *total* market for the product, our share of that market, the price we will get for our product, and the amounts of all the various costs involved in producing and distributing it. We can't be sure what the outcome will be for any of these variables. What we can do is work out how much difference it makes if any of these forecasts turns out to be wrong. Each of the forecasts is varied in turn, first to a more optimistic value and second to a more pessimistic one. All the other forecasts are kept unchanged at their original values. The NPV of the project is recalculated under these different assumptions and the results are set out in a table such as the one below, which represents part of Table 10-2 of the text.

	Net present value ($000,000)		
Variable altered	Pessimistic	Expected	Optimistic
Market size	11	34	57
Market share	−104	34	173
Unit price	−42	34	50
Unit variable cost	−150	34	111
Fixed cost	4	34	65

Stop and look at this table. What does it show? Clearly, we will have a disaster on our hands if the pessimistic values of the unit variable cost or the market share are realized. On the other hand, it seems to be relatively less important to have an accurate assessment of the total market size or of the project's fixed costs. That's all very well, you may say, but how can the manager benefit from having this information? The answer is that it points out the potential "weak links" in the project, and the manager can now consider actions that might strengthen them. For example, it may be worth investing in a further market survey to reduce the uncertainty about market share: a pessimistic survey would allow the project to be abandoned before any massive expenditure was incurred. Perhaps a different advertising campaign would bolster market share. At the very least management is alerted to the importance of keeping a sharp eye on what happens to market share. Similarly, it is alerted to the crucial nature of its variable costs. Perhaps the uncertainty about these can be reduced by hedging in commodity futures markets, or by an additional design study.

Break-Even Analysis   The manager is likely to want to know how low the expected level of sales will have to be before the NPV of the project falls to zero and the project has no value to the firm. Break-even analysis provides the answer. In the example we looked at just now, the assumptions of the base case were of a NPV of $34 million from sales of 100,000 units. The sensitivity analysis showed that subtracting 10,000 units of sales (by reducing the total market size by 10 percent) reduced the NPV by $23 million (from $34 million to $11 million). To reduce the NPV from $34 million to zero would therefore take a reduction in sales of $34/23 \times 10,000 = 15,000$ units. The break-even level of sales must be 100,000 − 15,000 = 85,000 units.

Notice, though, that many companies calculate break-even on a rather *different basis:* as the level of sales that gives a zero accounting profit. In the example above, accounting profits are made when sales exceed 60,000 units. This level of sales would be *very* unsatisfactory. In fact our sensitivity analysis tells us that if we expect sales at this level, the NPV of the project is $34 million − [$23 million × (40,000/10,000)] = −$58 million.

Scenario Analysis   One drawback to sensitivity analysis is that the company is likely to have to accept a low unit price *just when* its volume of sales is lowest. In other words, altering the variables one at a time ignores the fact that they are usually interrelated. One way around this problem is to look at how the project would fare under a number of different plausible scenarios of the future. Forecasts are made for *all variables* so as to be consistent with a particular view of the world. In the text, for example, the forecasters are asked to consider the effects of an immediate 20 percent rise in the price of oil, and the NPV of the project is recalculated on the resulting assumptions.

Monte Carlo Simulation   Monte Carlo simulation (or simulation for short) may be regarded as a logical extension of the idea of scenario analysis. In scenario analysis we look at a small number of specially chosen scenarios. In simulation we generate a large number of possible scenarios as they might occur if we could keep on winding back time and starting again. This usually involves a computer. The forecaster must specify probability distributions for all the factors that affect the success of the project. The computer then generates random numbers (this is its way of rolling dice) to produce a value for each factor. This provides one scenario, which has been selected as a random sample from the continuum of possibilities. The "dice rolling" procedure is then repeated a large number of times to build up a complete picture of what may happen to the project.

That is the broad outline, but you need to know more about some of the details. As an example, suppose that we give the computer instructions on how to generate plausible forecasting errors for the market size. In a given simulation the computer may then decide that market size is 10 percent higher than the expected value; so it adds 10 percent to this to get the "actual" market size for that simulation. We can do the same thing for the unit price and all the other key variables. Notice, though, that in order to take account of interrelationships, these too have to be specified to the computer. For example, we might decide that a 10 percent increase in market size results on average in a 3 percent increase in the unit price. In this case we could tell the computer to calculate the forecasting error for the price as

Percentage error in unit price = 0.3 × percentage error in market size + randomly generated error

Look for the three stages involved in simulation. First, we must choose the best form of equations to model the cash flows of the project. Second, we must specify the probability distributions of all the error terms. Finally, we must run the simulations and assess the results. Look at the distributions of cash flows given in Figure 10-5 of the text. These are part of the results of a simulation analysis, and they provide information both about the expected (average) cash flows and about how far they are likely to deviate from their averages. Notice that the average cash flow is different from what you might have expected from the average unit sales and the average profit per unit. This is because the interrelationship between unit sales and unit price means that the average level of revenues (unit sales times unit price) *is not equal to* the average unit sales times the average unit price. One of the advantages of simulation is that it is able to take account of these kinds of effects. Its disadvantage is that it can be costly and difficult to implement.

We now have better estimates of expected cash flows; so the NPV can be calculated more accurately. We also have an accurate picture of how uncertain the cash flows are. If we like, we can even obtain a probability distribution for the IRR of the project over its life. Beware, though, of so-called probability distributions of NPV. Even though the results of a project are uncertain, the project still has only one value in the marketplace today. Since the NPV of the project represents the difference between its value and its cost, *there can only be one NPV.*

Decision Trees The final technique described in the chapter is the use of decision trees. Look at the example decision tree we give in our summary. As time elapses we can make various decisions, and various events may occur over which we have no control. The decision tree provides a way to represent these different possibilities so that we can be sure that the decisions we make today take proper account of what we can do in the future. A project is more likely to be worth undertaking if we can bail out of it later if things go wrong, than if we can't. The example decision tree illustrates this. If at the end of a year things have gone badly, the plant can be sold for $700, whereas in use by us it will be worth only $500. If things go well it will be worth $1400 in year 1. Its expected value is found by weighting the values of these possible outcomes by their probabilities. It is given by

$$(\$1400 \times 0.6) + (\$700 \times 0.4) = \$1120$$

and this must be discounted to give its present value. If the discount rate is 10 percent, the NPV of the project is

$$\frac{\$1120}{1.1} - \$1000 = \$18$$

Notice that we had to work out what the best decisions would be at the second stage before we could choose the best first-stage decision. The process of working back through the decision tree from the future to the present is sometimes called rolling back the decision tree.

Finally, you may want to make sure you understand the principle of sensitivity analysis by working through the worked example.

Worked Example

Problem

The following forecasts have been prepared for a new investment of $20 million with an 8-year life:

	Pessimistic	Expected	Optimistic
Market size	60,000	90,000	140,000
Market share, %	25	30	35
Unit price	$750	$800	$875
Unit variable cost	$500	$400	$350
Fixed cost ($000,000)	7	4	3.5

You use straight-line depreciation, pay tax at 46 percent, and have an opportunity cost of capital of 14 percent. Calculate the NPV of this project and conduct a sensitivity analysis. What are the principal uncertainties of the project?

Solution

The first step is to calculate the annual cash flows from the project for the base case (the expected values). These may be calculated as shown in the following table:

Description	How calculated	Value ($000,000)
1. Revenues	(90,000 × 0.30 × $800)	21.60
2. Variable cost	(90,000 × 0.30 × $400)	10.80
3. Fixed cost	($4,000,000)	4.00
4. Depreciation	($20,000,000/8)	2.50
5. Pretax profit	(Item 1 − items 2 + 3 + 4)	4.30
6. Tax	(Item 5 × 0.46)	1.98
7. Net profit	(Item 5 − item 6)	2.32
8. Net cash flow	(Item 7 + item 4)	4.82

This level of cash flow occurs for each of the 8 years of the project. The present value of an 8-year $1 annuity is 4.639 at 14 percent. The NPV of the project is therefore given by

$$NPV = \$4,820,000 \times 4.639 - \$20,000,000 = \$2,359,980$$

Now that the base case has been completed, the next step is to alter the forecasts one at a time to their optimistic and pessimistic values. The easiest way to do this is to work out how much each change affects the net cash flow, and then use the annuity factor as before to work out the NPV. For example, the optimistic value of the market size increases the pretax revenues by $50,000 \times 0.30 \times \$800 = \$12$ million; so it increases the (after-tax) net cash flow by \$12 million $\times 0.54 = \$6.48$ million, to \$11.30 million. The NPV now becomes

$$NPV = \$11,300,000 \times 4.639 - \$20,000,000 = \$32,420,700$$

The following table shows the net cash flows and NPVs corresponding to the pessimistic and optimistic forecasts for each of the variables.

Forecast of	Net cash flow ($000,000)		NPV ($000,000)	
	Pessimistic	Optimistic	Pessimistic	Optimistic
Market size	0.50	11.30	−17.67	32.43
Market share	2.88	6.77	−6.65	11.39
Unit price	4.09	5.92	−1.01	7.44
Unit variable cost	3.36	5.55	−4.39	5.75
Fixed cost	3.20	5.09	−5.15	3.62

The table clearly shows that the most crucial variable is the total market size. This is much more important than even the possible 75 percent increase in the level of fixed costs. The second most crucial variable is the market share. Obviously for this project the volume of sales matters much more than either the unit price or the costs.

Summary

Sensitivity Analysis This chapter covered three important techniques to evaluate further investment projects. First was *sensitivity analysis*, whose *purpose* is to calculate the effect of misestimating each factor that goes in NPV calculations. The *method* for accomplishing this is to identify the key variables that determine the success of the project, such as sales volume, fixed cost, unit variable cost, and selling price. Taking one variable at a time and replacing its expected value with both an optimistic and a pessimistic estimate, cash flows and NPVs are recalculated. In this way financial managers can identify those variables which affect NPV most. Research to reduce the uncertainty of those variables, as well as other, overlooked factors, may then be in order. The *value of* this *information* is worthwhile, however, only if the expected value of the information exceeds its cost, calculated thus:

Expected value of information = sum of (PV of change in CF due to new information × probability of that change)

Note that information that cannot affect any decisions is valueless.

The strength of sensitivity analysis lies in its ability to highlight key variables and key assumptions, to expose inconsistencies, and to identify where additional information is worthwhile.

Sensitivity analysis is limited, however, because of the subjectivity of the optimistic and pessimistic forecasts and because it ignores interrelationships among variables.

Scenario Analysis One way to overcome the problem of interrelated variables is to present *scenarios*. Rather than alter variables one at a time, alternative scenarios are employed where, for each scenario, values are given to every variable to be consistent with one particular realization of the future.

Break-Even Analysis Break-even analysis is a variation of sensitivity analysis and is used to determine how low sales can go before the NPV becomes negative. We do this by working out *either* what level of sales will equate the PVs of inflows and outflows *or* (equivalently) what level of sales will equate the annual cash inflow to the equivalent annual cost of the investment (investment/annuity factor). Break-even is often calculated as the sales level needed to give a zero accounting profit. This is misleading, as a zero accounting profit is really a big loss: it indicates a failure to earn *any* return on capital, and that represents a loss equal to the opportunity cost of capital.

Monte Carlo Simulation The second technique employed to evaluate projects is *Monte Carlo simulation*, itself really an extension of scenario analysis except that a computer is used to generate a large number of possible outcomes for a project. Three stages produce the desired results:

1. Establish equations to model the cash flows of the project. These must reflect any interdependencies between variables.
2. Specify the probabilities of forecast errors of different magnitudes for each variable.
3. Sample outcomes. The computer samples from the distribution of forecast errors, calculates the cash flows, and records them. This is repeated a large number of times until an accurate picture of the distribution of possible outcomes has been built up.

As with all models, Monte Carlo simulation has its good and bad points. On the positive side, simulation forces explicit specification of interdependencies, such as, for example, that sales and margins move together. It can be used also to explore possible modifications to a project.

On the negative side, simulation can be time-consuming and expensive. Realism means complexity; building the model may have to be delegated, and this can diminish its credibility to the decision maker. It may replace one "black box" with another.

Beyond these points a common misuse of simulation arises when it is used to obtain distributions of "NPVs," which are calculated by discounting at the risk-free rate. The object is to avoid prejudging the risk of the project, which is reflected in the spread of the distribution. This practice is dangerous because:

1. "NPVs" calculated in this way no longer represent market values of the project.
2. The distribution does not give the information which would be needed to work out the market value of the project.
3. The method ignores the investor's ability to diversify.
4. It offends the value-additivity principle.
5. Distributions of IRRs are more useful.

Decision Trees   The third and final technique employed to evaluate investment projects is decision trees. They are used to analyze a sequence of different possible uncertain events and decisions through time.

To draw a decision tree, branches from points marked with squares (□) are used to denote different possible decisions. Branches from points marked with circles (○) denote different possible outcomes (with their probabilities often indicated in brackets).

To analyze a decision tree, calculate the expected values of the most distant branches first. "Roll back" to the immediate decision by accepting the best decision at each of the later stages. Take the following example of an abandonment option. Accepting the best second-stage decisions shows that:

High demand gives a value of $1400 with probability 0.6.

Low demand gives a value of $700 with probability 0.4.

The expected value of the investment at the end of a year is $(0.6 \times \$1400) + (0.4 \times \$700) = \$1120$; so its expected IRR is 12 percent. The option to sell the plant if demand turns out to be low saves $200 with probability 0.4. This option may be sufficient to swing the decision to invest.

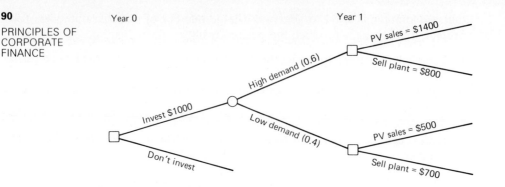

The *limited liability* of shareholders represents a similar sort of option.

Decision trees are valuable because they display the links between today's and tomorrow's decisions. Moreover, they force implicit assumptions to be expressed. Decision trees are limited, however, because they very quickly become unmanageably complex.

List of Terms

Abandonment value
Break-even analysis
Decision tree
Limited liability
Monte Carlo simulation
Probability
Project analysis
Scenario
Sensitivity analysis

Exercises

Fill-in Questions

1. Sensitivity analysis, simulation, and decision trees are three different forms of _____ analysis.

2. _____ enables the manager to see the effect of errors in forecasting sales, costs, etc., on the value of an investment project.

3. The analysis of a project under different _____ gives us a way to do a kind of sensitivity analysis which takes the interrelationships among variables into account.

4. _____ analysis tells the manager how low sales can go without making the project unprofitable.

5. The method of modeling the uncertainty about the level of sales and other important aspects of a project in order to discover the likelihood of various possible outcomes arising is called _____.

6. Sequential decisions can be analyzed by constructing a _____.

7. One of the difficulties of using a decision tree or simulation is that it becomes necessary to specify the _____ of different future outcomes.

8. The problem of whether to terminate a project before the end of its normal economic life is called the _____ problem.

9. _____ means that shareholders risk only the money that they invest and cannot be held responsible for any debts of their company.

Problems

1. Colorful Creams Cosmetics Corporation (CCCC) is considering an investment of $500,000 in a new plant for producing fluorescent disco makeup. The plant, which has an expected life of 4 years, has a maximum capacity of 700,000 units per year, and sales are expected to be 85 percent of this in each of the 4 successive years of production. Fixed costs are $200,000 per year and variable costs are $1.20 per unit produced. The product will be sold at a unit price of $2. The plant will be depreciated straight-line over 4 years, and it is expected to have a zero salvage value. The required rate of return on the project is 15 percent, and the corporation tax rate is 46 percent.
   a. Calculate the NPV of this project under the assumptions given above.
   b. Calculate how sensitive the NPV of the project is to variation in the level of sales, the unit price, the unit variable cost, and the level of fixed costs.
   c. CCCC is uncertain how to price its new product. What price would give a zero NPV?

2. In the investment project of problem 1 calculate what level of sales would give break-even in terms of (a) zero NPV, (b) zero accounting profit.

3. In problem 1, CCCC estimated that the annual sales would be 595,000 units, but there is some chance that the sales level will be inadequate to justify the capital expenditure. By commissioning a market survey, CCCC can hope to reduce this risk. CCCC's marketing department has some experience of such surveys. They estimate that there is a 20 percent chance that the survey will change the forecast sales to 515,000 or less, in which case the project would not be worth undertaking. If this does not occur (the remaining 80 percent of the time), they would expect the sales forecast to be revised upward to 620,000 units. What is the maximum amount that CCCC should be prepared to pay for a survey of this kind?

4. CCCC has another investment project with the following characteristics:
   Cost of investment, $800,000
   Expected sales volume, 21,000 units per year for 7 years
   Unit price, $150

Unit variable cost, $120
Annual fixed costs, $380,000
Life of investment, 7 years (zero salvage value)
Tax rate, 46 percent
Required rate of return, 17 percent
Calculate the NPV of this investment and perform a sensitivity analysis (use straight-line depreciation).

5. Analyze the project of problem 1 under the following two scenarios:

	Pessimistic scenario	Optimistic scenario
Sales volume	Expected value −20%	Expected value +50%
Unit price	Expected value −10%	Expected value +5%
Variable cost	Expected value +10%	Expected value −5%
Fixed cost	Expected value +10%	Expected value −5%

6. Analyze the project of problem 4 under the scenarios described in problem 5.

7. In problem 3, the first year of operation would give CCCC the same information as their market survey. After that year, if things go badly (with expected sales of 495,000 units), they can abandon the project to obtain a salvage value of $400,000 (less $11,500 tax) by selling the plant to another company. What value does the market survey have in the light of this option to abandon the project after it has been started?

8. The Transatlantic Toffee Company has to decide what size of new plant to build. A large plant will provide economies of scale but is also likely to lead to a reduced selling price. The capital costs and annual fixed and variable operating costs for different sizes of plant are as follows:

Capacity (million units)	Investment required ($000,000)	Annual fixed cost ($1000s)	Unit variable cost ($)
0.4	1.0	200	2.00
0.6	1.4	270	1.95
0.8	1.7	330	1.90

Transatlantic will discover how the market is receiving their product after the first year of operation. In the meantime they assess the prospects of being able to obtain various unit prices for their product at different levels of output as follows:

Quantity sold (million units)	Unit price ($)	
	Favorable	Unfavorable
0.4	3.05	2.60
0.6	2.90	2.45
0.8	2.75	2.30

The two possible market conditions are thought to be equally likely. After the first year Transatlantic can adjust to the market conditions. They can build an additional $400,000 unit plant. Alternatively, they can reduce the capacity of a larger plant by 200,000 units, which will realize $150,000 immediately and reduce the annual fixed costs by $40,000. In this case the advantages of the lower variable cost are retained. The company has a required rate of return of 10 percent and does not pay any corporate taxes. The plants have an indefinite life. Draw a decision tree and work out what decisions Transatlantic should take.

Essay Questions

1. Describe the technique of sensitivity analysis as applied to the appraisal of capital investment projects. What reservations do you have about its usefulness?

2. Describe how to calculate the break-even point for a capital investment project. Why is it misleading to calculate break-even in terms of accounting profit?

3. "You can prove anything with figures, can't you? I may be old fashioned but I don't see the point in all this sensitivity analysis stuff. As I see it, the job of the manager is to see that the forecasts are achieved. All this fiddling about is just a waste of time." Give a measured response to this statement.

4. Work out and describe in detail how you would produce and use a Monte Carlo simulation model to represent the purely financial aspects of buying a house instead of renting one. Assume you know you will be forced to sell it in order to relocate in a few years. Bear in mind the initial outlay costs, the various running costs (interest on the loan, taxes, repairs, insurance, heating), and the potential gain or loss on selling. Assume realistic values for these. Make sure to build appropriate interrelationships between variables into the model where necessary.

5. "What possible use to us," said the Ancient and Venerable Comptroller, "is a technique that pulls numbers out of a hat and adds them together? Sure! There are risks in this business, but we expect our managers to know what they're doing: if they don't, then they're out. It's all a matter of judgment, and there's nothing random about that." Is this a valid criticism of Monte Carlo simulation? How would you respond to his argument?

6. A decision must be taken whether to launch a new product immediately or subject it to further market research or abandon the idea altogether. Your boss has heard that decision trees can help with this kind of problem. Write a report on how a decision tree might be used in this situation. Make sure that you describe what sort of information you would need to apply this in practice, and how it would be used.

Answers to Exercises

Fill-in Questions

1. project
2. sensitivity analysis
3. scenarios
4. break-even

5. Monte Carlo simulation

6. decision tree

7. probabilities

8. abandonment value

9. limited liability

Problems

1. a. The following table derives the cash flows and the NPV for the base case and also for the pessimistic and optimistic scenarios of problem 5:

Item (in $1000s)	Year 0	Years 1 to 4		
		Expected	Pessimistic	Optimistic
Investment	−500			
Revenue		1190	856.8	1874.3
Variable cost		714	628.3	1017.5
Fixed cost		200	220.0	190.0
Depreciation		125	125.0	125.0
Pretax profit		151	−116.5	541.8
Tax		69.5	0.	249.2
Net profit		81.5	−116.5	292.6
Net cash flow		206.5	8.5	417.6
NPV at 15%		89.7	−475.7	692.2

b. The next table shows how given changes in sales, variable cost, unit price, and fixed cost affect the net cash flow and the NPV. The final column also shows the levels which give break-even (i.e., zero NPV):

Sensitivity to change of	Effect on cash flow	Effect on NPV	Break-even level
100,000 sales	43.20	123.34	522,270 units
10 cents variable cost	−32.13	−91.73	$1.9
10 cents unit price	32.13	91.73	$1.9
$10,000 fixed cost	−5.4	−15.42	$158,200

c. The final column indicates that a price of $1.9 gives a zero NPV.

2. a. The final column of the previous table also shows that the level of sales required for break-even in terms of zero NPV is 522,270 units per year.

b. The base case gave a pretax profit of $151,000 at sales of 595,000. Each unit reduction in sales reduces pretax profits by $0.80; so sales will have to fall by $151,000/0.80 = 188,750$ to eliminate profits entirely. That is, break-even sales are 406,000.

3. Without the extra information, the value of the project is its usual NPV of $89,700. With the information, there is a 20 percent chance of a zero NPV and an 80 percent chance of $120,500. The expected new NPV is equal to $96,400 minus the cost of the information; so the information must be worth $6700.

4.

Item (in $100s)	Year 0	Years 1 to 7		
		Expected	Pessimistic	Optimistic
Investment	−800			
Revenue		3150	2268.0	4961.3
Variable cost		2520	2217.6	3591.0
Fixed cost		380	418.0	361.0
Depreciation		114.3	114.3	114.3
Profit before tax		135.7	−481.9	895.0
Tax		62.4	0.	411.7
Profit after tax		73.3	−481.9	483.3
Cash flow		187.6	−367.6	597.6
NPV at 17%		−64.2	−2242	1544

The sensitivity analysis looks as follows:

Sensitivity to change of	Effect on cash flow	Effect on NPV	Break-even level
1000 unit sales	16.2	63.5	22,010 units
$1 variable cost	−11.3	−44.5	$118.6
$1 unit price	11.3	44.5	$151.4
$10,000 fixed cost	−5.4	21.2	$349,700

5. See the answer to problem 1.

6. See the answer to problem 4.

7. Without the abandonment option, we found in problem 3 that the project had a NPV of $96,400 less the cost of the survey, or $89,700 without the survey. This gave the survey a value of $6700.

   With the abandonment option, there is now a 20 percent chance of abandoning at a NPV of −$20,174. This is calculated as follows: the expected first year sales of 495,000 will give cash flow of $163,300 and there will be $400,000 less $11,500 tax from selling the plant. This makes an expected $551,800 in year 1, which means an NPV of $551,800/1.15 − $500,000 = −$20,174. There is also an 80 percent change of $120,500. Combining the two figures, we find that the abandonment option increases the NPV of the project to $92,365. This reduces the value of the survey information to $2665.

8. The following decision tree indicates that Transatlantic Toffee should build the 0.6 million unit plant, which has a NPV of $318,000 as compared with $300,000 for the 0.4 million plant and $295,000 for the 0.8 million one. All figures on the tree are shown in $1000s.

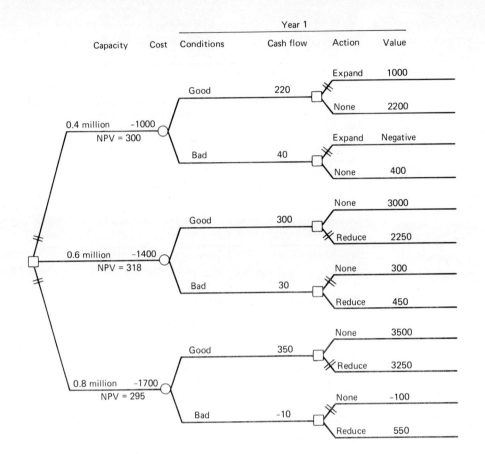

11 *Where positive net present values come from*

Introduction

No matter how much we know about the theory of making capital budgeting decisions, we will end up making bad decisions if our forecasts of cash flows turn out badly. Chapter 11 tells us how we can ensure that these forecasts are as good as it is possible to make them. The first part of the chapter deals with some general issues concerning forecasts of any kind. Forecasts may on average be too high (or too low), or they may exhibit too wide a range of high and low. The financial manager must be aware of these possibilities and able to make allowances for them. Problems may also be caused by different managers having different (and inconsistent) views, and the criteria used for assessing performance can produce further distortions of attitudes and objectives. Good management procedures based on an understanding of these problems can avoid their worst effects. The second part of the chapter focuses on the market in which the firm operates. This is discussed in the context of a small case study (Marvin Enterprises). Firms have to compete continually with each other, and they can never assume that the market will stay as it is for any length of time. Your company can *only* expect a positive NPV from a given project if it has some relative advantage in undertaking it compared with other companies. Remember, too, that new developments (of your own or of other companies) may affect the values of your existing assets.

What to Look For in Chapter 11

This chapter is quite short, and it hardly introduces any new terms. Nevertheless it is one of the most important chapters in the book. The biggest practical difficulty in applying the NPV criterion is in establishing reliable cash-flow forecasts. Although the text cannot provide firm rules to cover specific situations, it does illustrate the most important dangers and difficulties in forecasting cash flows, and it provides advice on how best to combat them. Try to take from the chapter an understanding of what is necessary to get unbiased forecasts that are based on consistent assumptions. Look out too for the key idea: that you can only *expect* a positive NPV if you have some kind of relative advantage.

Inconsistencies between forecasts (or attitudes) can take many forms. They usually arise from some failure of communication (such as, for instance, when the production manager's cost estimates are based on different assumptions about inflation from the marketing manager's forecasts of sales revenues). Obviously the larger the corporation the more likely these problems are to arise. Notice that there can be damaging effects even before projects begin to be evaluated, because of the process by which new projects are initiated. Establishing a framework which explicitly communicates basic economic forecasts and assumptions is an essential task of senior management. The objective is to reduce the scope for individual inconsistencies.

Bias is far more intractable: it is difficult to detect and even more difficult to eliminate. First, make sure you understand what we mean by the two different types of bias. These are overoptimism and exaggeration, and they are illustrated diagrammatically below.

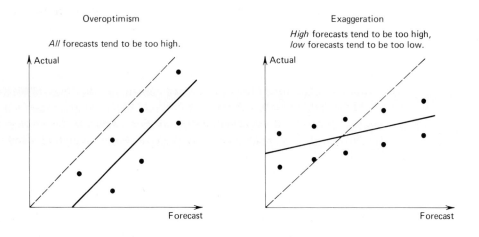

Of course, you can also get both kinds of bias occuring at once:

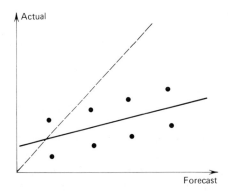

If you are able to monitor a manager's forecasts over a long enough period, you may be able to make allowances for any personal biases of these kinds: but be careful that your actions don't result in a change of your manager's behavior. Second, remember that when managers are rewarded for being optimistic, they will be optimistic: people tend to tell you what they think you want to hear, and it is all too easy to create situations in which you are bound to get biased forecasts.

Forecasting errors can never be eliminated entirely. When you estimate a positive NPV, there is always a chance that it is simply your estimate that is wrong. How can you tell if your positive NPV is a forecasting error or if it represents a genuinely attractive project? The text suggests two useful approaches. *First,* if you can't be sure about future cash flows, as far as possible try to avoid having to discount them to get a present value: while this is correct in theory, in practice it can lead to large (random) errors which could be avoided. Instead, then, look at market values (when you can) to see the market's opinion of what various assets are worth in use. Then, if you can use your assets more efficiently than your competitors can, adjust their market value by an amount that reflects the value of your extra efficiency. *Second,* look for situations where your company has relative advantages. Even if your competitors keep on investing until their new projects have zero NPVs, you will still be able to earn what are called *economic rents*—that is, profits in excess of your opportunity cost of capital.

Marvin Enterprises is an extended and useful illustration of the nature of firms' economic behavior. Although this section is starred, there is really nothing very frightening about it, and it is well worth taking the time to work through it in detail. Don't be put off by the rather unreal and futuristic framework of the case. Certainly, the story is a piece of science fiction, and in some ways it shouldn't be taken too literally. At the same time, the problems it confronts are very real and have many parallels in today's world.

The main argument of the case runs as follows. The price of a product is determined by the total amount of it that is produced. Producers compete with each other and will expand their capacity until new investment has a zero net present value. From this it follows that any single producer can only expect to find positive NPV projects if he or she has some kind of relative advantage over the competition. Such advantages certainly exist: a company may be unusually efficient in the way it operates its plant, or it may have built up a good reputation for its brand name in the marketplace. You can see that these advantages are hard-won and must be protected tenaciously.

The Marvin Enterprises example is about a company that has developed a new technology, but there are other firms hot on its heels and its relative advantage is expected to last for only 5 years. After 5 years, new investment will come in and drive the price of the product (gargle blasters) down to its equilibrium level. The company will therefore earn abnormally high profits (economic rents) only over the first 5 years.

The case raises two other important issues. The first is the effect of Marvin Enterprise's new investment on its existing business. Its proposed expansion is sufficiently large to affect the price of the product it is selling. Marvin must worry about the loss of revenue on its existing operations and include this in its calculation of the NPV of the new project. In more extreme situations this could lead to the company's wishing to suppress its new technology completely.

Second, the less efficient producers play an extremely important role. As the capacity of the industry is increased, the price of the product falls and it becomes increasingly difficult for these producers to stay in business. If the price falls far enough, some producers may withdraw from the market, and other *marginal* producers may be on the point of doing so. In this situation the price of the product will be at the point where it just pays the least efficient remaining producer to stay in business. The size of the economic rent obtained by a more efficient producer will simply reflect the difference between their costs (including the opportunity cost of the capital employed).

Look out too for the misleading argument that a fully depreciated plant is cheaper to run than an otherwise identical undepreciated one. This argument is often made, but it is falsely based on interpreting accounting income as if it were cash flow. Remember, it is only cash flows that matter, and not accounting numbers. Since in this example there are no taxes, there is absolutely no difference between the cash flows of a depreciated plant and an undepreciated one. If we were talking about two plants that had received different amounts of tax depreciation, that would be another matter—and problem 5 gives an example of that.

So much for the concepts behind Marvin Enterprises. The worked example gives you a further opportunity to check that you understand how to work out the numbers.

Worked Example

Problem

The Red Robbo Rubber Company is considering a new investment in a fully automated tire plant. Its existing plant produces 1 million tires a year. It cost $80 million 5 years ago and it could be scrapped for $30 million at any time. The production costs per tire of the old and new plants can be broken down as follows:

	Old plant	New plant
Raw materials and energy	$15	$17
Labor	$10	$3
Other direct costs	$5	$5
Total direct costs	$30	$25

The new plant would be able to produce 500,000 tires a year, and it would cost $35 million. The current price of tires is $38 each. Red Robbo's new investment is not expected to affect this, but the price may fall when other companies complete their modernization programs in 2 years' time. If Red Robbo's cost of capital is 10 percent and there are no corporate taxes:

1. What is the NPV of the new plant?
2. When will the old plant be scrapped, and what is its value today?
3. The costs of raw materials and energy suddenly double. The price of tires changes to $50. What are the answers to **(1)** and **(2)** now?

Solution

1. The capital outlay required on the new plant is $70 per annual tire capacity. The break-even price to give a zero NPV is therefore (10 percent × $70) + $25 (direct costs) = $32. This is the price that we should expect to see in 2 years' time. With the price now at $38, Red Robbo can expect economic rents of $6 per tire per year for 2 years. The NPV of the new plant is therefore

$$500,000 \times \left(\frac{\$6}{1.1} + \frac{\$6}{1.1^2} \right) = \$5,206,612$$

2. The old plant should be scrapped when it can no longer earn the opportunity cost of its salvage value, i.e., 10 percent $\times$ $30 million, or $3 on each tire produced. It will be scrapped when the price falls below $33, i.e., in 2 years' time. Meanwhile it will produce cash flows of $8 million for 2 years. Its value today is therefore

$$\frac{\$8,000,000}{1.1} + \frac{\$8,000,000 + \$30,000,000}{(1.1)^2} = \$38,677,686$$

3. The change in energy and materials costs modifies the direct costs to $45 and $42 for the old and new plants, respectively. This increases the break-even price on the new plant to $49, just $1 below the current price of $50. The economic rent is now only $1 per tire produced (for 2 years); so the NPV of the new plant is

$$500,000 \times \left(\frac{\$1}{1.1} + \frac{\$1}{1.1^2}\right) = \$867,769$$

The old plant will now be scrapped only if the price of tires falls below $45 + $3 = $48. It is now sensible for manufacturers to build only sufficient new plants to push the price down to $49. The old plant is no longer expected to be scrapped but will earn $5 per tire for 2 years, and $4 per tire after that. In year 2 it will be worth 4/0.1 = $40 million; so *today* it is worth

$$\frac{\$5,000,000}{1.1} + \frac{\$5,000,000 + \$40,000,000}{1.1^2} = \$41,735,537$$

Summary

Good investment decisions require good cash-flow forecasts. Watch out for inconsistencies and bias.

Inconsistencies can arise when:

1. Different managers expect different behavior of the economy: many companies establish a set of macroeconomic assumptions (e.g., figures for inflation, interest rates, GNP) to form the basis of all project analyses.
2. Different managers (or different divisions of a company) have different attitudes to risk.
3. Performance criteria affect managers' risk attitudes: a good reward system should have some tolerance for mistakes and be able to discriminate between good decisions and lucky ones.

There are *two kinds of bias*:

1. Optimism/pessimism: when forecasts on average are too high/low.
2. Exaggeration/understatement: when the expected differences between projects are over- or understated.

The net present value rule assumes *unbiased* forecasts. To control bias use these three guides:

1. Avoid such game situations in which managers are encouraged to produce either a "rosy picture" or forecasts which they can subsequently meet.

2. Make adjustments if you know something about the forecaster's track record.
3. Use ad hoc rules when necessary: imposing divisional budgets can limit the effect of overoptimism, and using payback may help if forecasters exaggerate their ability to make accurate long-term forecasts.

Forecasting errors can never be eliminated. An investment may look good *either* because it is good, *or* because you have made a forecasting error.

In order to reduce the chance of forecasting errors swamping the genuine information, look first at *market values* to find the best available valuation of commonly known information. Information that is not generally known can be analyzed separately and added to (or subtracted from) the market value.

Look for *economic rents,* by which we mean profits in excess of the cost of capital. Remember the following three points:

1. When an industry is in a long-run *competitive* equilibrium, all assets just earn their opportunity cost of capital, their NPVs are zero, and economic rents are zero.
2. Firms may earn temporary (or permanent) economic rents if there is temporary disequilibrium, or if they have some degree of monopoly or market power.
3. Don't accept that a project has a positive NPV unless you understand why your firm has a special advantage in doing it.

The *Marvin Enterprises* case illustrates the following salient points.

1. Anticipated and prolonged economic rents are uncommon.
2. High economic rents usually attract competitors; try to estimate the timing and extent of new entry.
3. Identify your firm's comparative advantages and try to capitalize on them.
4. Successive generations of technology will tend to reduce the value of earlier generation assets.
5. The NPV of a project may be reduced by the impact it has on the firm's existing business. This can provide an incentive to slow down the speed of innovation.
6. A marginal producer is one who will quit if the price goes any lower, i.e., for whom price *equals* manufacturing cost plus opportunity cost of not selling out. The economic rent to a more efficient producer is simply the *difference* between its costs and those of a marginal producer.

List of Terms

Bias
Economic rents
Marginal producer

Exercises

Fill-in Questions

1. A _____ is a producer who will cease production if there is any fall in the price at which the product is sold.

2. Profits which are in excess of the competitive equilibrium level are called _____.

3. Forecasts which tend on average to be too high are said to have an upward _____.

Problems

1. Which of the following are true and which are false:
   a. A monopoly can obtain permanent economic rents unless it is regulated in some way.
   b. The average forecasting error for the cash flow of a project is zero.
   c. New capacity decisions must take account of the effect on sunk costs, such as investment in existing plant.
   d. No firm can earn economic rents if it has to buy inputs at a price which reflects their value to the firm.
   e. Marginal producers have assets with zero market value.
   f. Fully depreciated assets always have a present value of zero.
   g. Stock prices reflect the value of growth opportunities only after the firm has announced its plans to invest in new capacity.

2. The following figures show the outcomes of one of your manager's last eight forecasts of the percentage change in the sales of his product:

Forecast	Outcome
10	−1
40	15
−10	−5
10	5
20	11
40	25
−10	−15
20	5

   a. Do his forecasts appear to be biased? Are they exaggerated?
   b. If he is now forecasting that sales will rise by 30 percent, how much would *you* expect them to rise by?

3. Universal Communicators, Inc., makes intergalactic message capsules that sell at $6 million each and cost $4 million each to manufacture. Their existing plant produces 2000 capsules per year, which represents a significant part of the total market. They are considering investing in a new plant that will increase their capacity by 500 additional units. When the increased volume of production hits the market, the market price of message capsules is expected to fall to $5.5 million. Universal is currently negotiating contracts for the construction of its new plant, which will reduce production costs to $3 million. The cost of capital for this project is 10 percent.
   a. What is the maximum price that Universal should be prepared to pay for its new plant, assuming that it can expect to retain a monopoly of the more efficient production technology indefinitely?

b. What would the plant be worth to another company that did not already produce message capsules?

4. The manufacture and sale of Brand X is highly competitive. The industry is composed of three firms with the following capacities and manufacturing costs:

Firm	Sales (million units)	Unit cost ($)
A	8	8
B	6	9
C	4	10
Total	18	

The demand curve for Brand X is given by the following equation: Price (in dollars) = $24 − 0.5 × (quantity in millions). The industry opportunity cost of capital is 10 percent, and new plant costs $70 per unit of capacity. All the plants have indefinitely long lives but could be scrapped at salvage values of $30 per unit of capacity. Firm C discovers a way of reducing unit manufacturing costs to $7, keeping capital costs unchanged. It manages to secure monopoly rights to the technique for an extremely long period, and decides to challenge Firm A's market leadership by immediately adding 5 million units of the new capacity.

a. What is the present value of Firm C's existing plant after the new capacity is added?

b. What is the maximum addition to capacity before it is worthwhile to scrap Firm C's original plant?

c. What is the NPV of Firm C's new investment project?

d. Can Firm C make *any* profitable investment without first disposing of its old plant?

5. Companies Y and Z have identical plants which can each manufacture 100,000 "giggle chips" a year, at a unit cost of $6. These plants could be scrapped at any time with a scrap value of $1.5 million. Company Y's plant has been fully depreciated for tax purposes, whereas Company Z's plant has been depreciated only to a book value of $1 million, and will give rise to annual $500,000 depreciation allowances for the next 2 years. Since both companies pay tax at 50 percent, Company Y would realize only a net $750,000 from scrapping its plant immediately, while Company Z would realize $1.25 million net. At what prices for "giggle chips" will each company find it economic to cease production immediately and scrap its plant? (Assume the opportunity cost of capital is 10 percent.)

*6. The market for shipping crude oil can be represented in terms of a number of types of tanker serving a number of different routes. One very simplified representation is given below. It shows, in millions, the available tonnage of each class of tanker, the total tonnage required on each route, and the operating costs of each tanker on each route.

Tanker type	Tonnage	Annual operating costs (per ton)		
		Route 1	Route 2	Route 3
VLCC	500	$30	$34	Too large
MLCC	400	35	37	$38
Other	300	40	40	40
Tonnage required		300	500	250

All tankers are available for charter in a competitive market, and the price mechanism will allocate them to routes so as to minimize the total costs of transporting crude. All tankers have a useful life of 15 years and can be sold for scrap at any time for $150 per ton. Assume the cost of capital is 10 percent.

a. What type or types of tanker will be used on each route?
b. What will be the annual rental (per ton) for chartering each type of tanker?
c. What will be the market price (per ton) for purchasing each type of tanker?
d. What could happen to the usage and prices of each type of tanker if the tonnage of VLCCs increased to 700?
e. What would happen if (with no increase in the tonnage of VLCCs) an environmental lobby succeeded in banning VLCCs from 50 percent of the required tonnage of route 1?

Essay Questions

1. Describe the different kinds of biases in forecasts that can affect capital budgeting decisions. Give some guidelines for minimizing their effects.
2. Do you think that corporate management should make their own forecasts of the economy as a whole? Give your reasons.
3. Explain clearly why a company may have an economic incentive to suppress an improvement in technology.
4. Explain clearly what is meant by the statement "the level of economic rents is determined by the costs of the marginal producer."
5. In the Marvin Enterprises example, users of the earlier and more expensive technologies were prepared to continue to produce even at prices that gave negative profits after depreciation. Explain what factors determine their willingness to do so.
6. Describe an industry which has experienced the type of situation and decisions described in Marvin Enterprises. What are the most important similarities and differences between your example and the imaginary gargle blaster industry?
*7. Discuss whether a company can still have an incentive to suppress an improvement in technology if all its shareholders hold the market portfolio.

Answers to Exercises

Fill-in Questions

1. marginal producer   2. economic rents   3. bias

Problems

1. (a) T; (b) F; (c) T; (d) T; (e) F; (f) F; (g) F
2. (a) They are biased and exaggerated. (b) 14 percent. The simple linear regression of his outcomes onto his forecasts produces the following equation:

Outcome = −4 percent + 0.6(forecast)

which for his 30 percent forecast produces an expected 14 percent outcome [−4 percent + 0.6 (30 percent)].

3. a. Universal will gain net revenues of $2.5 million on each of its 500 new units a year, and it will lose $500,000 on each of its existing 2000 units of output. This gives an incremental cash flow of

$$(500 \times \$2,500,000) - (2000 \times \$500,000) = \$250,000,000$$

At a 10 percent discount rate the present value is $2.5 billion, and this is the maximum price Universal should be prepared to pay.

b. Another company would not stand to lose revenues on existing plant. The new plant would be worth $12.5 billion to such a company.

4. a. The extra capacity will drive the price down to $12.50, but it is best to scrap C's old plant at any price below $13. The existing plant is therefore worth only its salvage value of $120 million.

b. 4 million units

c. Assuming the equilibrium price is $13, the NPV of Firm C's project is given as

$$NPV = [5,000,000 \times (\$6/0.1 - \$70)] - [4,000,000 \times (\$5/0.1 - \$30)]$$
$$= -\$50,000,000 - \$80,000,000$$
$$= -\$130,000,000$$

If Firm C scraps all its old plant and the price goes to $14.50, the NPV is still negative (−$55 million).

d. It is not possible. When the price is $15, each unit of investment has a NPV of −$70 + $8/0.1 = $10, but unless the old investment has been scrapped, we also reduce the present value of the old plant by

$$4 \times \frac{\$0.5}{0.1} = \$20$$

5. The incremental cash flows from Company Y's decision to maintain production are as follows:

	Year 0	Year 1
Net revenues after tax		$0.5 \times (P - 6) \times 0.1$
Proceeds on disposal	−0.75	0.75

where P is the unit price in dollars, and the cash flows are expressed in units of millions of dollars. These cash flows will have a positive NPV if the price is greater than $7.50.

Similarly, the incremental cash flows from Company Z's decision to maintain production are:

	Year 0	Year 1
Net revenues after tax		$0.5 \times (P - 6) \times 0.1$
Depreciation tax shield		0.25
Proceeds on disposal	−1.25	1.00

These cash flows will have a positive NPV if the price is greater than $8.50.

6. a. We can figure out from the structure of operating costs that the total costs of transporting crude are minimized when the demands of each route are satisfied as follows:

Route 1: 300 VLCC
Route 2: 200 VLCC, 300 MLCC
Route 3: 100 MLCC, 150 other

b. Since 150 "Other" tankers are in use and the remaining 100 are idle, this category of tanker represents a marginal producer and its rent must equal the opportunity cost of salvage. Since the cost of capital is 10 percent and the salvage value is $150 per ton, the rental must be $15 per ton.

MLCCs and "Other" tankers are both used on route 3, but the MLCCs are cheaper to operate by $2 per ton. They can therefore command a $2 higher rental of $17 per ton.

VLCCs and MLCCs are both used on route 2, with a $3 cost advantage to the VLCCs. This gives them a $3 rental advantage, and the VLCC rental is $20 per ton.

c. Capitalizing the rentals of $20, $17, and $15, we find that the market prices of the VLCC, MLCC, and "Other" tankers are $200, $170, and $150.

d. Route 2: 400 VLCC, 100 MLCC; route 3: 250 MLCC. All "Other" would be scrapped, MLCC would drop to salvage value of $150 per ton, and VLCC to $180 per ton.

e. Compared with (a), 150 route 1 VLCC would switch with 150 route 2 MLCC. No change in tanker prices. Price for shipping oil on route 1 increases by $5 per ton.

12 *Organizing capital expenditure and evaluating performance afterwards*

Introduction

Chapter 12 describes how firms usually organize the investment process and subsequent performance measurement. Besides telling us what firms actually do, it also points out a number of weaknesses and shortcomings associated with the methods in common use. There are often four stages to the process of capital budgeting and expenditure:

1. Preparation of the capital budget: the list of investment projects planned each year.
2. Project authorization: to give authority to go ahead.
3. Procedures for the control of projects under construction.
4. Postaudits: to check on the progress of recent investments.

What to Look For in Chapter 12

The various sections of Chapter 12 do not correspond exactly to the four stages of the capital budgeting process described above. You may find it helpful to see in advance just how this chapter is laid out:

Section 12-1 describes the first two stages in capital budgeting: the capital budget and project authorization. These comprise the decision-making part of the process.

Section 12-2 discusses a number of problems that can arise in the decision-making part of the capital budgeting process, and suggests some solutions to them.

Section 12-3 describes the third and fourth stages in capital budgeting: the control of projects under construction and the measurement of performance afterwards. These represent the control part of the process.

Section 12-4 consists of a long numerical example which illustrates the pitfalls in using ROI to measure performance.

Section 12-5 is a short section which makes two suggestions for avoiding the biases that can mess up performance measures based on ROI.

Notice that three different elements are involved in this chapter. First, there are descriptions of the procedures that companies most commonly use. Look out for the use of techniques that are theoretically inappropriate (such as payback and book rate of return), and for the reasons why it can still make sense for companies to continue to use them. Second, there are descriptions of problems that can occur within the usual types of system. These can arise in a number of different ways. The worst problems originate either because the originator of a project has a commitment to see a pet idea approved, or else because of the limitations of a

109

ORGANIZING
CAPITAL
EXPENDITURE
AND EVALUATING
PERFORMANCE
AFTERWARDS

particular technique (such as ROI). Finally, the chapter suggests some solutions to the problems that it raises.

The Capital Budgeting Process   You will probably find that the descriptive nature of much of this chapter makes it fairly easy going. Don't let this fool you! Watch out for the complexity of the capital budgeting process. Much of this complexity arises because we are dealing with a management problem. Senior management has neither sufficient time nor the necessary information to undertake a detailed analysis of every project. It is simply not its job to do so. Instead it must delegate, and the problem is how far to delegate and in what way to do so. If it is thoughtless in the way it delegates these responsibilities, many wrong decisions may be made.

All sorts of problems can occur. Many of them originate from the difficulty of maintaining accurate communication both up and down the ladder of authority. These problems can be made worse by the way managers are judged. You can hardly expect managers to make decisions solely on the basis of NPV if you then judge them on ROI. Communication is also affected by commitment. Almost any manager is likely to exaggerate the advantages of a pet scheme when trying to sell the idea to the boss and to the boss's boss. Maintaining control over the capital budgeting process poses other problems. If there is a way to beat the system, your managers will probably find it, unless the formal system is similar to the informal way in which people think about and communicate decisions. For example, there is no point in having elaborate controls on capital expenditures if managers can evade them by leasing the same equipment instead of purchasing it. These management problems are both complicated and difficult. Don't expect to find a foolproof system that neatly wraps them all up. Do expect to get an understanding of how problems can arise, and of the sorts of action that can be taken to reduce them.

Evaluating Performance   You will probably find that the hardest sections of the chapter are those concerned with the problems of evaluating performance (Sections 12-3, 12-4, and 12-5). After a short description of the kinds of procedures that companies use for controlling expenditures and implementing postaudits, the rest of the chapter deals with the difficulties of evaluating operating performance. Look out for the two basic types of approach:

1. Compare actual performance with projected performance.
2. Compare actual profitability against some absolute standard of profitability.

The first approach is fairly self-explanatory. The second approach contains a number of pitfalls which are examined in some detail. The standard way of measuring the profitability of operating performance is to calculate the accounting rate of return (that is, accounting profit expressed as a percentage of the book value of the assets employed). Unfortunately this figure is usually different from the true rate of return that we would calculate (in terms of economic income) on the basis of market values of present values. *Economic income* is simply the cash flow minus any reduction in present value. The reduction in present value is often called *economic depreciation* (remember that we also reduce book value by book depreciation). Economic income is therefore cash flow minus economic depreciation, and to see what rate of return we have earned we must divide this by the present value at the beginning of the period:

$$\text{True return} = \frac{\text{cash flow} - \text{economic depreciation}}{\text{initial present value}}$$

Notice how similar this is to ROI. Book income is essentially cash flow minus book depreciation. We may therefore write

$$\text{Book ROI} = \frac{\text{cash flow} - \text{book depreciation}}{\text{initial book value}}$$

It is now quite easy to see how ROI can give a distorted picture of the true return. Any differences between book values and present values or between book depreciation and economic depreciation will make ROI different from the true return. Often, in the early years of a project's life, its economic depreciation is less than its book depreciation, so that ROI *understates* profitability. In the later stages of a project ROI often *overstates* profitability, as economic depreciation may then be less than book depreciation, and the book value may also be less than the present value of the project. You may find the worked example helpful in clarifying your understanding of the differences between economic depreciation and book depreciation.

The chapter suggests that some of the biases in using ROI as a performance measure can be reduced by calculating it with economic depreciation instead of book depreciation. While of course this is true, it is worth pointing out that with this suggestion we have come back almost full circle to the first approach of comparing actual with projected to evaluate performance. The expected schedule of economic depreciation depends on the original estimates of future cash flows. If these cash-flow forecasts were to come true exactly, each year the true return would be exactly equal to the expected return that we used as the discount rate. The extent to which the realized return differs from this measures how far the actual cash flow differs from its forecast.

Worked Example

Problem

The Multicash Corporation is still considering a $500,000 new investment that will produce after-tax cash flows of $140,000 each year for 5 years. (We used this as our worked example in Chapter 5.) The required rate of return for this project is 10 percent. Calculate its expected economic depreciation and economic income in each year. How do these figures compare with straight-line depreciation and the corresponding accounting income?

Solution

The easiest way to work this example is to set it out in the form of a table such as the one shown on the top of the next page.

111

ORGANIZING
CAPITAL
EXPENDITURE
AND EVALUATING
PERFORMANCE
AFTERWARDS

Row	Item (figures in $1000s)	Year					
		0	1	2	3	4	5
1	Cash flow		140	140	140	140	140
2	PV at end of year	530.7	443.8	348.2	243.0	127.3	0
3	Economic depreciation		86.9	95.6	105.2	115.7	127.3
4	Economic income		53.1	44.4	34.8	24.3	12.7

The table was calculated as follows. First, we set out the five annual cash flows of $140,000 in the first row. Second, we discount them back a year at a time to get the PV at the end of each year. These are given in row 2. The first number to be calculated here was for year 4 as $140/1.1 = 127.3. The next number was for year 3 as ($140 + $127.3)/1.1 = $243.0, and so on. Third, we calculate the economic depreciation for each year as the reduction in PV. Thus year 5 is $127.3 − 0 = $127.3, year 4 is $243.0 − $127.3 = $115.7, etc. Finally, the economic depreciation is subtracted from the cash flow each year to give economic income.

In this example economic depreciation increases each year, and economic income decreases each year. In contrast, straight-line book depreciation would give a depreciation figure of $100,000 each year, making accounting income a constant $40,000 every year. This understates true income in years 1 and 2 and overstates it in the remaining years. It may also be noted that the use of accelerated depreciation (such as the sum-of-the-years'-digits method) would increase this distortion. If the cash flow increased year by year, this would also increase the distortion.

Summary

Capital Budgeting and Project Authorizations The *capital budget* is a list of planned investment projects with their required outlays. It is usually prepared annually for review by senior management.

Project proposals usually come from the *bottom up,* being initiated at plant manager level and submitted upward for approval. Strategic planning may initiate proposals on a top-down basis.

The budget may contain estimates of likely expenditure for the next 5 years.

Project authorization is usually reserved for senior management. For example, one survey found division heads in companies with sales of $50 million were seldom permitted to authorize capital expenditure amounts above $5000.

. A formal *appropriation request* must usually be prepared for each project after it has been approved in the annual budget. Most firms use checklists to make sure that all relevant costs and alternatives are considered.

Some firms distinguish among four types of projects:

1. Safety or pollution-control outlays required by law or company policy.
2. Maintenance or cost reduction.
3. Capacity expansion in existing business.
4. New products or ventures.

Decision Criteria To evaluate investment projects, most companies use a combination of such different *decision criteria* as payback, ROI, and IRR. Many companies apply capital budgeting techniques incorrectly by treating, for example, depreciation as a cash flow.

In the process intuitive judgment may be as important as formal appraisal. Moreover, simple methods like payback make it easy to *communicate* an idea of project profitability. And, of course, we can't expect managers to concentrate on NPV if we judge their performance on book return.

Organizational Problems Some organizational problems stem from *commitment of sponsors* and *evasion of controls*. Appropriation requests may reflect their sponsor's eagerness to obtain approval. Senior management cannot evaluate individual projects, but they can use *corporate staff* to check the assumptions and to ensure that the authorization request draws attention to all likely contingent expenditures. Management can also impose expenditure limits on individual plants and divisions: this uses capital rationing as a way of *decentralizing* decisions.

Managers permitted to approve projects up to a certain value may sometimes evade this control by breaking a project down into a number of smaller requests.

A similar problem may arise with leased assets.

Partial solutions to these problems include:

1. Use of corporate staff (see above).
2. Planning: capital investments have to make sense in terms of the broader budgeting and planning cycle of operating budgets for plants and divisions, and planned marketing, research etc.
3. Strategic choices: Capital investment should reflect a combination of "bottom-up" and "top-down" processes.
4. Decentralization: decentralization may be dictated by a lack of information at the top. It can work only if plant and division managers are rewarded for doing the right things.

Control of Projects in Progress *Control of projects in progress* is necessary and takes the following steps:

1. Authorization: specifies how much money may be spent and when.
2. Accounting procedures: record expenditures as they occur.
3. Overruns: supplemental appropriation request required, but 10 percent overrun may be permitted without authorization.
4. Completion: formal notice of completion transfers accumulated costs to permanent accounts, and eliminates any hidden kitty.

Postaudits of capital expenditure are usually undertaken 1 year after construction is completed. This is usually too soon to provide a clear assessment of the project's success. Postaudits can provide useful insights into the next round of capital budgeting. It may be impossible to measure the incremental cash flows generated by a project. (Your records don't tell you what cash flows you would have had without the project.)

113

ORGANIZING
CAPITAL
EXPENDITURE
AND EVALUATING
PERFORMANCE
AFTERWARDS

Evaluation of Operating Performance   Performance can be measured in two ways:

1. Actual versus predicted. Compare actual operating earnings with what you predicted.
2. Actual profitability versus an absolute standard of profitability. The accounting rate of return is usually used for this. It is full of pitfalls.

The accounting rate of return is equal to the true "economic" rate of return only when book depreciation is the same as economic depreciation (i.e., the reduction in the present value of the project). In general these are different; so book profitability does not measure true profitability. We have

$$\text{Economic income} = \text{cash flow} + \text{change in present value}$$

$$= \text{cash flow} - \text{economic depreciation}$$

(Remember *reduction* in present value represents economic depreciation.)

$$\text{Book income} = \text{cash flow} - \text{book depreciation}$$

$$\text{Book ROI} = \frac{\text{cash flow} - \text{book depreciation}}{\text{initial book value}}$$

Some important problems were illustrated by the Nodhead Stores example. For example, discounted cash flow and book earnings gave conflicting signals. Even in the long run the errors do not wash out because:

1. Book measures often understate the profitability of new projects and overstate the profitability of old ones.
2. Errors still occur when a company is in a "steady state" with a constant mix of old and new projects.
3. Errors occur because of inflation.
4. Book measures can be further confused by "creative accounting."

What can we do about these biases? Since the biases all stem from not using economic depreciation, why not switch to economic depreciation? In other words, specify a depreciation pattern that matches expected economic depreciation and use this as the basis of performance measurement.

Much of the pressure for good book earnings comes from top management. This can affect attitudes and decisions down the line. Financial managers should not emphasize book earnings at the expense of more fundamental characteristics of the firm.

List of Terms

Appropriation request
Capital budget
Economic depreciation
Economic income
Postaudit
Project authorization
Return on investment

Exercises

Fill-in Questions

1. The first step in the investment process is the preparation of the annual list of planned investment projects called the _____.

2. Most companies stipulate that a formal _____ must be prepared before funds are granted for undertaking a project already listed in the budget.

3. The _____ approving expenditure on large investment projects is usually reserved for senior management.

4. Once they have begun to operate, most projects are subjected to an investigation, called a _____, to check on their progress.

5. Cash flow plus any change in present value measures _____.

6. Each year the book value of an asset is reduced by the amount of its _____.

7. The amount by which the present value of an asset falls over a period is called its _____.

8. Many firms use _____ to measure performance. This may be calculated as cash flow minus book depreciation divided by the initial book value of the assets.

Problems

1. Which of these statements are true and which are false?
   a. Postaudits are usually undertaken a year after project completion.
   b. ROI usually overstates the profitability of new projects and understates the profitability of old ones.
   c. The effect of inflation is to make ROI decrease through time.
   d. Most new capital investment projects are initiated from the "top down."
   e. Incremental cash flows cannot usually be calculated from accounting records.
   f. Safety or environmental outlays required by law do not usually pass through the formal capital budgeting process.

2. The ABC company projects the following after-tax cash flows from its investment of $500,000:

	Year							
	0	1	2	3	4	5	6	7
Cash flow ($1000s)	−500	95	105	110	120	135	150	173

115

ORGANIZING
CAPITAL
EXPENDITURE
AND EVALUATING
PERFORMANCE
AFTERWARDS

a. If ABC's cost of capital is 15 percent, what is the expected economic income from this project each year?

b. The above figures were based on depreciating the investment straight-line over 7 years to its estimated salvage value of $45,000. What is the project's book income in each year?

c. What is the true return on the project each year, and what is its ROI each year?

3. The ABC company in problem 2 pays tax at 46 percent. It decides to depreciate its investment using sum-of-the-years'-digits (instead of straight-line) for tax purposes, but to continue to report its earnings on the basis of straight-line depreciation. How does this alter your calculations for problem 2?

4. An asset costs $370,000, and it is expected to produce a cash inflow of $90,000 in each of the following 6 years. The cost of capital is 12 percent. Calculate economic depreciation, straight-line book depreciation, sum-of-the-years'-digits book depreciation, and double-declining-balance book depreciation.

5. An asset costs $600,000 and is expected to produce after-tax cash flows of $160,000 in each of the following 6 years. The cost of capital is 12 percent and the tax rate is 50 percent. Calculate the NPV, IRR, payback period, and average return on book value for the project.

Essay Questions

1. Describe briefly the various stages in a capital budgeting system, from the origination of the idea for an investment project through to its postaudit.

2. ROI is often used to measure operating performance. What are the pitfalls associated with this technique and how can they be avoided?

3. Describe some of the problems involved in managing and controlling the capital budgeting process so that the profitable new projects are suggested and later approved. What measures can be taken to minimize the effects of these problems?

4. "The only people qualified to make judgments about the likely outcomes of most of our new projects are the very managers who are involved in their implementation. This makes proper control quite impossible." Discuss.

5. Describe the differences between economic income and book income. Some people take the view that accountants should not even *try* to measure economic income. Why not, and what is your view?

Answers to Exercises

Fill-in Questions

1. Capital budget	5. Economic income
2. Appropriation request	6. Depreciation
3. Project authorization	7. Economic depreciation
4. Postaudit	8. Return on investment

Problems

1. (a) T; (b) F; (c) F; (d) F; (e) T; (f) F

2. a. We must discount the cash flows to get the present value each year. Eco-

nomic depreciation is given by the reduction in present value each year, and this must be subtracted from the cash flow to give the economic income. The working may be set out as in the following table (in $1000s).

		Year						
	0	1	2	3	4	5	6	7
Present value	500	480	447	404	345	261	150	0
Cash flow		95	105	110	120	135	150	173
Economic depreciation		20	33	43	59	84	111	150
Economic income		75	72	67	61	51	39	23

b. The book income is the cash flow minus book depreciation (in $1000s).

		Year						
	0	1	2	3	4	5	6	7
Book value	500	435	370	305	240	175	110	0
Cash flow		95	105	110	120	135	150	173
Depreciation		65	65	65	65	65	65	110*
Book income		30	40	45	55	70	85	63

*Includes write-off of salvage value on realization.

c.

True return, %	15	15	15	15	15	15	15
ROI	6	9	12	18	29	49	57

3. The effect of the change in the method of depreciation is to alter the depreciation amounts and the depreciation tax shields as follows (in $1000s).

		Year						
	0	1	2	3	4	5	6	7
Sum-of-the-years'-digits depreciation		114	98	81	65	49	33	16
Straight-line depreciation		65	65	65	65	65	65	65
Change in depreciation		49	33	16	0	−16	−33	−49
Increase in cash flow (depreciation tax shield)		22	15	7	0	−7	−15	−22

117

ORGANIZING
CAPITAL
EXPENDITURE
AND EVALUATING
PERFORMANCE
AFTERWARDS

The calculations now look as follows:

				Year				
	0	1	2	3	4	5	6	7
Present value	517	477	429	376	313	232	131	0
Cash flow		117	120	117	120	128	135	151
Economic depreciation		40	48	53	63	81	101	131
Economic income		77	72	64	57	47	34	20

				Year				
	0	1	2	3	4	5	6	7
Book value	500	435	370	305	240	175	110	0
Cash flow		117	120	117	120	128	135	151
Depreciation		65	65	65	65	65	65	65
Book income		52	55	52	55	63	70	41

	1	2	3	4	5	6	7
True return %	15	15	15	15	15	15	15
ROI	10	13	14	18	26	40	37

4. The cash flows are discounted back to give the present value at the end of each year. Each year the reduction in present value represents the amount of economic depreciation (in $1000s).

				Year			
	0	1	2	3	4	5	6
Cash flow		90	90	90	90	90	90
Present value	370	324	273	216	152	80	0
Economic depreciation		46	51	57	64	72	80

The book depreciation amounts are calculated by applying the usual formulas to the initial cost of $370,000. For the double-declining-balance method the depreciation is always a constant proportion of the depreciable value; so it is convenient to record the depreciable value each year (in $1000s).

Book depreciation	Year						
	0	1	2	3	4	5	6
Straight-line (1/6 each year)		62	62	62	62	62	62
Sum-of-the-years'-digits (6/21, 5/21, etc.)		106	88	70	53	35	18
Double-declining-balance:							
Depreciable value:	370	247	164	110	73	49	0
Depreciation amount: (2/6 of undepreciated value)		123	82	55	37	24	49

5. The annual cash flows (in $1000s) are as follows:

	year 0	years 1–6
Cash flow	−600	160

We can use the 6-year 12 percent annuity factor to calculate the net present value:

$$NPV = -\$600,000 + (\$160,000 \times 4.111)$$

$$= \$57,760$$

IRR: At 15 percent the NPV is $5440. At 16 percent the NPV is −$10,400. Interpolating, the IRR is 15 percent + [$5440/($5440 + $10,400)] = 15.3 percent.

Payback: The cash flow of $160,000 per year pays back the investment of $600,000 in $600,000/$160,000 = 3.75 years.

Average return on book: Annual depreciation = $100,000; so book income = $60,000 each year. Average investment = $300,000; so ROI = 20 percent.

13 *Corporate financing and the six lessons of market efficiency*

Introduction

This chapter marks the beginning of a whole new section of the book. Chapters 2 to 12 were about how companies should make capital investment decisions: the decisions on spending money. The next 12 chapters are about how companies should think about their financing decisions: the decisions on raising money.

Chapters 13 to 15 are particularly important. They provide a comprehensive introduction to the problems of financing. Chapter 13 sets us on the road with some cautions to bear in mind along the way. When we considered capital investment decisions, there was a good chance that our company had some kind of relative advantage in meeting the needs of its markets in a profitable way. These relative advantages enable a company to find investments it can make with positive net present values. However, when it comes to financing decisions, the company is much less likely to have a relative advantage as a participant in the financial markets. Financial markets are highly competitive, and firms should usually assume that the securities they issue will be fairly priced and that issuing them has a net present value of zero. Chapter 13 spells out a number of implications for financing decisions that follow from the competitive nature of financial markets.

Looking ahead to the later chapters, Chapter 14 describes the principal families of securities and explains how they are used by corporations to raise money, while Chapter 15 describes the processes that are involved in issuing those securities. Chapters 16 to 19 are concerned with the questions of what dividends a company should pay, how much debt it should have, and how the interactions between investment and financing decisions should be handled. Last of all, Chapters 20 to 24 go into more detail about how various forms of debt can be valued, so that at least they won't be issued at a negative net present value.

What to Look For in Chapter 13

The main point of this chapter is the simple one that there is no easy way to make money. We have already encountered this idea in earlier chapters, especially in Chapters 3 and 11. Chapter 13 describes the competitive nature of financial markets and draws out a number of implications for financial managers.

One essential distinction is the difference between the markets for physical assets and for financial assets. Back in Chapter 11 we saw that a company may expect to find positive net present value investments if it has some kind of superior resource compared with its rivals. For example, it may be able to design a better product, produce it more efficiently, or sell it more effectively. Differences of these kinds among firms mean that similar assets can have different values to different firms and will give positive net present values to the more efficient firms. In principle, the same argument applies when we consider purely financial markets—the markets for companies' stocks and bonds. If a company were consistently better than its competitors at dealing in the financial markets, it would be able to make money from its financing operations. It would obtain net present values by selling (or issuing) securities at high prices and buying (or retiring) them at low ones—which, of course, is a recipe for making money in any market. However, here comes the rub. While it's hard enough to maintain the kinds of relative advantages necessary to obtain positive net present values in the markets for the company's products, it is infinitely harder to do so in financial markets.

The reasons for this are not hard to see. If we want to compete in the market for making and selling washing machines, we need a factory, skilled engineers and managers, and a work force and sales force. On the other hand, if we want to compete in the financial market, all we need is some money, a copy of the *Wall Street Journal*, and a telephone; this makes financial markets very competitive.

Investors who think that our company's stock looks cheap will buy it, while those who think it looks expensive will sell it. Of course, an investor can buy a share only if some other investor is willing to sell it. The stock price therefore always adjusts until the same number of shares are demanded for purchases as are offered for sale. The market price represents a kind of consensus as to what the stock is worth. As a result we shall be able to make money consistently from our financial market operations only if we have consistently better information than the rest of the market as to what various securities are worth. However, information is widely disseminated in financial markets—through company reports, the financial press, and broker's circulars; and investors can also collect their own data and form their own judgments. This means that it is very unlikely that our company will be able to maintain a sufficient monopoly of information to earn economic rents from its financing operations. Companies should generally assume that their securities will be fairly priced.

Definitions of Efficient Markets   The previous section described what an efficient capital market is like. We usually define an efficient market as one in which the prices of all securities fully reflect all available information and no investor can expect more or less than a fair rate of return from purchasing any security. Economists sometimes like to spell out the conditions that will lead to a market of this kind. We can *expect* a market to be efficient if there are a large number of participants, all of whom have free access to all information that is available and who can trade without incurring significant transaction costs. While securities markets don't *exactly* meet these conditions, they very nearly do. There are a large number of investors, information is widely available, and transaction costs are low.

Look out for the three different forms of the efficient market theory. Of course, in one sense a market either is efficient or it isn't, but we often distinguish among different levels of efficiency on the basis of what categories of information are efficiently impounded in prices. Thus if past prices cannot be used to make superior profits, we can conclude that security prices reflect all the information contained in the record of past prices. This type of market efficiency is called *weak form* efficiency. The other two forms are the *semistrong* form, when consistently superior profits cannot be made on the basis of published information,

121

CORPORATE
FINANCING AND
THE SIX LESSONS
OF MARKET
EFFICIENCY

and the *strong* form, when prices reflect all the information that can be obtained by even the most painstaking analysis.

Finally, look out for the various sorts of implications that follow from market efficiency—the six lessons of market efficiency. Some of the lessons are bad news for financial managers. You can't expect to earn economic rents by "clever" financing. For example, repurchasing bonds or splitting stock is unlikely to do much to change the value of your company, and manipulating reported earnings by the choice of accounting method is unlikely to have much effect either.

Finally, if markets are efficient, you won't be able to find companies to acquire at bargain prices, and neither will investors pay a premium for your company to diversify on their behalf, when they are perfectly able to construct diversified portfolios for themselves. On the other hand, not all the lessons are bad news. If markets are efficient, the financial manager can expect to be able to issue shares at a fair price at any time, and the high elasticity of demand for shares means that even very large issues may be made with a good deal of confidence. Further, since the prices of securities reflect investors' expectations about the future, we can use these prices to find out how investors expect interest rates or earnings to change in the future. Last of all, remember that efficient capital markets do *not* mean that financial managers can let financing take care of itself: there is still a great deal of work for the financial manager to do!

Worked Example

The board of the Eyeball Glazing Corporation is trying to decide on an issue of new shares. The company already has 4 million shares outstanding, and it is authorized to issue up to a further 1 million shares. What proportion of the company will have to be sold in order to raise $8 million if shares can be sold (1) at $32 each, (2) at only $20 each? (3) If the shares are really worth $32 but can be issued only at $20, what loss would existing shareholders suffer if they did not subscribe to such an issue? (4) What is the relevance of market efficiency to the board's decision?

Solution

1. To raise $8 million at $32 a share requires selling $8,000,000/32 = 250,000 shares. The company will then have 4.25 million shares issued, and 0.25 million/4.25 million = 5.88 percent of the company will have to be sold to new shareholders.
2. Similarly, at a price of $20 a share, 400,000 shares must be issued, and this will represent 9.09 percent of the issued capital of the company.
3. Suppose that the company raises $8 million by selling 400,000 shares. If the original 4 million shares were worth $32 each (or $128 million in total), the company is now worth $136 million, which is divided among its 4.4 million shares. Each share will be worth $30.91 ($136,000,000/4,400,000 shares); so the original shareholders have a 3.41 percent loss from the previous value of $32. This drop seriously understates the true significance of their loss, for their total shareholdings are now worth only $123.64 million (4,000,000 shares × $30.91),

$4.36 million below the previous figure. They have paid $12.36 million for $8 million worth of cash.

4. If the market is efficient, the situation described in 3 above cannot arise. The board can expect to issue new shares at very close to their true value and should therefore not be reluctant to issue new shares.

Summary

About Financing Decisions So far we have learned how companies decide to spend money on capital investment projects. Now we will learn how they raise the money to finance their investments. The financing choices include the following:

- What proportion of earnings should be retained and what proportion paid out in dividends?
- Should money be raised by borrowing or by issuing stock?
- Should borrowings be short-term or long-term?
- Should an issue of debt be made convertible into the stock of the company?

In many circumstances we can take the firm's investments as given and then determine what the best financing strategy is. The two kinds of decisions are independent of each other and can be dealt with separately. Sometimes decisions about capital structure depend on project choice (or vice versa), and then the financing and investment decisions have to be considered jointly.

A financing decision has an NPV (which measures how attractive it is) just as an investment decision does. For example, if we can borrow $100,000 for 10 years at 3 percent interest (making 10 annual interest payments of $3000 before repaying the $100,000 principal), where we would normally have to pay 10 percent, then this loan has an

$$\text{NPV} = +\$100,000 - \left[\sum_{t=1}^{10} \frac{\$3000}{(1.1)^t}\right] - \frac{\$100,000}{1.1^{10}} = \$43,012$$

Financing decisions differ from investment decisions in that they are easier to reverse and are more likely to have a zero NPV. If a company is to get a positive NPV from selling a security, it must persuade the buyer to accept a negative NPV—not an easy thing to do. If capital markets are *efficient*, the purchase or sale of a security at the current market price is a zero NPV transaction.

What Is an Efficient Market? Economists say that a security market is *efficient* when information is widely and cheaply available and all relevant information is always reflected in security prices. This *implies* that the purchase (or sale) of any security has a zero NPV.

The theory of efficient markets developed from statistical studies of the movements of stock prices. Such studies show that stock prices do *not* follow predictable cycles. Instead, the successive price changes of a stock appear to be independent of each other: today's price change will not help us to predict tomorrow's price change. This *random walk* of stock prices was first discovered by Maurice Kendall in 1953.

At first economists were surprised at this randomness (that is, unpredictability) of stock price movements. However, it turns out that they should not have been

123

CORPORATE
FINANCING AND
THE SIX LESSONS
OF MARKET
EFFICIENCY

surprised. We should expect this kind of price behavior in a security market that is efficient. In an efficient market prices reflect all relevant information, and price changes are caused by new information. If this new information could be predicted ahead of time, it wouldn't be new information, and the prices would already have adjusted to it. In other words, in an efficient market stock prices already reflect all that is predictable. Changes in stock prices are caused by new information that could not have been predicted.

The investment analysis carried out by investors helps to make price changes random. For example, if investors can forecast that a stock which sells at $50 today will go up to $60 next month, they will *immediately* rush to buy it until they have pushed the price up to the point where the stock offers a normal rate of return. There are two types of investment analysis: *Fundamental analysis* uses information about a company's business and profitability to appraise the value of its stock. *Technical analysis* simply uses the past price record to look for predictable patterns in the price series.

We sometimes distinguish among three forms of market efficiency. The *weak* form of efficiency means that prices reflect at least all the information contained in the record of past prices—this implies that it is impossible to make consistently superior returns by just using technical analysis. The *semistrong* form of efficiency means that prices reflect all published information, such as published accounting reports or published forecasts of earnings or dividends. Finally, the *strong* form of efficiency means that prices reflect all information that can be acquired by even the most painstaking fundamental analysis of the company and economy, including gathering information that is not publicly disseminated.

Empirical studies provide support for the weak and semistrong forms. They indicate that price changes seem to be random and that public announcements of many specific items of news are rapidly and accurately impounded in the price of the stock. Studies of the performance of professionally managed portfolios conclude that no group of institutions has been able to outperform the market consistently, after taking account of differences in risk. However, there do appear to be some inefficiencies in the stronger forms. Some researchers have found that investors could have made small but significantly superior profits by buying low P/E stocks or after a favorable earnings announcement; there is also evidence of superior returns to New York Stock Exchange specialists and to company managers trading in their own stock.

Finally, there are three common misconceptions about the efficient market hypothesis. To avoid them, remember that an efficient market *does not*:

- Imply perfect forecasting ability
- Mean that portfolio managers are incompetent (because of their inability to achieve superior returns)
- Mean that the market is irrational (because price changes are random)

The Six Lessons of Market Efficiency

1. *Markets have no memory*, and the history of the stock price is no guide as to whether it is overpriced or underpriced. Financial managers sometimes appear to ignore this. They tend to issue stock when their stock price is historically high and are reluctant to issue stock after a fall in price.

2. *Trust market prices*. There is no way for most investors to find bargains consistently that are underpriced. This should be borne in mind when considering the management of the firm's pension funds or its decision to acquire another company or its decision to repurchase its own securities. The Northwestern Bell decision to repurchase its bonds at a price of $1160 in 1977 (following a fall in interest rates) *did* reduce future interest charges but nevertheless had a negative NPV. The company would apparently have done better to wait until 1979, when it could have exercised its valuable option to call the bonds at the lower price of $1085.70.

3. *There are no financial illusions*. Investors are concerned with the firm's cash flows and the portion of those cash flows to which they are entitled. It is unlikely that a firm can increase its market value by merely cosmetic changes such as stock splits or by manipulating the earnings reported to shareholders.

4. *The do-it-yourself alternative*. Investors will not pay others for what they can easily do themselves. What advantage is there to a company in pursuing a diversification policy when its shareholders can (and should) hold diversified portfolios of stocks themselves? What advantage is there to a company borrowing to provide financial leverage for its shareholders when they are free to borrow on their own accounts? This last question is examined in more detail in Chapters 17 and 18.

5. *Seen one stock, seen them all*. Investors don't buy a stock for its unique qualities; they buy it because it offers the prospect of a fair return for its risk. This means that a very slight increase in the expected return from one particular stock should be sufficient to induce a lot of investors to switch to it. Economists describe this situation by saying that stocks are almost perfect substitutes for each other, and the demand for any given company's stock is very elastic. This has the following important implication: contrary to popular belief, you can sell large blocks of stock at close to the market price as long as you can convince other investors that you have no private information. Myron Scholes' study of secondary offerings confirmed that large offerings had only a very small depressing effect on the price.

6. *Reading the entrails*. Security prices reflect what investors expect to happen in the future. They can therefore be used as a guide to what people expect. The return offered by a company's bonds, and the variability of its common stock are good indicators of the probability of its going bankrupt. The Dow Jones average is a leading indicator of the level of economic activity. Finally, the difference between long-term and short-term interest rates tells something about what investors expect to happen to the short-term rate in the future (Chapter 21 gives more details of this).

List of Terms

Call provision	Semistrong form efficiency
Efficient market	Stock dividend
Elasticity of demand	Stock split
Fundamental analysis	Strong form efficiency
Maturity	Technical analysis
Random Walk	Weak form efficiency

Exercises

Fill-in Questions

1. A securities market is said to be _____, if the securities in it are fairly priced and reflect all known information.

2. The prices of securities appear to follow a _____ in which each successive price change is independent of all previous price changes.

3. Investment analysis to determine the worth of a company's shares by studying the company's business and trying to uncover information about its profitability is called _____ .

4. Investment analysis based on studying the record of past prices is called _____ .

5. If prices reflect all the information contained in the history of past prices, the market is _____ .

6. If prices reflect all published information, the market satisfies the conditions for _____ .

7. In the _____ of efficiency prices reflect all information that investors can obtain from any sources.

8. The _____ for any article measures the percentage change in the quantity demanded for each percentage increase in its price.

9. The _____ of a bond is when its original face value will be repaid.

10. A _____ on an issue of bonds provides the company with an option to repurchase its bonds at specified prices on specified dates.

11. A company makes a _____ when it increases the number of outstanding shares by subdividing the stock that is already outstanding.

12. A _____ occurs when a company issues more shares of stock as dividends to its shareholders.

Problems

1. The Catalytic Cracking Corporation is about to split its stock on a 4-for-1 basis. Before the split its share price is $76. What would you expect it to be afterwards?

2. High Potential Electronics Corporation believes that its stock is overvalued by the market. Its shares are selling at $80, although management believes they

are worth only $60. There are currently 1.2 million shares outstanding, and the company plans to raise $7.5 million by issuing a further 100,000 shares at $75 each. The existing shareholders can sell their rights to subscribe to this issue for $461,500. If they do so and all the new shares are taken up by new investors, how much will the original shareholders have benefited (a) if the shares were worth only $60 before, and (b) if they were worth $80?

3. A company is eligible for a subsidized 5-year loan of $1 million at 8 percent interest where the usual market rate is 12 percent. The loan is to be repaid in five equal annual payments (of interest plus principal). What is the net present value of this loan?

4. Today I can buy an 11-percent-coupon, 10-year bond at face value. I believe that in a year's time interest rates will have come down so that this bond (which will then be a 9-year bond) will be yielding only 8 percent. (a) If I am correct, what return will I have earned on my investment? (b) What implications does this have for forecasting interest rates in terms of (i) its usefulness and (ii) its difficulty? Assume interest is paid annually.

5. The highly respected economic forecasting department of a major United States bank announces that their latest forecast predicts a significant upturn in economic activity and corporate profits starting in 2 years and lasting for 3 or 4 years. What effect on share prices do you expect this to have: (a) immediately; (b) in 2 years; and (c) in 6 years?

6. Identify for which two of the following items demand is least elastic with respect to price, and for which two it is most elastic: (a) steak, (b) tobacco, (c) a financial security, (d) gasoline, (e) tuxedos, (f) shortening.

7. Company A has a market value of $40 million. Company B has a market value of $20 million. A proposed merger between them seems likely to reduce the standard deviation of their equity returns from 40 percent individually to 35 percent combined. What would you expect the market value of the combined company to be after the merger?

8. Which of the following is most likely to result in an increase in the value of the company's shares: (a) It announces that its long-awaited contract with the federal government has now been finalized, and production will begin as soon as a satisfactory specification can be agreed upon. (b) As a result of a change in its depreciation policy the earnings figure in its newly released annual report is almost double the figure for the previous year. (c) It announces a 50 percent increase in its dividend. (d) Its main competitor announces a price cut.

9. A random number generator provides me with the following sequence of random numbers: 18, −10, 12. Which of the following series most resembles the prices of a security on three successive dates in the future, where its price today is $50: (a) 50×1.18, $50 \times 1.18 \times 0.90$, $50 \times 1.18 \times 0.90 \times 1.12$; (b) 50×1.18, 50×0.90, 50×1.12; (c) Other: specify.

Essay Questions

1. Explain what is meant by an "efficient securities market," and describe the three forms of efficiency that are commonly distinguished.

127

CORPORATE
FINANCING AND
THE SIX LESSONS
OF MARKET
EFFICIENCY

2. Describe the most important implications of efficient financial markets for the corporate financial manager.

3. "This idea of market efficiency just doesn't make any sense to me at all. Why, I know of a dozen or more fortunes that have been made or lost on the stock exchange." Explain carefully why those two sentences are not incompatible.

4. "We can't afford to accept that the market might be efficient. If we accepted that, we'd have nothing to say to the investors who come to us for advice." Discuss.

5. "Even if the market is efficient, there's no need to lose money unnecessarily. I can still reduce my losses by making sure I always buy after a fall in price rather than after a rise in price." Discuss.

Answers to Exercises

Fill-in Questions

1. efficient		**7.** strong form	
2. random walk		**8.** elasticity of demand	
3. fundamental analysis		**9.** maturity	
4. technical analysis		**10.** call provision	
5. weak form efficient		**11.** stock split	
6. semistrong form efficiency		**12.** stock dividend	

Problems

1. $19.

2. (a) Before the issue the shareholdings were worth $72 million. Afterward, the shareholders have $461,500 in cash plus a 12/13 [1,200,000 shares/(1,200,000 shares + 100,000 shares)] claim on $72 million plus $7.5 million. This gives them a total value of $73,846,115; so they have benefited by $1,846,115. (b) Before the issue the shareholdings were worth $96 million. Afterward, the value to the original shareholders is

$$\$461{,}500 + \frac{12}{13} \times (\$96{,}000{,}000 + \$7{,}500{,}000).$$

This is still $96 million; so there is no benefit (or loss) to the original shareholders.

3. To give the loan an 8 percent interest rate the annual payments must be $1,000,000/3.993 = $250,438 (3.993 is the 5-year annuity factor at 8 percent). Discounting those payments at 12 percent produces a PV of $902,829 ($250,438 × 3.605); so the NPV of the loan is $97,171.

4. (a) The price of the bond will be $1187.17 [($110 × 6.247) + ($1000 × 0.500)] at the end of a year, and in addition I will have $110 cash. This gives a total return of 29.72 percent.
(a) (i) If I *could* forecast interest rates accurately, I could make a lot of money, but (ii) this makes forecasting extremely competitive and *very* difficult.

5. (a) A slight increase in share prices if this represents good news. (b) and (c) no effect

6. Least elastic: (b) tobacco, (d) gasoline. Most elastic: (c) a financial security, (f) shortening

7. $60 million. (The market price already represents market-related risk as measured by beta.)

8. (c)

9. (a)

14 *An overview of corporate financing*

Introduction

As you might expect from its title, Chapter 14 provides the kind of introduction to corporate financing that you just can't afford to miss. The first part of the chapter describes the four main families of securities that companies can issue: common stock, debt, preferred stock, and options of various kinds (such as warrants and convertible bonds). The emphasis is on explaining the wide variety of methods that companies can use to raise money and on explaining the different terms that are used to describe them. The remainder of the chapter describes how securities are actually used by corporations. It examines the relative importance of various sources of finance for corporations in the United States and comments on some patterns in financing behavior.

What to Look For in Chapter 14

Chapter 14 could change your life! After you have read this chapter, you may find that you begin to talk a strange new language using phrases like "shares that are issued but not outstanding" and "convertible subordinated debentures."

That is what this chapter is about. It doesn't contain any difficult new ideas but it does contain a large number of new terms that you have to be able to use if you want to speak the language of financing. In learning these new terms, you may want to devote more time than usual to our list of the main new terms and to the corresponding set of fill-in questions.

Here is a brief guide to where the majority of new terms arise. First, a number of terms arise in connection with common stock. There are terms to describe how much stock a company has been authorized to issue, to describe how much stock it has and hasn't issued, and stock that has been issued which has subsequently been repurchased by the company. Finally, there are terms for describing the arrangement by which shareholders vote for their board of directors, and sometimes we even have to distinguish between classes of common stock that have different rights to vote and receive dividends.

Second, a lot of new terms are needed to describe the enormous variety of debt that can be issued. The most common differences between debt issues concern their maturity, the kinds of provisions that are made for their retirement, their position in the pecking order of financial claims on the firm (their seniority), and whether they are secured; for, if they are, in the event of a default they have a direct claim on assets of the firm. Debt issues can also pay either a fixed rate of interest or a floating rate and may be denominated in currencies other than United States dollars.

Preferred stock introduces only a few new terms, but more are introduced by the different kinds of options that companies can issue. In particular we have warrants, which are simply a firm's securities that give the holder the right to purchase a set number of shares of common stock, at a set price, on or before a set date in the future. We also have convertible bonds, which are bonds that give their holder a similar right to exchange them for a fixed number of shares at a future date or dates.

Look out, too, for differences in the tax treatment of different securities. Notice that while interest payments on debt are paid out of pretax income, dividends on both common and preferred stock are paid out of after-tax income. On the other hand, companies that hold securities pay corporate income tax on the whole of their interest income from bonds but pay tax on only 15 percent of the dividends they receive from common or preferred stock. Can you guess what this means for those who issue preferred stock and who hold it? If you can't guess, Section 14-3 will tell you.

Sections 14-1 through 14-5 should give you a pretty good idea of the variety of different securities that a company can issue. Remember too that companies don't have to confine themselves to issuing the same kinds of securities that have already been issued by other companies. They are perfectly free to create entirely new securities; so if your company thinks that investors would like to buy a floating-rate Deutschemark bond that is convertible into its (dollar) common stock, there is no reason not to issue one.

Section 14-6 is about companies' requirements for external funds and how the different kinds of securities are used in practice. We shouldn't be surprised that a large proportion of firms' capital requirements come from internally generated cash. Remember that cash flow includes depreciation and if none of this were reinvested there would be a rapid decline in the country's stock of capital investment. Equally, internally generated cash is not sufficient to meet companies' expenditure requirements, and additional funds are raised by debt issues and issues of stock. The funds are supplied by pension funds and other financial intermediaries such as mutual funds, as well as by individual investors.

While, as we saw in the last chapter, we cannot predict future changes in the levels of stock prices, we can observe systematic and predictable patterns in firms' financing behavior. The amount of external money that companies require (their financial deficit) is linked to the general level of economic activity. This deficit is lowest when the economy is pulling out of a recession. At this stage of the business cycle companies have spare capacity and increases in sales have a big effect on their cash position, since inventories are reduced and major new investments are unlikely to be undertaken. The deficit is usually largest when economic activity begins to turn down, and investment that is already committed continues to be made. We may also observe patterns in the way companies choose between debt or equity financing. There is a pronounced tendency for companies to make equity issues when the stock market is historically high. Notice that neither of the patterns described conflicts with the efficient markets idea—there is no way that anyone can make superior profits from knowing about these regularities in the volumes of money raised.

Summary

The first five sections of our summary describe the main types of securities that firms can issue. The final section is about how firms tend to use these securities.

Common Stock A company is allowed to issue shares up to the amount specified by its *authorized share capital*, which can only be increased with the permission of the shareholders. *Outstanding* shares are ones that are held by investors. Shares that have been issued but subsequently repurchased by the company (and held in its treasury) are called *treasury shares*. They are said to be *issued but not outstanding*. All issued shares are entered in the company's accounts at their *par* (or *stated*) *value*. Because some states do not allow companies to sell shares below par value, par value is generally set at a low figure which has no economic significance.

The common stockholders are the owners of the company and have a general preemptive right to anything of value that the company may wish to distribute. Their control over the company's affairs is manifested by their right to vote on appointments to the board of directors and on some other issues. Voting may be on a majority basis or on a cumulative basis. Cumulative voting makes it more likely for minority groups to obtain representation on the board. Under this system shareholders may, if they wish, allot all their votes to one candidate. For example, if six directors are to be elected, a shareholder can allocate all six votes from each share to a single candidate and does not have to choose six candidates to vote for. Finally, a few companies separate classes of stock (for example, class A and class B) which are distinguished by having different rights to vote.

Corporate Debt There is a great variety of ways in which companies can borrow money. The common feature is that the company promises to make regular interest payments and to repay the principal amount according to an agreed schedule. The company's liability is limited; so lenders can only look to the earnings and assets of the company for their payment. Lenders cannot look beyond those assets to the shareholders for repayment. Any debt can be classified along the following six dimensions:

- *Maturity* The length of time before the debt is due to be completely repaid. Long-term debt which does not mature for more than a year is called *funded* debt. Short-term debt due in less than a year is called *unfunded*.
- *Provision for repayment* Long-term loans may be repaid in a single "bullet" payment on their maturity date, or they may be repaid steadily over a period of time. A *sinking fund* is often used to retire publicly traded bonds gradually. The borrower may also have a *call* provision which provides the right to repay all or part of the debt issue before maturity at some specified premium above its face value.
- *Seniority* Debt may be junior or senior. If the company goes bankrupt, its junior (or *subordinated*) debt is not eligible to receive payment until all senior debt has been paid in full.
- *Security* Debt which (in the event of default) has first claim on specified assets is said to be *secured* on those assets. A mortgage is an example of this, while long-term bonds which are unsecured are called debentures.
- *Fixed rate or floating rate* The interest rate may be fixed for the whole term of the loan when it is issued, or it may be determined from time to time during the term according to an agreed formula such as "1 percent above prime."
- *Country and currency* While most borrowing by United States corporations is

done in the United States and in United States dollars, firms may also borrow in foreign countries or in foreign currencies.

Preferred Stock   Every company has common stock. Most companies have debt. Relatively few have preferred stock, which has some of the characteristics of common stock and some of debt. Legally, preferred stock is part of the ownership of the company, but (like debt) it promises a fixed dividend every year. This dividend is payable at the discretion of the directors, with the provision that no dividends may be paid on the common stock until the preferred dividend has been paid. There is no final repayment date, but many issues provide for the periodic retirement of stock. Preferred stock rarely confers full voting privileges. In seniority it is senior to the company's common stock but junior to everything else.

A Note on Taxation   Interest payments on debt are regarded as a business expense and come out of pretax income. We can therefore think of debt as receiving a subsidy from the government. Dividends (whether on common stock or on preferred stock) are regarded as a distribution of income to the owners of the firm. Accordingly, they come out of after-tax income. Interest received is part of a company's income and is taxable. However, to reduce the incidence of double taxation, companies have to pay tax on only 15 percent of their dividend income. As a result most preferred stock is held by corporations (favorable treatment of dividend income), and most is issued by regulated utility companies (who would be made to lower their rates if they used subsidized debt instead).

Other Securities   The most important other securities issued by companies are:

• *Warrants*   These give their owner the right (known as a *call option*) to purchase one share of common stock at a specified price on or before a specified future date.

• *Convertible bonds*   These are bonds issued by the company that can be exchanged for (or *converted* into) a specified number of shares on specific future dates if the holder wishes.

There may also be call options on the company's stock other than warrants, but these are issued (or written) by third parties and *not* by the company itself. In addition, corporate debt and equity can be analyzed in terms of options. This makes options an important topic, which is studied at length in Chapter 20.

Patterns of Corporate Financing   The figures for 1977 show the following percentage uses and sources of funds in nonfinancial corporations:

Uses		Sources	
Capital expenditure	64%	Cash flow from operations	57%
Increase in inventories	6%	Net issues of:	
Increase in receivables	14%	Stock	1%
Other	16%	Long-term debt	21%
		Short-term debt	11%
		Increase in payables	10%
		Total external Funds	43%
Total uses	100%	Total sources	100%

The high predominance of internally generated funds (57 percent) is typical and not surprising, because the cash flow from operations includes depreciation provisions. There is still a substantial requirement for external funds. This requirement is sometimes called the *financial deficit*. It is usually largest when economic activity begins to turn down and smallest when the economy is pulling out of a recession.

The volume of new issues of stock varies substantially from year to year: the 1 percent figure for 1977 is unusually low, and around 4 percent would be more typical. Companies tend to issue more equity when stock prices are at historically high levels. Similarly, the volume of long-term debt issued is (inversely) related to the level of interest rates. Over the last 20 years companies' balance sheets show a marked increase in the proportion of debt to total assets (34 percent in 1954 to 47 percent in 1977). However, at least part of the reason for this is that progressive inflation has increased the market values of assets relative to their book values.

List of Terms

Authorized share capital	Outstanding shares
Call option	Par value
Convertible bond	Preferred stock
Cumulative voting	Prime rate
Debenture	Proxy contest
Eurobond	Secured
Eurodollar	Senior
Floating rate	Sinking fund
Funded debt	Subordinated
Lease	Treasury shares
Majority voting	Warrant

Exercises

Fill-in Questions

1. The maximum number of shares that a company can issue is known as its

   _____ .

2. Shares that have already been issued and are held by investors are called

   _____ .

3. _____ are shares that have been repurchased by the company.

4. The _____ of a security is the value at which it is entered in the company's books.

5. _____ is the name for the voting system under which each director is voted on separately.

6. The voting system under which a stockholder may cast all his or her votes for one candidate is known as _____ .

7. A _____ arises when the firm's existing management and directors compete with outsiders for the votes of the shareholders in order to control the corporation.

8. _____ debt is debt that matures after more than 1 year.

9. To repay its long-term loans in an orderly fashion over an extended period of time, a company may pay each year a sum of cash into a _____ which is then used to repurchase the bonds.

10. In the event of bankruptcy, _____ debt must be repaid before subordinated debt receives any payment.

11. _____ debt represents a junior claim which, in the event of default, is paid only after all senior creditors are satisfied.

12. In the event of default _____ debt has first claim on specified assets.

13. A _____ is a long-term bond that is unsecured.

14. The interest on a _____ loan varies with the short-term interest rate.

15. Banks will lend to their most favored customers at the _____ rate.

16. A _____ is a dollar that has been deposited with a bank outside the United States.

17. A _____ is an issue of debt that is sold simultaneously in several countries.

18. A long-term rental agreement, known as a _____, can provide an alternative to borrowing.

19. _____ stock is an equity security which offers a fixed dividend that must be paid before any dividend can be paid on the common stock.

20. A _____ option provides the right to purchase an asset at a specified price on or before a specified exercise date.

21. A _____ is a long-term security issued by a company which gives the holder the right to purchase one share of common stock at a set price on or before a set date.

22. A bond that may be converted into the company's common stock at the discretion of the holder is called a ———————.

Problems

1. The authorized share capital of Shady Enterprises is 400,000 shares. The equity is currently shown in the company's accounts as follows:

Common stock ($0.25 par value)	$ 60,000
Additional paid-in capital	200,000
Retained earnings	20,000
Common equity	$280,000
Treasury stock (15,000 shares)	10,000
Net common equity	270,000

   a. How many shares are issued?
   b. How many are outstanding?
   c. How many more shares can be issued without the approval of the share-holders?
   d. What is the share price, if it is twice its book value?

2. Shady Enterprises of problem 1 issues a further 80,000 shares at an issue price of $0.90 a share. How will the equity be shown in the company's books after the issue?

3. There are nine directors to be elected and I own a round lot of 100 shares. What is the maximum number of votes I can cast for my favorite candidate under (a) majority voting, and (b) cumulative voting?

4. The shareholders of Shady Enterprises need to elect five directors. There are 305,000 shares outstanding. How many shares do you need to own to ensure that you can elect at least one director (a) under majority voting and (b) under cumulative voting?

5. The Shifty Transportation Company has the following income for the year:

Taxable income from operations	$253,000
Interest income	42,000
Dividends from preferred stock	20,000
Dividends from common stock	10,000
Total income	$325,000

   It has paid interest charges amounting to $59,000 and dividends on its preferred and common stock of $35,000 and $50,000. If it pays tax at 46 percent, what is its tax bill for the year?

6. The Shifty Transportation Company of the last problem had the following income and payments in the previous year:

Income from:	
Operations	$224,000
Interest	32,000
Preferred dividends	40,000
Common dividends	40,000
	$336,000

Payments:

Interest	$ 44,000
Preferred dividends	$ 35,000
Common dividends	$ 45,000

How much tax should it have paid?

7. Which of the following are true and which are false?
   a. The financial deficit is usually largest when the economy is pulling out of a recession.
   b. Firms tend to issue more equity when stock prices are historically high.
   c. If a bond is secured, the company makes a regular payment of cash into a sinking fund.
   d. The firm's capital expenditure requirements are usually more than covered by internally generated cash.

Essay Questions

1. Explain how issued share capital is shown in a company's accounts, and describe what rights and privileges shareholders enjoy.

2. Describe the variety of different types of debt that a company can issue.

3. What is preferred stock, who issues it, who buys it, and why?

4. Describe the main sources and uses of companies' funds. What is meant by the financial deficit and how is it affected by the behavior of the economy?

5. "It's only when a company goes to the market to raise new equity that it's forced to earn the cost of capital on its funds." Discuss.

Answers to Exercises

Fill-in Questions

1. authorized share capital	12. secured
2. outstanding shares	13. debenture
3. treasury shares	14. floating-rate
4. par value	15. prime rate
5. majority voting	16. eurodollar
6. cumulative voting	17. eurobond
7. proxy context	18. lease
8. funded	19. preferred
9. sinking fund	20. call
10. senior	21. warrant
11. subordinated	22. convertible bond

Problems

1. (a) 240,000; (b) 225,000; (c) 160,000; (d) $2 \times (\$270,000/\$225,000) = \$2.40$

2.

Common stock ($0.25 par value)	$ 80,000
Additional paid-in capital	252,000
Retained earnings	20,000
Common equity	$352,000
Treasury stock	10,000
Net common equity	$342,000

3. (a) 100; (b) 900

4. (a) More than half the outstanding shares are needed, that is, 152,501 shares.
(b) As long as your candidate gets at least a fifth of the total votes cast, she is
bound to be elected. To ensure this, you need only 61,000 shares. Even this is
more than you really need. One more than a sixth, that is, 50,834, is sufficient.

5. Shifty's taxable income is calculated as follows:

Income from operations	$253,000
Interest income	42,000
15 percent of dividends	4,500
	$299,500
Less interest expense	59,000
Taxable income	$240,500

Its tax bill is 46 percent of $240,500 which is $110,630.

6. Taxable income is given by:

Income from operations	$224,000
Interest income	32,000
15 percent of dividends	12,000
	$268,000
Less interest expense	44,000
Taxable income	$224,000

Tax is 46 percent of $224,000, which is $103,040.

7. (a) F; (b) T; (c) F; (d) F

15 *How corporations issue securities*

Introduction

This chapter outlines how companies raise new long-term funds in the capital market. It not only covers a wealth of institutional material, but it also guides managers through the many decisions they face when embarking on any long-term funding exercise. Since in recent years United States companies have funded well over a third of their operations through external financing, more than two-thirds of which has taken the form of long-term security issues, it is clear that this chapter deals with a very important topic in corporate finance. It is important, therefore, that you should have a good understanding of this area and be conversant with the language and procedures involved.

What to Look For in Chapter 15

This chapter is structured around the two major methods used to acquire capital:

1. *Public issues*, where the securities issued will be traded on the securities markets. There are two types: *General cash offers*, which are issues sold to investors at large, and *Privileged subscription or rights issues*, which are offered to existing stockholders.
2. *Private placements*, where the securities issued are not traded on the securities markets.

This chapter contains both descriptions of the different issue methods and procedures in use and prescriptions for how they should be used by financial managers. The descriptive material is straightforward, but you will meet a lot of new terms—more even than in the last chapter. Although most of those terms mean much what you might expect them to mean, you may find it worthwhile to make sure you are reasonably familiar with the various issue procedures and the terms used to describe them before you start to worry too much about the implications for financial managers.

Managers concerned with raising money need to decide:

- What issue method to use
- How large issues should be and how often to make them
- What the selling price should be
- Whether they should buy insurance (called underwriting) against an issue's failing
- How the market will react to the issue

These are interesting and important questions. On the whole, they are easy to understand, but where they are not, we will try to help you. The chapter will be easier to follow if you remember some of the lessons of market efficiency developed in Chapter 13. It's fair to point out, however, that you don't need to be a fully converted believer in market efficiency to accept the validity of the following points:

Financing Decisions and Stockholder Wealth Financing decisions seldom affect total security holders' wealth. Furthermore, it is reasonable to assume that most financing decisions have a net present value of zero. This is because a positive NPV financing decision is one where the money raised exceeds the value of the liability created. In the highly competitive capital market, it is very unlikely that any firm could consistently fool investors in this way.

Financing Decisions and the Distribution of Wealth Financing decisions can, however, affect the distribution of wealth between security holders. If new securities are underpriced, new holders will obtain a bargain at the expense of existing holders. This is not a problem, however, in the case of rights issues where existing holders are given rights to subscribe in proportion to the size of their holdings. The worked example should help you to handle the kind of calculations that arise in connection with rights issues.

The Importance of Market Prices When deciding on the issue price for new securities, the best guide to what a company can hope to obtain is the price of closely comparable securities which are already traded.

There Are No Financial Illusions It is the effect of financing decisions on stockholders' wealth that matters, and it is difficult to imagine that stockholders will believe one share at $20 is worth more than two shares at $10. Bear this in mind when you read about rights issues.

It Is Helpful to Separate Investment and Financing Decisions If the market believes the investment projects for which the issue proceeds are destined will provide inadequate returns, the stock price will fall. However, this is the result of a poor investment decision and has nothing to do with the financing operation or the issue method employed. Keep this in mind when you read the section entitled A Word on Dilution.

With these points in mind, you should now read the chapter. On a first reading, you could easily skip the sections on Competitive Bidding and Pricing General Cash Offers in Other Countries. On the other hand, read How Rights Issues Work very carefully, since this is the key to understanding the sections which follow.

Worked Example

Pobble Footwear Corporation is making a rights issue to raise $10 million. Just before the issue Pobble's stock price was $42 and the terms of the issue are 1 for 5 at a subscription price of $33. Calculate (1) the expected price of the stock ex rights, and (2) the value of one right. (3) Mrs. Cobble owns 405 Pobble shares. How many rights will she have to sell to maintain the same ($17,010) investment in the company? (4) Show that in general the value of a right is given by the formula (rights-on price $-$ issue price)/$(N + 1)$ when the terms of the issue are 1 for N.

Solution

1. After the issue is completed, all shares will be ex rights. For every 5 shares worth 42×5 before the issue, there will correspond 6 shares worth $42 \times 5 + \$33$ ($= \$243$) after the issue. Each share will therefore be worth $243/6$; so the ex-rights price is $40.50.

2. The value of one right is the difference between the rights-on price (the share price before the issue) and the ex-rights price. This is $1.50.

3. If Mrs. Cobble were to sell all her rights at $1.50 each, the total value of her holding would fall by $405 \times \$1.50 = \$607.50$. To make this up, she must subscribe to $\$607.50/\$40.50 = 15$ new shares (since after the issue each share will be worth $40.50). For each new share she will need 5 rights. She should therefore sell $405 - (15 \times 5) = 330$ rights, which will realize $495.

4. Proceeding in the same way as in the answer to part 1, we note that to every N shares at the rights-on price is added an additional share subscribed to at the offer price. This gives the basic equation.

$$N \times (\text{rights-on price} + \text{issue price}) = (N + 1) \text{ ex-rights price}$$

Alternatively, this can be written as

$$[(N + 1) \times \text{rights-on price}] - (\text{rights-on price} + \text{issue price}) = (N + 1) \times \text{ex-rights price}$$

from which it follows immediately that since the value of a right is the difference between the rights-on and ex-rights prices:

$$\text{Value of a right} = \text{rights-on price} - \text{ex-rights price}$$
$$= (\text{rights-on price} - \text{issue price})/(N + 1)$$

In part 2 above, we would have used this formula to give value of right $= (\$42 - \$33)/(5 + 1) = \$1.50$.

Summary

This summary covers all the material in the chapter but structures it in a rather different way. It deals first with the descriptive sections on issue procedures and then moves on to the prescriptive content by looking at the questions facing managers who are making new issues. In this way, material from different parts of the chapter is brought together on a topic-by-topic basis. For revision purposes, we think you will find this the most useful approach.

Descriptive Information: Issue Procedures

1. *Public issues* The first formal step is approval of the issue by the board and also by stockholders if an increase in authorized capital is necessary.

A registration statement is then prepared for submission to the Securities and Exchange Commission (SEC). This statement presents information about the proposed financing, the firm's history, existing business, and plans for the future.

The statement, once accepted, is effective 20 days later. During this period, the company is prohibited from selling securities.

After registration, the final prospectus is issued giving the issue price, which is fixed at this stage.

From this point the procedures differ, depending on the type of offer:

a. *General Cash Offer* The marketing of a general cash offer is handled by the underwriters, who also provide advice and usually *underwrite* or guarantee the issue's subscription. Their remuneration is the spread between the issue price and the price at which they buy the securities from the company.

Large issues are usually handled by a syndicate of underwriters. The latter cannot sell securities below the issue price, although they may be allowed to "support" the market. If the issue cannot be sold, the syndicate will be broken.

b. *Privileged Subscription or Rights Issue* Existing stockholders receive one right for every share they hold. These rights can be either sold or exercised.

At the end of the subscription period (roughly 3 weeks later), the holders of the rights will exercise them if the offer price is below the stock price. Otherwise the issue will fail unless it has been underwritten.

Rights issues can be underwritten for a fee.

2. *Private Placements* Private placements involve no registration, and in general there will be no more than 12 buyers. Securities issued in this way are very illiquid and are held for long-term investment rather than resale.

Bond issues account for the bulk of private placements. A third are negotiated directly with the lender, while for larger issues, an investment banker will act as agent.

Prescriptive Information: Problems Facing the Manager

1. *Choice of Issue Method*
   a. *Stock Issues*

   Public issues account for the vast majority of all stock issues. These will be by either

   General cash offer, which is the most popular method for seasoned companies and the only method for companies "going public," or by a *Rights issue*, which, although less common, is cheaper and fairer, involving no loss to existing holders

   Private placements of "letter stock" are normally limited to small, closely held companies.

   b. *Bond Issues*

   Public issues tend to be used by the larger companies and account for about 75 percent of bond issues.

   Private placements are suitable for small- to medium-sized companies, particularly if risky or if they require specialized, flexible loans. Issue costs are lower, but coupons are about ½ percent higher because of illiquidity.

2. *Issue Size, Frequency, and Costs* Flotation costs such as the costs of registration, printing, mailing, and underwriters' fees can be a significant consideration for a company in deciding how often to make issues and how much to raise each time.

The high fixed-cost component makes a policy of frequent small issues very expensive. Because of the economies of scale from larger issues, it makes sense for companies to "bunch" issues, using short-term funds until a large issue is justified. Furthermore, companies should issue more than is dicated by their current needs in order to avoid frequent subsequent issues.

3. *Issue Pricing*
   a. *Consequences of Incorrect Pricing*   Pricing is important since, if an issue is *overpriced*, it will fail unless it has been underwritten and if it is *underpriced*, buyers will gain at the existing holders' expense.

   Underpricing, however, is irrelevant for rights issues, since the offer is made to existing holders in proportion to their current stockholding.
   b. *Some Pricing Guidelines*   The golden rule is to use existing market prices as guidelines wherever possible.

   For *seasoned stock issues* this is simple, since the issuer's stock price is already known. Furthermore, it is always possible to make a rights issue, where the degree of underpricing is irrelevant.

   Pricing is far more difficult for *unseasoned stock issues*, since a rights issue cannot be made and since the stock is as yet untraded. The price is usually set by a combination of explicit valuations (See Chapter 4) and an examination of the prices of comparable stocks.

   In pricing *bond issues*, guidelines can be obtained from recent issues by other companies, and from past issues by the issuing company.

4. *Underwriting* Underwriting is just like insurance. The underwriters guarantee the issue's success, promising full subscription at the issue price in return for a fee. It is worthwhile as long as the value of the guarantee is worth at least as much as the fee paid.

The value of the guarantee depends on the risk of the issues failing. We will learn how to value guarantees of this sort when we study options in Chapter 18.

Underwriter's remuneration is usually 20 to 30 percent of the spread. In the case of rights issues, they are paid a fixed standby fee plus a take-up fee for any shares for which they have to subscribe.

If underwriting appears expensive, there is a simple remedy in the case of rights issues, since the issue price can be set low enough to minimize the chance of failure. For other issues, more reasonable quotations may possibly be obtained by shopping around or by competitive bidding. The latter seems to reduce spreads, but it is unclear whether it leads to any real net benefits.

5. *Effect on the Stock Price*
   a. *Underpricing* If new securities are issued at a price below their market price, it will lead to a fall in the price of their stock. In the case of a rights issue this is of no consequence, as stockholders receive a corresponding benefit from their rights to subscribe. The extent of underpricing does not

affect the total value of the company, and this makes it possible to derive the value of a right as the amount by which the stock price will fall:

Value of one right = (rights on price − issue price)/(N + 1)

In the case of a general cash offer, the total value of the company is again unchanged but the fall in stock price represents a transfer of wealth from the existing stockholders to the purchasers of the new (and cheap) securities. Underpricing is not usually a serious consideration with seasoned issues.

b. *Dilution* Because underpricing does not affect the value of the company, the only sense in which dilution can have any meaning is if the proceeds of the issue are to be used to finance poor investment projects. However, any share price fall which this may give rise to on the issue announcement is due solely to the poor investment decision and has nothing to do with the financing decision. Always try to avoid confusing the effects of the investment and financing decisions.

c. *Price Pressure* The widely held belief that an increase in the supply of stock at the time of a new issue will depress the price appears to be largely a myth.

List of Terms

All-or-none	Registrar
Best efforts	Registration statement
Blue sky laws	Regulation A issue
Competitive bidding	Rights issue
Dilution	Seasoned stock issue
General cash offer	Spread
Letter stock	Standby fee
Negotiated underwriting	Take-up fee
Preemptive rights	Tombstone
Private placement	Transfer agent
Privileged subscription	Underwriting
Prospectus	Underpricing
Red herring	

Exercises

Fill-in Questions

1. An issue of securities that is offered to investors as a whole is called a

   _____ .

2. An issue of securities that is offered to current stockholders is usually called a

   _____ .

3. Rights issues are also known as _____ issues.

4. For most public issues a _____ _____ must be submitted to the Securities and Exchange Commission.

5. Loans maturing within 9 months and issues involving less than $400,000 are partially exempt from the usual requirements of the SEC and are known as _____ issues.

6. Information about an issue is provided in its _____, which must be sent to all purchasers and to all those who are offered securities through the mail.

7. The preliminary prospectus is called a _____.

8. A _____ is an advertisement which lists the underwriters to an issue of securities.

9. A financial institution is usually appointed as _____ to record the issue and ownership of the company's securities.

10. A _____ may be appointed to look after the transfer of newly issued securities.

11. The state laws covering the issue and trading of securities are known as the _____.

12. The sale of a public issue is normally handled by an _____, who provides financial and procedural advice and usually buys the security for less than the offering price and accepts the risk of not being able to re-sell it.

13. The underwriter's _____ is the difference between the price at which the underwriter buys an issue from a company and the price at which it is offered to the public.

14. When a rights issue is underwritten, the underwriters receive a _____ fee for agreeing to purchase any stock that is not purchased by the stockholders.

15. Underwriters of a rights issue may also receive a _____ fee as a fixed percentage on any stock that they are obliged to purchase.

16. Occasionally the underwriter does not guarantee the sale of an entire issue but handles the issue on a _____ basis, promising only to sell as much of the issue as possible.

17. _____ underwriting is where the entire issue is canceled if the underwriter is unable to resell it all at the offer price.

18. _____ occurs in a general cash offer when securities are sold at an offer price which is below their market price.

19. Public utility holding companies are required to choose their underwriters by _____.

20. Most firms use _____ underwriting and don't require underwriters to bid formally against each other.

21. Stock for which there is an existing market goes by the spicy name of _____ stock.

22. The _____ right of common stockholders to anything of value distributed by the firm includes the right to subscribe to new offerings.

23. When new shares are issued, each existing share is entitled to a smaller proportion of the income and assets of the firm than formerly. This phenomenon is called _____.

24. The _____ _____ provides an alternative to making a public offering.

25. Privately placed common stock cannot easily be resold. It is often called _____ because the SEC requires a letter from the purchaser stating that the stock is not intended for resale.

Problems

1. The Continuous Funding Corporation is making a privileged subscription stock issue to raise $15 million. The terms of the issue are 1 for 9 at $15, and the corporation's current stock price is $20. Calculate the following:
   a. The market value of the corporation's equity prior to the issue
   b. The percentage increase in market value due to the issue
   c. The expected price of one right
   d. The expected price of the stock ex rights
   e. The number of rights which a stockholder who owned 975 shares would have to sell in order to take up her remaining rights and thus maintain a $19,500 investment in the company.
   f. The loss per share to stockholders who are on vacation and fail to take any action with regard to the issue

2. Continuous Funding decides instead to issue the new stock via a general cash offer. The board believes the principal advantage of this is that the new shares can be sold at the higher price of $18 per share and thus that fewer new shares

will have to be issued to raise the $15 million the company requires. Ignoring the underwriter's spread, calculate the following:

a. The number of new shares which Continuous Funding will have to offer
b. The expected price of the shares after the issue
c. The loss per share to existing holders
d. The percentage reduction in value of an existing stockholder's preissue holding in the company
e. The net present value of purchasing 100 shares via the general cash offer

Finally, make use of the figures you have calculated above to write two or three sentences explaining to the board of Continuous Funding why existing holders may lose rather than gain from the higher issue price.

3. Cordial Beverages is planning to purchase plant and equipment for manufacturing a new line of fruit concentrates. The equipment has a 5-year life, and the new product line will increase the company's after-tax earnings from $6 million to $7 million per year, and provide incremental cash flows of $3 million per year. Cordial's investment bankers have suggested that the $10 million needed to finance the project should be raised by a one-for-five rights issue at $50 per share. The current stock price is $60. Cordial's management, however, is hesitating. Although the project appears sound on the basis of the 10 percent required rate of return, equity finance for the concentrate project will dilute earnings per share (EPS), and they are concerned about the effect of this on the stock price. Help Cordial's management to clarify the issues involved by calculating:

a. EPS both before and after the issue
b. The NPV of the concentrate project
c. The impact of the announcement of the rights issue on the share price (assume the market has no prior knowledge of the concentrate project)
d. The NPV of the financing decision
e. The expected "ex-rights" stock price
f. The return on Cordial's stock from the day before the announcement to the first day the shares are traded ex rights

Finally, make use of the figures you have calculated to explain to Cordial's board why dilution is irrelevant and to recommend to them the best course of action.

4. Persuaded by the arguments in your excellent answer to question 2, the vacillating board of Continuous Funding have reverted to their original intention to make a rights issue. Since they are unwilling to pay the seemingly high price of a standby arrangement, they are worried about the possibility of the issues failing. The board were only too aware that Continuous Funding was a fairly volatile stock and that monthly stock price declines of 10 percent or more were not uncommon, occurring on average once in every 6 months. Assist the board by

a. Calculating the probability of the issues failing if the originally proposed terms of one for nine at $15 were adopted
b. Suggesting a set of terms for the issue which will give approximately a 1 in 200 chance of failure

    Hint: You will need to use statistical tables for the cumulative normal distribution in order to answer this question. Assume that the issue period is 1 month.

5. United Fasteners is issuing a 20-year bond to raise $10 million. The corporation can either

a. Issue the bond publicly, in which case it will be sold at par and will carry a 9 percent coupon. The underwriter's spread would be ½ percent, and there are no other issue costs.

b. Issue the bond through a private placement, in which case it will be sold at par and carry a 9⅛ percent coupon. The total cost of the private placement will be $20,000.

Which option should United Fasteners choose?

Essay Questions

1. Discuss the relative merits of a public issue versus a private placement for a company wishing to raise new debt finance. What factors should be taken into account in pricing the bond issue?

2. Compare and contrast the role of the investment banker (or underwriter) in

a. general cash offers of either stock or bonds, (b) privileged subscription issues of stock, (c) private placements of bonds.

3. What factors affect the choice between the general cash offer and the privileged subscription method for stock issues by seasoned companies?

4. "If the firm has good projects and needs equity capital to finance them, then dilution should not bar it from going to the market." Discuss.

Answers to Exercises

Fill-in Questions

1.	general cash offer	14.	standby fee
2.	rights issue	15.	take-up fee
3.	privileged subscription	16.	best efforts
4.	registration statement	17.	all-or-none
5.	Regulation A	18.	underpricing
6.	prospectus	19.	competitive bidding
7.	red herring	20.	negotiated
8.	tombstone	21.	seasoned stock
9.	registrar	22.	preemptive right
10.	transfer agent	23.	dilution
11.	blue sky laws	24.	private placement
12.	underwriter	25.	letter stock
13.	spread		

Problems

1. a. Number of new shares issued = $15,000,000/$15 = 1,000,000.
   Number of shares before issue = 1,000,000 × 9 = 9,000,000 (issue is 1 for 9)
   Value of equity before issue = 9,000,000 × $20 = $180,000,000

   b. Increase in value = ($15,000,000/$180 × 100 percent = 8.33 percent

   c. Value of right = (rights-on price − issue price)/$(N+1)$
$$= (\$20 - \$15)/10 = \$0.50$$

   d. Ex-rights price = (rights-on price − value of right) = $20 − $0.5 = $19.5

   e. Investment before issue = 975 × $20 = $19,500

      To maintain $19,500 investment after issue, must hold $19,500/$19.5 = 1,000 shares. To obtain 25 new shares, must exercise (25 × 9) = 225 rights

      Thus number of rights sold = 975 − 225 = 750

      (*Note*: Proceeds of sale = 750 × $0.50 = $375 covers cost of exercising 225 rights = 25 × $15 = $375)

   f. Loss per share = value of right = $0.50

2. a. Number of new shares = $15,000,000/$18 = 833,333 shares

   b. Value of company after issue = $180,000,000 + $15,000,000 = $195,000,000

      Share price after issue = $195,000,000/9,000,000 = $19.83

   c. Loss per share to existing holders = $20 − $19.83 = $0.17

   d. Percentage reduction in value = ($0.17/$20) × 100 percent = 0.85 percent

   e. NPV purchasing shares via offer = $19.83 − $18 = $1.83

The underpricing in the general cash offer ($18 rather than $20) results in a wealth transfer from existing to new holders. The latter gain $1.83 per share purchased, while existing holders lose $0.17 per share held, or 0.85 percent of their original holding. This wealth transfer could be avoided by employing the rights issue method.

3. a. Number of new shares to be issued = $10,000,000/$50 = 200,000

      Number of shares before issue = 200,000 × 5 = 1,000,000

      EPS before issue = $6,000,000/1,000,000 = 6,000,000

      EPS after issue = $7,000,000/1,200,000 = $5.83

   b. NPV of project = −$10,000,000 + $3,000,000 × $A_{5,10\%}$

      $11,373,000 − $10,000,000 = $1,373,000

   c. Project increases value of company by $1,373,000

      Therefore, effect on price per share = $1,373,000/1,000,000 = 1.37 *increase*

   d. NPV of financing decision = $0

   e. Rights price = (rights-on price − issue price)/$(N+1)$
$$= (\$61.37 - \$50)/6 = \$1.90$$

      Thus, ex-rights price = rights-on price − rights price
$$= \$61.37 - \$1.90 = \$59.48$$

   f. Return = ($1.37/$60) × 100 percent = 2.28 percent

To avoid confusion, the investment and financing decisions should be kept separate. The project has a positive NPV, and the news of the project should cause a 2.29 percent increase in the share price. The financing decision as such is neutral and will have no effect on shareholders' wealth. Although EPS falls, this is irrelevant. EPS confuses investment and financing, focuses on earnings rather than cash flows, and fails to reflect changes in risk. It is a totally inappropriate criterion.

4. a. Standard deviation of returns on stock is approximately 10 percent per month.

      Issue price is $15 and expected ex-rights price is $19.50.

      Issue will fail if price declines by more than [($19.50 − $15) × 100]/$19.5 =

23.1 percent or 2.31 standard deviations from normal tables; probability of this occurring is approximately 1 percent.

b. From normal tables, a probability of 1 in 200 corresponds to 2.57 standard deviations; i.e., the terms must be set so that the issue price is 25.7 percent below the implied ex-rights price. We know that

Issue price = ex-rights price − (N × rights price)
= ex-rights price − [N × (rights-on price − ex-rights price)]
= [(N + 1) × ex-rights price] − (N rights-on price)

assuming that the issue is 1 for 9 (as originally planned),

Issue price = (10 × ex-rights price) − $180

But we know that (issue price/ex-rights price) = 1 − 0.257 = 0.743

So that issue price = $\dfrac{\$180 \times 0.743}{9.257}$ = $14.44

That is, a 1 for 9 issue at $14.44 will give an approximately 1 in 200 chance of failure.

(A note for the fussy reader: this answer assumes an issue period of 1 month, a zero expected return on the stock during this period, and a normal (rather than a lognormal) distribution of returns)

5. a. Cost of public issue = $10,000,000 × ½ percent = $50,000

b. Cost of private placement = $20,000 + additional interest cost
Additional interest = $10,000,000 × ⅛ percent = 12,500 per year for 20 years

If we discount these interest payments at 9 percent, i.e., the market rate for identical cash flows which are traded in the capital market, we obtain

Total cost of private placement = $20,000 + ($12,500 × 9.129)
= $134,113

That is, shareholders will be better off if United Fasteners makes a *public* issue.

16 *The dividend controversy*

Introduction

The central point of this chapter is whether and to what extent dividend policy affects the value of a firm. You should know that this is an unresolved issue. You should make it a point to understand the controversial elements which surround dividend policy. After all, financial managers cannot make intelligent decisions if they do not understand dividend policy.

What to Look For in Chapter 16

This chapter's emphasis is on the financial manager's choices of obtaining equity capital: either by retaining earnings or by paying them out and issuing new shares. The issues are: which policy affects the firm's value, how, and to what extent? The question is usually analyzed under the assumption that the firm's investing and borrowing decisions are given.

Terminology To familiarize yourself with the landscape of dividend policy, you should know such nuts-and-bolts concepts as record dates, with-dividend transactions, ex-dividend transactions, legal limitations on the payment of dividends, the various forms in which dividends are paid—regular cash dividends, extra dividends, and stock dividends—and the repurchase of shares.

Established Dividend Policies Knowing how companies decide on dividend policy is important, and Lintner's early, still very relevant work indicates that most financial managers zero in on a target payout ratio, which is the ratio of target dividends to earnings per share. Moreover, evidence tends to confirm Lintner's contention that current dividends depend in part on current earnings and in part on the dividends for previous years, with more distant years being given less weight than more current years.

Information Content of Dividend Policy Cash dividend policies may transmit important information to shareholders, because they may indicate management's assessment of future sustainable earnings.

The Dividend Controversy Next know the essence of the dividend controversy, which centers on the extent to which dividend policy affects the value of the enterprise. Know the three main views in this controversy.

One view says that dividend payouts increase firm value; the other says it has no influence on value; and the third says that it reduces value. The dividend irrelevancy argument rests on Miller and Modigliani's (MM's) position in which they argue convincingly that in a world of perfect capital markets dividend policy has no influence on value. As long as a firm's investment and borrowing policy are fixed and capital markets are efficient, dividends result in a transference of value among old and new shareholders. In MM's view increased cash dividend payments are offset by stock issues as long as the firm's investment and borrowing policies are fixed. To put it still a third way, shareholders finance the extra dividends by purchasing new shares. The opposite line of reasoning also holds.

MM's middle-of-the-road position flies in the face of traditional financial literature which says that high payout ratios tend to increase the value of the firm. One of the cornerstones of this position is that cash dividends today are valued more highly than cash dividends in the future because future cash dividends are more risky. The rebuttal to this position is: as long as investment and borrowing policies are fixed, the firm's total cash flows are the same regardless of payout policy; the risk of the enterprise is the same; and all shareholders accept that risk. Consequently, as long as markets are efficient, the riskiness of the cash dividend stream does not the change the irrelevancy argument of Miller and Modigliani.

If criticisms are to be placed at the feet of the MM position, they must rest on market imperfections or inefficiencies. For example, does a special clientele prefer high-payout stocks? Or, do cash dividend policies transmit important information to investors? In the first instance, legal restrictions, for example, may establish such clientele effects. In the latter instance, MM would argue that the information content of dividends is a temporary phenomenon because it is quickly absorbed by market participants and reflected in share prices. On net, the evidence in favor of generous payout policies is rather skimpy. Hence, as intuitively appealing as this policy may be, it remains nonetheless intuitive and without firm standing in either the theoretical or empirical literature.

The third position in the dividend controversy focuses primarily on the tax effects which influence the preference for cash dividends. The argument is this: Cash dividends are taxed more heavily than capital gains; this fact is a compelling reason to retain the cash; invest it in presumably highly profitable projects, which in turn generate increased earnings; and, when the earnings are properly evaluated, price appreciation in the shares will result. Those persons requiring cash may then sell off some of their shares, and because capital gains are taxed at a lower rate than the cash dividends, they will be better off. The extreme position of this argument is to pay no cash dividends whatsoever.

There is a tad of evidence which supports the position of those who advocate low payouts. Indeed, low-payout stocks should be and seem to be owned by investors in high marginal tax brackets, and high-payout stocks should be and seem to be held by investors in low marginal tax brackets.

A Still Unresolved Issue   Where does this leave the financial manager? Back to those who hold the middling position that dividend policy does not affect the value of the firm, that's where. For example, the clientele effect is answered thus: If every conceivable clientele for cash dividends is satisfied, it makes no difference to any one firm which dividend policy it adopts, because each investor is free to choose that firm which best satisfies his or her needs. Moreover, taxes, which are market imperfections, may be deferred as long as investors choose investment vehicles, such as life insurance and pension funds, which are not highly taxed or which are not taxed at all. The middle-of-the-road position, however, does indicate that there is an uncertainty effect which deters investors from preferring low-payout stocks. Notwithstanding, the conclusion is that the dividend controversy persists unresolved.

Worked Examples

Problem 1

In the third quarter of 1979 Minnesota Mining & Manufacturing Company (MMM, or The Three-M Company) paid a cash dividend of $0.60. Match each of the following dates:

(A) Monday, August 13　　　　　(a) record date
(B) Friday, August 24　　　　　　(b) declaration date
(C) Wednesday, September 5　　(c) ex-dividend date
(D) Wednesday, September 12　(d) payment date

Solution

To answer problems such as these, you must know the meaning of the terms in the right-hand list. The first date on the left-hand side is the declaration date, the day on which the cash dividend is publicly announced. The next date, Friday, August 24, is the record date, the date on which the list of shareholders eligible to receive the cash dividends is made up. The third date (C) is the date on which the stock is traded without the cash dividend; it is the ex-dividend date and comes five business days before the payment date, which is the last date, September 12.

Problem 2

Assuming for the moment that the Three-M Company pays $0.60 per quarter throughout 1979, calculate the stock's dividend yield based on its December 19 market price of $50.

Solution

The formula for calculating dividend yields is

Dividend yield = yearly cash dividends ÷ current market price per share

$$= (4 \times \$0.60) \div \$50$$

$$= \$2.40 \div \$50$$

$$= 0.048 = 4.80 \text{ percent}$$

Problem 3

If MMM's 1979 earnings per share were $5.40 and per share cash dividends were $2.40, what was the company's estimated dividend payout?

Solution

Payout ratio = estimated cash dividends per share ÷ estimated earnings per share

$$= \$2.40 \div \$5.40$$

$$= 0.444 = 44.4 \text{ percent}$$

Problem 4

If MMM declared a stock dividend of 15 percent, its market price was $60, and nothing else changed, what would you expect the price of the shares to be after the new stock is distributed?

Solution

There are several ways to approach this answer, but all must emphasize that the stock dividend, by itself, has no expected effect on the value of the shares. We conclude, then, that the aggregate value of the shares after the stock dividend must equal the aggregate value of the shares before it. Say you own 100 shares of MMM. The value of your holding is $6000 (100 shares × $60 per share). After the stock dividend you have 115 shares [100 original shares + (15 percent of 100)], the total value of which is still $6000. The value per share of the new set of shares is $52.17 ($6000 ÷ 115 shares), or 52⅛ to the nearest one-eighth of a point. Alternatively,

$$\frac{100\% + \text{percentage}}{\text{stock dividend}} \times \frac{\text{price per share after}}{\text{stock dividend}} = \frac{\text{price per share before}}{\text{stock dividend}}$$

$$(100\% + 15\%)\,(x) = \$60$$

$$115\%x = 1.15x$$

$$x = \$60 \div 1.15$$

$$= \$52.17$$

or 52⅛ to the nearest eighth.

Problem 5

What Not, Inc.'s financial numbers, as the financial community likes to call them, are as follows:

Net income	$5 million
Earnings per share	$1
Number of shares outstanding	5 million
Price-earnings ratio	10

The management plans to repurchase 20 percent of the company's outstanding shares at the going market price. What effect does the stock repurchase have on the above numbers? What effect does it have on the value of the firm? Explain.

Solution

The stock repurchase is similar to the reverse of a stock split, *except* cash is needed to buy up the stock. Let's proceed to determine what happens to the numbers. First, the company has to have $10 million in cash in order to repurchase 1 million shares at $10 each. In order to do this it will have to sell a fifth of its assets. If it sells typical assets, its net income will subsequently shrink to $4 million. Second, the number of shares outstanding decreases to 4 million. Third, earnings per share remains at $1 ($4 million ÷ 4 million shares). And fourth,

153

because the price-earnings ratio stays the same, the value of the shares also stays at $10 each. Look at it this way. Prior to the repurchase, the value per share was $10, 5 million shares were outstanding, and the firm's value was $50 million. After the repurchase, the value of the shares remains at $10 each, which, when multiplied by the 4 million then outstanding, results in a total value of $40 million. The size of the firm has contracted with no gain or loss to its shareholders.

Summary

Dividend policy is really a matter of determining how financial managers obtain equity capital. The central issue is whether and to what extent dividend policy influences the value of the firm. This remains an unresolved issue, and the controversy surrounding dividend policy, although having waned in recent years, nonetheless continues.

What seems to be known with some certainty is that firms aim for a target payout ratio based on target or achievable earnings; cash dividend policies transmit important information to the marketplace, for they tell investors what management realistically expects sustainable earnings to be; and low payout ratios are favored by those in high marginal income tax brackets.

List of Terms

Dividend policy	**Par value**
Ex-dividend	**Record date**
Extra dividend	**Regular cash dividends**
Legal capital	**Special dividend**
Liquidating dividend	**Stock dividend**
Market efficiency	**With dividend**

Exercises

Fill-in Questions

1. Dividend policy is concerned with the trade-off between _____ and paying out cash and _____.

2. The _____ is the date on which the list of registered shareholders who are to receive cash dividends is made.

3. Shares bought and sold before the _____ are said to be transacted _____, whereas those bought and sold after the _____ are said to be transacted _____.

4. A firm's _____ consists of the par value of all its outstanding shares.

5. _____ are cash dividends which a company usually expects to be able to maintain in the future; _____ are cash dividends paid irregularly and are not necessarily expected to be maintained in the future.

6. _____ are similar to stock splits in that neither makes shareholders better off.

7. The percentage ratio of cash dividends to earnings is called the _____ .

Problems

1. On August 13, 1979, Superior Oil Co. announced a stock split of 5-for-1 and an increase in cash dividends from 70 to 88 cents per share before the stock split. At the time of the announcement, the stock closed on the New York Stock Exchange at $434 a share, the highest price of any stock on any United States exchange. (a) What would you expect the price of the stock to be after the split, assuming nothing else changes? (b) The amount of the quarterly dividend? (c) Could the adjustments in per share price and cash dividends have been accomplished by a stock dividend? (d) If so, what size would the stock dividend have had to be to accomplish this goal?

2. On August 13, 1979, Waverly Press, Inc., announced a quarterly dividend of 12.5 cents and a stock dividend of 10 percent payable on September 12, 1979, to shareholders of record on August 27, 1979. (a) If the August 13 market price of $16½ remains the same, at what price would you expect the stock to sell after the cash and stock dividends? (b) When would you expect the stock to go ex-dividend? (c) Assuming that the quarterly cash dividend of 12.5 cents per share will continue after the stock dividend, what is the effective percentage increase in the cash dividend? What is the expected annual dividend yield using your estimate of the ex-dividend price and the 12.5-cent quarterly cash dividend? (d) If expected annual earnings per share are $3, what is the annual expected dividend payout?

Essay Questions

1. Explain the mechanics of paying dividends.

2. "I've heard it said a million times that dividends are paid out of surplus. Yet just the other day I heard this financial expert say that dividends can only be paid out of cash. What I would like to know is which of these is correct." Formulate an answer for this bewildered person.

3. Why would a firm repurchase its common shares? (That is, what economic or financial significance is attached to share repurchases?)

4. "This dividend controversy stuff really bothers me. First off, I'm not even sure what the controversy is about. Second, *everybody* knows that dividend policy is really important. Finally, as investors, let's face it, it's the after-tax return that really counts!" Formulate a one-page response to this statement.

5. How can it be said that cash dividends are financially equivalent to stock issues, once investment and financing policies are fixed? Explain fully.

Answers to Exercises

Fill-in Questions

1. retaining earnings, issuing new shares
2. record date
3. record date; with dividend; record date; ex-dividend
4. legal capital
5. regular cash dividends; extra dividends
6. stock dividends
7. payout ratio

Problems

1. (a) $86.80 or 86⅞ to the nearest one-eighth of a point; (b) 17.6 cents; (c) Yes; (d) 400 percent
2. (a) ($16.5 − $0.125)/1.1 = $14.89; (b) September 5, 1979; (c) 10 percent; 3.33 percent; (d) 16.7 percent

17 *Does debt policy matter?*

Introduction

This chapter emphasizes Modigliani and Miller's (MM) argument that debt policy does not matter, the conditions under which their case is made, and the counterargument put forth by the more traditional view. MM argue from two fundamental propositions. Proposition I states that regardless of the way in which a firm's total cash flows are split between debt and equity, the total value of the firm remains unchanged. If Proposition I holds, debt policy does not matter, financing and investing decisions are separable.

Proposition II states that the expected rate of return on and risk of common stocks of a firm that has debt increases in proportion to the ratio of debt to equity. Proposition II's major implication is that the weighted cost of capital to the firm remains unchanged as the capital structure mix changes. This is another way of saying that the value of the firm does not change as debt policy changes.

What to Look For in Chapter 17

This chapter sets forth the famous Modigliani-Miller (MM) propositions concerning the capital structure of business firms. Their first argument, Proposition I, says that the style by which a firm is financed, as expressed by its mix between debt and equity, does not affect the value of the firm. Proposition II follows from the first, namely, that the rate of return required by equity shareholders increases as debt increases so that both the weighted average cost of capital and the value of the firm remain constant.

Perfect Markets Assumption   Know that the MM argument rests on the assumptions of perfect capital markets and the absence of taxes. In this world all investors, regardless of their feeling toward risk and expected returns, agree that the value of an unlevered firm is equal to the value of a levered firm, provided the two firms are alike in operating characteristics. This position in turn rests on the *law of conservation of value,* which says that the present value of combined and independent cash flows is equal to the present value of each of the separate cash flows. The principle at work here is called *value additivity.*

Magnification Effects of Financial Leverage   Financial leverage tends to magnify returns and risk to common shareholders. Because of the magnification effects resulting from going into debt, MM's Proposition II emerges: the expected rate of return on common shares of a financially levered firm increases proportionally to the debt-equity ratio, as measured by market values. Increased risk results in increased expected returns by shareholders, and the increased expected returns, which are really required rates of return, are used to evaluate the shares of the financially levered firm.

The Traditional Position   The traditional position conflicts with the MM position. Traditionalists begin their argument with the weighted average cost of capital, which is the sum of two products: the required return on debt, weighted by the proportion of debt to the total market value of the firm, plus the required return on equity, weighted by the equity relative to the total market value of the firm. Although the weighted average cost of capital may be an incorrect benchmark for financial decision making, the traditional view uses it as the basis for arguing that the Modigliani-Miller positions do not hold up. The traditional view argues that the cost of capital will tend to decrease initially as debt is added to the capital structure but that it will increase only after a market-determined intolerable threshold level of risk is passed. At that point the cost of equity and the cost of debt increase significantly.

Some Possible Flaws in the MM Position   Although Chapter 18 explores these notions in greater detail, violations in MM's propositions are to be found in the lack of perfect capital markets. Also, unsatisfied clienteles, seeking a package of debt securities, likewise may violate the MM position. AT&T's efforts to sell the equivalent of a savings bond is an example of catering to special needs of special clienteles.

MM and the CAPM   That the capital asset pricing model may be invoked to substantiate the Modigliani-Miller Proposition I is demonstrated in the Appendix.

Worked Examples

Problem 1

What Not, Inc., operates in perfect capital markets with no corporate or personal taxes. Calculate its expected return on assets, given the following information: 40 percent debt financed, 10 percent expected return on debt, 60 percent equity financed, and 15 percent expected return on equity.

Solution

$$r_A = \left(\frac{D}{D + E} \times r_D\right) + \left(\frac{E}{D + E} \times r_E\right)$$

$$= (0.40 \times 0.10) + (0.60 \times 0.15)$$

$$= 0.04 + 0.09$$

$$= 0.13 = 13 \text{ percent}$$

Problem 2

Macbeth Spot Removers' expected operating income is $2000 and the market value of all its all-equity financed securities is $12,000. Assuming that it operates in perfect capital markets with no corporate or personal taxes, what happens to the rate of return on equity capital when it decides to sell $4800 of debt and retire an equal amount of equity? The return debtholders expect is 9 percent.

Solution

The return on assets is

r_A = expected operating income/market value of all securities

= $2000/$12,000

= 0.1667 = 16.67 percent

In an all-equity financed firm the return on equity is equal to the return on assets; so

$r_E = r_A = 16.67$ percent

After the borrowing, the return on equity will change but the return on assets will remain the same, because the value of the firm does not change—the expected operating income does not change and the value of the outstanding securities does not change. The return on equity is calculated thus:

$$r_E = r_A + \frac{D}{E}(r_A - r_D)$$

$$= 0.1667 + \frac{\$4800}{\$7,200}(0.1667 - 0.09)$$

$$= 0.1667 + 0.667(0.0767)$$

$$= 0.1667 + 0.0512$$

$$= 0.2179 = 21.79 \text{ percent}$$

Problem 3

Given the information in problem 2 and assuming the beta of the firm is 1.2 before the debt financing, what is the beta of the equity after the financing? Assume the beta of the debt is 0.5. What would the beta of the equity be if the debt-equity ratio were 30, 50, 60, and 70 percent?

Solution

The answer before the debt financing is straightforward: the beta of the equity is the same as the beta of the firm, because there are no other securities outstanding. After the financing, the beta of the equity changes as follows:

$$\beta_E = \beta_A + \frac{D}{E}(\beta_A - \beta_D)$$

$$= 1.2 + 0.667(1.2 - 0.5)$$

$$= 1.2 + 0.667(0.7)$$

$$= 1.2 + 0.467$$

$$= 1.667$$

For the other debt proportions, β_E is

$\frac{D}{E}, \%$	β_E
30	1.41
50	1.55
60	1.62
70	1.69

Problem 4

Using the data in problems 2 and 3, what are the betas of the equity if the beta of the debt is zero, that is, risk-free? What would they be if the beta of the debt were equal to the beta of the firm before debt financing? Compare these results with those of problem 3.

Solution

$\frac{D}{E}, \%$	β_E		
	$\beta_D = 0$	$\beta_D = 1.2$	$\beta_D = 0.5$
30	1.56	1.2	1.41
40	1.68	1.2	1.48
50	1.80	1.2	1.55
60	1.92	1.2	1.62
70	2.04	1.2	1.69

Although the data are contrived, several interesting relations emerge. First, if the beta of the debt is equal to the beta of the firm when it is all-equity financed, for all practical purposes the company has issued another dose of equity and not debt. Consequently, the beta of the equity does not change.

If the company were able to issue debt at the zero beta level, the risk-free rate, the betas of the equity would tend to increase substantially over the all-equity scheme of financing. In almost all instances, the beta of corporate debt is greater than zero but less than the beta of the all-equity-financed firm.

Problem 5

"The way I see it," says the financial manager of Milk 'Em Dry, Inc. (MED, Inc.), "if I buy half of the 10,000 outstanding common shares with the proceeds from the sale of debt, I can increase earnings per share. After all, I can borrow at 10 percent and I am currently earning 20 percent on my all-equity-financed firm. I estimate the risk of the borrowed money at 0.4 and the beta of my equity before borrowing is 1.2. The price-earnings ratio of the common shares is 5 on operating income of $25,000, and I expect to continue to generate that amount of operating income after the debt financing. Seems to me this will be a good deal for shareholders. And that's the way I am supposed to behave, isn't it, on behalf of the shareholders? In fact, it seems dumb not to go into debt." Formulate the answer for this financial manager, assuming operation in perfect capital markets with no corporate or personal taxes.

Solution

Begin by placing a value on the firm before the debt financing. The operating earnings are capitalized at 20 percent; so the value of the firm when it is all-equity-financed is $125,000 ($25,000 ÷ .20). The value per share is $12.50; earnings per share are $2.50 ($25,000 ÷ 10,000 shares).

Next, determine the earnings per share after the debt financing. The financial manager must sell $62,500 of debt at the going market rate of 10 percent in order to repurchase an equivalent amount of equity. Remember, because the operating income remains unchanged, the firm's total value remains unchanged at $125,000. The equity earnings change, however, as follows:

Operating income	$25,000
Interest	6,250
Equity earnings	$18,750

With 5000 shares now outstanding, earnings per share increase to $3.75 ($18,750 ÷ 5000 shares). Now here's the trap in this thought process. *If* the price-earnings ratio remains unchanged at 5, the shares have a market price of $18.75 (5 × $3.75). But going into debt entails additional risk to shareholders. How much more risk? Work it out in terms of the betas before and after the debt financing.

The formula:

$$\beta_E = \beta_A + \frac{D}{E}(\beta_A - \beta_D)$$

Before

$$\beta_E = 1.2 + 0.0(1.2 - 0) = 1.2$$

After

$$\beta_E = 1.2 + 1.0(1.2 - 0.4)$$
$$= 1.2 + 0.8 = 2.0$$

And we all know that with increased risk comes increased expected (required?) returns. What is the return now required by equity holders? Look at it this way. If the return on assets stays the same, as it does, the required return on equity is affected by the riskiness of the debt financing. In formula format, the result is

$$r_E = r_A + \frac{D}{E}(r_A - r_D)$$

$$= 0.20 + 1.0(0.20 - 0.10)$$

$$= 0.20 + 0.10 = 30 \text{ percent}$$

So the answer to the financial manager is: "While it is true that earnings per share increase, so does the risk. Hence the rate at which the increased earnings are evaluated is increased as well, and proportionally at that, thereby mitigating the hoped-for results of increased share prices." The new price-earnings ratio is the reciprocal of the earnings yield. The earnings yield is 30 percent, the reciprocal of which is 3.333. When the price-earnings ratio of 3.333 is multiplied by the new earnings per share of $3.75, we obtain a market price per share of common of $12.50, which is where we were at the beginning.

These phenomena are depicted in Figure 17–1. Because the relations are linear,

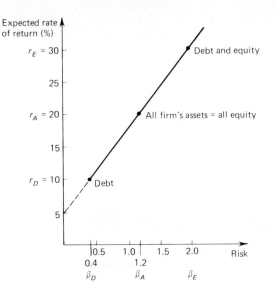

Figure 17-1 The risk-return trade-off for Milk 'Em Dry, Inc.

the implied risk-free rate is 5 percent, as represented by the dashed line extending down from the 10 percent, beta = 0.4 portion of the graph.

Summary

Every financial manager must eventually come to terms with the issue of whether going into debt and the extent to which the firm goes into debt affect the value of the firm. Under a perfect capital markets assumption, Modigliani and Miller argue that the amount and kind of debt does not influence the total value of the firm, although the component parts may be affected. The traditional view is that going into debt may not matter up to a certain, market-determined level, but after that threshold level of debt to total capital is surpassed, the level of debt affects adversely the value of the firm. In the MM view the cost of debt and equity changes as the level of debt changes, so that the average cost of capital does not change, thereby leaving the total value of the firm unchanged. In the traditional view, after that threshold level of acceptable debt is surpassed, both the cost of debt and the cost of equity increase, thereby increasing the average cost of capital and lowering the value of the firm.

List of Terms

Capital structure	Money funds
Earnings-price ratio	Proposition I
Financial leverage	Proposition II
Gearing	Value additivity
Law of conservation of value	Weighted-average cost of capital
Levered equity	

Exercises

Fill-in Questions

1. A firm's mix of debt and equity is called its _____ .

2. Proposition I states that the _____ of the firm is not changed by the mix of debt and equity.

3. A firm that borrows is said to engage in _____.

4. The law of conservation of value states that the _____ of an asset is preserved regardless of the nature of the _____ on it.

5. The weighted average cost of capital is equal to the _____ multiplied by the ratio of debt to the _____ of the firm plus the return on equity multiplied by the ratio of _____ to the market value of the firm.

6. Proposition II states that the _____ on the common stock of a financially levered firm _____ in proportion to the _____ ratio.

Problems

1. What is the expected return on assets for a firm that is 60 percent debt financed and pays an expected return on debt of 9 percent and has required return on equity of 20 percent? Assume the firm operates in perfect capital markets with no corporate or personal income taxes. Show all calculations.

2. Your firm's expected operating income is $5000 and the market value of its outstanding securities is $25,000, when it is all-equity-financed. If the firm operates in perfect capital markets with no corporate or personal taxes, what will happen to its return on equity after it sells enough debt to repurchase half the outstanding equity? Assume that bondholders require a 10 percent return on their money. An 8 percent return. A 12 percent return.

3. Using the data in problem 2 above, a beta for the firm of 1.5, and a beta for the debt of 0.6, what is the beta of the equity after the financing?

4. The financial manager of Ballpoint, Inc., estimates that she will increase the earnings per share of her presently all-equity-financed firm if she borrows at the going market rate of 8 percent. She estimates the debt's beta to be 0.3 and the beta of the all-equity firm is 0.8. A return of 12.5 percent is expected on the all-equity firm, the price-earnings ratio of 8 is expected to persist, expected operating income is $300,000, and 100,000 shares are outstanding. She plans to replace 40 percent of her equity with debt. She feels the argument is so compelling that she is chomping at the bit to borrow money. "After all," she

argues, "the price of debt is not going to get any cheaper. So now is the time to get the value of the shareholders up." If she operates in perfect capital markets in which there are also no corporate and personal income taxes, what reasonable evaluation should you make of her financing scheme? Show all calculations you may make.

Essay Questions

1. What is Modigliani and Miller's (MM) Proposition I, and what implications does this have for financial managers?
2. "The way I see it, financial leverage tends to magnify the potential returns to equity shareholders. I know, it also tends to magnify losses. But any rational shareholder has gotta like firms that engage in financial leverage more than those than don't. And, to make my long story short, that has to reduce the cost of capital to the firm because shareholders will prefer to pay more for equal amounts of earnings in firms that have debt outstanding as compared to those that don't. And, finally!, that means the value of the firm will increase. Doesn't it?" Articulate your evaluation of this statement.
3. "I guess what bothers me the most about Modigliani and Miller's position is that they hang their hat on perfect capital markets in a way that really ticks me off. 'Cause *everybody* knows that capital markets ain't perfect. How come Modigliani (I can't even pronounce the guy's name) and Miller can't figure that out?" Give a detailed response to that statement.
4. How can individual investors augment or undo the debt policy of firms in which they wish to invest? Explain fully. Also explain why this concept is important to the Modigliani-Miller position regarding debt policy.
5. What is Modigliani and Miller's Proposition II? What implications does that have for financial managers who must deal with these knotty problems day in and day out?
6. Demonstrate how the beta of a firm is dependent on the beta of the capital structure components.

Answers to Exercises

Fill-in Questions

1. capital structure
2. value
3. financial leverage
4. value; claims
5. return on debt; value; equity
6. expected return; increases; debt-equity

Problems

1. 13.4 percent
2. All-equity firm: 20 percent; 10 percent debt: 30 percent; 8 percent debt: 32 percent; 12 percent debt: 28 percent
3. 1.95
4. Take this one in stages. The analysis is the same as that for problem 5 of the Worked Examples.
   Stage 1, all-equity firm:
   Value = $300,000 ÷ 12.5 percent = $2,400,000

Value per share: $24
Earnings per share: $3
Stage 2, effect of debt financing on earnings per share:
Amount of required debt: 0.4($2,400,000) = $960,000

Operating income $300,000
Interest (0.08 × $960,000)   76,800
Equity earnings $223,200

Earnings per share: $223,200 ÷ 60,000 = $3.72
Stage 3, beta of equity:
Before-debt financing: 0.8; after: 1.133
Stage 4, return on equity, after-debt financing:

$$r_E = r_A + (D/E)(r_A - r_D)$$
$$= 0.125 + (0.4/0.6)(0.125 - 0.08) = 15.5 \text{ percent}$$

Stage 5, market price of equity after debt financing:
Price/earnings ratio = 1/earnings yield = 1/0.155 = 6.452
Market price per share = price earnings ratio × earnings per share
$$= 6.452 \times \$3.72 = \$24$$
Value of equity = market price per share × number of shares
$$= \$24 \times 60,000 = \$1,440,000$$
Stage 6, value of firm after-debt financing:

Value of debt $ 960,000
Value of equity   1,440,000
Value of firm $2,400,000

18 *How much should a firm borrow?*

Introduction

The point of this chapter is to combine some practical and relevant issues with the analysis of Chapter 17. Capital markets work well, but corporate and personal income taxes, the probability of bankruptcy and other forms of financial distress, differing goals of management and shareholders, and possible nonseparable investing and financing decisions complicate debt-policy decisions.

What to Look For in Chapter 18

This chapter's major point is that *debt policy does matter,* once taxes, the probability of bankruptcy, financial distress, potential conflicts of interest between the firm and its security holders, potential conflicts of interest among the firm's security holders, to say nothing of the interactions of investing and financing decisions, are included.

Notwithstanding the above noted imperfections, capital markets function remarkably well, but the variety of institutional constraints on them gives rise to the statement: debt policy counts, but only within the context of the specific considerations.

Corporate Taxes The existence of corporate taxes is the first complication to the position that debt policy does not count. Because interest on debt is deductible before corporate taxes are paid, a *tax shield*, which tends to enhance the value of the firm, emerges. Indeed, tax shields are valuable assets, their value being the present value of the reduced taxes as determined by the corporate tax rate and the amount of permanent debt. Although MM corrected it to include tax shields, Proposition I continues to be flawed because it leads to the conclusion that all firms should be 100 percent debt-financed. Mere observation indicates that this is incorrect.

Corporate and Personal Taxes In an attempt to correct for this view not only are corporate taxes to be considered but also personal income taxes. In that analysis, however, recognize that cash dividends are taxed more heavily than capital gains. Because interest income is taxed at the personal level and equity income is taxed at the corporate level, if the personal tax on bond interest is higher than equity income, corporate borrowing may reduce the firm's market value. In any event, the object is how to minimize the total tax from business operations, both the tax on business income as well as the tax on the income to shareholders.

Miller's Capital Structure View Merton Miller's view of capital structure effects on firm values when investors have different tax rates states that as companies borrow more and more, investors can be persuaded to hold corporate debt, rather than common stock, only by offering bondholders higher interest rates than they can obtain from holding common stock. Miller's model indicates that there is an optimal debt-equity ratio for all corporations. Although Miller's model is not without its problems, it is another step forward in trying to explain the way in which business firms decide on a proper debt-equity ratio.

Financial Distress   Other considerations impinging on the debt-equity decision are the costs of financial distress. Because promises made to creditors may be broken, or honored only with substantial difficulty, a firm is not able to borrow as much as it may choose. Consequently, the negative aspects of the present value of the cost of financial distress influence the value of the firm. Such costs include the cost of bankruptcy as well as such indirect costs of time and effort to resolve a financially distressed condition. Financial distress may arise without bankruptcy, especially when a firm has insufficient capital to meet its obligations.

Stockholders and Financial Distress   Whenever financial distress arises, there are a variety of games in which stockholders may engage in order to minimize their risk exposure, such as risk shifting, refusing to contribute equity capital, taking cash out of the enterprise, and making decisions which defer the day of reckoning. All may be very costly to creditors. To forestall the possibility of such maneuvers, restrictive provisions are often incorporated into bond contracts, the most typical being dividend limitations, limitations on additional borrowing, restrictions on selling assets, specific accounting procedures, and constraints on operating and investment decisions.

One Last Thought   When the firm's debt-equity ratio is chosen, taxes, the risk of financial distress, and such intangible assets as management and research and development capabilities are incorporated into the firm's financial plans and are manifested in pro forma income statements and balance sheets.

Worked Examples

Problem 1

Demonstrate how interest paid on debt is a tax shield.

Solution

To make this demonstration, take two firms alike in all respects except that one firm is 100 percent financed by common stock and the other is 50 percent equity-financed and 50 percent debt-financed at 9 percent a year. The balance sheets of the two firms are as follows:

All-equity				Equity and debt			
Assets	$10,000	Equity	$10,000	Assets	$10,000	Debt, 9%	$ 5,000
						Equity	5,000
Total	$10,000	Total	$10,000	Total	$10,000	Total	$10,000

Their income statements are as follows:

	All equity	Equity and debt
Earnings before interest and taxes	$1500	$1500
Interest expenses		450
Pretax income	1500	1050
Tax at 46 percent	690	483
Net income to stockholders	$ 810	$ 567
Total income to both bondholders and stockholders	$0 + $810 = $810	$450 + $567 = $1017
Interest tax shield (0.46 × interest)	$0	(0.46) × ($450) = $207

Problem 2

What is the present value of the tax shield as calculated in problem 1?

Solution

It is assumed that the risk of the investment in the tax shield requires a rate of return equal to that paid on the debt, namely, 9 percent. If the financing is considered permanent, the problem is one of solving for the present value of a perpetuity.

$$\text{Present value of tax shield} = \frac{\$207}{0.09} = \$2300$$

Because the total amount of the debt is $5000, the present value of the tax shield is the amount of the total debt which the government underwrites when it allows interest to be deducted as an expense. The difference between the total debt and federal subsidy, $2700 ($5000 − $2300), is the amount the company underwrites. Also note that the present value of the tax shield is independent of the return on the debt. The cash difference between taxes paid, $207 ($690 − $483), makes going into debt a profitable investment, and worth $2300. Restated

$$\text{Present value of tax shield} = \frac{\text{corporate tax rate} \times \text{expected interest payment}}{\text{expected return on debt}}$$

$$= \frac{T_c(r_D D)}{r_D}$$

$$= T_c D$$

$$= 0.46 \times (0.09 \times \$5000)/0.09$$

$$= 0.46 \times \$5000$$

$$= \$2300$$

Problem 3

Demonstrate how interest tax shields contribute to the value of stockholders' equity.

Solution

To solve this problem, begin with a firm that has no long-term debt. International Business Machines Company (IBM) was such a company prior to November

Table 18-1a Simplified balance sheets for IBM September 30, 1979. In millions

Book values				Market values			
Net working capital	$ 4,510	$ 286	Long-term debt	Net working capital	$ 4,510	$ 286	Long-term debt
Long-term assets	9,511	241	Other long-term liabilities	Long-term assets	36,844	241	Other long-term liabilities
		13,494	Equity			40,827	Equity
Total assets	$14,021	$14,021	Total liabilities and equity	Total assets	$41,354	$41,354	Total liabilities and equity

Table 18-1b Balance sheets for IBM with $1 billion of long-term debt substituted for stockholders' equity. In millions

Book values				Market values			
Net working capital	$ 4,510	$ 1,286	Long-term debt	Net working capital	$ 4,510	$ 1,286	Long-term debt
Long-term assets	9,511	241	Other long-term liabilities	Long-term assets	37,304	241	Other long-term liabilities
		12,494	Equity			40,287	Equity
Total assets	$14,021	$14,021	Total liabilities and equity	Total assets	$41,814	$41,814	Total liabilities and equity

1979; so let's take it. First, construct simplified book and market value balance sheets, such as those in Table 18-1a. The next step is to estimate the value of the firm if it were to borrow $1 billion in permanent long-term debt, as IBM did in November 1979. Because of the tax-shield effects, assuming a 46 percent tax rate, this financing scheme should increase the firm's value by T_cD, the corporate tax rate T_c times the amount of permanent long-term debt D. Since the additional debt is $1 billion, the market value of the firm should increase by $0.46 \times \$1,000,000,000 = \$460,000,000$. If the MM theory, corrected for taxes, holds, the value of the firm must increase by $460 million to $41.814 billion. The new balance sheets will be those in Table 18-1b. The value of the equity declines by $540 million, which is $(1 - T_c)(D)$, just the obverse of the increase in the value of the firm, which is T_cD. The question of the moment of course is: Are the shareholders better off? If you, as the financial manager, purchased $1 billion of stock and it dropped in value by only $540 million, the stockholders are ahead on the deal to the tune of $460 million ($1 billion $-$ $540 million). To put it another way, the shareholders received $1 billion in exchange for $540 million, not a bad deal by anybody's standards.

Summary

Even your intuition probably tells you that no financial manager can continue to take on more and more debt without impunity. Well, the real-world capital markets say roughly the same thing, with the result that in this chapter we conclude that debt does count, at least to the extent that it poses a bankruptcy cost. When taxes, financial distress, and the interactions between investment and financing decisions are allowed to enter the picture, the perfect capital markets assumptions are violated and debt looms large in the picture of financial decision making. Even at that, there may be relevant ranges of the debt-equity ratio that do not materially affect the value of the firm, and shrewd financial managers will seek to determine that range.

List of Terms

Bankruptcy
Bankruptcy costs
Capital gains
Default
Financial distress
Pro forma balance sheet
Pro forma income statement
Tax shield

Exercises

Fill-in Questions

1. The main advantage to corporate debt is that the interest is _____ expense whereas cash dividends are not.

2. If a company has permanent long-term debt carrying an interest rate of 9 percent and is in the 40 percent tax bracket, the tax shield amounts to _____ for every $1000 of debt.

3. The present value of a tax shield of $46 is _____ when the effective long-run interest rate is 9 percent.

4. The new MM Proposition I says that _____ is equal to _____ + _____ .

5. If investors are willing to lend at a before-tax return of 9 percent, they must be equally willing to lend at an after-tax return of _____, if they are in a 35 percent marginal income tax bracket.

6. In Merton Miller's "Debt and Taxes" scheme of the financial world, migrations between stocks and bonds continue to take place up to the point where _____ tax losses are just equal to _____ tax savings.

7. Once we add the cost of financial distress to the analysis of a firm's value, we find that the value of the firm is equal to _____ if

the present value of the tax shield is equal to the present value of

_____ .

8. Bankruptcy is _____ problem and not

_____ problem.

9. The expected cost of bankruptcy is equal to the _____ of

bankruptcy times the cost of bankruptcy as a _____ of the

firm's current _____ value.

10. In a financially distressed firm stockholders (gain, lose) _____

when the business risk is increased.

11. In a finacially distressed firm, a project whose net present value is $200 will

add (exactly, less than, more than) _____ $200 to the

value of shareholders.

12. The bondholders of a financially distressed firm have (more, less)

_____ to gain from investments which increase firm value,

the greater the probability of default.

Problems

1. Compute the present value of interest tax shields resulting from each of the
following debt issues. Consider only corporate taxes, the marginal rate of
which is 40 percent. Show all calculations.
   a. A $1000, 1-year loan at 9 percent.
   b. A 7-year loan of $1000 at 9 percent. Assume no principal is repaid until
maturity.
   c. A $1000 perpetuity at 8 percent.

2. Consider the following book and market value balance sheets of PaperWeight,
Inc.:

Book value				Market value			
Net working capital	$ 40	Debt	$ 70	Net working capital	$ 40	Debt	$ 70
Long-term assets	70	Equity	40	Long-term assets	110	Equity	80
	$110		$110		$150		$150

Answer the following questions in light of these assumptions: (**1**) The MM
theory holds except for taxes. (**2**) No growth. (**3**) The debt is permanent. (**4**) 42
percent corporate tax rate. (**5**) The interest rate on debt is 8 percent.
   a. How can the market value of the firm be greater than its book value?
   b. Demonstrate the extent to which the stockholders would be better off if the
company were to sell additional debt at 8 percent, using the proceeds to
purchase $40 of stock.

c. Demonstrate the effects of replacing $40 of permanent 8 percent debt with equity.

3. Compute the total corporate and personal taxes paid on debt and equity income for each of the following cases. In which cases does the tax advantage lie, with a levered or unlevered firm? For convenience assume a corporate income tax rate of 44 percent; realized capital gains are taxed at one-half the rate on cash dividends; the interest rate on debt is 10 percent; earnings before interest and taxes are $1000; and the levered firm borrows $1000.

Case	Bondholders' tax bracket	Stockholders' tax bracket	Form of equity income
1	0	0	All dividends
2	0.20	0.20	All dividends
3	0.20	0.20	All realized capital gains
4	0.45	0.45	All dividends
5	0.45	0.45	All unrealized capital gains
6	0.45	0.45	All realized capital gains
7	0.56	0.56	All dividends
8	0.56	0.56	All unrealized capital gains
9	0.56	0.56	All realized capital gains

In addition, contrast the all-dividends, realized capital gains, and unrealized capital gains cases for each of the several different tax brackets. What noticeable differences, if any, do you observe? What implications do the differences you observe have to making financial decisions of the firm? For individual investors?

4. PaperWeight, Inc., has fallen onto hard times and is bankrupt; its market value balance sheet is as follows:

Net working capital	$500	Bonds	$650
Long-term assets	200	Equity	50
	$700		$700

You are brought in to evaluate each of the following possible actions the financial manager is contemplating. Present an objective evaluation of each action. Assume each action is independent of all other actions.

a. The company pays a cash dividend of $75.

b. The company sells its long-term assets for $100, collects $450 from its net working capital, closes its doors, and invests the cash of $550 in U.S. Treasury bills at the going rate of 8 percent.

c. The company is confronted with an investment opportunity which has a net present value of $200 but decides not to undertake it.

d. The company is confronted with an investment project whose net present value is $200 and sells new equity to undertake it.

e. The company is confronted with an investment opportunity whose net present value is $200 and borrows $200 to undertake it.

f. The lenders agree to extend the due date of its debt from 1 year to 2 years. From 1 year to 5 years.

g. The lenders agree to extend the due date of its debt from 1 year to 2 years, provided the lenders control all working capital and investment decisions, as well as prohibiting the issuance of any further debt.

Essay Questions

1. Explain why tax shields are valuable assets.
2. What is MM's Proposition I, as corrected? Why was the correction necessary?
3. "This much I know, as more and more debt is taken on the chances of bankruptcy increase. It only stands the test of reason that the value of a firm which has 'too much' debt is likely to be less than a firm that has 'just the right amount' of debt." Evaluate this statement.
4. How can it be said that: "It may not be in the stockholders' self-interest to contribute fresh equity capital even if that means forgoing positive net present value investment opportunities"?

Answers to Exercises

Fill-in Questions

1. a tax-deductible
2. $36
3. $511.11
4. the value of the firm; the value of an all-equity firm; the present value of the tax shield
5. 5.85 percent
6. personal; corporate
7. the value of an all-equity firm; the cost of financial distress
8. an operating; a financial
9. probability; proportion; market
10. gain
11. less than
12. more

Problems

1. (a) Interest tax shield: $0.4 (\$1000 \times 0.09) = \$36$; present value of tax shield = $\$36/1.09 = \$33.03$; (b) Present value of tax shield = $\$36 \times 5.033 = \$181.19$; (c) $400

2. a. Book values are based largely on historical costs, whereas market values are based on expected productivity.

   b. $T_cD = 0.42 \times \$40 = \$16.80$, the amount by which total assets increase. The decline in equity is $(1 - T_c) D = \$23.20$. In sum,

Amount received by shareholders	$40.00
Decline in shareholder value	23.20
Net gain to shareholders	$16.80

   Market value balance sheet after the debt issue:

Net working capital	$ 40.00	Debt	$110.00
Long-term assets	126.80	Equity	56.80
	$166.80		$166.80

c. Assets now decline by $16.80 and equity increases by $23.20. In sum,

Increase in shareholder value	$23.20
Amount paid by shareholders	40.00
Net loss to shareholders	$16.80

Market value balance sheet after the equity issue:

Net working capital	$ 40.00	Debt	$ 30.00
Long-term assets	93.20	Equity	103.20
	$133.20		$133.20

3. Take case 4.

	Income statements	
	Unlevered firm	Levered firm
Earnings before interest and taxes	$1000	$1000
Interest	0	100
Pretax income	$1000	$ 900
Tax at 44 percent	440	396
Net income to stockholders	$ 560	$ 504
Total income to both bondholders and stockholders	0 + $560 = $560	$100 + $504 = $604
Tax on the firm	$440	$396.00
Tax on bondholders	0	45.00
Tax on stockholders	252	226.80
Total tax	$692	$667.80

For case 6:

Tax on the firm	$440.00	$396.00
Tax on bondholders	0	45.00
Tax on stockholders	126.00	113.40
Total tax	$566.00	$554.40

All the cases are:

1	$440.00	$396.00
2	552.00	516.80
3	496.00	466.40
4	692.00	667.80
5	440.00	441.00
6	566.00	554.40
7	753.60	734.24
8	440.00	452.00
9	596.80	593.12

4. a. Bond value falls, stockholders gain
   b. Bondholders will get $550; stockholders will get nothing.
   c. Everyone loses
   d. Bondholders gain because the debt ratio improves; stockholders also gain.
   e. Bondholders could gain or lose, depending on the risk of the project.
   f. Bondholders lose in both instances.
   g. Bondholders may win in this case.

19 *Interactions of investment and financing decisions*

Introduction

This chapter takes us off in a new direction, because we drop the assumption that investment and financing decisions are separable and independent of each other. This important shift in emphasis forces us to search for a method of valuing the firm which includes the interplay between investment and financing decisions. The preferred valuation method is called adjusted present value (APV), because it incorporates the capital mix decision into the investment decision and it always leads to correct answers.

What to Look For in Chapter 19

To this point we lived in the idealized Modigliani-Miller financial world in which (1) investment decisions were separated from financing decisions, (2) financing decisions were irrelevant to the value of the firm, and (3) an all-equity financed firm was assumed. We now shift our emphasis to include the influence of financing decisions on the value of the firm. Retained is the value-additivity assumption, which states that individual investment projects, when each is viewed independently of the others, may be added together to derive the total value of the firm.

Adjusted Present Value Is Preferred   To trace the impact of financing decisions on the value of the firm, several approaches are taken, including adjusted net present value, the Modigliani-Miller formula, and the weighted-average cost of capital formula. The adjusted-present-value formula is preferred.

How APV Works   The adjusted-present-value (APV) rule is applied by first determining the present value of a project assuming the firm is all-equity-financed. The project's resulting base-case net present value is thereafter adjusted for the influence of financing decisions. Issue costs, for example, are evaluated; their present value tends to reduce the base-case net present value, and APV decreases. If subsidized financing is obtainable, the net present value of the subsidized loan is added to the base-case net present value, and APV increases.

Debt Capacity and APV   Additions to the firm's debt capacity also tend to add to the project's adjusted net present value. Debt capacity depends on the firm's target debt ratio and expands as new investment projects are undertaken, although the target debt ratio is maintained. Not all investment projects, however, make the same marginal contribution to borrowing power. The tangibility of assets, the relative independence of an investment project of the firm's overall fortunes, the profitability of the investment project, and the stability of the future cash flows are important influences on debt-capacity expansion. Expansion of debt capacity is valuable because it generates the tax shield of which we made quite a to-do in Chapter 18. The present value of the tax shield is added to the base-case net present value so that the adjusted net present value increases.

Adjusted-Discount-Rate Approaches   The adjusted-discount-rate approach to the valuation of investment opportunities is an alternative to adjusted present values. The discount rate is adjusted upward or downward to accommodate the specific riskiness of the investment. In this scheme, the adjusted cost of capital becomes the minimum acceptable rate of return, because it reflects the opportunity cost of capital and the side effects of the project's financing.

MM and Adjusted Discount Rates   Two ways to adjust discount rates are the Modigliani-Miller (MM) formula and the weighted-average cost of capital. The MM formula takes into account the opportunity cost of capital for the firm under an all-equity condition but adjusts for the tax shield arising from debt financing. The MM formula may be adjusted for the opportunity costs of the specific project being evaluated. On theoretical grounds, the MM formula is deficient because it requires perpetual cash flows and permanent debt financing. Consequently, the MM formula either is not useful or applies only as a rough approximation to evalution of short-term investment projects.

Weighted-Average Cost of Capital   The weighted-average cost of capital approach to adjusting discount rates says the proper discount rate used to evaluate projects is the market-value weighted cost of capital. This approach assumes that all projects possess the same risk as the firm. Consequently, the weighted-average cost of capital may not be used to evaluate investment projects whose risk is different from the entire firm. Moreover, the weighted-average cost of capital formula suffers from the same infirmities as the MM formula; namely, perpetual cash flows and a permanent debt ratio are assumed.

Worked Examples

Problem 1

What-Not, Inc., is considering an investment project which will generate a level after-tax cash flow of $500,000 a year in the next 5 years. Returns on comparable-risk investment opportunities are 14 percent. The investment requires a cash outlay of $1.5 million. Compute the net present value of this project.

Solution

This straightforward capital budgeting problem requires you to find the present value of the $500,000 a year for each of 5 years, using the discount rate of 14 percent. The cash outlay is then deducted from the present value of that stream of cash to obtain NPV. The calculations are

$$\text{NPV} = -\$1,500,000 + \sum_{t=1}^{5} \frac{\$500,000}{(1.14)^t}$$

$$= -\$1,500,000 + (\$500,000)(3.433)$$

$$= -\$1,500,000 + \$1,716,500$$

$$= \quad \$216,500$$

Problem 2

Because What-Not, Inc., does not have the cash available to undertake the project, it is investigating the possibility of selling stock. The financial manager discovered that for issues of that size, the effective cost to the firm would be 16 percent of the gross proceeds to the company. How much must the company raise in order to net $1.5 million and what impact does the cost of issuing common stock have on the project's NPV?

Solution

This is a problem of determining the adjusted present value (APV) of the investment, taking into account the costs incurred when external financing is needed. To find the amount of money that must be raised so that the company obtains the needed $1.5 million, simply set up the problem in this way: The company will receive only 84 percent of the amount raised; $1.5 million is 84 percent of what unknown (x) amount to be raised? Algebraically it is set up thus:

$$\$1,500,000 = 0.84x$$

Solving for x by dividing both sides of the equation by 0.84, the result is $1,785,714. To obtain the needed $1.5 million, the company must raise $1,785,714 because that amount, when adjusted for the cost of selling the issue, results in the desired amount, that is, $[\$1,785,714 - (\$1,785,714 \times 0.16)] = \$1,500,000$. Or equivalently $\$1,785,714 \times 0.84 = \$1,500,000$. So the issue cost is $285,714 ($1,785,714 − $1,500,000). Because this is an additional cash outlay prompted by this project, it must be included in the analysis. The APV is

APV = base-case NPV − issue cost

$$= \$216,500 - \$285,714$$

$$= -\$69,214$$

The issue cost makes the project unacceptable

Problem 3

Now say that What-Not, Inc., is able to pick up half of the needed $1.5 million from the government by a subsidized 5-year, 5 percent loan, whereas were it to borrow from the public it would pay 9 percent. The loan will be repaid in equal annual installments. What impact does this have on the APV, again taking into account the issue costs as set forth in problem 2? Be sure to determine first your required annual installments to amortize the loan.

Solution

Neat deals come with subsidized loans, always! Let's see why. First, determine the amount of common stock the company must sell to pick up the required $0.75

million. The procedure for doing this is the same as that in problem 2. The answer is $892,857 ($750,000 ÷ 0.84), and the issue cost is $142,857 ($892,857 − $750,000).

Next evaluate the subsidized loan by determining its net present value. To determine the amount of annual payments, principal and interest, use the formula, $i/[1 − (1 − i)^{-n}]$, where i is the rate of interest, to determine the annual payment per dollar borrowed. The rest of the arithmetic looks like this:

$$\text{Annual payments} = \text{amount of loan} \times \text{payment factor, 5 percent}$$

where the "factor payment" is equal to the reciprocal of the usual annuity factor

$$= \$750,000 \times \frac{.05}{1 − (1.05)^{-5}}$$

$$= \$750,000 \times 0.231$$

$$= \$173,250$$

The next step is to find the NPV of the subsidized loan by subtracting from the amount of the loan the present value of the loan installments.

$$\text{NPV of subsidized loan} = \text{PV of loan} − \text{PV of loan installments}$$

$$= \$750,000 − \sum_{t=1}^{5} \frac{\$173,250}{(1.09)^t}$$

$$= \$750,000 − (\$173,250)(3.890)$$

$$= \$750,000 − \$673,943$$

$$= \$76,058$$

This amount must then be added to the NPV of the base-case project. And the issue cost must be subtracted.

$$\text{APV} = \text{base-case NPV} − \text{PV of issue costs} + \text{PV of subsidized loan}$$

$$= \$216,500 − \$142,857 + \$76,058$$

$$= \$149,701$$

With this financing scheme, the project becomes acceptable.

Problem 4

Now that we are having so much fun with What-Not, Inc., and its financing schemes, let's add another twist. Say financial management is comfortable with a 65 percent target debt ratio, based on the book value of its assets. Say it borrows 15 percent of the needed $1.5 million at the rate of 9 percent, obtains 50 percent of the needed money from the subsidized loan, and obtains the remainder from a stock sale, the issue costs being those of problem 2. The company's marginal tax rate is 46 percent. What does this do to APV?

Solution

This is merely an extension of the basic problem, only this time you have to incorporate the present value of the tax shield to make it complete. Let's go through it in steps.

- *Step 1:* We already know the NPV of the subsidized loan; it is $76,058 (thank you, Uncle Sam).
- *Step 2:* To calculate the issue cost of common stock, determine how much will be needed. It is $525,000 ($1.5 million × 35 percent). Now determine how much must be raised to obtain that amount; it is $625,000 ($525,000 ÷ 0.84). Then determine the issue cost; it is $100,000 ($625,000 − $525,000).
- *Step 3:* Determine the present value of the tax shield. Before you can do that, however, you must determine the annual installment payments, the annual interest payable in each year, the annual tax shelter, and the present value of the annual tax shelter. Setting up a table is the best way to accomplish that goal. The annual installments are $45,000 plus interest on the remaining balance. The table is as follows:

Year	Debt outstanding at start of year	Interest	Interest tax shield	Present value of tax shield
1	$225,000	$20,250	$9,315	$ 8,546
2	180,000	16,200	7,452	6,272
3	135,000	12,150	5,589	4,316
4	90,000	8,100	3,726	2,640
5	45,000	4,050	1,863	1,211
				Total $22,985

Combine all the NPVs to obtain APV.

APV = base-case NPV − PV of issue cost + PV of subsidized loan + PV of tax shield

= $216,500 − $100,000 + $76,058 + $22,985
= $215,543

Once again, accept the project. But also notice the role the government plays in making this a good deal; it subsidizes a loan directly through lower interest rates on the loan it makes and it subsidizes publicly offered debt issues through the tax-deductible provisions of the Internal Revenue Code.

Problem 5

Now the financial manager engages you to study the impact of basing his borrowing decisions on market rather than book values. After all, you persuaded him that to exclude common stock on a market value basis is convoluted thinking. Let's assume for the sake of peace that the debt ratio remains the same, so that you can concentrate your efforts on the publicly offered debt issue of $225,000 at the going rate of 9 percent. The question, of course (you do know that, don't you?), is the impact on APV when market values are used instead of book values.

Solution

To solve this problem, redo the table in problem 4, this time taking into account the extent to which the total present (market) value of the firm has been increased as a result of undertaking the project. Because the project costs $1.5 million and has a present value *without* the tax shield of $216,500, the total present value at the beginning of the period is $1,716,500 ($1,500,000 + $216,500, from problem 1).

This is now how the financing breaks down:

Total present value to be financed	$1,716,500
Amount to be financed by debt:	
Total debt = 0.65 × $1,716,500	1,115,725
Subsidized debt	750,000
New debt	365,725
Amount to be financed by equity:	
0.35 × $1,716,500	600,775

Armed with that information, the calculations follow.

- *Step 1:* We already know the NPV of the base-case project is $216,500.
- *Step 2:* We already know the net present value of the subsidized debt is $76,058.
- *Step 3:* We now have to recalculate the issue cost (PV) of the equity capital. We will need to float $715,208 of equity capital ($600,775 ÷ 0.84) in order to net the required amount. The issue cost is $114,433 ($715,208 − $600,775).
- *Step 4:* It now remains for us to determine the PV of the tax shield. This is accomplished by replicating the table in problem 4, this time factoring in the forecasted base-case PV at the beginning of each year because the amount of debt outstanding depends on the market value of the firm, itself contingent on the present values of its projects. For the sake of argument, let's assume that the base-case present value declines by equal amounts so that by the *end* of the fifth year its value is zero. The yearly decline is $343,300 ($1,716,500 ÷ 5). This means that the amount of new debt outstanding will decline by the same $73,145 ($365,725 ÷ 5) a year. The setup is:

Year	Forecasted base-case PV at start of year	Debt outstanding at start of year	Interest	Interest tax shield	PV of tax shield
1	$1,716,500	$365,725	$32,915	$15,141	$13,891
2	1,373,200	292,580	26,332	12,113	10,195
3	1,029,900	219,435	19,749	9,085	7,015
4	686,600	146,290	13,166	6,056	4,291
5	343,300	73,145	6,583	3,028	1,968
					$37,360

Combining all the relevant numbers, we obtain

$$APV = \$216,500 - \$114,430 + \$76,058 + \$37,360$$

$$= \$215,488$$

which is less than that obtained using book values! Why? Because the subsidized loans are carrying less of the total NPV and the additional money must come from the higher-cost equity segment. But even at that, the reevaluated NPV of the tax shield generated an additional $14,375 ($37,360 − $22,985), when market values were used instead of book values, and that's 62.5 percent more. But because market values are used as the basis for deciding the debt-equity mix, and because the government loan is fixed in absolute amount, the publicly issued debt no longer is 15 percent of the total, but rather 21.31 percent.

Problem 6

Let's take the case of Forever and Ever Company, which is considering an investment project that costs $2 million and is expected to generate savings of $200,000 a year, forever and ever, naturally. The business risk of this project warrants a rate of return of 12 percent.

In successive steps, your task as financial manager is to calculate the net present value of the project, assuming no tax shields. Then calculate the project's NPV assuming tax shields which arise because additional 8 percent debt may be issued in amounts equal to 30 percent of the cost of the project. Your marginal tax rate is 45 percent. Finally, determine the minimum acceptable base-case NPV as well as the minimum internal rate of return.

Solution

The solution to this problem is straightforward. The base-case NPV is

$$\text{Base-case NPV} = \text{cash outlay} + \text{present value of a perpetuity}$$
$$= -\$2,000,000 + (\$200,000/0.12)$$
$$= -\$2,000,000 + \$1,666,667$$
$$= -\$33,333$$

Obviously you must reject this project, for it takes away more from the value of the firm than it adds to it.

Now add the effects of the financing scheme. A total of $600,000 ($2 million × 30 percent) is borrowed at the 8 percent rate. The tax shield is

$$\text{Tax shield} = \text{debt} \times \text{interest} \times \text{marginal tax rate}$$
$$= \$600,000 \times 0.08 \times 0.45$$
$$= \$21,600$$

This annual tax shield lasts, remember, forever and ever; so to find the present value of this perpetuity, divide it by the required rate of return of 8 percent, the resulting answer being $270,000. Now the project is acceptable, its APV being

$$\text{APV} = \text{base-case NPV} + \text{PV tax shield}$$
$$= -\$33,333 + \$270,000$$
$$= \$236,667$$

Finding the minimum acceptable level of income for the project alone, that is, without the tax shield, is another story. What you want to know is the annual income that is needed to make the project acceptable. To find the minimum acceptable level of income needed to generate the minimum acceptable NPV of $-$270,000$ set up the problem this way.

Base-case NPV = cash outlay + (annual income/required rate of return)

$$-$270,000 = -$2,000,000 + (\text{annual income}/0.12)$$

Solving for annual income, we obtain

Annual income = ($2,000,000 - $270,000) × 0.12

= $207,600

This is the minimum annual income this project must generate in order to make it acceptable.

The minimum acceptable internal rate of return is

$207,600 ÷ $2,000,000 = 0.1038 = 10.38 percent

Problem 7

Use the MM formula to determine the adjusted cost of capital in problem 6.

Solution

Their formula for projects is

$$r^*_j = r_j(1 - T_cL_j)$$

where r^*_j = adjusted cost of capital

r_j = discount rate appropriate for project j under all-equity financing

T_c = corporate tax rate

L_j = firm's target debt ratio

The target debt ratio from problem 6 is 0.3 and the completed equation is

$$r^*_j = 0.12[(1 - (0.45)(0.3)]$$

$$= 0.1038 = 10.38 \text{ percent},$$

which is precisely the answer we obtained.

Problem 8

As our last problem we will use the weighted-average cost of capital approach to evaluate investment projects. Let's use the information of problem 6, except that now the firm will earn $467,100 in perpetuity. First, determine the value of the firm as if it were all-equity-financed. Second, determine its value when it has a debt ratio of 0.3. Third, calculate the equity income and return on equity.

Solution

The problem is solved, as always, in several steps. The value of the all-equity firm is

$$V = \text{income/appropriate discount rate}$$

Here the discount rate is the firm's opportunity cost of capital. The answer is

$$V = \$467{,}100/0.12$$

$$= \$3{,}892{,}500$$

Now say the firm changes its capital structure by selling \$1,350,000 at 8 percent debt. The tax shield created is

$$\text{Tax shield} = \text{marginal tax rate} \times \text{interest} \times \text{amount of debt}$$

$$= 0.45 \times 0.08 \times \$1{,}350{,}000$$

$$= \$48{,}600$$

a year, which has a present value of \$607,500 (\$48,600 ÷ 0.08). Thus the value of the firm increases to \$4,500,000 (\$3,892,500 + 607,500). The value of the equity must be

$$E = V - D$$

$$= \$4{,}500{,}000 - \$1{,}350{,}000$$

$$= \$3{,}150{,}000$$

and the debt ratio is

$$\text{Debt ratio} = \text{debt} \div \text{value of the firm}$$

$$= D \div V$$

$$= \$1{,}350{,}000 \div \$4{,}500{,}000$$

$$= 0.3 = 30 \text{ percent}$$

The equity income is

$$\text{Equity income} = \text{profit} - r_d(1 - T_c)D$$

$$= \$467{,}100 - 0.08(1 - 0.45)\$1{,}350{,}000$$

$$= \$467{,}100 - 0.08(0.55)(\$1{,}350{,}000)$$

$$= \$467{,}100 - \$59{,}400$$

$$= \$407{,}700$$

The rate of return on equity is

$$\text{Return on equity} = \text{equity income/equity}$$

$$= \$407{,}700/\$3{,}150{,}000$$

$$= 0.1294 = 12.94 \text{ percent}$$

Summary

Both investing and financing decisions must be analyzed together. All financial managers seem to know that, although that is something we have not done heretofore.

Of the three ways to incorporate the interaction of investment and financing decisions, adjusted present value (APV) is preferred to the Modigliani-Miller formula and the weighted-average cost of capital. APV produces correct results, formally forces financial managers to isolate the causes of the adjustment, and is comparatively easy to use. The other, less preferred approaches adjust the discount rate used to evaluate expected cash flows.

List of Terms

Adjusted cost of capital
Adjusted discount rate
Adjusted net present value
Corporate debt capacity
Subsidized financing
Target debt ratios
Value additivity
Weighted-average cost of capital

Exercises

Fill-in Questions

1. The adjusted net present value is equal to _____ plus _____.

2. If the net present value of a base-case investment project is $100,000 and equity is issued to finance it at a cost of $125,000, the project may be (accepted, rejected) _____ under the strict Modigliani-Miller scheme of the world, whereas it would be (accepted, rejected) _____ when viewed under the adjusted-present-value scheme.

3. Subsidized financing tends to (increase, decrease) _____ adjusted present value.

4. Corporate borrowing power is (increased, decreased) _____ when an investment is made in tangible assets which are highly related to the firm's fortunes.

5. The opportunity cost of capital is dependent on the _____ of the investment project to be undertaken.

6. The adjusted cost of capital reflects _____ and

_____ .

7. Using the adjusted cost of capital approach to investment analysis, the lowest
return a firm is willing to accept from projects of comparable risk occurs when
the internal rate of return is such that the adjusted present value is

_____ .

8. If the minimum acceptable internal rate of return is 9 percent, a project
which has a 10 percent rate of return will produce a (positive, negative)
_____ adjusted present value.

9. The MM formula for calculating the adjusted cost of capital applies to projects
which are equal in riskiness to the firm as well as to projects which have their
own unique risk characteristics, whereas the weighted-average cost of capital
formula applies only to _____ .

10. The Modigliani-Miller formula is correct only for projects whose cash flows
and debt are _____ .

Problems

1. If-Not, Inc., is evaluating a $1 million investment project which is expected to
generate level, after-tax cash flows of $300,000 a year in each of the next 6
years. Rates of return obtainable on investments of comparable risk are 12
percent. Compute the net present value of this project.

2. If-Not, Inc., will finance the project in problem 1 entirely by the sale of stock.
The cost of floating the stock is 12 percent of the gross proceeds. How much
must the company raise and what impact do the flotation costs have on the net
present value of the project?

3. If-Not, Inc., is now able to finance $250,000 of the investment project in
problem 1 with a 6 percent subsidized federal loan. Its alternative borrowing
rate is 10 percent. The loan will be repaid in equal annual installments. The
remainder of the project will be financed by the sale of stock, the flotation costs
of which will be 12 percent of the gross proceeds to the company. (a) Determine the annual installments required to retire the debt at maturity. (b) Trace
the impact of the government loan on the adjusted present value of the project.

4. The management of If-Not, Inc., sets a target debt ratio, based on book values,
of 40 percent. The company now plans to finance the project in problem 1 with
the total amount of debt allowed by its target debt ratio, $250,000 coming from
the 6 percent government loan of problem 3 and the remaining debt coming
from a 10 percent bank term loan. The government loan will be repaid in the
same way as set forth in problem 3, but the annual payments of the bank loan
will be $25,000 plus interest due on the unpaid balance. The remainder of the
financing will come from the sale of stock, the issue costs of which will be 12
percent of the gross proceeds. As the financial manager your task is to trace the

impact of this additional twist in the company's adjusted present value. The company's marginal tax rate is 40 percent.

5. As another permutation on the issues raised in problems 1 to 4, you want to know the implications of setting your target payout ratio based on market values as opposed to book values. As you make your analysis, assume that it is only the debt portion which will be based on market values. What conclusion do you come to as a result of "working through the numbers"? Show all calculations.

6. The Perpetual Motion Company is evaluating a $6 million plant expansion which it estimates will generate $750,000 in after-tax cash, year in and year out, perpetually. The return obtainable on investments of comparable risk is 13 percent. (a) Calculate the net present value of the project, assuming no tax shields. (b) Calculate the project's net present value, assuming tax shields produced by the issuance of 9 percent debt in amounts equal to 40 percent of the project's cost. The company's marginal tax rate is 40 percent. (c) Determine the minimum acceptable base-case NPV. (d) Determine the minimum acceptable internal rate of return.

7. Use the MM formula to determine the adjusted cost of capital in problem 6.

8. This is a weighted-average cost of capital problem. Use the information in problem 6. (a) Determine the value of the firm as if it were all-equity-financed. (b) Determine its value when it changes to a financing scheme whereby it borrows 40 percent of the project's cost at 9 percent. (c) Calculate the equity income and the return on equity. Show all calculations.

Essay Questions

1. What are issue costs and what bearing do they have on adjustment present value? Demonstrate as well as explain your answer.

2. Demonstrate the influence of subsidized financing on adjusted present values.

3. Contrast the weighted-average cost of capital formulation with Modigliani and Miller's formula and the adjusted-present-value formula. Wherein are they similar? Dissimilar? Explain fully.

Answers to Exercises

Fill-in Questions

1. base-case net present value; net present value of financing decisions caused by project acceptance
2. accepted; rejected
3. increase
4. decreased
5. business risk
6. the opportunity cost of capital; the project's financing side effects
7. zero
8. positive
9. projects which are comparable in risk to the firm
10. permanent

Problems

All the answers below were determined with a hand-held calculator. If you use the tables in the Appendix of the text, your answers will be slightly different.

1. $233,422

2. $1,136,364; it is reduced to $97,058

3. (a) $50,841; (b) APV = $159,723

4. Amount of common stock needed: $681,818; flotation costs: $81,818; present value of tax shields: $16,447; present value of government loan: $28,574; APV = $196,625.

5. Total present value with tax shield: $1,016,447; financing: total debt = $406,579, subsidized debt = $250,000, private debt = $156,579, and equity to be raised = $693,032; flotation costs = $83,164; present value of government loan = $28,574; present value of new tax shield = $17,168; APV = $196,000.

6. (a) Base-case NPV: −$230,769; (b) Tax shield: $86,400; APV = $729,231; (c) $655,200; (d) 10.92 percent

7. 10.92 percent

8. (a) $5,769,231; (b) $6,433,846; (c) Equity income: $620,400; equity return: 17.23 percent

20 *Corporate liabilities and the valuation of options*

Introduction

This chapter focuses on the valuation of options. When making financial decisions, financial managers are faced with many options. Knowing the nature of options and how to evaluate them helps financial managers make better decisions. The value of options depends on the exercise price, the expiration date of the option, the price of the shares, the variability in the rate of return on the stock, and the return on the risk-free asset.

What to Look For in Chapter 20

As you traverse the landscape of this chapter, keep in mind that every issue of corporate securities creates an option.

What They Are A call option gives its owner the right to buy an asset at a specified exercise, or striking, price during a specified time period; a put option gives its owner the right to sell an asset at a specified striking price during a specified time period. Although this chapter focuses primarily on options on stocks, the ideas may be extended to all assets and liabilities.

The difference between European and American calls lies in the timing at which they may be exercised, the latter being exercisable anytime before the option's expiration date and the former being exercisable only on the expiration date.

Option Combinations Calls, puts, and shares may be held in combination. For European options the value of a call plus the present value of the exercise price is equal to the value of the put plus the share price. The present value of the exercise price is equivalent to borrowing. Consequently, by being able to hold calls, puts, and shares, and to borrow and lend, combining any three creates the fourth. The process of creating one from the three others is called an option conversion. This leads to the conclusion that whenever a firm borrows, the lender in effect acquires the company and shareholders obtain the option to buy it back by paying off the debt. Because shareholders may not wish to exercise their option to buy back the firm (for example, when it is not profitable), the option creates the value of the limited-liability feature of the corporate form of doing business.

Applications Options concepts were applied to standby underwriting agreements and the issuance of warrants. The standby agreement assures the firm that the shares will be sold. The call options in the case of newly issued stocks are called rights. Warrants, by contrast, are long-term call options which entitle the holder to purchase shares at a specified price within a specified time period.

Valuation When considering the value of options, several things stand out. First, when the stock is worthless, the option is worthless. Second, when the stock price becomes large, the option price approaches the stock price, less the present value of the exercise price. Third, the option price always exceeds this minimum value except when the stock price is zero.

The Black-Scholes Model The Black-Scholes formula says that the present value of the call option depends on the exercise price of the option, the time remaining to the exercise date, the price of the stock now, the per period variance in the rate of return on the stock, and the risk-free rate of interest.

Hedged Portfolios A hedge may be established by combining long positions in stock and selling call options. The portfolio of the long stock and sold call options is called a hedged portfolio which has a beta of zero. The hedged portfolio in well-functioning capital markets produces returns equal to the risk-free rate of interest.

Worked Examples

Problem 1

Find the value of a call option, given that the present value of the exercise price is $10, the value of the put is $15, and the share price is $25.

Solution

To find the answer to this exercise, use the formula

Value of call + present value of exercise price = value of put +
$$\text{share price} \qquad (1)$$

Rearranging,

Value of call = value of put + share price −
$$\text{present value of exercise price} \qquad (1a)$$

$$= \$15 + \$25 - \$10$$

$$= \$30$$

Problem 2

Find the implied present value of the exercise price of a 13-week call, given that the value of the call option is $19, the value of the put option is $5, and the market price is $30.

Solution

Rearranging equation (1) to solve for the present value of the exercise price, we have

Present value of exercise price = value of put + share price −
$$\text{value of call} \quad (1b)$$
$$= \$5 + \$30 - \$19$$
$$= \$16$$

Problem 3

If the present value of the exercise price on a call option is $23, the call option is selling for $5, the put option is selling for $10, and the market price of the stock is $20, should a call or a put on the stock be purchased, if you wish to take a position in the issue?

Solution

Using equation (1b) as the starting point, determine the implied present value of the exercise price and compare that with the actual present value. The implied present value of the exercise price is

Present value of exercise price = $10 + $20 − $5
$$= \$25$$

Because the actual present value ($23) is less than its implied present value ($25), one would expect either the call option to be bid up, the put option bid down, or the share price to decline. To what price? To prices which equilibrate the value on both sides of equation (1). Assuming that the give in the system will be in the call option, the value of the call will have to increase to $7, the $5 present call option value plus $2 for the difference between the implied present value of the exercise price and the actual present value.

Summary

Option theory plays a unique role in financial management. A call option gives you the right to purchase an asset at a fixed exercise price in the future and to decide not to purchase it at that price if its value is less than the exercise price. Many financial decisions involve elements of options. For example, options occur when we decide to issue debt or equity and when there is a chance to expand the scale of a capital investment project at a later date. The theory is not as nicely developed as one would like, but advances are coming rapidly. The Black-Scholes option-valuation model contains the major variables financial managers should consider when analyzing financial decisions within the options context.

List of Terms

American call
Black-Scholes option-pricing model
Call option
European call
Hedged portfolios

Option conversions
Put option
Short sale
Striking or exercise price
Warrants

Exercises

Fill-in Questions

1. The second largest security market in terms of dollar value is the _____.

2. A _____ gives its owner the right to buy stock at a specified price; a _____ gives its owner the right to sell stock at a specified price; and the specified price is called the _____.

3. _____ call options may be exercised only on the expiration day, whereas _____ call options may be exercised on or before the expiration day.

4. Selling stock which an investor does not yet own is called a _____.

5. For European options the value of a call option plus _____ equals the _____ plus the share price.

6. _____ allow call options to be transformed into put options, and vice versa, thereby eliminating the need for the presence of calls, puts, shares, and borrowing.

7. When a firm borrows, _____ acquire the company and _____ obtain an option to buy it back.

8. The value of limited liability lies in the option to default and is the value of a _____ option on the firm's assets with an exercise price equal to the promised payment to _____.

9. Long-term options which entitle their owners to purchase from the company a specified number of shares at a specified price on or before a specified date are called _____.

10. The value of an option (increases, decreases, remains unchanged) _____ when both the rate of interest and the time to maturity decrease.

11. The probability of a large stock-price change during the remaining life of an option depends on _____ and _____.

12. If you own one share of stock and the price of the call option against it

rises or falls by 25 cents for each dollar move in the stock, you may protect yourself against any small change in stock price by (selling, buying) _____ four call options. Such a combination of holding one share long and selling four call options is called a _____, the beta of which is _____. Consequently, were capital markets in equilibrium, the call option would be priced such that the return on the portfolio will equal the _____.

Problems

1. Find the value of a call option, given that the present value of the exercise price is $6, the value of the put is $5, and the share price is $16.
2. Find the implied present value of the exercise price of a 26-week call, given the value of the call option is $12, the value of the put option is $12, and the market price is $55.
3. If the present value of the exercise price of a call option is $20, the call option is selling for $5, the put option is selling for $7, and the market price of the stock is $22, should a put on the stock be purchased? Why or why not?

Essay Questions

1. Explain why financial managers should be interested in options, as they are traded on the Chicago Board Options Exchange, and the means by which to place a value on such options.
2. "As soon as we sold some bonds, I felt as though we gave away the firm. That is, it now seems as though bondholders own the firm, not the stockholders, and stockholders have a claim on the firm. When I took corporate finance courses many years ago, I was taught that bondholders have a claim on the firm and shareholders own it. I no longer believe that is true." In what sense is this statement correct?
3. What are warrants and what rationale can you give for their use by financial managers?
4. List the key elements which determine the value of options.
5. What is a hedged portfolio and of what value is this to financial decision making?

Answers to Exercises

Fill-in Questions

1. Chicago Board Options Exchange
2. call option; put option; exercise or striking price
3. European; American
4. short sale
5. present value of exercise price; value of put option
6. option conversions

7. lenders; shareholders
8. put; bondholders
9. warrants
10. decreases
11. the variance of the stock price per period; the number of periods until the option expires
12. selling; hedged portfolio; zero; risk-free rate of interest

Problems

1. $15
2. $55
3. No, don't buy: the put is only worth $3 relative to the other securities.

Valuing risky debt

Introduction

The most important things to be learned from this chapter are: a term structure of interest rates exists; nominal rates of return must be adjusted for inflation; and wise financial managers must comprehend the nature of bond pricing in order to understand capital markets, however efficient they may be. Intelligent financial decisions can be made only when the financial manager is conversant with the many nuances of the bond markets and the way in which bonds are valued, regardless of whether a public offering of bonds is made, but especially if bonds are offered privately.

What to Look For in Chapter 21

The chapter begins with the classical theory of interest as set forth by Irving Fisher. He postulated that real rates of return are determined by the equilibration of the supply of and demand for capital. He also postulated that real rates of return on bonds must include an adjustment for anticipated inflation. This insight has carried over to the present day in that nominal, money, or stipulated rates of interest clearly must be adjusted for prospective rates of inflation. Even after the fact, nominal rates of return on bonds, or the returns on any other asset for that matter, must be adjusted for inflation. The commonplace method used by financial managers to adjust nominal rates of return is to subtract from that rate the rate of inflation.

Nominal Rate and Inflation   Picking up on Fisher's idea, Professor Fama found that nominal interest rates appear to be unbiased forecasters of changes in the inflation rate. He also found that changes in inflation expectations are the principal cause of changes in nominal interest rates. This is important to financial managers who are considering offering bonds and must negotiate the offering terms.

Spot Rates and the Term Structure   We saw that the spot rate is the rate of interest obtainable on a bond at the present, or spot, time period. The series of spot rates today to different dates results in a term structure of interest rates; typically, the term structure is upward sloping, with long-term rates higher than short-term ones.

Yield to Maturity   As much as the investment community uses yield to maturity to evaluate bonds, it suffers from all the infirmities of the internal rate of return concept, which it is. The yield to maturity assumes that the same rate is used to discount all payments to bondholders; that is, each spot rate is equal. The evidence suggests that spot rates are not all equal.

Explaining the Term Structure   The three primary explanations of the term structure of interest rates are the expectations hypothesis, the liquidity preference theory, and the inflation premium theory. The expectations hypothesis says that the expectations of investors that future spot rates will be higher than the current spot rates is the only reason for an upward-sloping term structure. The liquidity preference theory says that a liquidity premium, which is the difference between forward rates and expected future spot rates, is required because of the uncertainty regarding the reinvestment rate when bonds mature. The inflation premium argument says that the typically upward-sloping term structure is attributable to the risk associated with uncertainty about the inflation rate. None of these explanations is totally satisfactory, although the expectations hypothesis is the least satisfactory of all.

Default Risk   When the value of bonds and the term structure of interest rates are determined, default risk must also be considered. The threat of default on bonds, similar in all respects except their expected ability to pay interest and principal, is another reason different rates of return exist. Bonds are evaluated by financial services whose ratings are good predictors.

Debt as Options   When option pricing is extended to debt analysis, corporate bonds become the equivalent to lending money with no chance of default while giving stockholders a put option on the firm's assets. Thus the value of a bond consists of the value of the assets less the value of the put option.

Guaranteed Debt   Finally, we saw that government loan guarantees are valuable because they lift the onus of default from the borrower. Thus a loan guarantee is valued as a put option on the firm's assets. The value of the loan without the guarantee is equal to the value assuming no chance whatsoever of a default less the value of the put.

Worked Examples

Problem 1

Find the real rate of interest given that the nominal rate is 10 percent and the inflation rate is 8 percent.

Solution

The solution is obtained by using the formula

$$1 + r_{\text{money}} = (1 + r_{\text{real}})(1 + i) \tag{1}$$

where r_{money} = nominal or money rate of interest
r_{real} = real rate of interest
i = inflation rate

Substituting in the equation, we obtain

$$1 + 0.10 = (1 + r_{\text{real}})(1 + 0.08)$$

We then solve for r_{real}.

$$1 + r_{real} = (1 + r_{money})/(1 + i)$$
$$= (1 + 0.10)/(1 + 0.08)$$
$$= (1.10)/(1.08)$$
$$= 1.0185, \text{ so}$$
$$r_{real} = 0.0185 = 1.85 \text{ percent}$$

Problem 2

If the money rate of interest is 9 percent and the real rate is expected to be 4 percent, what is the assumed inflation rate?

Solution

The answer is obtained from equation (1) by solving for i.

$$1 + i = (1 + r_{money})/(1 + r_{real})$$
$$= (1 + 0.09)/(1 + 0.04)$$
$$= 1.09/1.04$$
$$= 1.0481, \text{ so}$$
$$i = 0.0481 = 4.81 \text{ percent}$$

Problem 3

If the real rate of interest is expected to be 5 percent and the inflation rate is expected to be 8 percent, what nominal interest rate would you expect?

Solution

Once again use equation (1) and solve for the money or nominal rate of interest.

$$1 + r_{money} = (1 + r_{real})(1 + i)$$
$$= (1 + 0.05)(1 + 0.08)$$
$$= (1.05)(1.08)$$
$$= 1.134, \text{ so}$$
$$r_{money} = 0.134 = 13.4 \text{ percent}$$

Problem 4

In December 1979 the nominal rate of interest on 1-year U.S. Treasury notes was 11.2 percent. Assuming that the real rate on such bills continues at its historical average of 0.2 percent, what is the forecasted inflation rate for the year ahead?

Solution

One way to solve this problem is to subtract the real interest rate from the nominal rate to obtain the estimated 1-year inflation rate.

Forecasted inflation rate = nominal interest rate − real interest rate

$$= 11.2 \text{ percent} - 0.2 \text{ percent}$$

$$= 11.0 \text{ percent}$$

Problem 5

Calculate the yield to maturity on a 10-year bond carrying a coupon rate of 8 percent. Assume that the interest is payable annually and the bond is selling at 87.

Solution

The setup for the solution of this problem is similar to every other internal-rate-of-return problem, for that is what solving for the yield to maturity is, an internal rate-of-return problem. Using the present value of an annuity formula allows you to find the present value of the 10 equal interest payments. You also have to calculate the present value of the maturity value of $1000. All this requires a hunt-and-peck method, unless your hand-held calculator contains this routine, because the object is to find the present value that sums to the present market price of $870.

Taking some arbitrary interest rate, such as 10 percent, is a good place to start. (We know that the yield to maturity must be higher than the coupon rate, for the price of the bond is selling below its face value. Were it selling at its face value, the yield to maturity would be 8 percent. And, remember, interest rates and bond prices fluctuate inversely so that when prices go down, yields increase.) Using that 10 percent rate we find

PV of interest   = $80 × 6.145   = $491.60

PV of principal = $1000 × 0.386   =   386.00

the sum of which is $877.60, which is so very close to the market value of 87 that further calculations are not worthwhile. (The actual yield to maturity is 10.13 percent, derived from the internal-rate-of-return calculations from a hand-held calculator.)

Problem 6

It is 1982 and you notice that the yield to maturity of your company's two bonds, 5s of '86 and 9s of '86, are selling at 87.44 and 100.71, which results in yields to maturity of 8.87 and 8.78 percent. You are a recently hired finance major and are asked to explain this phenomenon. "After all," says the financial manager, "the bonds are of the same quality and come due at exactly the same time. Consequently, they should have the same yield to maturity, shouldn't they?" What reasonable answer will you give?

Solution

The answer lies in estimating the spot rates for each of the remaining years and taking the present value of the payments to be received. This is done in Table 21–1, where a set of assumed spot rates are presented.

Although this assumption is not necessary to the analysis, it should be clear that the yield to maturity does not tell the entire story about the period-by-

Table 21-1
Present value of two comparable risk bonds with different coupon rates

		Present-value calculations			
		5s of '86		9s of '86	
Period	Interest rate, r_t	C_t	PV at r_t	C_t	PV at r_t
$t = 1$	0.06	$ 50	$ 47.17	$ 90	$ 84.91
2	0.07	50	43.67	90	78.61
3	0.08	50	39.69	90	71.44
4	0.09	1050	743.85	1090	772.18
Totals			$874.38		$1007.14

period spot rates on the bonds. And it is the spot rates that count, not yield to maturity.

Problem 7

Given that there are two bonds, alike in all respects except coupon rates, calculate the estimated spot rate in the fifteenth year of two 15-year bonds, one of which has a coupon rate of 5 percent and a price of 60 and the other of which has a coupon rate of 10 percent and a price of 100. Assume interest is payable annually.

Solution

To solve this problem, begin by finding the present value of the cash flow, using 10 percent as the discount rate for each. Calling the first bond 1 and the second 2,

$$PV_1 = \frac{\$100}{1 + r_1} + \frac{\$100}{(1 + r_2)^2} + \cdots + \frac{\$1100}{(1 + r_{15})^{15}}$$

$$= \$1000$$

$$PV_2 = \frac{\$50}{1 + r_2} + \frac{\$50}{(1 + r_2)^2} + \cdots + \frac{\$1050}{(1 + r_{15})^{15}}$$

$$= \$600$$

Next compare two investment strategies, one which purchases one 10 percent bond at 100, the other which purchases two 5 percent bonds at 60 (for a total of $2 \times \$600 = \$1200$). Each strategy generates $100 a year in income, although in the fifteenth year the first produces $1100 in cash whereas the second produces $2100 ($2 \times \$1050$). Strategy 2 generates an advantage in cash flows over strategy 1 only in the fifteenth year, and a disadvantage at the beginning of the first year because an additional $200 is required to undertake the investment. The problem is one of comparing the value of the advantages with the disadvantages; that is, compare the present value of $1000 to be received 15 years from now with the present value of the additional present cash outlay of $200. This procedure determines the fifteenth year's spot rate and is set up in this way:

$$PV = \frac{\$1000}{(1 + r_{15})^{15}} = \$200$$

or $200 = \dfrac{\$1000}{(1 + r_{15})^{15}}$

This is how to solve for r_{15}:

$$(1 + r_{15})^{15}(\$200) = \$1000$$

$$= \dfrac{\$1000}{\$200}$$

$$= 5.00$$

We may solve this directly in several ways. First, use a table of future values of $1, by going across the 15-year column until you find a value close to 5.00. Chances are the exact value will not be found, so that interpolation between two adjacent values is required. It turns out that the interest rate required to get $200 to grow to $1000 at the end of 15 years is between 11.0 and 11.5 percent, which is close enough for our purposes.

A second solution involves logarithms. Because most hand-held calculators now have logarithmic functions, this is convenient. The solution follows this setup:

1. Take the natural logarithms of both sides:

$$(1 + r_{15})^{15} = 5.00$$

$$15 \ln (1 + r_{15}) = 1.6094$$

2. Divide by 15:

$$\ln (1 + r_{15}) = 0.1073$$

3. Take the antilog of both sides:

$$1 + r_{15} = 1.1133$$

4. Subtract 1 and multiply by 100:

$$r_{15} = 0.1133$$

$$= (0.1133)(100) = 11.33 \text{ percent}$$

The third way in which to solve this problem is to use a hand-held calculator's present value/future value routine and solve for the interest rate in percent. As expected, the answer is 11.33 percent.

Problem 8

Determine the better financial strategy when confronted with a 2-year spot rate of 9 percent, a 1-year spot rate of 8 percent, and an expected spot rate on 1-year bonds 1 year from now of 10 percent. Assume you do not need your money for 2 years and are not bothered by risk.

Solution

To find the answer to this, you want to know the expected return of each strategy. The setup is

$1000(1 + r_1)[1 + E(_1r_2)]$ compared with $1000(1 + r_2)^2$

where r_1 = 1-year spot rate

$E(_1r_2)$ = expected spot rate on 1-year bonds 1 year from now

r_2 = 2-year spot rate

Substituting the values above, we obtain

$1000(1 + 0.08)(1 + 0.10)$ compared with $1000(1 + 0.09)^2$

$1000(1.08)(1.10)$ compared with $1000(1.09)^2$

$1000(1.188)$ compared with $1000(1.1881)$

1188 compared with 1188.10

For all practical purposes there is no difference between the two outcomes; therefore, you would be indifferent about this investment.

If you wish to lock in the final outcome of $1188, say, because of your queasiness about the expected 1-year spot rate, choose the 9 percent 2-year spot rate. You should also note that the implied forward rate is

$$(1 + r_2)^2 = (1 + r_1)(1 + f_2)$$

where f_2 is the implied forward rate. Substituting the above values, we obtain

$$(1 + 0.09)^2 = (1 + 0.08)(1 + f_2)$$
$$(1.09)^2 = (1.08)(1 + f_2)$$
$$1.1881 = 1.08(1 + f_2)$$
$$1 + f_2 = 1.1881/1.08$$
$$= 1.1001$$
$$f_2 = 0.1001 = 10.01$$

As expected, the implicit forward rate is almost exactly equal to the expected future spot rate, again indicating a condition of relative indifference.

Problem 9

As you proceed to explain to the nonfinancial managers in your organization the nature of the term structure of interest rates, the following question is posed: "Say I want to invest for only 1 year. Am I better off buying a 2-year bond and selling it at the end of the year, or buying a 1-year bond and cashing it in at the end of the year?" On June 29, 1979, the quoted 2-year spot rate on Treasury issues was 8.98 percent, whereas the quoted spot rate on a 1-year Treasury bill was 9.42 percent. What response would you give?

Solution

The answer begins with a determination of the present value of the 2-year bond at the end of the 1-year period.

$$\text{PV of 2-year bond at year 1} = \frac{\$1000(1 + r_2)^2}{1 + _1r_2}$$

$$= \frac{\$1000(1 + r_1)(1 + f_2)}{1 + _1r_2}$$

Because we have too many unknown variables to solve this equation, we must make an assumption about one of them, typically $_1r_2$. We can determine the implied forward rate, however:

$$(1 + r_2)^2 = (1 + r_1)(1 + f_2)$$

$$(1 + 0.0898)^2 = (1 + 0.0942)(1 + f_2)$$

$$1.1877 = (1.0942)(1 + f_2)$$

$$1 + f_2 = 1.1877/1.0942$$

$$= 1.0854$$

$$f_2 = 0.0854 = 8.54 \text{ percent}$$

We will only benefit from purchasing the 2-year bond if next year's 1-year rate $_1r_2$ is less than this value of f_2. Say you expect $_1r_2$ to be 9.2 percent, the present value of the 2-year bond 1 year from now is

$$\text{PV} = \frac{\$1000(1 + r_2)^2}{1 + {_1r_2}}$$

$$= \frac{\$1000(1 + 0.0898)^2}{1 + 0.092}$$

$$= \$1000(1.187664)/1.092$$

$$= \$1187.66/1.092$$

$$= \$1087.60$$

Alternatively, compare the payoff from buying the 1-year bond which generates a 9.42 percent return for certain with the payoff from investing in a 2-year bond and selling it at the end of the first year. That means we must forecast the expected future spot rate $E(_1r_2)$. Say we think it will most likely be the 9.2 percent assumed above. The solution then is

Certain payoff		Expected payoff
$\$1000(1 + r_1)$	compared with	$\dfrac{\$1000(1 + r_2)^2}{1 + E(_1r_2)}$
$\$1000(1 + 0.0942)$	compared with	$\dfrac{\$1000(1 + 0.0898)^2}{1 + 0.092}$
$\$1000(1.0942)$	compared with	$\dfrac{\$1000(1.0898)^2}{1.092}$
$\$1094.20$	compared with	$\$1187.66/1.092$
$\$1094.20$	compared with	$\$1087.60$

The certain payoff should be taken; invest in the 1-year bond.

Summary

Let's retrace some of the preceding steps. Wise financial decisions are made only after a thorough understanding of the term structure of interest rates. The beginning point for determining the discount rate to be applied to any investment is the term structure of interest rates. The term structure relates the going rates of return on bonds of comparable risk over varying durations.

Irving Fisher postulated that returns on bonds should include a premium for inflation and Fama found that Fisher's position was essentially correct, with the result that the nominal returns on very short-term, high-grade bonds are good forecasters of changes in inflation rates.

Among other things to remember is that the spot rates in each period, when butted up against each other, constitute the term structure; yield to maturity, although widely used in practice, is deficient; that three major explanations for the term structure exist, none of which is totally satisfactory; default risk must be incorporated into debt analysis; all debt may be analyzed within the option-pricing model framework; and government loan guarantees, an ever-more-popular sport of late, are valuable put options.

List of Terms

Expectations hypothesis
Forward rate
Inflation premium
Liquidity preference theory
Liquidity premium
Money rate of interest

Nominal interest rate
Real interest rate
Spot rate
Term structure of interest rates
Yield to maturity

Exercises

Fill-in-Questions

1. Interest rates that include a premium for anticipated inflation are called _____ rates.

2. The nominal rate of interest must equal the _____ rate plus the _____ rate of inflation.

3. If the money (nominal) rate of interest is 10 percent and the anticipated inflation rate is 10 percent, the real rate of interest is _____.

4. Under Fisher's scheme of interest rates, if the forecasted inflation rate is 12 percent and the real interest rate is 0.2 percent, the nominal interest rate is _____.

5. The real rate of interest is equal to the _____ minus the _____.

6. Any interest rate which is fixed today is called the _____.

7. The term structure of interest rates is a series of _____ on bonds of comparable risk.

8. A bond's internal rate of return is called _____.

9. Ordinarily the term structure of interest rates presents a condition in which the _____ rates are higher than the _____ rates and therefore the term structure slopes _____.

10. The _____ rate in the second year of a 2-year bond is the rate implied by the 2-year spot rate.

11. Ignoring risk considerations, a person who desires a 2-year investment should purchase 1-year bonds in each of the 2 years if the _____ exceeds the forward rate.

12. Ignoring risk considerations, if you wish to make a 1-year investment but are considering a 2-year bond to be sold at the end of that 1 year, the 2-year bond should be purchased if the forward rate is (less than, greater than, equal to) _____ the future spot rate.

13. Ignoring risk considerations—on the one hand, if the forward rate of a 2-year bond exceeds the expected spot rate, you should be (willing, unwilling) _____ to hold 2-year bonds, whereas if the forward rate were less than the expected future spot rate, you should be (willing, unwilling) _____ to hold 2-year bonds.

14. The _____ of the term structure of interest rates says the only reason for an upward-sloping term structure is that investors expect future spot rates to be higher than current spot rates.

15. The difference between forward rates and expected future spot rates is called _____.

16. The _____ theory of term structure of interest rates takes into account risk, whereas the _____ explanation does not.

17. The _____ theory of the term structure of interest rates assumes that the risk from holding bonds comes only from uncertainty about expected inflation rates.

18. When the risk of bond investing arises from uncertainty about the real rate of

interest, the safest strategy you should follow is to hold bonds that match your _____.

19. If the risk from holding bonds comes from uncertainty about expected inflation rates, the safest strategy is to hold (short, long) _____ bonds.

20. The history of bond ratings indicates that they are (good, poor) _____ indicators of overall quality.

21. When one assumes that bonds create options, the bond value is equal to the value of the bond assuming no chance of default minus _____.

22. A loan guarantee may be valued as a _____ on the firm's assets.

Problems

1. Find the real interest rate, given that the nominal rate is 9 percent and the inflation rate is 5 percent.

2. If the money rate of interest is 9.3 percent and the real rate is expected to be 5 percent, what is the assumed inflation rate? How realistic is it to assume that the real rate will be 5 percent?

3. If the expected real rate of interest is 2 percent and the expected inflation rate is 7 percent, what is the expected nominal interest rate?

4. If the nominal rate of interest on 1-year Treasury bills is 8.2 percent, what is the likely estimate of the inflation rate for the year ahead?

5. Calculate the yield to maturity on a 15-year bond carrying a coupon rate of 9 percent. Assume that the interest is payable annually and the bond is selling at 92.

6. Retain all the conditions in problem 5 except that interest is payable semiannually. Now compute the yield to maturity. Are the results significantly different from those obtained in problem 5 for decision-making purposes? Why or why not? Explain fully.

7. As the financial manager of Ink, Inc., you estimate the following spot interest rates on Treasury securities:

Year	Spot interest rate, %
1	$r_1 = 4.00$
2	$r_2 = 5.00$
3	$r_3 = 5.60$
4	$r_4 = 7.20$
5	$r_5 = 6.50$

Your company's bonds carry a coupon rate of 11 percent and interest is payable annually, and mature in exactly 5 years.

a. What is the present value of the bonds when the scheme used in Table 21–2 of Brealey and Myers is used?

b. Calculate the present values of the following Treasury issues: (1) 5 percent, 3-year bond; (2) 8 percent, 3-year bond; (3) 6 percent, 5-year bond.

c. Determine the yield to maturity of each of the bonds.

d. What differences between the yields to maturity do you observe and how might you explain them to the board of directors, who also happen to have noticed the differences?

8. Ink, Inc.'s board of directors are hard at it trying to learn more about the bond markets. They ask you to explain how to estimate tenth-year spot rates, given that there are two 10-year bonds, alike in all respects except one carries a 6 percent coupon and the other carries a 12 percent coupon. The price of the 6 percent bond is 74; that of the 12 percent bond is 111. How would you make your presentation?

9. Ink, Inc.'s board of directors simply cannot get enough of this good bond markets stuff. Now they ask you to explain which of two financial strategies is better: a 2-year investment horizon, with a 2-year spot rate of 8 percent, a 1-year spot rate of 9 percent, and the expected 1-year spot rate 1 year from now of 7 percent. Give them the analysis they seek.

10. Ink, Inc.'s directors are really warming up to the term structure of interest notions, enlightened as they are by your sterling presentations, and now they wish to know which investment strategy should be followed, given the following conditions: they desire to invest for 1 year; the 1-year spot rate is 6 percent; the 2-year spot rate is 7.5 percent; and the expected spot rate 1 year from now is 9 percent. Go to it!

Essay Questions

1. Differentiate between real rates of interest and nominal rates of interest.

2. How are nominal rates of interest adjusted for the effects of inflation? Explain fully, using whatever equations you feel are necessary.

3. First explain the concept of yield to maturity and then evaluate its usefulness.

4. "The book says that yields to maturity do not determine bond prices; rather it is just the other way around. What I want to know is: How come?" Present an explanation for this comment.

5. Why are there bond ratings and what influence do you think they have on the value of bonds?

6. How do you think bond-rating agencies determine the ratings they place on bonds?

Answers to Exercises

Fill-in Questions

1. nominal
2. real; anticipated
3. zero
4. 12.2 percent
5. nominal rate on Treasury bills; expected inflation rate
6. spot rate
7. spot rates
8. yield to maturity
9. long; short; upward
10. forward
11. expected future spot rate

12. greater than
13. willing; unwilling
14. expectations hypothesis
15. liquidity premium
16. liquidity preference;
expectations hypothesis

17. inflation premium
18. liabilities
19. short
20. good
21. value of a put
22. put option

Problems

1. 3.81 percent
2. 4.10 percent. Unrealistic; the real rate has usually been lower.
3. 9.14 percent
4. 8.0 percent
5. 10.06 percent
6. 10.04 percent compounded semi-annually or 10.29 percent annually.
7. (a) $1185.12; (b) (1) $985.08, (2) $1066.62, (3) $982.17; (c) (1) 5.55 percent, (2) 5.53 percent, (3) 6.43 percent.
8. Buying two 6 percent bonds requires $370 more than buying one 12 percent bond and gives an extra $1000 in year 10. The estimated spot rate is 10.45 percent.
9. Compare these two sets of numbers: $1000(1 + 0.09)(1 + 0.07) and (1 + 0.08)^2 or $1166.30 and $1166.40. They should be indifferent.
10. The implied forward rate is 9.02 percent, almost identical to the 9.00 percent expected future spot rate. They should be indifferent.

22 *The many different kinds of debt*

Introduction

We know some argue that debt does not increase the value of the firm and others say it does. Regardless of which position you take, as a budding financial manager you cannot escape the realities of the various types of debt available for your use, the rationale for the various provisions contained in debt contracts, and the methods of selling debt. These three topics are the sum and substance of this chapter.

What to Look For in Chapter 22

Debt was differentiated between straight bonds, private debt, and project financing. All are promissory notes, although each has characteristics peculiar to it. The bond contract contains the specific terms, called covenants, to which borrowers and lenders agree. Bonds contain such features as being fully registered, unsecured, subordinated, mortgage, collateral trust, and a variety of repayment provisions.

Legal Security and Seniority The significance of the legal security and seniority of bonds depends largely on the extent to which assets and earnings are available to meet the legal obligations of semi-annual interest payments as well as the repayment of principal at maturity. Debenture bonds are general creditors of the company and have no legal security other than the general bill-paying ability of the company. Mortgage bonds, by contrast, have a specific claim on a specific set of tangible assets. Subordinated debt has its claim for repayment of principal in the event of default subordinated to all other specified debt.

Call Provision For most industrial firms, but not for public utility companies, repayment provisions are commonplace. Perforce, the call provision which allows the corporation to call in (retire) its bonds before they mature is a valuable option because when it is invoked under the proper conditions—when the market price equals the call price—it tends to minimize the value of the bonds, which is equivalent to saying that it tends to maximize the value of the firm's stock.

Sinking Funds A sinking fund, which is a provision that stipulates that cash must be set aside periodically during the life of the bond and used to retire bonds from time to time, is another method of retiring bonds before they mature. Sinking funds increase the security behind the remaining outstanding bonds and improve the overall creditworthiness of the company, provided all else stays the same.

Reactions to Default Options Because the company has the valuable option to default on its bonds, restrictive bond provisions are the order of the day. Maintaining an adequate ratio of assets to debt, minimum working capital require- ments, ensuring that all subsequent debt will be subordinated to existing debt, incorporating a negative pledge clause, restricting the amount of cash dividends paid, and requiring a minimum level of net worth are typical restrictive provisions, all of which are intended to enhance the security of bondholders.

Project Loans   In the Appendix we discussed project finance, loans that finance particular projects through a parent company or one of its major subsidiaries. Project loans, as they are sometimes called, rely on the project itself for repay- ment of principal and payment of interest. Because that may not be sufficient security for lenders, tangible property, production payments, completion guaran- tees, and recourse to stockholders are commonly incorporated into the lending agreement. The major advantage of project loans lies in the insurance against risks which may have significant adverse affects on the firm's other operations.

Leftovers   Finally, three less commonly used types of bonds were discussed: income bonds, which depend on the presence of earnings for payment of interest; floating-rate bonds, the interest on which is pegged to another interest rate such as that on Treasury bills; and indexed bonds, which maintain the real rate of return by pegging principal repayments to an index of inflation.

Worked Examples

Problem 1

If Whozits Company's 8 percent debenture bonds mature in 10 years and the yield on comparable-risk bonds is 6 percent, at what price would you expect the Whozits bonds to be selling?

Solution

The object here is to determine the present value of the bond, the formula for which is

$$PV = \sum_{t=1}^{n} \frac{C_t}{(1 + r)^t}$$

where PV $= $ present value
$C_t = $ per period cash flow
$r = $ required rate of return on assets of this risk level
$t = $ number of periods over which the cash flows will be forthcoming

Inasmuch as interest is paid semiannually, the cash flow per period C_t is $40 ($80/2) and the total number of periods t over which the cash flows will be forthcoming is 20(2 × 10 years). Using the remaining data, the completed for- mula is

$$PV = \sum_{t=1}^{20} \frac{\$40}{(1 + 0.06/2)^t} + \frac{\$1000}{(1 + 0.06/2)^{20}}$$

$$= \sum_{t=1}^{20} \frac{\$40}{(1 + 0.03)^t} + \frac{\$1000}{(1 + 0.03)^{20}}$$

$$= \sum_{t=1}^{20} \frac{\$40}{(1.03)^t} + \frac{\$1000}{(1.03)^{20}}$$

Next use the present-value tables. The first term on the right-hand side of the equation is the present value of an annuity of $40 for 20 periods at 3 percent. The second term is the present value of a lump sum of $1000 to be received at the end of the twentieth period. The arithmetic of the matter looks like this:

$$PV = (\$40)(14.877) + \$1000(0.554)$$

$$= \$595.08 + \$554.00$$

$$= \$1149.08$$

Problem 2

If the bonds in problem 1 are callable at 106, what should the financial manager do?

Solution

The financial manager should call the bond because the present value of the bond is greater than the present value of the call price. If needed, a new issue of bonds may be sold at the going rate of 6 percent, thereby lowering the firm's cost of capital, reducing the drain on cash, and improving its interest coverage ratio, all to the benefit of shareholders.

Problem 3

If the call provision of problem 2 exists, what is the maximum price you would expect the bond to achieve when bonds of comparable risk are selling to yield 6 percent?

Solution

The bond will sell for no more than the call price, which is $1060 a bond. The difference between the present value of the bond without the call provision and $1060 is the value of the call provision, or $89.08.

Problem 4

Whozits Company's bonds have a provision which stipulates that senior debt will never fall below a ratio of senior debt to total assets of 40 percent. Say the company is at the limit of that ratio and it wishes to issue still another $5 million in senior debt. How much additional equity capital must it raise to comply with this restrictive provision?

Solution

Begin by setting up the problem as a proportion, which it is. The required ratio of 40 percent senior debt implies that equity must be 60 percent. So the ratio of senior debt to equity is 40 percent to 60 percent, or two-thirds. If they desire to issue $5 million of new debt, the amount of new equity required x will be determined thus:

$$\frac{0.40}{0.60} = \frac{\$5 \text{ million}}{x}$$

$$0.4x = 0.6(\$5 \text{ million}) \qquad \text{(cross-multiplying)}$$
$$= \$3 \text{ million}$$
$$x = \$7.5 \text{ million}$$

Summary

Debt counts when financial managers obligate themselves and their companies to repay the principal amount borrowed as well as the interest due on the loan. So all financial managers must know what they are letting themselves in for when they borrow. This chapter set forth the major provisions commonly found in loan contracts. Most long-term bonds sold to the public contain call provisions and sinking funds, to say nothing of the other provisions intended to protect the interests of bondholders.

List of Terms

Call provision	Mortgage bonds
Collateral trust bonds	Negative pledge clause
Debenture bonds	Private debt
Equipment trust certificates	Project finance
Floating-rate bonds	Registered bonds
Income bonds	Serial bonds
Indenture	Sinking fund
Indexed bonds	Subordinated bonds

Exercises

Fill-in-Questions

1. Private placements are (easier, more difficult) _____ to float than publicly issued contracts.

2. Private placements are more likely to possess (nonstandard, standard) _____ loan features.

3. The contract provisions of private placements are (more, less) _____ stringent than public issues, but they are (more, less) _____ difficult to renegotiate.

4. The document in a public issue of bonds which incorporates all the contract provisions between the borrower and lender, through an agreement with a trust company, is called an _____.

5. Bondholders whose names appear on the records of the company as being owners of the bonds and to whom bond interest and principal will be paid

hold _____ bonds, whereas those who must clip coupons in order to collect their interest and turn in the bond for repayment of principal are called _____ bonds.

6. A bond which is unsecured and relies on the general credit of the corporation is called _____.

7. If an issue of bonds has a _____ , then, if interest rates fall, the company may be able to retire them for less than their present value.

8. A provision which allows debenture bondholders to become mortgage bond-holders, when mortgage bonds are issued after the debentures were sold, is called _____.

9. Bonds, the interest on which is payable only if earnings are present, are called _____; bonds whose rate of interest is contingent on the rate of interest paid on Treasury bills are called _____; and bonds which maintain the real rate of return for bondholders are called _____.

Problems

1. If Whatsits Company's 6 percent debenture bonds mature in 8 years and the yield on comparable-risk bonds is 10 percent, at what price would you expect the Whatsits bonds to be selling, all else the same?
2. If Whatsits Company has 10 percent mortgage bonds maturing in 9 years, and comparable-risk bonds are selling to yield 8 percent, at what price would you expect the Whatsits bonds to be selling if they were noncallable? If they were callable at 105?
3. What is the value of the right to call a 10-year 10 percent coupon bond at a price of 106, when bonds of comparable risk yield 6 percent?
4. Whatsits Company's bond indenture contains a provision stipulating that the ratio of senior debt to total assets must be kept at 30 percent at all times. If the company is at the limit of that ratio, determine how much more additional equity capital it must raise in order to float an additional $40 million of bonds.

Essay Questions

1. Differentiate between a debenture bond, a subordinated bond, and a mortgage bond.
2. In what sense, if any, can subordinated debt be viewed as equity capital?
3. Why does a call provision have value to the financial manager?
4. Explain what a sinking fund is and how it is most likely to work.
5. Why is the option to default on a corporate bond valuable? Explain fully.

Answers to Exercises

Fill-in Questions

1. easier
2. nonstandard
3. more; less
4. indenture
5. fully registered; bearer
6. a debenture
7. call provision
8. a negative pledge clause
9. income bonds; floating-rate bonds; indexed bonds

Problems

1. $783.20
2. 112.7; 105
3. Value of bond less the call price = value of call provision

   $1294.00 − $1060.00 = $234

4. $93.3 million

23 *Warrants and Convertibles*

Introduction

As compared with convertible securities, warrants are typically of shorter duration, are detachable from the securities from which they are issued, and carry an exercise price which requires a cash payment when used. The Black-Scholes option-valuation formula may be used to place a value on warrants, but care must be taken to allow for the effects of dividends and changes in the number of shares outstanding.

The owner of a convertible bond must give it up when exercising the option to acquire common stock, whereas a detachable warrant holder does not. The value of a convertible bond depends on its value as a bond standing apart from the conversion feature as well as the value of the conversion feature itself. Forced conversion may result when the value of convertible securities exceeds the call price. The financial manager's rule for calling convertible securities is: Call them when, and only when, the value of the convertible security reaches the call price.

What to Look For in Chapter 23

Warrants and convertible securities are studied in this chapter. Warrants are a long-term option to buy common stock for cash. Convertible securities give their owners the right to exchange the securities for stock.

Warrants   Warrants are usually detachable, meaning that they may be exercised apart from the security with which they were offered. Warrant holders are not entitled to vote nor do they receive cash dividends. Their interest in the company is usually protected against stock splits and stock dividends. Often the exercise price is stepped up over the life of the warrant. Usually the life of a warrant is shorter than the conversion feature of a convertible bond. The Black-Scholes option-valuation formula may be used to place a value on a warrant. Cash dividends and potential dilution arising from the additional shares potentially outstanding, however, present difficulties in using the Black-Scholes valuation model. Consequently, adjustments for dilution are required. To avoid the cash dividend problem, valuation between the cash payment dates is necessary.

Convertible Securities   Convertible securities resemble warrants because they are options to acquire common stock. The warrant and convertible options differ in that warrants are exercised by the payment of cash to the issuing firm whereas holders of convertible securities exchange them for common stock on predetermined terms. The value of convertible bonds consists of the value of the bond as a bond, and the value of the conversion feature, itself being evaluated as an option. Thus, the price of convertible securities has two lower bounds: the value as a security standing apart from the conversion feature and the value of the conversion feature itself. The conversion option is evaluated just as warrants are, making certain to adjust for cash dividends and potential dilution. The bonds are evaluated just as any other bond would be.

Forced Conversion   Holders of convertible securities may be forced to convert by calling the bonds in. Even though the appropriate decision rule is to call the bond when its value reaches the call price, the evidence indicates that the rule is not consistently followed by financial managers.

Differences between Warrants and Convertibles   You should know that the major differences between warrants and convertibles are:

1. Warrants are usually issued privately, whereas convertibles are usually issued publicly.
2. Warrants are usually detachable and exercisable alone, whereas when a convertible bond is exercised both the bond and the option are given up.
3. Warrants may be issued alone, whereas convertible securities always consist of the security and the conversion option.
4. Warrants are exercised for cash, whereas convertible securities are not, the holder of a convertible giving up the security in exchange for the stock.
5. The cash receipts from exercised warrants may be taxable, whereas there are no unusual tax features with convertible securities.
6. Financial managers cannot call warrants, whereas generally all bonds are callable.

Reasons for Using Them   Historically, the superficial reasons given for issuing warrants and convertible securities were that they were a rather cheap source of debt and they were often regarded as a deferred sale of stock at an attractive price. Both reasons are difficult to defend. Circumstances arise, however, under which it makes eminently great sense to issue either convertible securities or warrants, as, for example, when it is unusually costly to assess the risk of debt or when investors are worried that management may not act in the bondholder's interests.

Worked Examples

Problem 1

Sometime Leisure Products, Inc., issued 1 million warrants 5 years ago as part of a financing package which included $50 million of subordinated debenture bonds. The exercise prices of the warrants are $30 for the first 4 years; $35 for the next 4 years; and $40 for the final 3 years, at which time the warrants expire. The current market price of the stock is $32 for each of its outstanding 9 million shares.

1. If the common stock were split two-for-one, what adjustment in the exercise price would you expect? What if the split were five-for-three?
2. Would an adjustment in the number of shares the warrant holder may purchase provide the same results as an adjustment in the exercise price? If so, why? How much must the adjustment be?

3. What is the theoretical value of the warrant?

4. Should the warrants be exercised now?

Solution

1. A two-for-one split indicates that twice as many shares will be outstanding after the split than were outstanding before. To maintain the warrant holders' proportionate claim after the split like the one they had before it, the exercise price must be adjusted. Their claim beforehand was on one share at the price of $35. Afterward, their claim must represent two shares; so the exercise price must be cut in half to $17.50. In the case of the five-for-three split, the principles are the same. Before the split, a holder of three warrants had a claim on three shares of stock, exercisable at $35 each, making a total value of $105 (3 × $35). After the split, the value of the claim must stay the same, although the warrant holders' claim is on five shares. Thus the value of each warrant will be $21 ($105 ÷ 5).

2. Yes, the number of shares on which the warrant holders have a claim must simply always be two afterward to be equal to one before the split. So, the exercise price of $35 may be retained, but the claim should be doubled, to two shares instead of one share. In the five-for-three case, the claim is now 1.67 shares (5 ÷ 3).

3. The theoretical value of the warrant is the value it would have if it expired immediately. For $35 the warrant gives us the right to buy stock at $32—not an enormous privilege if the option expires immediately. The theoretical value is therefore zero. This provides a lower bound on how much the warrant is worth. The warrant has some value because the stock price may increase above $35 in the future.

4. If we exercise immediately, we simply lose $3. The warrant should not be exercised as long as the share price is less than the exercise price. Even when the share price is above the exercise price, to delay exercising it as long as possible usually pays, unless its value is threatened either by dividends on the stock or by an increase in the exercise price.

Problem 2

Flying Colors Airlines issued a 5½ percent convertible bond which matures 25 years from now. The conversion price is $36 and the bonds are callable at 106.25. The market price of the common stock is $42 per share.

1. What is the conversion ratio of the bonds?

2. If the conversion ratio were 33.33, what would be the conversion price?

3. At the current market price for common shares, what is the minimum price at which you would expect the bond to sell? Explain your answer.

4. If all other bonds comparable with those of Flying Colors were selling to return 10 percent, at what price would you expect the bond to be selling if it did not have the conversion feature? Assume interest is payable annually.

5. Based on your answer in 4, what part of the bond's total value is ascribable to

the value of the bond alone and what part is ascribable to the conversion feature? Explain fully.

6. Should the financial manager call the bonds? Why or why not?

Solution

1. Conversion ratio $= \dfrac{\text{face value of convertible security}}{\text{conversion price}}$

   $= \$1000/\$36 = 27.78$ shares

2. $33.33 = \$1000/\text{conversion price}$
   Conversion price $= \$1000/33.33 = \$30$

3. Conversion value of the convertible security $=$ conversion ratio $\times$ market price of common shares

   $= 27.78$ shares $\times \$42$ per share

   $= \$1166.76 = 116.68$

   In other words, one convertible bond may be exchanged for $1166.76 worth of common stock and must be worth at least this value.

4. Using present-value tables, we obtain the PV of $55 a year for 25 years and the present value of $1000 to be received at the end of the twenty-fifth year.

   $9.077 \times \$55 \quad = \$499.24$

   $\underline{0.092 \times \$1000 = \quad 92.00}$
   $\ \$591.24$

5. Conversion value of bond $\quad \$1166.76$
   Value of bond alone $\qquad\quad \underline{\ 591.24}$
   Value of conversion feature $\quad \$\ 575.53 = 5$ (at least)

6. Yes, because the price of the bond exceeds the call price.

Problem 3

One of the directors of Sometime Leisure Products, mentioned in problem 1, expressed concern about the possible dilution that will result if all the warrants are exercised. Specifically, she is concerned about the following considerations:

1. The current market value of old equity, new equity, and exercise price.
2. How much will the warrant holders' share of the new equity be worth if they are exercised immediately?
3. By how much must the old equity increase before the warrant holders are likely to exercise at a profit? The warrants currently trade at $3 each and the stock price is $32.

Solution

1. Old equity $=$ common stock $+$ warrants
   $= (9,000,000$ shares $\times \$32) + (1,000,000$ warrants $\times \$3)$

$$= \$288,000,000 + \$3,000,000$$
$$= \$291,000,000$$

New equity $=$ old equity $+$ exercise money
$$= \$291,000,000 + (\text{warrants} \times \text{exercise price})$$
$$= \$291,000,000 + (1,000,000 \times \$35)$$
$$= \$291,000,000 + \$35,000,000$$
$$= \$326,000,000$$

2. $1/10(\text{new equity}) = 1/10(\text{old equity} + \text{exercise money})$
$$= 1/10 \times \$326,000,000$$
$$= \$32,600,000$$

3. Only when

$$[(1/10 \times \text{old equity})] \text{ exceeds } [9/10(\text{exercise money})]$$

So, a point of indifference arises when they are equal, that is,

$$(1/10 \times \$291,000,000) = (9/10 \times \$35,000,000)$$

Presently,

$$\$29,100,000 < \$31,500,000$$

So the old equity must increase by more than

$$\$24,000,000 \ [= 10 \times (\$31,500,000 - \$29,100,000)]$$

Summary

Financial managers should view warrants and convertible securities in much the same way as they view options. Warrants are options just like those studied earlier in the text, except that their duration is longer and the company receives additional cash when the warrant is exercised. The convertible feature is an option held by the holder of the convertible securities.

Because these provisions may be viewed as options, the Black-Scholes option-valuation model may be used to evaluate them, provided proper adjustments for potential dilution are made. There are many differences between warrants and convertible securities, and every financial manager should trace through the implications of using either or both.

List of Terms

Bond value	**Detachable warrant**
Call premium	**Dilution**
Call price	**Exercise price**
Conversion price	**Nondetachable warrants**

Conversion ratio　**Overhanging convertibles**
Conversion value　**Warrant**
Convertible bond

Exercises

Fill-in Questions

1. A _____ gives its owner the right to buy _____ for cash, whereas a convertible security gives its owner the right to _____ the bond for stock.

2. The price at which common stocks may be purchased with warrants is called the _____.

3. A warrant which is sold originally with bonds but which may be resold apart from the bonds is called a _____ warrant.

4. If the Whozits Corporation has a number of $1000 convertible bonds outstanding, each of which is convertible into 40 shares of common stock, the (conversion ratio, conversion price) _____ is _____ dollars and the (conversion ratio, conversion price) _____ is _____ shares.

5. The value of a convertible bond depends on both its _____ and its _____.

6. The value of a convertible bond depends on both its value as a bond as if it (were, were not) _____ converted and its _____ as if the bond were converted.

7. A convertible bond which is callable at 106 percent is callable at a _____ over its face value.

Problems

1. What-Not, Inc., issued 250,000 warrants 5 years ago. The warrant exercise price is $15 and the stock's current market price is $40. There are 2.5 million shares outstanding. The warranties are about to expire.
   a. If the stock is split four-for-three, what adjustment in the exercise price is necessary to maintain the warrant holders' position?
   b. If the stock is split three-for-one, and management wishes to adjust the

number of shares the warrant holders may purchase, what adjustment is needed?

  c. What is the value of the warrant?

  d. Should the warrants be exercised?

2. How-Not, Inc., issued an 8 percent convertible subordinated debenture bond 9 years ago at a price of 99.95. The bonds mature in 20 years and contain a sinking fund which begins next year and which requires annual cash payments equal to 5 percent of the outstanding face amount of bonds. The conversion price at the time of issuance was $35 and is stepped up as follows: $40 five years after issuance, $45 ten years after issuance, and $50 thereafter. The bonds are presently callable at 105, and the common stock's current price is $55 a share.

  a. What is the bond's present conversion ratio?

  b. What is the conversion ratio in each of the other periods?

  c. At the current market price for common shares, at what price would you expect the bond to sell? Explain fully.

  d. If the market price of the common shares declined to $25 a share, and comparable bonds were selling to return 8 percent, what is the lowest price at which you would expect How-Not's bonds to sell?

  e. If the market price of the common shares were $50 and comparable bonds were selling to return 11 percent, at what price would you expect the bonds to be selling, if they did not contain the conversion feature? Assume interest is payable annually.

  f. Based on your answer in e, what part of the bond's minimum value is ascribable to the value of the bond alone and what part is ascribable to the conversion feature? Explain fully.

  g. Is it financially smart to call the bonds in, given the conditions in e above?

3. Use the data from problem 1 to answer the following questions.

  a. What is the current market value of old equity, new equity, and exercise price?

  b. How much will the warrant holders' share of the new equity be worth before they exercise?

  c. By how much must the old equity increase before the warrant holders are likely to exercise at a profit?

Essay Questions

1. How should one adjust for dilution in valuing warrants?

2. Compare the major characteristics of a convertible bond with a bond possessing a detachable warrant.

3. It has been well stated that convertible bonds have a floor or lower limit to their price. What is this floor and how is it determined? Is there also an upper bound? If so, what is it and how is it determined?

4. "The way I see it, financial managers should call in outstanding convertible bonds when their value reaches the call price. Yet, empirical evidence suggests that many financial managers don't do this. And I would like to know how come." Explain.

5. Under what conditions do convertible securities and warrants make sense? Are they really a lower cost of capital source? Do they really defer the sale of common stock?

Answers to Exercises

Fill-in Questions

1. warrant; common stock; exchange
2. exercise price
3. detachable
4. conversion price; 25; conversion ratio; 40

5. bond value; conversion value
6. were not; conversion value
7. premium

Problems

1. (a) $11.25; (b) Option is now on three shares instead of one; (c) $25; (d) Yes, because the value of old equity exceeds the exercise money.
2. (a) 25; (b) 28.57, 25.00, 22.22, 20.00; (c) $1375; (d) not much above $1000; (e) $711.04; (f) at least $663.96; (g) Yes.
3. (a) Old equity: $106,250,000; new equity: $110,000,000; exercise money: $3,750,000; (b) $10,000,000; (c) Not at all.

24 *Leasing*

Introduction

Almost all of this chapter's major points focus on financial leases, that is, leases that extend over almost all of an asset's estimated economic life and that are noncancellable by the lessee or cancellable only if the lessor is reimbursed for expected losses arising from forgone income. The list of important things to know is contained in the summary.

What to Look For in Chapter 24

The central feature of this chapter is the evaluation of a lease to determine whether and to what extent it tends to enhance the value of the firm. The decision rule which emerges is: A financial lease is superior to buying and borrowing if the financing provided by the lease exceeds the present value of the liability it creates. And therein lies the crux of the major thrust of this chapter.

Terms to Know Before you embark on an analysis of leases, you must know a variety of terms: lessor; lessee; operating leases; financial leases; full-service leases; net leases; direct leases; leveraged leases; and, if that were not enough, the sale and lease-back arrangement, to mention some.

Some Background Ideas Financial leases are studied in depth because they are a source of financing, they displace debt, and all other leases may be analyzed in exactly the same way.

On the path to determining how to analyze a lease, you discovered that sometimes it makes a difference who owns the assets: when the lease expires, the owner obtains its salvage value; when bankruptcy and reorganization occur, the lessee loses the asset's use whereas the lessor does not.

The Internal Revenue Service and the accounting profession must be given their due when structuring leases and reporting them to the investing public. Regardless of the reporting or recording method used, the value of the firm will not be materially affected if capital markets are efficient.

When Leasing Pays Typically, leasing pays when the asset is needed only for a short period, cancellation options are available, maintenance is more easily provided by a lessor, standardized and low administrative and transactions costs are better provided by the lessor, or lessors can make better use of the tax shields arising from depreciation and investment tax credits.

Evaluation The evaluation of financial leases assumes the same format as the evaluation of any other asset: the direct cash flows are discounted at a rate appropriate to the level of risk, which is typically assumed to be the firm's present borrowing rate. The present borrowing rate is used because the lease displaces debt in the company's financial structure but has no effect on the required amount of equity financing.

The beginning point in the evaluation process is to determine the equivalent loan that must be taken out to buy the equipment to be leased. Financial leases are then evaluated by one of three methods, all of which produce the same results. The three methods are: (1) comparison of the financing provided by the lease with the financing provided by the equivalent loan, (2) adjusted present value, and (3) adjusted discount rate.

Leasing versus Buying and Borrowing   Leasing is preferable to buying and borrowing when: (1) the financing generated by the lease exceeds the financing that could have been generated by an equivalent loan, (2) the lease's adjusted present value is positive, or (3) the lease's net present value is positive when computed at the adjusted discount rate.

Leasing pays only when the lessor and lessee are in different tax brackets.

Worked Examples

Problem 1

What-Not, Inc., is evaluating the lease of a mini-computer which if purchased would cost $150,000. Its estimated useful life is 5 years, at the end of which time it will be obsolete. The annual lease payments are $35,000. Set up a direct cash-flow statement. The company is in the 42 percent marginal income tax bracket. If it purchased the machine, the sum-of-the-year's-digits depreciation method would be used. The current investment tax credit is 10 percent.

Solution

What you want to do is determine, line-by-line, the cash flows in each of the years, as contained in Table 24–1.

Problem 2

If What-Not, Inc.'s borrowing rate on long-term debt is 12 percent, estimate the net present value (NPV) at 12 percent of the lease arrangement in problem 1.

Solution

Because leasing displaces debt and the riskiness of the cash flows from leasing, approximate the riskiness of the cash flows that would have been incurred had the

Table 24–1
Direct cash-flow statement of What-Not, Inc.
$000 omitted

	Year					
	0	1	2	3	4	5
Cost of new computer	+150.0					
Lost investment tax credit		−15.0				
Lease payment	−35.0	−35.0	−35.0	−35.0	−35.0	
Tax shield of lease payment		+14.7	+14.7	+14.7	+14.7	+14.7
Lost depreciation tax shield		−21.0	−16.8	−12.6	− 8.4	− 4.2
Totals	+115	−56.3	−37.1	−32.9	−28.7	+10.5

firm borrowed, the current borrowing rate appears to be the appropriate rate at which to evaluate the lease. The arithmetic is:

$$NPV = +\$115,000 - \frac{\$56,300}{1.12} - \frac{\$37,100}{(1.12)^2} - \frac{\$32,900}{(1.12)^3} - \frac{\$28,700}{(1.12)^4} + \frac{\$10,500}{(1.12)^5}$$

$$= +\$115,000 - \$50,268 - \$29,576 - \$23,418 - \$18,239 + \$5958$$

$$= -\$543$$

Remember, this *does not* give the value of the lease to What-Not, Inc., because it ignores the tax benefits associated with borrowing.

Problem 3

At the recent board of directors meeting of What-Not, Inc., one member of the board is quoted as having made the following statement: "I've been reading this book on corporate finance called, oh, what's-its-name, by these two professors, Brealey and Myers. And you know what? They claim that leasing displaces the same amount of debt as the leased asset but that it does not affect the amount of equity financing. They gave an example, but I didn't follow it too closely. But that does not matter. Assuming they are correct, I'd like the numbers produced for our firm. Until I get them, I'm not going to pass judgment on leasing that computer. No siree! And remember, we have a target debt-equity mix of 60–40."

Using the balance sheet in Table 24–2 as the starting balance sheet, demonstrate to this board member the effects of leasing as opposed to borrowing and buying.

Solution

(Remember that the symbols have the following meanings: NWC is net working capital, FA is fixed or long-term assets, D is debt, LL is lease liability, and E is equity.)

As illustrated above, the lease liability (LL) displaces an exact amount of debt (D) in order to maintain the desired mix between debt and equity. In order to accommodate that goal, $60,000 of equity must be raised and $60,000 of debt must be reduced. The total debt is $990,000 ($840,000 + $150,000), which is what it would have been had the firm borrowed. The difference between the debt found in Balance Sheet 2, Normal financing, and the debt found in Balance Sheet 3, Lease financing, is exactly equal to the amount of the lease; it is ($990,000 − $840,000) = $150,000. It is in this sense that leasing displaces debt but does not affect the amount of equity financing, for the latter remains unchanged.

Problem 4

"Okay, okay, now I see what they mean about debt displacing debt. But what I really don't understand is how this equivalent loan stuff works. It looks like it is very important on the one hand and a lot of mumble-jumble on the other hand." As the financial manager, it is your task to lead this poor babe out of the woods of ignorance. What is your response?

Solution

Begin by setting up a table similar to Table 24–3. Before you get to that point, however, you must determine how much you will need at the outset. That amount

Table 24-2
Comparison of capital structures under lease and normal financing for What-Not, Inc.
$000 omitted

Normal Financing	Lease Financing

1. Starting balance sheet

NWC	300	900	D
FA	1200	600	E
	1500	1500	

↓

Buy computer

↓

1. Starting balance sheet

NWC	300	900	D
FA	1200	600	E
	1500	1500	

↓

Lease computer

↓

2. New balance sheet

NWC	300	990	D
Computer	150		
FA	1200	660	E
	1650	1650	

2. New balance sheet

NWC	300	900	D
Computer	150	150	LL
FA	1200	600	E
	1650	1650	

3. New balance sheet after adjustment to regain target debt ratio

NWC	300	840	D
Computer	150	150	LL
FA	1200	660	E
	1650	1650	

is obtained by working back from the final number in the lower right-hand corner of the table, $10,500. The setup of the column for the fifth year goes like this. Because the $10,500 is the sum of rows 5 to 7, we can formulate the problem thus:

Table 24-3
Equivalent loan analysis
$000 omitted

	Year					
	0	1	2	3	4	5
1. Amount borrowed at year-end	126.38	78.88	47.26	17.65	0	0
2. Amount lent at year-end					9.82	0
3. Net borrowing, (1) − (2)	126.38	78.88	47.26	17.65	(9.82)	0
4. Interest paid (received) at 12 percent		15.17	9.47	5.67	2.12	(1.18)
5. Interest paid (received) after tax at 42 percent		8.80	5.49	3.29	1.23	(0.68)
6. Principal repaid		47.50	31.61	29.61	17.65	0
7. Amount lent (reduction in lending)					9.82	(9.82)
8. Net cash flow of borrowing = initial borrowing (1) − [(5) + (6) + (7)]	126.38	−56.30	−37.10	−32.90	−28.70	+10.50

$10,500 = amount lent + (amount lent)(interest rate)(1 − tax rate)

$$= \text{amount lent } [1 + (0.12)(0.58)]$$

$$= \text{amount lent } (1.0696)$$

Solving for the amount lent, we obtain $9817 or $9.82 thousand. The difference between $10.50 thousand and $9.82 thousand is the after-tax amount of interest; it is $0.68 thousand. The before-tax amount of interest is obtained by dividing the after-tax amount by (1 − tax rate) or 0.58. Doing that, the amount of $1.18 thousand is obtained. Because that represents a 12 percent return, the amount on which that interest was paid must have been $9.82 thousand ($1.18 ÷ 0.12), the amount shown in the fourth-year column.

To derive the values for the entire fourth-year column, we know that the amount required at the bottom line is −$28.70. We also know we are lending $9.82 thousand. The difference between the two is $18.88, which must be split between the after-tax interest paid and the amount of principal repaid. The solution lies in setting up the problem in this way:

$$\$18.88 = P + (P)(r)(1 - T)$$

where P = principal,
$\quad r$ = rate of interest paid, i.e., 12 percent
$\quad T$ = the firm's marginal tax rate

Substituting the proper values and solving for P, we obtain

$$\begin{aligned} P + (P)(r)(1 - T) &= \$18.88 \\ P + P(0.0696) &= \\ P(1 + 0.0696) &= \\ P(1.0696) &= \\ P &= \$17.65 \end{aligned}$$

Because the total amount involved for both interest and principal was $18.88, the interest amount must have been $1.23 thousand before taxes. After-tax interest is $2.12 thousand [($1.23 ÷ (1 − T)]. The same procedure is used to generate all the other values in the table.

As you make all these calculations, do not lose sight of why you are doing them. You want to know the equivalent loan value of the lease payments. And you must start with the initial year 0 amount that would have to be borrowed. The details are contained in Table 24–3.

Problem 5

This board member is really persistent, for now he wants you to calculate the value of the lease. And, as if that were not bad enough, he wants you to use the three methods he says Brealey and Myers use.

Solution

The first method is to compare the financing provided by the lease with the financing provided by the equivalent loan, as follows.

			Year			
	0	1	2	3	4	5
1. Cash flows from leasing	+$115,000	−$56.30	−$37.10	−$32.90	−$28.70	+$10.50
2. Cash flows of equivalent loan	+126.38	−56.30	−37.10	−32.90	−28.70	+10.50
3. Difference (1) − (2)	−11.38	0	0	0	0	0

The only difference occurs in the first period in which the loan generates $11,370 more in cash.

Adjusted-present-value method (APV) is the second method, where

APV = base-case NPV + PV of side effects resulting from undertaking the project.

The base-case NPV is evaluated at the opportunity cost of capital as if it were an all-equity-financed mini-firm. So we want to find the NPV of the after-tax cash flows of the equivalent loan. Line 8 of Table 24–3 contains the numbers we work with, and the setup of the problem is as follows:

$$\text{NPV} = +\$126.38 - \frac{\$56.30}{1.12} - \frac{\$37.10}{(1.12)^2} - \frac{\$32.90}{(1.12)^3} - \frac{\$28.70}{(1.12)^4} + \frac{\$10.50}{(1.12)^5}$$

$$= \$126.38 - \$50.27 - \$29.58 - \$23.42 - \$18.24 + \$5.96$$

$$= \$10.84 = \$10,840$$

To obtain the APV of the lease, use

APV of lease = base-case NPV − NPV of equivalent loan

$$= -\$0.54 - \$10.84 = -\$11.38$$

which is exactly the results obtained in the first method.

The third method uses adjusted discount rates.

The general formula is

NPV at adjusted discount rate = APV = NPV at opportunity cost of capital + Present value of financing side effects

To obtain an approximation to the adjusted discount rate, use Modigliani and Miller's formula:

$$r_j^* = r_j(1 - T_c L_j)$$

where r_j^* = adjusted discount rate for project j

r_j = opportunity cost of capital for this level of risk

T_c = marginal corporate tax rate

L_j = project's proportional contribution to the firm's borrowing power

In this instance L_j is the amount of debt displaced per dollar of lease liability. Assume that a dollar of lease liability displaces a dollar of debt, so that $L_j = 1$. Filling in the numbers, we obtain

$$r_j^* = 0.12[1 - (0.42)(1)]$$
$$= 0.12(1 - 0.42)$$
$$= 0.12 \times 0.58$$
$$= 0.0696 = 6.96 \text{ percent}$$

This adjusted discount rate is then used to calculate the NPV of the direct cash flows resulting from leasing. The numbers are taken from Table 24–1, and the setup is as follows:

$$\text{NPV at } 6.96\% = \$115 - \frac{\$56.3}{1.0696} - \frac{\$37.1}{(1.0696)^2} - \frac{\$32.9}{(1.0696)^3} - \frac{\$28.7}{(1.0696)^4} + \frac{\$10.5}{(1.0696)^5}$$
$$= \$115 - \$52.64 - \$32.43 - \$26.89 - \$21.93 + \$7.50$$
$$= -\$11.38$$

SURPRISE!

Summary

The analysis of leasing is best summarized by remembering the following list of important things to know about leasing.

1. The *lessor* always retains *legal ownership* of the leased *asset*.
2. The *lessee* obtains *use* of the asset.
3. Because a financial lease is equivalent to a secured loan, the legal ownership makes a difference: when the lease expires the lessor obtains the asset as well as its salvage value.
4. The legal ownership of an asset also makes a difference in bankruptcy or reorganization: a bankrupt lessee loses the use of the asset whereas a bankrupt owner does not.
5. As long as the requirements of the Internal Revenue Service and the accounting profession are satisfied, the most important financial issue is to determine whether to lease assets in the first place, a decision that can be made only after the lease is properly evaluated.
6. Financial leases are evaluated just as any other investment opportunity is, although the precise way in which that is accomplished varies because of the differences in determining the cash flows.
7. Financial leases displace debt.
8. Leasing has no effect on the required amount of equity financing.
9. The proper way by which to evaluate a lease is to compare it with a buy-and-borrow decision.
10. The decision rule is: A financial lease is superior to the buy-and-borrow alternative only if the financing provided by the lease exceeds the present value of the liability it creates.

List of Terms

Adjusted discount rate
Adjusted present value
Base-case net present value
Capital (financial, full-payout) lease
Capital leases
Direct lease
Equivalent loan
Full-service (rental) lease
Lease

Lessee (user)
Lessor (owner)
Leveraged leases
Net lease
Nonrecourse loan
Off-balance-sheet financing
Operating lease
Sale and lease-back
Tax shields

Exercises

Fill-in Questions

1. A lease is a _____ agreement that extends for a year or more and involves a series of _____ payments.

2. The user of a leased asset is called the _____, whereas the owner of a leased asset is called the _____.

3. Leases which are short-term and cancellable during the contract period at the option of the _____ are called _____ leases.

4. Leases which are long-term or extend over the economic life of the asset and which cannot be canceled or can be canceled only if the _____ is reimbursed for losses are called _____ leases.

5. When the lessors promise to maintain and insure the leased assets and pay property taxes on it, they have taken out a _____ lease.

6. When the _____ agrees to maintain the leased asset, insure it, and pay property taxes due on it, the lease is known as a net lease.

7. When the lessee identifies the equipment to be used and arranges for the leasing company to buy it from the manufacturer, the signed contract is called a _____ lease.

8. When a firm sells an asset it owns and leases it back to the buyer, the arrangement is known as _____.

9. When lessors borrow part of the purchase price of a leased asset, they use the lease contract as _____ for the loan, and the entire financing scheme is known as a _____ lease.

10. Generally accepted accounting standards no longer allow _____ financing under certain circumstances; rather lease payments of _____ leases must be _____, which is to say that the _____ of the lease payments must be estimated and shown as debt on the right-hand side of the balance sheet.

11. An _____ is one that exactly matches the lease liability, or to put it another way, one which commits the firm to exactly the same cash outlays as a lease would.

Problems

1. What-If, Inc., decided to lease additional production equipment for the next 5 years. The deal requires annual lease payments of $75,000. Had the equipment been purchased, it would have cost $325,000 and the sum-of-the-year's-digits depreciation method would have been used. The company's marginal tax bracket is 40 percent, its target debt-equity mix is 50–50, its starting balance sheet is that shown below, and the current investment tax credit is 10 percent.

Starting balance	NWC	$ 540	Debt	$ 900
sheet	FA	1260	Equity	900
$000 omitted		$1800		$1800

a. Set up a direct cash flow statement.
b. The company can issue 5-year debentures at 2 percent above the prime rate, which is presently 12 percent. Calculate the net present value of the lease.
c. What amount of debt was displaced by the lease?
d. What is the equivalent loan for this lease?
e. Calculate the value of the lease, using the three methods set forth in Brealey and Myers. Assume a dollar of lease displaces a dollar of debt.

2. What-If, Inc.'s second alternative required annual lease payments of $35,000, $40,000, $40,000, $45,000, and $250,000. Evaluate this proposal using the data from problem 1. Replicate the steps followed in problem 1 a to e.

3. A third alternative faced What-If, Inc., which was the same in all respects as that contained in problem 1 except the year-by-year lease payments are now $180,000, $75,000, $30,000, $30,000, and $30,000. Evaluate this proposal and compare it with those in problems 1 and 2. Assume all other conditions are the same.

Essay Questions

1. How can it be said that financial leases are a source of financing? Explain fully.
2. What is meant by off-balance-sheet financing?
3. In what sense may lease payments be viewed as the equivalent of interest payments, especially when viewed in terms of the financial leverage of the firm?

4. Some people say that long-term lease obligation should be regarded as debt, even though they may not appear on the balance sheet. What rationale can you give for this point of view?

5. Make a list of reasons that make leasing dubious, and provide an explanation for each item.

6. Usually the direct cash flows from the lease are assumed to be safe and are discounted at roughly the same rate of interest obtainable on a secured bond issued by the lessee. Why?

Answers to Exercises

Fill-in Questions

1. rental; fixed

2. lessee; lessor

3. lessee; operating

4. lessor; capital, financial, or full-payout

5. full-service or rental

6. lessee

7. direct

8. sale and lease-back

9. security; leveraged

10. off-balance-sheet; capital; capitalized; present value

11. equivalent loan

Problems

1. (a)

Direct cash flow statement of What-If, Inc.	Year					
	0	1	2	3	4	5
Cost of new equipment	+$325,000					
Lost investment tax credit		−$32,500				
Lease payment	−75,000	−75,000	−75,000	−75,000	−75,000	
Tax shield of lease payment		+30,000	+30,000	+30,000	+30,000	+30,000
Lost depreciation tax shield		−43,333	−34,667	−26,000	−17,333	−8,667
Totals	+$250,000	−$120,833	−$79,667	−$71,000	−$62,333	+$21,333

$$\text{(b) NPV} = +\$250,000 - \frac{\$120,833}{1.14} - \frac{\$79,667}{(1.14)^2} - \frac{\$71,000}{(1.14)^3} - \frac{\$62,333}{(1.14)^4} + \frac{\$21,333}{(1.14)^5}$$

$$= \$250,000 - \$105,994 - \$61,301 - \$47,923 - \$36,906 + 11,080$$

$$= \$8,956$$

(c)

Starting balance sheet $000 omitted	NWC	$ 540		Debt	$ 900
	FA	1260		Equity	900
		$1800			$1800

NWC	$ 540	D	1063	NWC	$ 540	D	$ 900
Equipment	325			Equipment	325	LL	325
FA	1260	E	1063	FA	1260	E	900
	$2125		$2125		$2125		$2125

Adjusted debt ratio

NWC	$ 540	D	$ 738
Equipment	325	LL	325
FA	1260	E	1063
	$2125		$2125

(d)

Equivalent loan analysis

			Year			
	0	1	2	3	4	5
1. Amount borrowed at year-end	$265,900	$167,402	$101,797	$39,348	0	0
2. Amount lent at year-end					19,680	0
3. Net borrowing (1) − (2)	265,900	167,402	101,797	39,348	(19,680)	0
4. Interest paid (received) at 14 percent		37,226	23,436	14,252	5,509	(2,755)
5. Interest paid (received) after tax		22,336	14,062	8,551	3,305	(1,653)
6. Principal repaid		98,497	65,605	62,449	39,348	0
7. Amount lent (reduction in lending)					19,680	(19,680)
8. Net cash flow [1(year 0 only)] − (5 + 6 + 7)	265,900	−120,833	−79,667	−71,000	−62,333	+21,333

(e) Value of the lease = −$15,900.

2. (a) Net cash flows are +$290,000, −$101,833, −$58,667, −$55,000, −$249,333, +$91,333. (b) NPV (at 14 percent) = $18,217; (c) Value of lease = −$16,604.

3. (a) Net cash flows are +$145,000, −$78,833, −$34,667, −$44,000, −$35,333, +$3,333. (b) NPV (at 14 percent) = $285. (c) Value of lease = −$15,133.

25 *Short-term financial planning*

Introduction

Firms finance their operations from both long- and short-term sources of capital. Usually short-term assets are financed from short-term sources of capital, and long-term assets are financed from long-term sources. The analysis of short-term assets and their financing, as well as the interconnection between short- and long-term financing are the major topics of short-term financial planning.

What to Look For in Chapter 25

The focus of this chapter is on the major classes of short-term assets and short-term liabilities, how long-term financing decisions affect short-term financial planning, and how financial managers come to grips with cash and working capital problems. The components of working capital are cash, marketable securities, accounts receivable, and inventory. Although short-term financial decisions almost always involve short-lived assets, there is a linkage between long- and short-term financing decisions because of the firm's cumulative capital requirements. Ordinarily financial managers try to obtain capital sources whose maturities coincide with the need for the funds, with permanent working capital requirements ordinarily being financed by long-term sources and temporary financial requirements being financed by temporary short-term sources.

Sources and Uses of Funds In order to trace changes in cash and working capital, usually a sources and uses of funds statement is generated, the purpose of which is to identify the major sources and uses of funds which have been used in the past so that future financial decisions may be made. Because profits and cash flows are not the same, frequently measures of short-term liquidity are used, most notably the current and quick ratios.

Cash Forecasting Forecasting future cash needs is typically encompassed in a weekly, monthly, or quarterly cash budget. The purpose of the cash budget is to indicate where there may be deficiencies or excessive cash balances. When it is anticipated that such deficiencies or excesses will result, financing decisions are more easily formulated.

Short-Term Financial Planning These financing decisions are encompassed in the short-term financial plan of the firm. For the sake of simplicity, in this chapter it was assumed that the financial manager was confronted with just a handful of short-term financing choices, namely, unsecured bank borrowing, stretching payables, and financing through a commercial finance company.

It was noted that financial planning schemes are the best guess a financial manager can make. By trial and error several iterations are made and each proposed plan is evaluated for its compatibility and costs to the enterprise as a whole. Although there are simulation and optimization schemes for short-term financial planning, all of them rely heavily on the reality of the assumptions underlying them.

Worked Examples

Problem 1

Below are the balance sheets and income statement for Up-Beat Music, Inc. Complete a statement of sources and uses of cash and sources and uses of funds for 1981.

Year-end balance sheets for Up-Beat Music, Inc. In millions

	1980	1981	Impact on sources and uses
Current assets:			
Cash	$ 15	$ 13	+ 2
Marketable securities	5	0	+ 5
Inventory	25	17	+ 8
Accounts receivable	20	35	−15
Total current assets	$ 65	$ 65	0
Fixed assets:			
Gross investment	$ 75	$ 85	−10
Less depreciation	−15	−17	+ 2
Net fixed assets	60	68	− 8
Total assets	$125	$133	− 8
Current liabilities:			
Bank loans	$ 10	$ 15	+ 5
Accounts payable	35	30	− 5
Total current liabilities	$ 45	$ 45	
Long-term debt	$ 15	$ 20	+ 5
Net worth (equity and			
retained earnings)	65	68	+ 3
Total liabilities and net worth	$125	$133	+ 8

Income statement for 1981 for Up-Beat Music, Inc. In millions

		Impact on sources and uses
Sales	$266	
Operating expenses	−245	
	$ 21	
Depreciation	− 2	+2
	$ 19	
Interest	− 3	
Pretax income	$ 16	
Tax at 50 percent	− 8	
Net income	$ 8	+8
Note: Dividend	$ 5	−5
Retained earnings	3	+3

Solution

The object of analyzing both these statements is to determine how management derived the funds and cash to finance its operations during this period. Because such information may be valuable for future financial planning, the method for composing such statements is important. To determine the sources and uses of cash, the differences between the two balance sheet dates as well as the cash generated from operations must be analyzed.

- *Step 1:* Compare the differences in each balance sheet account.
- *Step 2:* Determine whether the differences between each balance sheet increase or decrease the cash or funds of the firm.
- *Step 3:* Under the caption "Sources," list all the items which increased the amount of cash or funds. Under the caption "Uses," list all the items which decreased cash or funds.
- *Step 4:* Sum up both sources and uses.
- *Step 5:* Take the difference between sources and uses to determine the net changes in the cash position of the firm.

Applying these steps to Up-Beat Music, Inc., the right-hand column of the comparative balance sheets indicates both the amount of the changes from year to year as well as the impact each change has on the uses and sources of funds, plus or minus. These results are then summarized, as below, along with the similar pluses and minuses from the income statement.

As you review the pluses and minuses of those statements, remember this: anything that increases the sources of funds is a plus; anything that uses funds is a negative. For example, a reduction of accounts payable is a use of funds, because funds were needed to pay off the payables.

Sources and uses of funds and cash for 1981 for Up-Beat Music, Inc. In millions

Sources:	
Sold marketable securities	$ 5
Reduced inventories	8
Increased bank loans	5
Issued long-term debt	5
Cash from operations:	
Net income	8
Depreciation	2
Total sources	$33
Uses:	
Increased accounts receivable	$15
Invested in fixed assets	10
Reduced accounts payable	5
Dividend	5
Total uses	$35
Decrease cash balance	$ 2

Problem 2

What changes in net working capital took place in problem 1?

Solution

Tracing these changes in terms of their impact on net working capital results in the following statement:

Sources:	
Issued long-term debt	$ 5
Cash from operations:	
Net income	8
Depreciation	2
	$15
Uses:	
Invested in fixed assets	$10
Dividends	5
Changes in net working capital	$ 0

Because it is the difference between current assets and current liabilities, *changes* that result in net working capital stem from factors other than the current assets and short-term liabilities; they stem from long-term financing and investment decisions as well as from current operations.

Problem 3

Calculate the two most commonly used liquidity ratios for Up-Beat Music using data from problem 1.

Solution

To calculate the two most frequently used liquidity ratios for each period, we take the ratio of current assets to current liabilities to calculate the current ratio. To calculate the acid test, or quick ratio, we subtract the least liquid of all the company's short-term assets, inventories, and relate that result to the sum of the current liabilities. The ratios for the two years are as follows:

$$\text{1980} \qquad\qquad \text{1981}$$

$$\text{Current ratio} = \frac{\text{current assets}}{\text{current liabilities}}$$

$$= \frac{\$65}{\$45} \qquad\qquad = \frac{\$65}{\$45}$$

$$= 1.44 \qquad\qquad = 1.44$$

$$\text{Quick ratio} = \frac{\text{current assets less inventories}}{\text{current liabilities}}$$

$$= \frac{\$65 - \$25}{\$45} \qquad\qquad = \frac{\$65 - \$17}{\$45}$$

$$= \frac{\$40}{\$45} \qquad\qquad = \frac{\$48}{\$45}$$

$$= 0.89 \qquad\qquad = 1.07$$

Problem 4

The following is the 1982 sales forecast for Up-Beat Music, Inc.:

	Quarter			
	First	Second	Third	Fourth
Sales in millions	$92.5	$80.5	$135.8	$165.2

Use the following assumptions to construct a cash budget for the company:

1. 85 percent of sales are realized in cash in the quarter sales are made.
2. The remaining 15 percent of sales are collected in cash in the following quarter.
3. The sales prior to the forecasted first quarter were $88.3 million.
4. Receivables carried into the first quarter were $17 million.
5. Accounts payable are to be paid on time.
6. All labor and administrative expenditures are paid when due.
7. The capital expenditures are those indicated in the budget below.
8. The firm's financial manager feels "comfortable" with a cash cushion of $10 million.

Solution

Your task is to complete the cash budget for 1982. You accomplish this task in the following steps:

1. Formulate a statement of expected receivables.
2. Formulate a cash budget in which the expected cash sources and cash uses are combined, with the end result being an estimate of the deficiency or excess of cash in each quarter.

Forecast of sales, collection rates, and accounts receivable of Up-Beat Music, Inc. In millions

		First quarter	Second quarter	Third quarter	Fourth quarter
1.	Receivables at start of period	$17.000	$17.630	$ 15.830	$ 24.125
2.	Sales	92.500	80.500	135.800	165.200
	Collections:				
	Sales in current period (85 percent)	78.625	68.425	115.430	140.420
	Sales in last period (15 percent)	13.245[a]	13.875	12.075	20.370
3.	Total collections	$91.870	$82.300	$127.505	$160.790
4.	Receivables at end of period, (4) = (1 + 2 − 3)	$17.630	$15.830	$ 24.125	$ 28.535

[a] Sales in the fourth quarter of 1981 were $88.3 million.

To construct the 1982 cash budget, data from both the foregoing statement of sales, collections, and accounts receivable and from the assumptions made above are needed.

Up-Beat Music, Inc.'s 1982 Cash Budget In millions		First quarter	Second quarter	Third quarter	Fourth quarter
Sources of cash:					
	Collections on accounts receivable	$ 91.870	$82.300	$127.505	$160.790
	Other	6.000	10.000	0.0	0.0
Total sources		$ 98.870	$92.300	$127.505	$160.790
Uses of cash:					
	Payments on accounts payable	$ 84.000	$36.000	$ 48.000	$ 80.000
	Labor, administrative, and other expenses	35.000	35.000	35.000	35.000
	Capital expenditures	20.000	10.000	0.0	0.0
	Taxes, interest, and dividends	9.000	9.000	9.000	9.000
Total uses		$148.000	$90.000	$ 92.000	$124.000
Sources minus uses		− 50.130	2.300	35.505	36.790

Calculation of short-term financing requirements		First quarter	Second quarter	Third quarter	Fourth quarter
1.	Cash at start of period	$ 13.000	−$37.130	−$34.830	0.675
2.	Change in cash balance (sources less uses)	−50.130	2.300	35.505	36.790
3.	Cash at end of period (1 + 2 = 3)	−37.130	−34.830	0.675	37.465
4.	Minimum operating cash balance	10.000	10.000	10.000	10.000
5.	Cumulative short-term financing requirement (5 = 4 − 3)	−47.130	−44.830	9.325	27.465

Summary

Short-term financial planning is best understood by working through some problems. When doing so, however, remember that cash budgeting is central to the planning process, for it is the forecast of needed cash for the planning period. Knowing what sources of capital were employed in the past and how the capital was deployed in the past is valuable to financial planning. Usually it is wise financial management to match the need for permanent capital with permanent capital sources, and temporary needs should be financed from temporary sources.

List of Terms

Accounts receivable
Cash budgeting
Compensating balance
Current ratio
Line of credit
Marketable securities
Net working capital
Permanent working capital
Quick ratio
Sources and uses of cash
Sources and uses of funds
Working capital

Exercises

Fill-in Questions

1. Working capital consists of _____ and _____, whereas net working capital is the difference between _____ and _____.

2. The planned-for permanent level of net working capital is called _____.

3. The ratio of all the current assets to the current liabilities is called the _____ ratio, whereas the quick ratio relates _____ less _____ to current liabilities.

4. In order to make up a cash budget, _____ must be forecasted.

5. A prearranged maximum borrowing capability at specified interest rates is known as a _____.

6. Not paying bills when they are due in order to finance short-term operations is called _____.

Problems

1. Work out a short-term financial plan for Up-Beat Music, Inc. Use the data from the worked examples.

2. Using the balance sheets and income statement below for Up-Beat Music, Inc., work out a complete sources and uses of cash and a sources and uses of funds statement for 1982.

Year-end balance sheets for Up-Beat Music, Inc. In millions

	1981	1982
Current assets:		
Cash	$ 13	$ 2
Marketable securities	0	5
Inventory	17	22
Accounts receivable	35	48
Total current assets	$ 65	$ 77
Fixed assets:		
Gross investment	$ 85	$ 85
Less depreciation	−17	−19
Net fixed assets	$ 68	$ 66
Total assets	$133	$143
Current liabilities:		
Bank loans	$ 15	$ 13
Accounts payable	30	37
Total current liabilities	$ 45	$ 50
Long-term debt	$ 20	$ 18
Net worth (equity and retained earnings)	$ 68	$ 75
Total liabilities and net worth	$133	$143

Income statement for 1982 for Up-Beat Music, Inc. In millions	Sales	$320
	Operating expenses	−289
		$ 31
	Depreciation	−2
		$ 29
	Interest	− 3
	Pretax income	$ 26
	Tax at 50 percent	13
	Net income	$ 13
	Cash dividends	$ 6

3. Using the data for 1982 contained in problem 2, answer the following:
   a. The company's current liabilities were _____.
   b. The company's current assets were _____.
   c. The company's current ratio was _____.
   d. The company's quick ratio was _____.
   e. The company's net working capital was _____.

4. If the rate of return obtainable on the marketable securities portfolio of Up-Beat Music, Inc., in problem 2 is 9 percent, demonstrate that the net present value of that investment is, at best, zero.

5. Up-Beat Music, Inc.'s revised 1982 sales forecast is as follows:

	Quarter			
	First	Second	Third	Fourth
Sales in millions	$85	$75	$100	$150

Assumptions:

1. 87 percent of sales are realized as cash in the quarter in which they are made.
2. The remaining 13 percent of sales are collected as cash in the following quarter.
3. Sales prior to the first quarter of this forecasting period were $130.
4. Receivables carried into the first quarter were $17 million.
5. All accounts payable are paid when due.
6. All labor and administrative expenses are paid when due.
7. Capital expenditures of $15 million and $5 million will be made in the first and third quarters.
8. The firm's financial manager has changed her comfort level of cash to $8 million.

Complete the cash budget for 1982—found at the top of page 242—and work out a financing scheme for Up-Beat Music, Inc.

Essay Questions

1. What is meant by matching maturities?
2. What rationale can you give for the statement, "We think that firms with a *permanent* cash surplus ought to go on a diet!"

1982 cash budget for Up-Beat Music, Inc. In millions	First quarter	Second quarter	Third quarter	Fourth quarter
Sources of cash:				
Collections				
Other	$ 5.00	$ 6.00	$ 7.00	$10.00
Uses of cash:				
Accounts payable	72.00	63.00	76.00	84.00
Labor, administrative, and other expenses	42.00	42.00	42.00	42.00
Capital expenditures				
Taxes, interest, and dividends	19.00	19.00	19.00	19.00
Total uses				
Sources minus uses				
Short-term financing requirements:				
Cash at start of period				
Change in cash balance				
Cash at the end of period				
Minimum operating cash balance				
Cumulative short-term financing requirement				

3. How might a financial manager trace changes in cash and working capital?
4. Put in words the value of a cash budget. Do you see the value of a cash budget applying to yourself?
5. What impact does a compensating balance have on (1) the cost of bank borrowings and (2) the amount that must be borrowed?

Answers to Exercises

Fill-in Questions

1. current assets (and) current liabilities; current assets; current liabilities
2. permanent working capital
3. current; current assets; inventories
4. sales
5. line of credit
6. stretching payables

Problems

1. Several schemes may be developed, although each of them must provide for covering the deficits developed in the cash budget.
2. From the balance sheet:

Cash	−11
Marketable securities	+ 5
Inventory	+ 5
Accounts receivable	+13
Total current assets	+12
Gross investment	0
Depreciation	+ 2
Net fixed assets	+ 2
Total assets	+10
Bank loans	− 2
Accounts payable	+ 7
Total current liabilities	+ 5

Long-term debt	− 2
Net worth	+ 7
Total liabilities and net worth	+10

From the income statement:

Depreciation	+ 2
Net income	+13
Cash dividends	− 6
Retained earnings	+ 7

Sources and uses of funds and cash:

Sources:	
Depreciation	2
Net income	13
Increased accounts payable	7
Total sources	$22
Uses:	
Bought marketable securities	$ 5
Increased inventories	5
Increased receivables	13
Decreased bank loans	2
Reduced long-term debt	2
Dividends	6
Total uses	$33
Reduction in cash	$11

3. (a) $50; (b) $77; (c) 1.54; (d) 1.10; (e) $27

4. Because shareholders may invest at the 9 percent rate, it is that rate that is used as the opportunity cost of capital. Then calculate the net present value of the *stockholders'* investment, assuming that the 9 percent rate is available in perpetuity.

$$\text{NPV} = -\$5,000,000 + \frac{\$450,000}{.09} = 0$$

This is the *best* that can happen, and corporate tax may give the investment a negative NPV.

5.

Financing scheme for Up-Beat Music, Inc. In millions	First quarter	Second quarter	Third quarter	Fourth quarter
Receivables at start of period	$ 17.00	$ 11.15	$ 9.85	$ 13.10
Sales	85.00	75.00	100.00	150.00
Collections				
Sales in current period	73.95	65.25	87.00	130.50
Sales in last period	16.90	11.05	9.75	13.00
Total collections	90.85	76.30	96.75	143.50

	First quarter	Second quarter	Third quarter	Fourth quarter
Receivables at end of period	$ 11.15	$ 9.85	$ 13.10	$ 19.60
Sources of cash:				
Collections	$ 90.85	$ 76.30	$ 96.75	$143.50
Other	5.00	6.00	7.00	10.00
Total sources	95.85	82.30	103.75	153.50
Uses of cash:				
Accounts payable	72.00	63.00	76.00	84.00
Labor, administrative and other expenses	42.00	42.00	42.00	42.00
Capital expenditures	15.00		5.00	
Taxes, interest, and dividends	19.00	19.00	19.00	19.00
Total uses	$148.00	$124.00	$142.00	$145.00
Sources minus uses	−$ 52.15	−$ 41.70	−$ 38.25	$ 8.50
Short-term financing requirements:				
Cash at start of period	2.0	− 50.15	− 91.85	−130.10
Change in cash balance	−52.15	−41.70	− 38.25	8.50
Cash at end of period	−50.15	−91.85	−130.10	−121.60
Minimum operating cash balance	8.0	8.0	8.0	8.0
Cumulative short-term financing requirement	−$ 58.15	−$ 99.85	−$138.10	−$129.60

It should be obvious that if the present conditions persist, permanent additions to working capital are in order. Chances are retained earnings or a stock sale is best for this company. Short-term financing does not seem to be in order because of the seeming chronic deficiency in cash flows.

26 *Credit management*

Introduction

As you study the nuts-and-bolts issues of credit management, remember that no clear-cut, scientific guidelines by which to make credit decisions exist. Reasonably sound financial decisions, however, will result if financial managers follow these steps: (1) determine the terms of sale, (2) determine the creditworthiness of customers, (3) determine how much credit should be extended to each customer, and (4) monitor each account after credit has been extended.

What to Look For in Chapter 26

As you study this chapter, look for the four considerations outlined in the preceding sections.

Terms of Sale   The terms of sale indicate the method by which customers pay for goods and services. Most goods and services are sold on credit, usually with a cash discount being offered if payment is received within a short period of time, but with the entire amount nonetheless due at the end of a specified time period. A variety of commercial credit instruments expedite the terms of sale. The chief commercial credit instrument is the open account, which is simply a record on the books of the firm indicating that credit has been extended. A variety of other credit instruments is used depending on the particular circumstances.

Credit Analysis   Ordinarily credit analysis precedes credit extension. To that end, financial managers may hire the services of a credit agency, such as Dun and Bradstreet, but that may not be enough. Financial ratio analysis is another method of checking customers' creditworthiness. This technique uses the data contained in financial statements to estimate the likely bill-paying ability of customers. Yet another method of analyzing the creditworthiness of customers is numerical credit scoring and risk indexes. Risk indexes often utilize highly sophisticated tools to set a minimum numerical screen or threshold which every customer must meet.

The Credit Decision   After the forgoing steps have been taken, the credit decision is made. In essence every credit decision estimates the present value of the difference between revenues to be received and cost expended from credit sales. The revenue and the cost must each be weighed by their probability of occurrence.

No credit manager can pursue the credit search without limit; after all, there is a cost of searching for additional information. Usually the probability of default as well as the size of the order, when compared with the gain from not extending credit, form the bases for the analysis. Repeat orders, however, in no instant may be ignored without hazard. To cultivate prospective business the financial manager must look beyond the immediate order in hand.

Credit Policy   A reasonable credit policy will be based on three general principles. First, the object of the credit manager, as it is with all managers, is to maximize expected profits and not to minimize the number of bad accounts. Second, credit managers should concentrate their efforts on those accounts most likely to pose a threat to the financial welfare of the firm, either because of their size or because of their doubtful paying ability. Third, repeat orders must be factored into the overall decision because they have a bearing on the total sales and production ability of the firm.

Collection Policy   After credit has been extended, a collection policy must be enforced. By aging accounts receivables those which are delinquent, and the extent to which they are delinquent, may be identified and appropriate measures taken. Another method of collecting accounts receivable is to sell them outright to firms that specialize in this practice. Factors, as they are called, may absorb the entire credit-collection function or parts of it, for a fee. To further assure that accounts receivable will be collected, credit insurance may be bought

Financial Ratio Analysis   Financial ratio analysis was discussed in Appendix B. Even though financial ratio analysis concentrates more on book values than on market values, overall it seems to have been a fairly good predictor of financial troubles. Usually there are more ratios available for calculation than it is feasible to do. All of them, however, may be compartmentalized in terms of the specific functions they are intended to perform. For example, ratios, which measure the overall financial leverage of the enterprise, focus on the total amount of long-term debt, the amount of interest payable, the operating leverage, and earnings variability of the firm.

A second set of ratios focuses on the firm's short-term assets and liabilities and liquidity. The object of all short-term liquidity ratios is to determine the extent to which a firm *may* have sufficient cash or other short-term assets on hand to pay off its short-term liabilities.

The third and final set of ratios focuses on the operational efficiency of the firm, because, so the story goes, a firm which is operationally efficient is more likely to pay its bills on time than one that is not.

Ordinarily financial ratios are neither to be assessed independently of each other nor necessarily related simply to industry averages. Rather all ratios are interdependent and should be reviewed over time as well as with respect to industry averages. Because they seem to possess some power to predict financial distress, it is precisely this intuitive feel for the financial integrity of a potential customer that financial ratios try to capture.

Worked Examples

Problem 1

Find the effective annual cost of forgoing taking cash discounts for each of the following terms of sale: 2/10, *n*/30; 5/20, *n*/45; 2/10, *n*/60; 5/20, *n*/60.

Solution

The object is first to determine the effective cost of the loan arising from not taking the cash discount. For convenience let's deal in increments of $100 of sales and let's take the case of 2/10, n/30. Recognize that the first 10 days you obtain a "free ride," on the seller's credit, although it is not cost-free, the cost of the free ride most probably being built into the sale price. Also note that if you do not take the cash discount, in effect you are borrowing the difference between the total amount billed, $100, and the amount of the cash discount, $2, which, of course is $98; it costs you $2 each time you borrow the $98. You are borrowing the $98 for 20 days. If you repeat this process throughout the year, you will borrow 18.25 times because there are 18.25, 20-day periods in a 365-day year (365 ÷ 20). (Sometimes for convenience and by convention, a 360-day year is used.)

Now for the calculations. The cost of the 20-day, $2 loan is

Per period
cost of loan = dollar cash discount/dollar amount of loan

$$= \$2/\$98$$

$$= 0.0204 = 2.04 \text{ percent}$$

You are paying 2.04 percent for each of the 18.25 periods. The effective annual cost is the compound return on the 2.04 percent, namely,

Effective annual cost
of not taking a cash
discount

$$= [(1 + \text{per period rate})^{\text{number of periods per year}} - 1] \times 100$$

$$= [(1 + 0.0204)^{18.25} - 1] \times 100$$

$$= [(1.0204)^{18.25} - 1] \times 100$$

$$= (1.4456 - 1) \times 100$$

$$= 0.4456 \times 100 = 44.56$$

which is very expensive money by anyone's standards. Note that it is incorrect to estimate the cost of not taking the discount by merely estimating the cost as 2 percent ($2 ÷ $100) and multiplying that by the number of periods to obtain an answer of 36.5 percent (2 percent × 18.25), because that procedure ignores the effective amount that is borrowed and the compounding effect of the forgone interest.

The calculations for the other terms of sale are as follows:
5/20, n/45:

Per period
cost of loan = $5/$95

$$= 5.26 \text{ percent}$$

Effective
annual cost $= [(1.0526)^{(365 \div 25)} - 1] \times 100$

$$= [(1.0526)^{14.6} - 1] \times 100$$

$$= (2.1137 - 1) \times 100 = 111.37 \text{ percent}$$

2/10, *n*/60:

Per period
cost of loan $= \$2/\$98$

$= 2.04$ percent

Effective
annual cost $= [(1.024)^{(365 \div 50)} - 1] \times 100$

$= [(1.0204)^{7.3} - 1] \times 100$

$= (1.15884 - 1) \times 100 = 15.88$ percent

5/20, *n*/60:

Effective
annual cost $= [(1 + \text{per period cost})^{(\text{number of periods})} - 1] \times 100$

$= [(1 + 0.0526)^{(365 \div 40)} - 1] \times 100$

$= [(1.0526)^{9.125} - 1] \times 100$

$= (1.5964 - 1) \times 100$

$= 0.5964 \times 100 = 59.64$ percent

Problem 2

Use Altman's multiple discriminant analysis results to estimate the Z-scores for each of the firms listed below.

	A	B	C	D
EBIT	$200	$ 600	$ 50	$ 5
Total assets	400	400	400	400
Sales	400	1900	1200	200
Market price per share	20	100	50	5
Number of shares	100	100	100	100
Book value of debt	100	100	100	100
Retained earnings	50	100	25	50
Working capital	100	200	10	10

Solution

The setup for this answer is as follows:

$Z = 3.3(\text{EBIT/total assets}) + 1.0(\text{sales/total assets}) + 0.6(\text{market value of equity/book value of debt}) + 1.4(\text{retained earnings/total assets}) + 1.2(\text{working capital/total assets})$

The solution for firm A is

$Z = 3.3(\text{EBIT/total assets}) + 1.0(\text{sales/total assets}) + 0.6(\text{market value of equity/book value of debt}) + 1.4(\text{retained earnings/total assets}) + 1.2 (\text{working capital/total assets})$

$$3.3(\$200/\$400) + 1.0(\$400/\$400) + 0.6[(\$20 \times 100)/\$100)] +$$
$$1.4(\$50/\$400) + 1.2(\$100/\$400)$$

$$= (3.3)(0.5) + (1.0)(1.0) + (0.6)(20) + (1.4)(0.125) + (1.2)(0.25)$$

$$= 1.65 + 1 + 12 + 0.175 + 0.3$$

$$= 15.125$$

For firms B, C, and D the solutions are:

Firm B:

$$Z = 3.3(\$600/\$400) + 1.0(\$1900/\$400) + 0.6[(\$100 \times 100)/\$100] +$$
$$1.4(\$100/\$400) + 1.2(\$200/\$400)$$

$$= 4.95 + 4.75 + 60 + 0.35 + 0.6$$

$$= 70.65$$

Firm C:

$$Z = 3.3(\$50/\$400) + 1.0(\$1200/\$400) + 0.6[(\$50 \times 100)/\$100] +$$
$$1.4(\$25/\$400) + 1.2(\$10/\$400)$$

$$= 0.4125 + 3.0 + 30.0 + 0.0875 + 0.03$$

$$= 33.53$$

Firm D:

$$Z = 0.04125 + 0.5 + 3.0 + 0.175 + 0.03$$

$$= 3.74625$$

Problem 3

What-Not, Inc.'s credit manager studied the bill-paying habits of its customers and discovered that 92 percent of them were prompt payers and 8 percent were slow payers. The records also showed that 18 percent of the slow payers and 3 percent of the prompt payers subsequently defaulted. The company now has 1500 accounts on its books, none of which has yet defaulted. What is the total number of expected defaults, assuming no repeat business is on the horizon?

Solution

To solve this problem, first categorize the number of prompt and slow payers. They are

Prompt payers = $1500 \times 0.92 = 1380$

Slow payers $\;\;= 1500 \times 0.08 = \;\;120$

Next multiply the probability of default for each class to obtain the expected number for each class.

Prompt payers: $1380 \times 0.03 = 41.4$

Slow payers: $\;120 \times 0.18 = \dfrac{21.6}{63.0}$

A total of 63 accounts (4.2 percent of the total) may be expected to default.

Problem 4

Given the data in problem 3, revenues from sales of $2000, and cost of the sales of $1740, what is the expected profit (loss) from extending credit to slow payers? Should credit be extended to both slow and prompt payers, regardless?

Solution

$$\text{Expected profit} = p \times \text{PV (revenues} - \text{cost}) - (1 - p)(\text{cost})$$

$$= 0.82(\$2000 - \$1740) - 0.18(\$1740)$$

$$= \$213 - \$313$$

$$= -\$100$$

Clearly, at this level of credit it is not profitable to extend credit to slow payers.

Problem 5

Estimate how much What-Not would have to increase prices to make it just worthwhile to extend credit to slow payers in problem 4.

Solution

This problem is solved by setting the entire equation equal to zero and solving for revenues. The answer is

$$0.82 \text{ (revenues} - \$1740) - \$313 = 0$$

$$0.82 \text{ revenues} - \$1740 = 0$$

$$0.82 \text{ revenues} = \$1740$$

$$\text{Revenues} = \$2122$$

At average revenues of about $2122, a price increase of 6.1 percent, the firm is likely to just break even from extending credit to all customers.

Problem 6

Is it worthwhile for the credit manager of What-Not, Inc., to engage in a credit search to determine whether customers are slow or prompt payers if the cost of search is $12, the probability of identifying a slow payer is 0.02, and the expected loss from a slow payer is $100?

Solution

To answer this, set up the problem in this way

Expected payoff from credit check = probability of identifying a slow payer × gain from not extending credit − cost of credit check

$$= (0.02 \times \$100) - \$12$$

$$= \$2 - \$12 = -\$10$$

It is not worthwhile to engage in the credit check.

Problem 7

At what level of sales per customer would the credit manager in problem 6 be indifferent?

Solution

If the expected loss from a slow payer were six times as large, the credit check pays. This occurs when a customer requires credit amounting to $12,000 or more (6 × $2000). Seems to be a mighty high level for a cost of $12, doesn't it?

Problem 8

We expect that one of our slow-paying customers in problems 3–7 will subsequently place a repeat order. If the customer pays on the first order, we estimate a probability of 0.95 of no default on the second order. How do we evaluate the original extension of credit?

Solution

Let's take this in steps. First, calculate the expected profit on the initial order.

$$\text{Expected profit on initial order} = p_1 \times \text{PV (revenues} - \text{cost)} - (1 - p_1) \text{ PV (cost)}$$

$$= (0.82 \times \$260) - (0.18 \times \$1740)$$

$$= \$100$$

Second:

$$\text{Next year's expected profit on repeat order} = p_2 - \text{PV (revenues} - \text{cost)} - (1 - p_2) \text{ PV (cost)}$$

$$= (0.95 \times \$260) - (0.05 \times \$1740)$$

$$= \$247 - \$87$$

$$= \$160$$

Third:

$$\text{Total expected profit} = \text{expected profit on initial order} + \text{probability of payment and repeat order} \times \text{PV of next year's expected profit on repeat order}$$

$$= \$100 + 0.82 \text{ PV (\$160)}$$

Fourth, assuming investments of comparable risk are expected to return 10 percent, the total expected profit (present value) is

$$\text{Total expected profit} = -\$100 + \frac{(0.82)(\$160)}{1.1}$$

$$= -\$100 + \$119$$

$$= \$19$$

Problem 9

Make a thorough financial ratio analysis of the balance sheets and income statements of Universal Paperclips, Inc.

Assets	December 1980	December 1979
Cash and marketable securities	$ 100	$ 75
Accounts receivable	350	300
Inventories	600	650
Current assets	$1050	$1025
Gross fixed assets	1000	800
Less accumulated depreciation	400	350
Net fixed assets	$ 600	$ 450
Total assets	$1650	$1475

Liabilities	December 1980	December 1979
Bank loans and notes payable	$ 100	$ 60
Accounts payable	350	275
Current liabilities	$ 450	$ 335
Long-term debt	375	400
Common stock	200	200
Surplus	625	540
Total stockholders' equity	$ 825	$ 740
Total liabilities	$1650	$1475

Year Ended December 1980	
Sales	$3465
Cost of goods sold	2252
Selling, administrative, and general expenses	346
Depreciation	173
Earnings before interest and tax (EBIT)	694
Interest	35
Earnings before tax	659
Income taxes	320
Earnings after tax	339
Common dividends	254
Retained earnings	85

Solution

The beginning of a thorough analysis lies with the set of ratios contained in Appendix B of the chapter.

1. Leverage indicators

    a. Financial leverage = long-term debt/(long-term debt + equity)

$$= \$375/(\$375 + \$825)$$

$$= \$375/\$1200 = 0.3125 = 31.2 \text{ percent}$$

or

Debt-equity ratio = long-term debt/equity

$$= \$375/\$825$$

$$= 0.45454 = 45.5 \text{ percent}$$

b. Times interest earned = EBIT/interest

$$= \$694/\$35$$

$$= 19.8 \text{ times}$$

c. Earnings variability: To calculate this ratio, we need to know past earnings (EBIT). Say they were $580, $602, $690, $640, $574, $660, and $655, for the years 1973–1979. The standard deviation of earnings changes, including 1980, is $56.3, and the average is $637. The relative earnings variability may then be presented as the ratio of the standard deviation to the mean, which is called the coefficient of variation CV.

$$CV = \$56.3/\$637 = 0.0883 = 8.83 \text{ percent}$$

d. Operating leverage $= \dfrac{\text{percent change in EBIT}}{\text{percent change in sales}}$

To calculate this we need to know both changes in sales and in EBIT. Say past sales were $3010, $3100, $3430, $3240, $3040, $3350, $3330, and $3465 for the years from 1973. This gives the following percentage changes in sales and EBIT.

Changes in sales	2.99	10.65	−5.54	−6.17	10.20	−0.60	4.05
Changes in EBIT	3.79	14.62	−7.25	−10.31	14.98	−0.76	5.95

The line of best fit is

Percent change in EBIT $= -0.22 + (1.45 \times$ percent change in sales), $(R^2 = 0.99)$

which gives an estimate of 1.45 for operating leverage.

2. Liquidity Indicators

e.

Net working capital to total assets $= \dfrac{\text{current assets} - \text{current liabilities}}{\text{total assets}}$

$$= (\$1050 - \$450)/\$1650$$

$$= \$600/\$1650$$

$$= 0.3636 = 36.4 \text{ percent}$$

f.

Current ratio = current assets ÷ current liabilities

$$= \$1050 \div \$450$$

$$= 2.33 \text{ times}$$

g.

$$\text{Quick (acid-test) ratio} = \frac{\text{current assets} - \text{inventories}}{\text{current liabilities}}$$

$$= (\$1050 - \$600)/\$450$$

$$= \$450/\$450$$

$$= 1.0 \text{ times}$$

h.

$$\text{Cash ratio} = \frac{\text{cash} + \text{marketable securities}}{\text{current liabilities}}$$

$$= \$100/\$450$$

$$= 0.22 \text{ times}$$

3. Efficiency indicators

i.

$$\text{Sales to total assets} = \text{sales/average total assets}$$

$$= \$3465/[(\$1650 + \$1475) \div 2]$$

$$= \$3465/\$1562.5$$

$$= 2.22 \text{ times}$$

j.

$$\text{Sales to net working capital} = \text{sales/average net working capital}$$

$$= \$3465/[(\$600 + \$690) \div 2]$$

$$= \$3465/\$645$$

$$= 5.37 \text{ times}$$

k.

$$\text{Return on total assets} = \frac{\text{EBIT} - \text{taxes}}{\text{average total assets}}$$

$$\text{Return on total assets} = (\$694 - \$320)/[(\$1650 + \$1475) \div 2]$$

$$= \$374/\$1562.5$$

$$= 0.23936 = 23.94 \text{ percent}$$

l.

$$\text{Return on equity} = \frac{\text{earnings available for common}}{\text{average common equity}}$$

$$\text{Return on equity} = \$339/[(\$825 + \$740) \div 2]$$

$$= \$339/\$782.5$$

$$= 0.4332 = 43.32 \text{ percent}$$

m.

$$\text{Net profit margin} = \frac{\text{EBIT} - \text{taxes}}{\text{sales}}$$

$$= (\$694 - \$320)/\$3465$$

$$= \$374/\$3465$$

$$= 0.1079 = 10.79 \text{ percent}$$

n.

$$\text{Inventory turnover} = \frac{\text{cost of goods sold}}{\text{average inventory}}$$

$$= \$2252/[(\$600 + \$650) \div 2]$$

$$= \$2252/\$625$$

$$= 3.60 \text{ times}$$

o.

$$\text{Average collection period} = \frac{\text{average receivables}}{\text{average daily sales}}$$

$$= [(\$350 + \$300) \div 2]/(\$3465 \div 365 \text{ days})$$

$$= \$325/\$9.49 \text{ per day}$$

$$= 34.25 \text{ days}$$

The above ratios do not provide us with a definitive statement concerning the financial soundness of the firm, but the credit managers never know with certainty the financial soundness of any firm to which they extend credit. Some observations may be made, however. First, the leverage appears acceptable, although earnings have fluctuated quite a bit around their positive trend. Second, by generally accepted standards the liquidity ratios are satisfactory. So are the efficiency indicators.

But this analysis would be more enlightening if data for comparable firms and for this firm for several past periods were available.

Summary

Because credit is often a substantial part of the grease that makes the machinery of business firms run, credit management looms large in most firms. Determining reasonable terms of sale, evaluating the creditworthiness of customers, estimating the probabilities of being paid, and establishing a credit policy that includes maximizing profits and scrutinizing accounts most likely to fail, and repeat orders that add value to the firm, are all the stuff of sound credit management.

List of Terms

Aging of receivables	**Commercial draft**
Banker's acceptances	**Credit insurance**
Cash discount	**Factor**

Multiple discriminant analysis   Progress payments
Open account credit   Terms of sale

Exercises

Fill-in Questions

1. _____ are often used to induce customers to pay their bills before the end of the free payment period.

2. When the credit terms are 2/10, $n/30$, this means that customers are entitled to a _____ percent cash discount provided they pay within the first _____ days, but in any event the entire bill must be paid in _____ days.

3. A financial manager who fails to take a cash discount on terms of 2/10, $n/30$ incurs an effective annual cost of _____ percent.

4. Granting credit depends on whether the _____ profit from doing so is greater than the _____ profit from refusing.

5. If the probability of identifying a slow-paying customer is 0.06, the customer places an order of $60, and the gain that results from not extending the credit is $7, the expected payoff of the credit check is _____ .

6. If the probability of detecting a slow payer is 0.07 and a customer places an order for $500, and the gain from not extending credit is $18, the expected payoff from the credit check is _____ .

7. Ordinarily a credit manager (does, does not) _____ subject each customer to the same credit analysis. Rather, efforts should be concentrated on the (large, small) _____ and doubtful orders.

8. A firm, usually part of a commercial bank, which purchases accounts receivable is called a _____ .

9. The times-interest-earned ratio relates _____ to _____ .

10. Fixed financial costs give rise to _____ , whereas fixed operating costs give rise to _____ .

11. The difference between current assets and current liabilities is known as _____ .

12. The evidence suggests that firms that fail had (higher, lower) _____ returns on sales and assets, (less, more) _____ cash, (less, more) _____ receivables, and (less, more) _____ inventory than most firms that did not.

Problems

1. Find the effective annual cost of not taking the cash discounts on the following terms of trade: 3/10, n/30; 3/10, n/45; 3/10, n/60; 4/10, n/30; 5/10, n/30; 6/10, n/30. What general phenomena seem to be at work?

2. Use Altman's multiple discriminant analysis to estimate the Z-scores for each of the following companies:

	1	2	3	4
EBIT	$ 200	$ 400	$ 600	$ 800
Total assets	1000	1200	1400	1600
Sales	2000	2400	2800	3200
Market price per share	40	48	56	64
Number of shares	50	100	150	200
Book value of debt	400	500	600	700
Retained earnings	400	500	600	700
Working capital	600	600	600	600

3. If-Not, Inc.'s credit manager studied the bill-paying habits of its customers and found that 90 percent of them were prompt payers and the remainder were slow payers. She also discovered that 22 percent of the slow payers and 5 percent of the prompt payers subsequently defaulted. The company has 2000 accounts on its books, none of which has yet defaulted. Calculate the total number of expected defaults, assuming no repeat business is on the horizon.

4. Given the data in problem 3, revenues from sales of $1300, and the cost of sales of $1100, what is the expected profit or loss from extending credit to slow payers?

5. Estimate the average level of revenues that makes it just worthwhile to extend credit to slow payers in problem 4.

6. Is it worthwhile for the credit manager of If-Not, Inc., to engage in a credit search to determine whether customers are slow or prompt payers if the cost of each search is $11, the probability of identifying slow payers is 0.06, and the expected cost of a slow payer is $55? Show all calculations.

7. At what sales level would the credit manager in problem 6 be indifferent? Show all calculations.

8. Say there is a 0.92 probability that a repeat customer of If-Not, Inc., will not default. How should the credit manager evaluate the original extension of credit to a customer who has been identified as a slow payer but also as certain to place a repeat order?

9. The following are the financial statements of If-Not, Inc. Make a complete financial ratio analysis of them and comment on the message they give.

Balance Sheets of If-Not, Inc. (December 31)		1980	1979
Assets:			
	Cash and marketable securities	$ 253	$ 234
	Accounts receivable	527	466
	Inventories	650	500
	Current assets	$1430	$1200
	Gross fixed assets	1500	1200
	Accumulated depreciation	325	300
	Net fixed assets	$1175	$ 900
	Total assets	$2605	$2100
Liabilities and net worth:			
	Bank loans	$ 700	$ 400
	Accounts payable	$ 500	$ 400
	Current liabilities	$1200	$ 800
	Long-term debt	375	500
	Common stock	100	100
	Surplus	930	700
	Total stockholders' equity	$1030	$ 800
	Total liabilities and net worth	$2605	$2100

Income Statement of If-Not, Inc., (December 31, 1980)		
Sales		$6450
Cost of goods sold		4385
Selling, administrative, and general expenses		968
Depreciation		258
Earnings before interest and taxes (EBIT)		$ 839
Interest		45
Earnings before taxes		$ 794
Income taxes		333
Earnings after taxes		$ 461
Common dividends		230
Retained earnings		231

For the years 1973–1979 earnings before interest and taxes were: $550, $615, $702, $690, $715, $795, $802 thousand. Sales during this period were $4410, $4850, $5470, $5400, $5590, $6140, and $6190.

Essay Questions

1. In what general way do financial managers proceed to analyze the creditworthiness of a potential customer? Would such analysis be different from that applied to present customers?
2. What role does financial ratio analysis play in credit evaluation? Explain both the advantages and disadvantages of financial ratio analysis.
3. What special role does numerical credit scoring play in evaluating credit risks? Explain fully.
4. What are Z-scores and how are they used in credit analysis?
5. "All I know," says the financial manager of What-Not, Inc., "is that sometimes it simply does not pay to continue a credit investigation of customers. There comes a time when you just stop looking." Evaluate this statement and set forth the analytical framework in which it applies.

6. "I don't know about other financial managers, but as the credit manager of What-Not, Inc., I consider maximization of profits, concentration on dangerous accounts, and repeat orders to be the most influential on my credit decisions." Evaluate this statement.

7. What is financial ratio analysis and how might it be applied to credit management?

8. What bearing does the use of book values in financial ratio analysis have on (1) the analysis itself and (2) credit management?

9. Differentiate between financial leverage and operating leverage and indicate the implications each of these has for credit management.

Answers to Exercises

Fill-in Questions

1. cash discounts
2. 2; 10; 30
3. 44.6
4. expected; expected
5. $3.40
6. $17
7. does not; large

8. factor
9. earnings before interest and taxes; interest expense
10. financial leverage; operating leverage
11. net working capital
12. lower; less; more; less

Problems

1. 74.26 percent; 37.36 percent; 24.88 percent; 110.77 percent; 154.86 percent; 209.17 percent
2. Firm 1, 6.94; firm 2, 10.04; firm 3, 12.93; firm 4, 15.68
3. 134
4. −$86
5. $1410
6. −$7.70
7. $183.33
8. Total expected profit = −$86.00 + (0.78)($76) = −$26.72
9. Leverage indicators;
   Financial leverage: 0.27
   Debt-equity ratio: 0.36
   Times interest earned: 18.6
   Earnings variability:
     Standard deviation of changes in EBIT: $34.74
     Coefficient of variation of EBIT: 4.87 percent
   The percent changes in sales and EBIT are as follows:

Changes in sales	9.98	12.78	−1.28	3.52	9.84	0.81	4.20
Changes in EBIT	11.82	14.15	−1.71	3.62	11.19	0.88	4.61

The line of best fit through the data produces the following equation.

$$\text{Percent change in EBIT} = -0.19 + (1.15 \times \text{Percent change in sales}),$$
$$(R^2 = 99.8)$$

which gives an estimated operating leverage of 1.15.

Liquidity:

Net working capital to total assets: 0.09

Current ratio: 1.19

Quick ratio: 0.65

Cash ratio: 0.21

Efficiency ratios:

Sales to average total assets: 2.74

Sales to average net working capital: 20.5

Return on average total assets: 22.51 percent

Return on equity: 50.38 percent

Net profit margin: 7.84 percent

Inventory turnover: 7.63 times

Average collection period: 27.93 days

27 *Cash management*

Introduction

It should come as no surprise to be told that efficient management of a firm's resources produces the desired value of the enterprise. What may be surprising to some of you is to be told that cash management is as important to the value and survival of the firm as the management of any of the firm's assets and liabilities. The object of efficient cash management, as always, is to ensure the solvency of the enterprise and to add to the value of the firm.

What to Look For in Chapter 27

Efficient cash management is the focus of this chapter. Financial managers knowingly forgo the interest return on invested money in exchange for liquidity. The object of cash management is the proper balance between too little and too much cash.

Cash as a Raw Material Because cash is another raw material needed to carry on the functions of a firm, several inventory models are used to solve the problem of how much cash or cash substitutes to keep on hand. In the Baumol model the three variables of concern are the interest forgone from holding cash, the fixed administrative expenses of buying and selling highly marketable securities, and the rate of disbursement of cash. The Miller-Orr model's major variables are the transactions costs in highly marketable securities, the variation in day-to-day cash flows, and the interest rate. The value of these models, as of all models, rests with insights they provide us regarding the important variables to consider.

Managing Float The date on which checks are received for payment of goods and services differs from the date they are cleared and gives rise to float. Financial managers estimate the net float between checks written and checks received and adjust cash balances accordingly. To minimize the amount of float working to the financial manager's disadvantage, a process of speeding up collections is necessary, concentration banking, wire transfers, and lock-box systems being the most prominent. To maximize the amount of float working to the financial manager's advantage, a process of slowing down the rate at which cash moves out of the business is necessary, mailing checks at the very last moment and paying for goods and services by drafts being commonplace.

Your Friendly Banker Good bank relationships are essential to efficient cash management. Nothing makes a banker happier than large deposits of cash. To ensure her happiness, a banker often requires financial managers to maintain compensating balances, in return for which a number of services are provided "free."

Worked Examples

Problem 1

Because of the unusual success of *Principles of Corporate Finance,* Everyman's Bookstore finds its demand doubled to 200 copies a year, its cost of money tied up in inventory increased to $1.20 per book, and the fixed, clerical, and handling expenses increased to $2.10 per book. You are asked to determine the optimal order size Q.

Solution

The formula for the solution to this problem is

$$Q = \sqrt{\frac{2 \times \text{sales} \times \text{cost per order}}{\text{carrying cost}}}$$

Filling in the relevant numbers,

$$Q = \sqrt{\frac{2 \times 200 \times \$2.10}{\$1.20}}$$

$$= \sqrt{\$840/\$1.20}$$

$$= \sqrt{700}$$

$$= 26.46 \text{ books}$$

Because fractional books cannot be ordered, the optimal order size is 26 books. This implies that orders will be placed about 7.7 times a year (200 books ÷ 26 books), or once about every 47 days (365 ÷ 7.7 times).

The equilibrium between the cost and benefits of ordering in this magnitude is further demonstrated by determining the marginal reduction in order costs and comparing them with the marginal carrying costs.

$$\text{Marginal reduction in order costs} = \frac{\text{sales} \times \text{cost per order}}{Q^2}$$

$$= (200 \text{ books} \times \$2.10)/(26.46)^2$$

$$= \$420/700.13$$

$$= \$0.60$$

$$\text{Marginal carrying costs} = \frac{\text{carrying cost per book}}{2}$$

$$= \$1.20/2$$

$$= \$0.60$$

$$\text{Marginal reduction in order costs} = \text{marginal carrying costs}$$

$$\$0.60 = \$0.60$$

Problem 2

On the assumption that cash is merely another inventory that must be replenished from time to time, Baumol extended the inventory ordering model to cash management. As the financial manager of What-Not Corporation you want to use the model to determine how frequently you should sell your U.S. Treasury bills in order to cover day-to-day cash outflows, which average $100,000 a month, or $1.2 million a year. If the annual rate of return on your bills is 8.5 percent, and it costs $50 each time you sell bills, what is the optimum number of times per year that you should sell the bills?

Solution

To solve this problem, determine the optimum amount of money that will be needed. Using Baumol's formula, the results are as follows:

$$Q = \sqrt{\frac{2 \times \text{annual cash disbursements} \times \text{cost per sale of Treasury bills}}{\text{interest rate}}}$$

$$= \sqrt{\frac{2 \times \$1,200,000 \times \$50}{0.085}}$$

$$= \sqrt{\$120,000,000/0.085}$$

$$= \sqrt{\$1,411,764,706}$$

$$= \$37,573.46$$

The optimal amount of bills to be sold is $37,573, rounded to the nearest dollar. Because $100,000 per month is needed, you should sell Treasury bills 2.66 times ($100,000 ÷ $37,573) a month, or about 31.9 times a year (2.66 × 1.2).

Problem 3

As financial manager of the What-Not Corporation you estimate that you will need new cash at the rate of $2 million per year. Say you estimate that you are able to obtain money at a cost of 12 percent and invest temporary excess cash balances at 9 percent. Say also you must pay $5000 every time you obtain new money, no matter how much is raised. How often should you go to the market for capital?

Solution

To solve this problem, you may use the Baumol cash management model, with a twist. First solve for Q, the optimal quantity of cash:

$$Q = \sqrt{\frac{2 \times \$2,000,000 \times \$5,000}{0.12 - 0.09}}$$

$$= \sqrt{\$20,000 \text{ million}/0.03}$$

$$= \sqrt{\$666,667 \text{ million}}$$

$$= \$816,496.58$$

The total amount needed is $816,497. Note that the denominator of the equation takes into account that cash not needed immediately will earn a positive rate of return and therefore has the impact of increasing the amount of money that should be obtained.

To determine the interval at which you should "take a trip to the capital markets," given the optimal quantity of money needed, divide the optimal quantity Q by the total amount needed ($2 million).

The results are

$$\text{Interval} = Q/\text{total needed per annum}$$

$$= \$816,497/\$2,000,000$$

$$= 0.408 \text{ year}$$

To determine the time interval in days between successive trips to the capital markets, multiply this by 365 days, to obtain

$$\text{Interval (years)} \times 365 \text{ days}$$

$$0.408 \times 365 = 149 \text{ days}$$

You should go to the capital markets for funds once every 149 days.

Problem 4

Now you are to determine the upper and lower cash balance limits using the Miller-Orr model of cash management. A minimum cash balance of $15,000 makes you comfortable, given that the variance of daily cash flows is $9,000,000 or the equivalent of a daily standard deviation of $3000. Additional information is (1) daily interest rate is 0.0236 percent and (2) the transaction cost for each sale or purchase is $25.

Solution

The lower limit LL is already established by you at $15,000.

The spread between the upper and lower limit is determined by the following formula:

$$\text{Spread} = 3 \left(\frac{\frac{3}{4} \times \text{transaction cost} \times \text{variance of cash flows}}{\text{interest rate}} \right)^{1/3}$$

Filling in the numbers, we obtain

$$\text{Spread} = 3 \left(\frac{\frac{3}{4} \times \$25 \times \$9,000,000}{0.000236} \right)^{1/3}$$

$$= 3 \left(\frac{0.75 \times \$25 \times \$9,000,000}{0.000236} \right)^{1/3}$$

$$= 3 \left(\frac{\$168{,}750{,}000}{0.000236} \right)^{1/3}$$

$$= 3(\$715{,}042{,}370{,}000)^{1/3}$$

$$= 3\ (\$8942.19)$$

$$= \$26{,}826.57$$

or about $26,820

The next step is to calculate the upper limit, using this formula:

Upper limit = lower limit + spread

$$= \$15{,}000 + \$26{,}820$$

$$= \$41{,}820$$

The next step is to calculate the return point, using this formula:

Return point = lower limit + (spread/3)

$$= \$15{,}000 + (\$26{,}820/3)$$

$$= \$15{,}000 + \$8940$$

$$= \$23{,}940$$

The *decision rule* which emanates from these calculations is: *When cash balances reach the $41,820 level, invest $17,880 ($41,820 − $23,940) in marketable securities; when cash balances fall to the lower limit of $15,000, sell $8940 ($23,940 − $15,000).* In both instances the return point is achieved by this decision rule.

Problem 5

As you continue to manage the cash of What-Not Corporation, you discover that there is a time lag among the dates on which you write, mail, and pay bills; the date when the check is received by the drawee of your check; and the date between the date your check is deposited in the drawee's checking account and the date on which it is finally cleared. On the date it is cleared, you know that your checking account will be reduced by the amount of each check, but you estimate that you have 2 days before this is likely to happen. If on average you send out $50,000 worth of checks a day and the average return obtainable in the year is 0.02 percent daily, what is the annual dollar return obtainable from investing the "unused" portion of your checking account?

Solution

The average daily float is $100,000 (2 days × $50,000 per day). This will earn $20 per day, $7300 per year.

However, if your accounts receivables also contain a 2-day time lag before your checking account is credited with payments, and if daily receipts average $30,000, what then is the dollar advantage to playing the float?

The solution lies in determining the net collection float, the difference between the payables float, arising from having written checks against your checking account, and the collection float, arising from checks received but not cleared. In this instant the net collection float is $20,000 ($50,000 − $30,000). If all else stays the same, you will now earn $4 per day, or $1460 a year. This process continues to be profitable up to the point where the total costs equal the total revenues to be gained from doing it.

Summary

Because the object of cash management is to make certain that just enough cash, but not too much, is available to satisfy the needs of the firm, it may be viewed as inventory, just as any other raw material is. Consequently, inventory models may be applied to the analysis of the stock of cash. Also, checks in the process of collection or being collected by others give rise to float. Efforts to slow collection by others of your checks and efforts to speed up collection of others' checks are the essence of sound management of float. Finally, your friendly banker is made happy by the amount of deposits left with her.

List of Terms

Baumol's cash model	Marginal reduction in order cost
Carrying costs	Miller-Orr cash model
Collection float	Money-market funds
Compensating balances	Net float
Concentration banking	NOW accounts
Float	Order cost
Lock-box system	Payment float
Marginal carrying costs	Playing the float

Exercises

Fill-in Questions

1. Cash provides (more, less) _____ liquidity than securities.

2. In equilibrium the _____ value of cash liquidity is equal to the _____ value of the _____ forgone on investments.

3. As a financial manager you wish to hold cash up to the point where the _____ value of the _____ liquidity is equal to the _____ value of the _____ forgone.

4. The two costs of holding inventory are _____ cost and _____ cost.

5. The optimal order size results when the _____ reduction in order cost is equal to the _____ carrying cost.

6. The main cost of holding cash is _____.

7. The (higher, lower) _____ the interest rate, the higher the optimum amount of Treasury bills sold.

8. In the Miller-Orr cash model, the three factors which determine the extent to which cash wanders randomly between upper and lower bounds are _____, _____, and _____.

9. The Miller-Orr cash-management model minimizes the _____ and _____ costs of holding cash and marketable securities.

10. The value of checks that have been written but have not yet cleared is called _____.

11. _____ banking requires customers to make payments to a local bank rather than directly to the company.

12. Renting a post office box to which customers make payments and from which the bank collects the payments is known as the _____ system of cash management.

Problems

1. What-Not Corporation has $2 million invested in Treasury bills yielding 8 percent per annum; this will satisfy the firm's need for funds during the coming year, in addition to the cash it has on deposit, of course. If it costs $50 to sell these bills, regardless of the amount, how much should be withdrawn at a time?

2. If What-Not Corporation needs $167,000 a month, under the conditions of problem 1, how frequently should the financial manager sell off Treasury bills?

3. If the interest rate obtainable on Treasury bills were to decrease to 7 percent, as compared with the 8 percent in problem 1, what bearing would this have on the answers to problems 1 and 2?

4. The financial manager of What-Not is explaining why it does not pay to hold more cash than is needed. The company currently has a total of $5 million in cash but estimates that it will need only $1.5 million during the next 3 months. If the cost of transacting in each is the same, what daily dollar return may the financial manager expect if the annual returns on marketable securities are as follows:

U.S. Treasury bills	9.55 percent
Federal agencies	9.75
Negotiable time CDs	10.00
Commercial paper	9.90
Bankers' acceptances	9.80

5. The demand for *Principles of Corporate Finance* exceeded everyone's wildest expectations, with the result that the demand for the book at Everyman's Bookstore increased to 400 copies a year. Concomitantly, the cost of money tied up in the inventory increased to $1.40 a book, whereas the fixed and clerical expense increased to $2.20 a book. What is the optimal order size?

6. Running Everyman's Bookstore is not without its financial headaches. After all, some books sell very rapidly, whereas others, equally important to the entire product line of books, move very slowly. A cash-management problem arises, and the owner has programmed the Miller-Orr model into her mini-computer. Using historical data, she finds that the variance in daily dollar cash flows is 4 million. She thinks it might be worthwhile to invest temporary excess cash balances, especially now that annual interest rates for a money fund are 9.2 percent, without a transaction cost, although the cost of her time is $5 per transaction. She feels that the lower cash limit that makes her comfortable is $3000. She then plugs this information into her mini-computer. Give the answers she would obtain for each of the following questions: (a) the lower limit, (b) spread, (c) upper limit, (d) return point, (e) decision rule. Show all calculations and explain fully.

7. The owner of Everyman's Bookstore finds that typical terms of sale in the book industry are 2/30, n/90 and that book companies are very slow to clear her checks. The average elapsed time between the time she mails her check for payment of books and the time they clear her bank is 10 days. She averages $4000 a day of checks that have not cleared her checking account. On the other hand, 60 percent of her average daily sales of $8000 is paid in cash, 20 percent by check, and 20 percent by credit card. Assume that the credit cards and check sales clear at the average rate of 3 days. If she obtains a daily rate of return of 0.015 percent, what is the annual dollar return obtainable from investing the unused portion of her checking account?

Essay Questions

1. What rationale can you give for holding cash, especially when it is considered that no interest is earned? Explain fully.

2. In Baumol's model the higher the interest rate one uses the lower the quantity Q of cash is optimal. Explain why this is so.

3. Put in words the essence of the Miller-Orr model.

4. Explain how float may work either for or against a business firm.

5. The financial manager of the Whozits Company, Inc., is contemplating establishing a lock-box system. She asks you to perform an analysis of the number of lock boxes which she should consider in order to make the system as profitable as possible. What answers might you provide her?

Answers to Exercises

Fill-in Questions

1. more
2. marginal; marginal; interest;
3. marginal; cash; marginal interest
4. carrying; ordering
5. marginal; marginal
6. the interest forgone
7. lower
8. transactions costs; variance of cash flows; the interest rate
9. transactions; interest
10. float
11. concentration
12. lock-box

Problems

1. $50,000
2. 3.34 times per month or once every 9 days
3. $53,450 at a time, 3.12 per month or once every 10 days
4. Treasury bills $874.73
   Federal agencies   892.23
   Negotiable time CDs   914.05
   Commercial paper   905.03
   Banker's acceptances   896.60
5. 35
6. Lower limit $ 3,000
   Spread   11,712
   Upper limit   14,712
   Return point   6,904
   Decision rule: When cash balances reach $14,712, invest $7808; when cash falls to $3000, sell $3904.
7. Revenues from payables

   $4000 \times 0.00015 \times 10$ days $\times 360$ = $2160.00

   Cost of receivables

   $8000 \times (0.20 + 0.20) \times 0.00015 \times 3$ days $\times 360$ = 518.40
   Annual net gain $1641.60

28 *Short-term lending and borrowing*

Introduction

Financial managers invest temporary excess cash balances in short-term securities. When financial managers have a shortfall of cash, they borrow, usually short-term if the deficiency is expected to be temporary. Efficient financial management therefore requires a working knowledge of the short-term securities in which financial managers may invest and the major aspects of borrowing short-term funds.

What to Look For in Chapter 28

This chapter brings together both the major instruments of short-term lending and borrowing and the ways in which financial managers use them. Some of their major characteristics are:

1. The marketplace in which the instruments of lending and borrowing are traded is known as the money market.
2. Short-term debt is usually less risky than corporate bonds.
3. The method of calculating yields on most money-market investments is different from that on other types of investment, because they are sold at a discount from their face value, the difference between the purchase price and the discount being the interest earned.

Money-Market Instruments The dominant money-market instruments are U.S. Treasury bills, which have maturities of 90, 180, 270, and 360 days and are sold at auction either competitively or at the average price of successful competitive bids. Next in importance are United States government agency securities. Although they are not backed by the full faith and credit of the United States government, their quality is impeccable. Next in order of quality are short-term securities of states and other municipalities. Because interest income is exempt from federal income taxation, municipals are very desirable for investors in a high marginal income tax bracket.

Deposits Although they are insured up to $100,000 by the Federal Deposit Insurance Corporation, regular time deposits are not typically thought of as money-market investments, are not sold at a discount from face value, and are not negotiable. Negotiable deposits at commercial banks are called certificates of deposit and have denominations of $100,000 or more, a minimum maturity of 30 days, and a maximum maturity of 270 days. Time deposits of dollars with foreign banks or foreign branches of United States banks are called Eurodollar investments.

Commercial Paper   Although still very, very high quality, commercial paper is another notch down in quality from the money-market investments already discussed. Commercial paper is issued directly by only the best-known, largest, and safest companies. Considerable cost savings are obtainable by issuing commercial paper.

Banker's Acceptances   Banker's acceptances were seen to be demands written on a bank which, when accepted, become negotiable money-market instruments. When the bank accepts them, they become high-quality and the returns on them are slightly more than those available on Treasury bills.

Repurchase Agreements   Repurchase agreements are frequently used for investing overnight monies because they are loans secured by a government security dealer and because they are highly liquid.

Bank Loans   When companies are short of cash, often they go to banks where they borrow on either an unsecured or a secured basis. Some unsecured loans are self-liquidating, for the sale of the goods and services for which the loan was made provides the cash to repay the loan; some are used for interim financing, being replaced when long-term financing is arranged. Frequently a line of credit, which specifies the limit of monies to be borrowed, is arranged.

Secured bank loans usually require collateral, either receivables or inventory. Although almost all trade accounts receivables are acceptable collateral for loans, not all kinds of inventory are.

Term Loans   Term loans are a final way in which firms finance their short-term needs, even though their duration is as long as 8 years. Often term loan interest rates vary with the prime rate. A revolving credit, which enables the firm to borrow up to an assured amount over a period of as much as 3 years, is frequently found.

Worked Examples

Problem 1

Beautiful Boats Corporation is preparing for the summer boating season and finds that it will need additional funds in December to build up inventory. The amount needed is $2 million and the company's bank has offered to make a loan at 10 percent annually provided the company maintains a 20 percent compensating balance. The manager of a competing bank, when he dropped in to purchase a boat, indicated that he would lend the company the needed monies for 11 percent with no compensating balance. Which bank is making the better offer? Explain fully. Would your answer be different if Beautiful Boats normally maintained a $50,000 cash balance?

Solution

The compensating balance is $400,000 ($2,000,000 × 0.2). The amount of interest charged is $200,000 ($2,000,000 × 0.1). The cost of the loan is 12.5 percent annually ($200,000 ÷ $1,600,000). The amount of funds actually available for use is $1.6 million and the dollar cost of using that sum is $200,000.

If the financial manager normally kept an average of $50,000 on deposit, the amount normally available for use increases to $1.65 million and the cost per annum is 12.12 percent ($200,000 ÷ $1,650,000).

In any event the 11 percent loan without the compensating balance is the better deal.

Problem 2

Beautiful Boats Corporation decides to take out a term loan in the amount of $5 million at a cost of 1 percent above the prime rate of interest. If the prime rate varies from 12, 13, 9, 7, and 6 percent per year in each of the years during which the loan is outstanding, what is the dollar interest cost of the loan? Assume the entire loan is paid off at the end of the fifth year.

Solution

$5 million × 0.13 = $ 650,000

$5 million × 0.14 = 700,000

$5 million × 0.10 = 500,000

$5 million × 0.08 = 400,000

$5 million × 0.07 = 350,000

$2,600,000

Problem 3

Compare the loan in problem 2 with a loan which has fixed 15 percent per year interest cost but which is payable in equal annual installments.

Solution

The formula for determining the annual payment on this loan is

$$\frac{i}{1 - (1 + i)^{-n}}$$

where i = rate of interest
n = number of repayment periods

Completing the formula

$$\frac{0.15}{1 - (1 + 0.15)^{-5}}$$

and solving, we obtain a factor of 0.2983156, which, when multiplied by the amount of the loan, $5 million, produces the annual payment of $1,491,578. Multiplying the annual payments by 5, the number of payments, we obtain $7,457,890. The total amount paid on the loan is $7,457,890 and the difference between that and the amount of the loan, $5 million, is the amount of interest paid, $2,457,890.

Problem 4

If a 90-day Treasury bill is quoted as a discount of 9.5 percent, at what price must it be selling? Show calculations.

Solution

The general formula is

$$\text{Percent discount} = \frac{100 - \text{price}}{100} \times \frac{360}{91}$$

Inasmuch as we wish to find price, we make that our unknown, x, and solve for it. Thus we have

$$0.095 = \frac{100 - x}{100} \times 3.956044$$

Solving for x, we obtain 97.5986, which means that a $10,000 Treasury bill sells for $9759.86.

Problem 5

If 90-day Treasury bills are quoted at a discount of 9.5 percent, what is the annual simple interest return? What is the effective compound annual rate of return?

Solution

The relative wealth earned over the 91-day period is given by

$$100/97.5986 = 1.0246$$

or a return of 2.46 percent. When this result is multiplied by (365/91), the annual simple interest return is determined. Thus

$$\text{Simple annual return} = 2.46 \text{ percent} \times (365/91)$$

$$= 9.87 \text{ percent}$$

The effective compound annual return is 10.24 percent and was found using this formula:

$$(1.0246)^{365/91}$$

Summary

When financial managers have temporary excess cash balances, they invest them in short-term money-market instruments, such as Treasury bills, banker's acceptances, and commercial paper. The quality of all money-market instruments is generally quite high, although there are gradations among the set.

When financial managers find they are likely to be short of funds for a short period, they borrow from banks or from the money markets. For example, some companies, because of their assumed impeccable credit rating, may borrow based on their commercial paper; they sell the commercial paper to investors wishing temporary investment of funds. When financial managers borrow from a bank, the loans are either secured by physical collateral, secured by accounts receivable, or unsecured. Term loans also are used to finance short-term needs, even though their duration is 5 to 10 years.

List of Terms

Balloon payments   Interim financing
Banker's acceptances   Line of credit
Commercial paper   Money market
Discount securities   Revolving credit
Eurodollar investments   Self-liquidating loans
Eurodollars   Trust receipt
Field warehouse   Warehouse receipt
Floor planning

Exercises

Fill-in Questions

1. In general the default risk for money-market securities is (greater, less) _____ than it is for long-term debt.

2. Money-market investments are _____ securities.

3. When Treasury bills are selling at a discount, their yield (is, is not) _____ the same as the discount.

4. Noncompetitive bids for Treasury bills are filled at the _____ price of the successful competitive bids.

5. The income from securities of states and other municipalities are _____ from federal income taxes.

6. Time deposits are invariably insured by the Federal Deposit Insurance Corporation up to _____.

7. Negotiable certificates of deposit come in denominations of _____ or more.

8. Commercial paper rates usually are (below, equal to, greater than) _____ the prime rate charged by banks.

9. A bank loan which enables a financial manager to borrow up to a preestablished limit is known as _____.

10. A loan collateralized by receivables, but giving the bank the right to require the firm to meet any deficiencies in collection of the receivables to repay the loan is said to be a loan (with, without) _____ recourse.

11. The major difference between a factor loan and the typical receivables loan of commercial banks is that the former _____ the receivables whereas the latter does not.

12. An automobile dealer usually employs _____ in order to finance inventory. As evidence of this arrangement the automobile dealer signs a _____, which is redeemed when the automobiles are sold.

13. The principal form of medium-term debt financing is called _____.

Problems

1. What-Not's bank has offered to lend the firm $5 million at an annual rate of 12 percent, provided the company maintains a compensating balance of 25 percent. Because the financial manager does not think this is the best deal he can obtain, he approached a competitor bank and it offered him a $5 million loan at 15 percent annually with a 10 percent compensating balance. Which is the better deal, expressed on an annual basis?

2. What would be the better deal, if the company in problem 2 usually kept on deposit an average of $100,000?

3. What-Not decided to take out a 5-year $10 million term loan whose rate of interest is 2 percent above the prime rate. If the prime rate is 12, 13, 14, 15, and 11 percent in each of the years the loan is outstanding, what is the dollar amount of interest paid?

4. How does the loan in problem 3 compare with a 16 percent loan, payable in equal annual installments? What is the dollar difference in interest paid? What is the dollar difference in interest paid?

5. In January 1980, 90-day Treasury bills were selling at a discount of 11.12 percent. At what price must the bills have been selling?

6. What is the annual simple interest of the bills discussed in problem 5? The annual compound rate of return?

7. From a current issue of the *Wall Street Journal* gather the money-market rates listed in Table 28-2 of the text. What changes do you observe and to what do you ascribe them?

Essay Questions

1. Briefly describe the money market and the investments that are traded there.

2. What does it mean when we say: "Money-market investments are pure discount securities"?

3. Discuss the following statement: "Because the middle man is eliminated, or at least most of his functions are eliminated, when commercial paper is issued, there is a significant reduction in the cost of funds when commercial paper is used."

4. What is meant by a self-liquidating loan? Interim financing? Line of credit?

5. What provisions are typically found in a line of credit? Explain why you think they are there.

6. What characteristics should be possessed by assets that are used as collateral for inventory loans?

Answers to Exercises

Fill-in Questions

1. less	6. $100,000	11. buys
2. discount	7. $100,000	12. floor planning; trust receipt
3. is not	8. below	
4. average	9. a line of credit	13. term loans
5. exempt	10. with	

Problems

1. The effective cost of the 12 percent loan is 16 percent. The effective cost of the 15 percent loan is 16.7 percent.
2. The effective cost of the 12 percent loan is 15.5 percent. The effective cost of the 15 percent loan is 16.3 percent.
3. $7,500,000
4. Annual payment = $3,054,094; total payments = $15,270,469; total interest paid = $5,270,469.
5. $9718.91
6. 11.60 percent; 12.12 percent

29 *Approaches to financial planning*

Introduction

The important thing to remember about financial planning is that it is both neces- sary and one of the most difficult tasks a financial manager faces. The two major purposes of financial planning are to avoid surprises and to anticipate the future.

What to Look For in Chapter 29

Because it melds all investing and financing decisions, a financial plan is the confluence of each of the previous chapters in which a topic here and a topic there were studied. As each of these decisions percolates up the organization and is amalgamated into the financial planning process, the risk aversion of financial management is fitted to the riskiness of all investing and financing decisions. In other words, financial planning is not concerned with minimizing risks; financial planning is concerned with which risks to undertake and which ones to avoid.

Forecasting Financial planning requires forecasting, but there is more to the story than that. Because every forecast is likely to be imprecise, the deviations around the forecast caused by both avoidable and unavoidable surprises must be planned for. During the financial planning process, financing and investment deci- sions are analyzed for their impact on the future welfare of the enterprise. Once this impact has been determined, alternative investments and financing schemes are formulated and goals are set.

Ordinarily financial planning is concerned with the long term, although short- term financing and investment decisions are a part of this process. At all times financial planning focuses on *all* the investment and financing decisions of a firm.

A Complete Financial Plan A complete financial plan usually includes pro forma financial statements, a statement of capital expenditures, overall business strategy, planned financing, a forecast of revenues and expenses, and an attempt to find the optimal financial plan which satisfies the risk-return expectations of shareholders and financial managers. Because each of the foregoing is an option to the financial manager, financial planning may devolve into managing a portfolio of options.

Financial Planning Models To achieve the goals of financial planning, corpo- rate financial models, ranging from very simple to complex systems, are often used. One of the major flaws of corporate financial models is their lack of finance theory. Consequently, a system of incorporating finance theory should be found. The appendix to this chapter provided such a system, a linear programming model called LONGER. This rather complete model indicates what may be accomplished when corporate financial planning considers the impacts of various alternative strategies. What a financial manager seeks is the net contribution to the value of the firm which is equal to the base-case net present value adjusted for the value of a project's marginal contribution to borrowing power—to give effect to the tax shelter—as well as the addition of the marginal cost of equity which is sold to finance a project.

Worked Examples

Problem 1

The financial statements of Book Ends, Inc., are set forth in Table 29-1.

As the financial manager of the company, your task is to set up a pro forma set of statements for 1981. The following assumptions are to be used:

1. Sales are forecasted to increase by 20 percent.
2. No new stocks will be issued.
3. The following coefficients are used:

$a_1 = \text{CGS} \div \text{REV} = 0.87$

$a_2 = \text{interest rate} = 10 \text{ percent}$

$a_3 = \text{tax rate} = 48 \text{ percent}$

$a_4 = \text{depreciation rate} = 10 \text{ percent}$

$a_5 = \text{payout ratio} = 50 \text{ percent}$

$a_6 = \text{NWC} \div \text{REV} = 16 \text{ percent}$

$a_7 = \text{FA} \div \text{REV} = 64 \text{ percent}$

**Table 29-1
1980 financial statements for Book Ends, Inc. (All figures in $1000s)**

Income statement	
Revenue (REV)	$4250
Cost of goods sold (CGS)	3655
Earnings before interest and taxes	$ 595
Interest (INT)	170
Earnings before taxes	$ 425
Tax at 48 percent (TAX)	204
Net income (NET)	$ 221

Balance sheet	
Assets:	
Net working capital (NWC)	$ 680
Fixed assets (FA)	2720
Total assets	$3400
Liabilities:	
Debt (B)	$1700
Book equity (EQ)	1700
Total liabilities	$3400

Solution

To solve this problem, compare the forecasted results with those of the most recent year. The setup takes two steps.

First, fill in each of the statements below with as much data as you can, starting with the income statement. It helps to use the equations contained in Table 29–3 of the Brealey-Myers text.

Pro forma income statement, Book Ends, Inc. ($1000s)

Revenue	$5100.0
Cost of goods sold	4437.0
Earnings before interest and taxes	$ 663.0
Interest	
Earnings before taxes	
Taxes (48 percent rate)	
Net income	

The balance sheet may be completed as follows:

Balance sheet, Book Ends, Inc.

	1981	1980	Change
Assets:			
Net working capital (NWC)	$ 816	$ 680	$136
Fixed assets (FA)	3264	2720	544
Total assets	$4080	$3400	$680
Liabilities:			
Debt (B)	$	$1700	$
Book equity (EQ)		1700	
Total liabilities	$4080	$3400	$680

And the sources and uses of funds statement looks like this:

Sources and uses of funds Book Ends, Inc.

Sources:	
Net income	$
Depreciation	326.4
Operating cash flow	
Borrowing	
Stock issues	0
Total sources	$
Uses:	
Increase in net working capital	$136.0
Investment	870.4
Total dividends	
Total uses	$

The following gaps exist:
Income statement:

1. Interest (INT)
2. Earnings before taxes
3. Taxes (TAX)
4. Net income (NET)

Balance sheet:

5. 1981 debt (B)
6. 1981 equity (EQ)
7. Change in debt (ΔB)
8. Change in equity (ΔEQ)

Sources and uses of funds statement:

9. Net income (NET)
10. Operating cash flow
11. Borrowing (B)
12. Total sources
13. Total dividends (DIV)
14. Total uses

A careful look at that list of 14 items reveals that many are self-determining, once some other information is available. What information? The change in debt (ΔB), that's what, and that is estimated in one of two ways. One may use the formula for change in debt, solve that, and then add the results to the prior year's debt of $1700. Here is the step-by-step process.

$$\Delta B = \Delta NWC + INV + DIV - NET - DEP - SI$$
$$= \$136 + \$870.4 + 0.5\ NET - NET - \$326.4 - 0$$
$$= \$680 - 0.5\ NET$$
$$= \$680 - 0.5[REV - CGS - INT - TAX]$$
$$= \$680 - 0.5[\$5100 - \$4437 - 0.1B - 0.48(REV - CGS - INT)]$$
$$= \$680 - 0.5[\$663 - 0.1B - 0.48(\$5100 - \$4437 - 0.1B)]$$
$$= \$680 - 0.5[\$663 - 0.1B - 0.48(\$663 - 0.1B)]$$
$$= \$680 - 0.5(\$663 - 0.1B - \$318.2 + 0.048B)$$
$$= \$680 - 0.5(-0.052B + \$344.8)$$
$$= \$680 + 0.026B - \$172.4$$
$$= \$507.6 + 0.026(\Delta B + 1700)$$
$$= \$507.6 + 0.026\Delta B + \$44.2$$
$$= \$551.8 + 0.026\Delta B$$
$$0.974\Delta B = \$551.8$$
$$\Delta B = \$566.5$$

$$B = \Delta B + B(-1)$$
$$= \$566.5 + \$1700$$
$$= \$2266.5$$

Debt financing (ΔB) is $566.5 and total debt (B) is $2266.5, which means that total equity is

$$EQ = \text{total assets} - D$$
$$= \$4080 - \$2266.5$$
$$= \$1813.5$$

Additional equity is $113.5($1813.5 − $1700).

The second solution is to find the amount of debt (B) which will be outstanding at the end of 1981. The change (ΔB) is obtained by taking the difference between that and the amount outstanding at the beginning of the period [(B(−1)] of $1700. The equally tedious calculations are set forth below.

$$B = \Delta B + B(-1)$$
$$= \Delta B + \$1700$$
$$= \Delta NWC + INV + DIV - NET - DEP - SI + \$1700$$
$$= \$136 + \$870.4 + 0.5\ NET - \$326.4 - 0 + \$1700$$
$$= \$2380 - 0.5\ NET$$
$$= \$2380 - 0.5(\$5100 - \$4437 - INT - TAX)$$
$$= \$2380 - 0.5(\$663 - INT - TAX)$$
$$= \$2380 - \$331.5 + 0.5\ INT + 0.5\ TAX$$
$$= \$2048.5 + 0.5\ INT + 0.5\ TAX$$
$$= \$2048.5 + 0.5(0.1B) + 0.5[0.48(REV - CGS - INT)]$$
$$= \$2048.5 + 0.05B + 0.5[0.48(\$663 - 0.1B)]$$
$$= \$2048.5 + 0.05B + 0.5(\$318.2 - 0.048B)$$
$$= \$2048.5 + 0.05B + \$159.1 - 0.024B$$
$$= \$2207.6 - 0.026B$$
$$0.974B = \$2207.6$$
$$B = \$2266.5$$

And

$$\Delta B = B - B(-1)$$
$$= \$2266.5 - \$1700$$
$$= \$566.5$$

which is precisely what we obtained before.

Armed with that information, the statements may then be completed. Begin by completing the balance sheet, at least the debt portion. Then complete the income statement, now that you know the total amount of debt is $2266.5, because you can put in the amount of interest to be paid. After you do that, the remainder of the income statement is straightforward. If you take half of the net income as retained earnings and add that to the prior year's equity of $1700, the new equity results. Completing the sources and uses of funds statements is the last step in this process.

Problem 2

Book Ends, Inc., will use LONGER to estimate how much to invest or borrow in the coming year. The firm faces the following conditions:

1. Available investment opportunities can absorb $500,000.
2. The expected cash flows are perpetual.
3. The internal rate of return on the cash flows is 10 percent.
4. The market capitalizes cash flows of this nature at 12 percent.
5. The firm plans to finance half of the new investment with debt.
6. The firm has $400,000 in cash.
7. Excess cash will be paid out as dividends.
8. Additions to debt and equity are expected to be permanent.
9. The company's marginal tax rate is 50 percent.

Set up a graphical solution to this problem, making sure you explain each part of the graph.

Solution

This is a linear programming problem, the solution to which begins with setting up the basic equation as well as the constraints imposed by the financial management of the firm. Begin by letting x equal the new investment and y equal new borrowing, both expressed as dollars. Next, use the Modigliani-Miller valuation formula, such that

$$V = V_o + TD$$

where V_o = market value of existing assets, if they were all-equity-financed
T = marginal corporate tax rate
D = amount of outstanding debt (does not include borrowing for the new project)

TD, then, is the present value of the tax shield arising from debt financing. So,

$$V = V_0 + 0.5D - 0.167x + 0.5y$$

We want to find what x and y will be. Because V_o and D are fixed, we may safely ignore them. We want to solve the following:

Maximize: $-0.167x + 0.5y$ (called the objective function)

Subject to: $x \leq \$500,000(100 \text{ percent invested})$

$y \leq 0.5x(\text{amount of debt issued})$

$x \leq y + \$400,000 \text{ (balance to be financed)}$

The graphical solution is contained in Figure 29–1. The steps in the solution are as follows:

1. Make each of the constraints equal to their limits, that is, $x = \$500,000$, $y = 0.5x$, and $x = y + \$400,000$.
2. Graph each of the constraints by solving for the indicated function.
3. The three graphed lines establish the boundary of the feasible set of solutions but do not find the optimal solution.
4. Set the maximization function equal to V, the value of the investing and borrowing decision, such that $V = -0.167x + 0.5y$.
5. To find the slope of the function, first set V equal to zero. The slope of the function is

$$\text{Slope} = \frac{\text{rise}}{\text{run}}$$

6. The solution works out thus:

$$V = -0.167x + 0.5y$$

$$0 = -0.167x + 0.5y, \text{ or } x = 3y$$

When $y = 0$, $x = 0$

When $y = 1$, $x = 3$

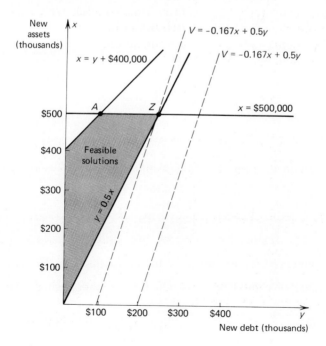

Figure 29-1

Slope = rise/run = $\Delta x/\Delta y$

where Δx and Δy mean change in x values and change in y values. For every two units of increase (rise) in x, there is one unit of increase (run) in y.

Increasing values of the objective function are given by shifting in a southeasterly direction (that is, increasing y and decreasing x), while keeping its slope equal to 3. We want to shift the line as far as possible in this direction until it only just touches the feasible region. This gives the point Z as the optimal solution, with y = $250,000, x = $500,000, and an adjusted net present value from the investment equal to $41,667 (or $41,500, if you rounded the ratio of 9 percent to 12 percent).

Summary

As obvious as it is to state that sound financial management calls for financial planning, it is a lot more easy to say than to pull off. Whatever the format for financial planning, it is likely that at the minimum pro forma financial statements will be formulated based on forecasts of different likely events occurring. Because no forecast will be perfect, each financial plan must provide for the contingency that it will be greater or less than originally formulated. More and more, sophisticated planning models are being used because they are able to incorporate more variables into the analysis than other, cruder techniques. Interestingly, it is not altogether clear that the more sophisticated models produce superior results.

List of Terms

Aggressive growth	LONGER
Divestiture	**Normal growth**
Financial models	**Pro forma financial statements**
Financial plan	**Retrenchment**
Financial planning	**Shadow price**
Linear programming	

Exercises

Fill-in Questions

1. One of the purposes of financial planning is to avoid _____.

2. Financial planning brings together the _____ and _____ choices open to the firm.

3. Forecasted financial statements are called _____ statements and are used to anticipate the future and link the present with the past.

4. The value of capital projects which have important financing side effects is called _____.

5. A _____ is defined as the change in the objective per unit change in the constraint.

6. When evaluating an investment decision using linear programming, a shadow price of 0.2 on the investment limit means that if we were to invest an additional dollar, _____ would increase by _____ .

Problems

1. What-Not, Inc.'s financial statements are set forth below.

Revenues	$5000
Cost of goods sold	4500
Earnings before interest and taxes	$ 500
Interest	120
Earnings before taxes	$ 380
Taxes	171
Net income	$ 209
Assets:	
Net working capital	$ 500
Fixed assets	2000
Total assets	$2500
Liabilities:	
Debt	$1500
Book equity	1000
Total liabilities	$2500

The financial manager estimates that sales next year will increase by 15 percent. The board of directors have decided not to issue more shares in light of the currently weak equity markets. The additional assumptions about the coefficients of the model to be used to determine how much must be borrowed are:

$a_1 = \text{CGS} \div \text{REV} = 0.90$

$a_2 = \text{interest rate} = 8 \text{ percent}$

$a_3 = \text{tax rate} = 45 \text{ percent}$

$a_4 = \text{depreciation rate} = 8 \text{ percent}$

$a_5 = \text{payout ratio} = 40 \text{ percent}$

$a_6 = \text{NWC} \div \text{REV} = 10 \text{ percent}$

$a_7 = \text{FA} \div \text{REV} = 40 \text{ percent}$

a. Set up the pro forma financial statements for the coming year.

b. If the depreciation rate were 18 percent instead of 8 percent, would the amount borrowed change?

c. If the payout ratio were increased to 60 percent, how much additional borrowing would be required?

d. What effect would a change in the coefficient a_1 have if it were 88 percent? If it were 95 percent?

2. What-Not, Inc., will use LONGER to estimate how much to invest or borrow in the coming year. The firm faces the following conditions:

a. Available investment opportunities absorb $5 million.

b. The expected cash flows are perpetual.

c. The internal rate of return on the cash flows is 12 percent.

d. The market capitalizes cash flows of this nature at 15 percent.

e. The firm wishes to finance 60 percent of the new investment with debt.

f. The firm has $4 million in cash.

g. Excess cash will be paid out as dividends.

h. Additions to debt and equity are permanent.

i. The company's marginal tax rate is 50 percent.

Set up the graphical solution to this problem. Label all relevant points. Explain, in words, the nature of the graph and the story it tells.

Essay Questions

1. "When you come right down to it, let's face it, good management provides for both expected and unexpected events and bad management does not. All this should be reflected in financial planning. After all, there is such a thing as contingency planning, ya know." Evaluate this statement in light of the principles of finance of which you are aware.

2. You have just been hired by the corporate strategy group of a large firm. The firm's outlook is uncertain. The vice-president for finance asks you to present a brief statement of how each of the following policies may affect your firm: aggressive growth, normal growth, retrenchment, and divestiture. Begin your answer by explaining what each of those terms means.

3. How does financial planning differ for a firm with generous operating cash flows, modest dividend payout policies, and only a handful of investment opportunities as compared with one that has considerably less operating cash flow because of rapid expansion, also has a moderate dividend payout policy, has stretched its borrowing power virtually to the limit, and is confronted with many investment opportunities?

4. Is it really possible that an investment may have no net present value and still be undertaken by firms simply to enter markets that heretofore were untapped? What financial sense, if any, does that make?

5. How is linear programming used in financial planning?

Answers to Exercises

Fill-in Questions

1. surprises
2. investment; financing
3. pro forma
4. adjusted present value
5. shadow price
6. net present value; 20 cents

Problems

1. a. Before working with the equations in worked problem 1, the partially completed pro forma financial statements are as follows:

Pro forma income statement, What-Not, Inc.		
Revenues	$5750	
Cost of goods sold	5175	
Earnings before interest and taxes	$ 575	
Interest		
Earnings before taxes		
Taxes		
Net income		

Pro forma balance sheet, What-Not, Inc.	This year	Last year	Change
Assets:			
Net working capital	$ 575	$ 500	$ 75
Fixed assets	2300	2000	300
Total assets	$2875	$2500	$375
Liabilities:			
Debt	$	$1500	$
Book equity		1000	
Total liabilities	$2875	$2500	$375

Sources and uses of funds, What-Not, Inc.	
Sources:	
Net income	$
Depreciation	184
Operating cash flow	
Borrowing	
Stock issues	0
Total sources	
Uses:	
Increase in net working capital	$ 75
Investment	484
Total dividends	
Total uses	

Using either of the equations in worked problem 1 results in new debt of $1731, or $231 more than last year. The completed statements follow.

	This year	Last year	Change
Assets:			
Net working capital	$ 575	$ 500	$ 75
Fixed assets	2300	2000	300
Total assets	$2875	$2500	$375
Liabilities:			
Debt	$1731	$1500	$231
Book equity	1144	1000	144
Total liabilities	$2875	$2500	$375
Revenues		$5750	
Cost of goods sold		$5175	
Earnings before interest and taxes		$ 575	
Interest		138	
Earnings before taxes		$ 437	
Taxes		196	
Net income		$ 240	
Sources:			
Net income	$ 240		
Depreciation	184		
Operating cash flow	$ 424		
Borrowing	231		
Stock issue	0		
Total sources	$ 655		
Uses:			
Increases in net working capital	$ 75		
Investment	484		
Total dividends	96		
Total uses	$ 655		

b. Yes, the equations in worked problem 1 indicate that, with $41 less debt being issued and $41 more in equity being retained, the revised payout ratio is now 24 percent, given the strictures of the model.

c. $22

d. In the 88 percent case the following happens:

New debt: $152, which is $79 less than the case in a.
New equity increases by $79 to $1223.
Net income increases to $244.
In order to increase equity from $1000 last year to $1223 this year, $233 of the $244 of net income must be retained; the payout ratio is then 4.5 percent.
In the 95 percent case, $57 additional debt over the case in a results, so that much less in equity is needed. Working through the income statement results in a payout ratio of 63 percent.

2.

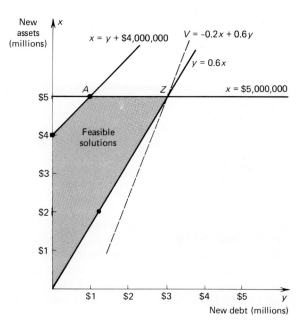

30 *Mergers*

Introduction

Mergers are evaluated in the same way as any other investment: as long as the merged firms are worth more when combined than when alone, the net present value of the fusion must be profitable and shareholders are better off. Mergers are popular today, as they have been in the past. It behooves financial managers to know when and under what conditions it pays to merge with another firm.

What to Look For in Chapter 30

Mergers are evaluated in the same way as any other investment decision, the decision rule remaining the same: if the investment (acquisition) adds more value to the firm than it costs, it should be undertaken. The problem lies in finding acquisitions that fill that bill of particulars.

Economic Gains   The chief economic gains from an acquisition, and therefore increases in the value of the firm, arise from economies of scale, for when they are present, two firms are likely to be worth more together than apart. When evaluating the net present value of an acquisition, a financial manager must evaluate the potential gains from the merger, the estimated cost, and the division of these gains between the two companies' shareholders.

Motives That Make Sense   Reasonable motives for mergers are horizontal integration, in which two firms in the same line of business are merged; vertical integration, in which firms which either consume another firm's output or supply its raw materials are merged; and conglomerates, in which companies in unrelated businesses are combined. Economies of scale may be found in all three types of mergers. Other merger motives include eliminating inefficiencies, using heretofore unused tax shields, using surplus funds, and combining complementary resources.

Motives That Do Not Make Sense   Contrariwise, diversification, bootstrapping, that is, attempting to increase earnings per share which are not based on the productivity of the assets employed, and allegedly lower financing costs do not hold up well as reasonable reasons for a merger.

Merger Costs   The cost of a merger is a premium that the buying firm pays for the selling firm over the value of a selling firm's value as a separate entity. Given the efficiency of markets in which publicly held stocks are traded, companies selling below their intrinsic value are not likely to be found. The costs of cash deals are straightforward. When stock is used to finance an acquisition, the apparent cost is equal to the difference between the number of shares exchanged times the value per share and the dollar value of the acquired firm. But this may not be the true cost, because the acquired firm's value as a separate entity may not be reflected in the value of its shares, the acquiring firm's value as a separate entity may not be the value of its shares, and most likely, the acquired firm's shareholders may receive some of the gains from the merger by virtue of becoming partners in the merged firm. Remember: when cash is used, the cost of the merger is unaffected by the merger gains; when stock is used, the cost depends on the gains because the gains are shared with the acquired firm's owners.

Merger Mechanics   Next, you studied the mechanics of mergers and saw that any large acquiring firm must pay heed to federal antitrust laws, the foremost of which is the Clayton Act of 1914, which in turn, focuses on the intent to lessen competition substantially or to create a monopoly. Also part of the mechanics is the form of the acquisition. A strictly defined merger, for example, takes place when the liabilities and assets of the selling company are transferred and absorbed by the buying company. Consolidations arise when two or more firms come together under the mantle of a new firm. Some tax considerations enter into the evaluation of mergers because some acquisitions are taxable and others are tax-free. In the former case shareholders are viewed as having sold their shares, and are taxed accordingly, whereas in the latter instance shareholders are viewed as exchanging their shares for new ones, there being no taxes recognized at the time of the fusion. Whereas mergers are usually negotiated between the managements of the buyer and the seller, another method of acquiring firms is by means of a tender offer in which the acquiring firm offers to purchase shares of the company it wishes to purchase. The final mechanical aspect of merging is the way in which the accounting books are kept. Two systems exist: a purchase of assets acquisition in which the assets are acquired for amounts usually in excess of their book value, thereby giving rise to goodwill; and a pooling of interest method whereby the firm's separate balance sheets are merged. The evidence suggests that regardless of which accounting technique is used, acquiring firms did no better under one system as opposed to another.

It would be foolhardy for financial managers to ignore the problems that may beset a firm which has acquired another one after the acquisition takes place.

Finally, you saw that mergers tend to ebb and flow. The crests of the major waves of merger activity seem to be coincident with high levels of stock prices, and selling companies tend to gain from mergers whereas acquiring firms do not.

Worked Examples

Problem 1

Sink, Inc., plans to merge with Swim Corp. The capital market places a value on Sink of $7.875 million and Swim is valued at $500,000, when they are evaluated separately. After the merger, economies of scale will result in additional cash flows, the present value of which is $250,000. What is the net present value (NPV) of the merger? The cost? Sink will buy Swim for $600,000 in cash. Sink has 150,000 shares outstanding.

Solution

The NPV is obtained by taking the difference between the gain from the merger and the cost.

$$\text{Cost} = \text{cash} - \text{PV}_{\text{Swim}}$$

$$= \$600,000 - \$500,000$$

$$= \$100,000$$

$$\text{NPV} = \text{gain} - \text{cost}$$

$$= [(\text{PV}_{\text{Sink + Swim}}) - (\text{PV}_{\text{Sink}} + \text{PV}_{\text{Swim}})] - (\text{cash} - \text{PV}_{\text{Swim}})$$

$$= [(\$7,875,000 + \$500,000 + \$250,000) - (\$7,875,000 + \$500,000)] - (\$600,000 - \$500,000)$$

$$= (\$8,625,000 - \$8,375,000) - \$100,000$$

$$= \$250,000 - \$100,000$$

$$= \$150,000$$

Problem 2

How did the shareholders of Sink and of Swim make out on the merger?

Solution

To determine how shareholders make out from a merger, begin by recognizing that the cost of the merger is a gain to Swim's shareholders; they capture $100,000 of the $250,000 gain. The NPV calculated above is the gain to Sink's shareholders. It works out this way:

$$\begin{aligned}\text{Net gain to acquiring}\\\text{firm's shareholders} &= \text{overall gain to the combination} - \text{gain}\\&\qquad \text{captured by acquired firm's shareholders}\end{aligned}$$

$$= \$250,000 - \$100,000$$

$$= \$150,000$$

As a check, use this formula:

$$\text{NPV} = \text{wealth with merger} - \text{wealth without merger}$$

$$= (\text{PV}_{\text{Sink + Swim}} - \text{cash acquisition outlay}) - \text{PV}_{\text{Sink}}$$

$$= [(\$7,875,000 + \$500,000 + \$250,000) - \$600,000] - \$7,875,000$$

$$= \$8,625,000 - \$600,000 - \$7,875,000$$

$$= \$150,000$$

Problem 3

Now say that Sink, Inc., is considering the acquisition of Float Company. The data for this deal are set forth in Table 30-1. Assuming there are no gains from the merger, complete the third column of that table.

Solution

The third column is completed. Because there are no economic gains from the merger, the combined values (line 6) of the two firms (PV of Sink and Float

**Table 30-1
Impact of merger
on market value
and earnings
per share of
Sink, Inc.***

	Sink, Inc. (premerger)	Float Company	Sink, Inc. (postmerger)
1. Earnings per share	$3.50	$3.50	$4.67
2. Price per share	$52.50	$26.25	$52.50
3. Price-earnings ratio	15	7.50	11.25
4. Number of shares	150,000	150,000	225,000
5. Total earnings	$525,000	$525,000	$1,050,000
6. Total market value	$7,875,000	$3,937,500	$11,812,500
7. Current earnings per dollar invested in stock (line 1 divided by line 2)	$0.067	$0.133	$0.089

*Because of rounding, not all the numbers are exact.

combined) is simply the sum of their separate PVs. Because Sink is selling at a higher multiple of earnings per share, it purchased Float with half again as many shares as Float had outstanding, making for a total of 225,000 after the merger. The firm's total earnings is the sum of the two entities. When both total earnings and total value are divided by the number of outstanding shares, lines 1 to 3 may be completed. Note that earnings per share increase as well as the current earnings per dollar invested (line 7), but that nothing else changes. Such bootstrapping is a myth and does not create value.

Problem 4

Now, suppose that just before the merger of Sink and Swim, the following conditions prevailed:

	Sink	Swim
Market price per share	$52.50	$20
Number of shares	150,000	25,000
Market value of firm	$7,875,000	$500,000

The problem is to determine the cost of the merger, assuming all the conditions in problems 1 and 3 continue to hold. Also assume that the market bids up the price of Swim's stock to $22 after the merger announcement.

Solution

The answer is exactly what we obtained in problem 1, that is, before the merger. After the announcement the numbers work out this way:

$$\text{Cost} = (\text{cash} - \text{MV}_{\text{Swim}}) + (\text{MV}_{\text{Swim}} - \text{PV}_{\text{Swim}})$$

$$= [\$600,000 - (\$22 \times 25,000)] + [(\$22 \times 25,000) - \$500,000]$$

$$= (\$600,000 - \$550,000) + (\$550,000 - \$500,000)$$

$$= \$50,000 + \$50,000$$

$$= \$100,000$$

We see (surprise!) that the total cost is the same as before, although its two components have changed.

Problem 5

Now let's say Sink, Inc., wishes to estimate the cost of a merger that entails an exchange of 11,429 (rounded to nearest full share) instead of $600,000 in cash. What are the apparent and true costs of the merger?

Solution

The apparent cost is straightforward.

$$\text{Apparent cost} = (\text{number of shares} \times \text{market price per share}) - PV_{Swim}$$

$$= (11,429 \times \$52.50) - \$500,000$$

$$= \$600,000 - \$500,000 = \$100,000$$

which is what we obtained in all previous cases.

The true cost is determined by the amount of the new value the Swim shareholders obtain in the deal. That is, we have to determine what x is.

$$x = \frac{\text{new shares issued to acquired firm's shareholders}}{\text{outstanding shares of acquiring firm} + \text{new shares issued}}$$
$$\text{to acquired firm's shareholders}$$

$$= 11,429/(150,000 + 11,429)$$

$$= 11,429/161,429$$

$$= 0.0708 = 7.08 \text{ percent}$$

Sink, Inc., gives up slightly more than 7 percent of its claim on the total value of the merged firm.

Now we proceed to determine the true cost of the merger in this way:

$$\text{True cost} = x PV_{Sink + Swim} - PV_{Swim}$$

$$= 0.0708(\$7,875,000 + \$500,000 + \$250,000) - \$500,000$$

$$= 0.0708(\$8,625,000) - \$500,000$$

$$= \$610,650 - \$500,000$$

$$= \$110,650$$

Problem 6

The book value balance sheets of Sink, Inc., and Swim Corp. are set forth at the top of Table 30-2. What would the ending balance sheets look like after the merger using both pooling of interest and purchase of assets accounting methods?

Table 30-2
Purchase of assets vs. pooling of interest accounting methods for merger of Sink with Swim
In millions

1. Initial balance sheets

Sink, Inc.

NWC	$1.0	$1.4	D
FA	2.5	2.1	E
	$3.5	$3.5	

Swim Corp.

NWC	$0.1	$0.1	D
FA	0.2	0.2	E
	$0.3	$0.3	

2. Pooling of interest

Sink, Inc.

NWC	$1.1	$1.5	D
FA	2.7	2.3	E
	$3.8	$3.8	

Purchase of assets (purchase price = $600,000)

Sink, Inc.

NWC	$1.1	$1.5	D
FA	2.7		
Goodwill	0.4	2.7	E
	$4.2	$4.2	

Solution

Section 2 of the table contains the answer.

Summary

Mergers generate economic gains if two firms are worth more when combined than when separated. Merger gains are most likely to be obtained from economies of scale, economies of vertical integration, improved efficiency, fuller use of tax shields, the combination of complementary resources, or redeployment of surplus funds. Decision rules for mergers are the same as those imposed on every major investment; namely, as long as the present value of the cash inflows exceeds the present value of the cost, the merger should be undertaken.

List of Terms

Amalgamation (consolidation)
Apparent cost of mergers
Bootstrapping
Clayton Act of 1914
Complementary resources
Conglomerate mergers
Consolidation (amalgamation)
Economic gains from
    the merger
Economies of scale
Federal Trade Commission
    Act of 1914

Goodwill
Horizontal mergers
Merger, loosely defined
Merger, strictly defined
Pooling of interest accounting
Proxy
Purchase of assets accounting
Sherman Act of 1890
Tender offer
True cost of mergers
Vertical mergers

Exercises

Fill-in Questions

1. If two merged firms are worth more together than apart, an
_____ gain results.

2. A _____ merger is one that takes place between two firms in the same line of business; a _____ merger is one in which the buyer expands forward or backward to the ultimate consumer or the supplier of raw materials; and a _____ merger involves companies in unrelated lines of business.

3. Bootstrapping (does, does not) _____ result in real gains created by a merger and there (are, are not) _____ increases in the two firms' combined value.

4. The (true, apparent) _____ cost of a merger between two firms may exceed the (true, apparent) _____ cost, if the stock prices observed (before, after) _____ the merger is announced do not reflect the merger gains or their division between the two firms' stockholders.

5. The Sherman Act of 1890 focuses primarily on _____ _____ _____ ; the Federal Trade Commission Act of 1940 focuses primarily on _____ _____ ; and the _____ _____ focuses primarily on acts that tend to lessen competition substantially or create a monopoly.

6. Strictly defined, a merger refers to the case in which the assets and liabilities of the selling company are transferred to the buying company and the (selling, buying) _____ company disappears as a separate entity.

7. When two companies are combined into a single new company, a _____ is said to have taken place.

8. The right to vote someone else's shares is called a _____ .

9. A _____ is a general offer made directly to a firm's shareholders to buy their stock at a specified price.

10. When a merger takes place and the two firms' separate balance sheets are added together, this is called a _____ from an accounting standpoint.

11. When the accounting technique used to give evidence to a merger gives rise to goodwill, it is safe to assume that a _____ method of accounting was used.

Problems

1. Use the data in Table 30-3 to answer the following questions. Answer each question independent of all other questions.

   a. What are the cost and net present value of the combination of What-Not, Inc., and If-Not, Inc., if, as a result of the merger, the economies expected are $400,000 and What-Not, Inc., plans to pay $3 million in cash for If-Not?

   b. If What-Not acquires If-Not for $3 million in cash, how will the shareholders of each make out on the deal?

   c. If What-Not, Inc., merges with Why-Not, Inc., there are no economic gains from the merger, and $1.2 million in stock is paid for Why-Not, demonstrate the bootstrapping effect of the merger.

   d. Calculate the apparent and true costs of the merger between What-Not, Inc., and If-Not, Inc., assuming expected economies of $400,000 and the shareholders of If-Not receive one share of What-Not for every two shares they hold. On the announcement of the merger, the shares of If-Not increase to $31.

   e. Show the results of accounting for the merger between What-Not, Inc., and If-Not, Inc., using both pooling of assets and a purchase of assets methods, where If-Not is acquired for $3 million.

Essay Questions

1. Explain why buying another company is just like any other investment decision financial managers make.

2. Explain how unused tax shields may be beneficial to an acquiring firm.

3. Set forth some doubtful reasons that are used to explain mergers, and explain why you selected those that you did.

4. It has been and still is argued that mergers are consummated in order to diversify a firm. Evaluate the diversification motive for mergers.

5. Is it true that mergers tend to lower financing costs?

6. Why do you think mergers come in waves, and why do you think that the crest of the waves coincides with high stock prices?

7. Who gains more from a merger, the selling company or the acquiring one? Explain the reasons why you think one gains more than the other. Is it possible that neither gains? Explain.

Table 30-3 Data for What-Not, Inc. In millions		What-Not, Inc.	If-Not, Inc.	Why-Not, Inc.
	Earnings per share	$4	$2	$2
	Price per share	$64	$28	$12
	Price-earnings ratio	16	14	6
	Number of shares	200,000	100,000	200,000
	Total earnings	$800,000	$200,000	$200,000
	Total market value	$12,800,000	$2,800,000	$2,400,000
	Book values:			
	NWC	$1.1	$0.4	$0.3
	FA	2.8	1.0	0.8
	D	2.0	0.7	0.3
	E	1.9	0.7	0.8

Answers to Exercises

Fill-in Questions

1. economic
2. horizontal; vertical; conglomerate
3. does not; are not
4. true; apparent; before
5. restraint of trade; unfair methods of competition; Clayton Act of 1914
6. selling
7. consolidation (amalgamation)
8. proxy
9. tender offer
10. pooling of interest
11. purchase of assets

Problems

1. (a) Cost = $200,000; NPV = $200,000; (b) What-Not's shareholders' gain: $200,000; If-Not shareholders' gain: $200,000;
   (c)

Bootstrapping effects of the merger between What-Not, Inc., and Why-Not, Inc.	What-Not, Inc. (premerger)	Why-Not, Inc.	What-Not, Inc. (postmerger)
1. Earnings per share	$4.00	$2.00	$4.21
2. Price per share	$64	$12	$64
3. Price-earnings ratio	16	6	15.20
4. Number of shares	200,000	200,000	237,500
5. Total earnings	$800,000	$200,000	$1,000,000
6. Total market value	$12,800,000	$2,400,000	$15,200,000
7. Current earnings per dollar invested in stock	$0.0625	$0.1667	$0.0658

(d) apparent cost: $400,000; true cost: $70,000

(e)

Purchase of assets vs. pooling of interest of What-Not, Inc., and If-Not, Inc.

1. Initial balance sheets

What-Not, Inc.			
NWC	$1.1	D	$2.0
FA	2.8	E	1.9
	$3.9		$3.9

If-Not, Inc.			
NWC	$0.4	D	$0.7
FA	1.0	E	0.7
	$1.4		$1.4

2. Pooling of interest

What-Not, Inc.			
NWC	$1.5	D	$2.7
FA	3.8	E	2.6
	$5.3		$5.3

Purchase of assets

What-Not, Inc.			
NWC	$1.5	D	$2.7
FA	3.8		
Goodwill	2.3	E	4.9
	$7.6		$7.6

299

31 *International financial management*

Introduction

Three additional problems are tacked onto financial decision making when firms operate in international markets: (1) financial managers must contend with more than one currency; (2) interest rates differ from country to country; and (3) financial managers must analyze international investments differently from national investments. Financial managers of firms dealing in international markets must formulate financial policies that incorporate these three additional considerations when they make investing and financing decisions.

What to Look For in Chapter 31

The foreign exchange market is the place in which foreign currencies are traded. Spot rates, which are rates of exchange on foreign currencies for immediate delivery, and forward rates, which are rates of exchange in foreign currencies deliverable in the future, form the basis for dealing in foreign currencies.

Four Fundamental Relations   Four fundamental relations add insight to foreign exchange markets: (1) those dealing with different rates of interest on different currencies; (2) differences between forward and spot rates of the same currencies; (3) determination of next year's expected spot rate of exchange between two currencies; and (4) rates of inflation between two foreign countries and their impact on exchange rates. All four are interdependent because: differences in interest rates between two currencies are equal to differences in expected inflation rates, which in turn are equal to expected changes in spot rates, which themselves are equal to differences between forward and spot rates of the same currency, which, finally, are equal to differences in interest rates between two different currencies. All of which is to say that the system for analysis is about as self-contained as one can imagine. These relations arise because the real rate of return on invested capital among all countries eventually equilibrates even though nominal interest rates may differ. The interest rate parity theory, the expectations theory of forward rates, the law of one price, and capital market equilibrium are the concepts underlying the solutions to the four fundamental relations.

Handling Currency Risk of Receivables in Foreign Currencies   Financial managers may insure themselves against currency risk by selling foreign currencies forward against the currencies they presently have. When financing foreign operations, financial managers have three options: (1) export capital from the domestic country; (2) borrow foreign currencies; and (3) borrow wherever interest rates are lowest. It should not be surprising to know that financial managers use all three. Moreover, to protect themselves against devaluations of currencies many financial managers finance their fixed asset requirements by exporting domestic capital. Their variable asset requirements, chiefly financial assets, are financed by borrowing foreign currencies or currencies that possess the lowest rate of interest.

International Capital Markets   Understanding international capital markets is essential to sound financial management. An important aspect of international financial markets are eurodollars, which are dollars deposited in banks located in Europe. (There is an Asian dollar market as well, although it is not nearly as large as the eurodollar market.) Because of domestic governments' regulations on lending, a eurocurrency market, where eurodollars are loaned, exists.

Long-term international financial markets give rise to eurobonds. Although eurobonds typically possess almost all the characteristics found in bonds sold in the United States, such differences as the currency in which the bonds are denominated exist. Companies dealing in international markets invariably finance part of their operations with their own currencies, but the repatriation of excess cash may be problematic and may well influence a company's decisions to invest abroad. Double-taxation agreements go a long way toward mitigating the potential adverse effects of being unable to repatriate invested funds.

International Investment Decisions   International investment decisions pose two problems which are not found in domestic investment decisions. The first problem is one of choosing the proper rate at which to discount international investment projects. To be sure, the concept of opportunity cost is paramount; the problem is: which opportunity cost? Typically the discount rate is the next best alternative rate of return available in the foreign country, notwithstanding the existence of world interest rates and a rate of return on a world market portfolio, which would lead to a different discount rate. The second problem of international capital budgeting is identification of incremental cash flows.

Because of these two problems, the investment decision cannot be separated from the financing decision. One way to see whether international investments are feasible is to make an analysis which separates international tax and currency effects.

Worked Examples

Problem 1

Using Figure 31–1, calculate the Monday forward discount or premium for the dollar against each of the following currencies: British pound; Canadian dollar; French franc; Japanese yen; Swiss franc; and West German mark.

Solution

To answer this problem, calculate the per period rate of discount or premium and then multiply by the number of periods in the year to approximate the annual discount or premium. For example, taking British pound, 30-day futures, we obtain

Forward discount (premium) = [(futures exchange rate − spot exchange rate) ÷ spot exchange rate] × 100

Foreign Exchange

Monday, May 5, 1980
The New York foreign exchange selling rates below apply to trading among banks in amounts of $1 million and more, as quoted at 3 p.m. Eastern time by Bankers Trust Co. Retail transactions provide fewer units of foreign currency per dollar.

Country	U.S. $ equiv. Mon.	U.S. $ equiv. Fri.	Currency per U.S. $ Mon.	Currency per U.S. $ Fri.
Argentina (Peso)				
Financial	.00056	.00056	1786.00	1783.00
Australia (Dollar)	1.1135	1.1135	.8981	.8981
Austria (Schilling)	.0781	.0772	12.81	12.96
Belgium (Franc)				
Commercial rate	.034686	.034270	28.83	29.18
Financial rate	.033580	.033534	29.78	29.82
Brazil (Cruzeiro)	.0205	.0205	48.86	48.86
Britain (Pound)	2.2810	2.2590	.4384	.4427
30-Day Futures	2.2710	2.2510	.4403	.4442
90-Day Futures	2.2605	2.2435	.4424	.4457
180-Day Futures	2.2485	2.2365	.4447	.4471
Canada (Dollar)	.8405	.8386	1.1898	1.1925
30-Day Futures	.8382	.8365	1.1930	1.1955
90-Day Futures	.8349	.8358	1.1978	1.1965
180-Day Futures	.8336	.8356	1.1996	1.1967
China (Yuan)	.6638	.6671	1.5065	1.4990
Colombia (Peso)	.0218	.0218	45.95	45.95
Denmark (Krone)	.1765	.1755	5.6660	5.6980
Ecuador (Sucre)	.0375	.0375	26.75	26.75
Finland (Markka)	.2680	.2690	3.7320	3.7170
France (Franc)	.2385	.2355	4.1930	4.2400
30-Day Futures	.2384	.2362	4.1940	4.2340
90-Day Futures	.2383	.2364	4.1960	4.2285
180-Day Futures	.2378	.2365	4.2060	4.2280
Greece (Drachma)	.0239	.0239	41.80	41.80
Hong Kong (Dollar)	.2028	.2024	4.9300	4.9400
India (Rupee)	.1250	.1250	8.00	8.00
Indonesia (Rupiah)	.00162	.00162	619.80	619.00
Iraq (Dinar)	3.40	3.40	.2941	.2941
Ireland (Pound)	2.0430	2.0450	.4894	.4890
Israel (Pound)	.0231	.0232	43.37	43.05
Italy (Lira)	.001181	.001172	847.00	853.60
Japan (Yen)	.004221	.004179	236.90	239.30
30-Day Futures	.004227	.004187	236.60	238.80
90-Day Futures	.004228	.004191	236.55	238.60
180-Day Futures	.004235	.004214	236.15	237.30
Lebanon (Pound)	.2935	.2935	3.4072	3.4072
Malaysia (Ringgit)	.4484	.4505	2.2300	2.2200
Mexico (Peso)	.0439	.0439	22.78	22.78
Netherlands (Guilder)	.5032	.4973	1.9875	2.0110
New Zealand (Dollar)	.9610	.9610	1.041	1.0406
Norway (Krone)	.2023	.2018	4.9445	4.9565
Pakistan (Rupee)	.1015	.1015	9.852	9.852
Peru (Sol)	.004	.004	250.00	250.00
Philippines (Peso)	.1360	.1360	7.353	7.353
Portugal (Escudo)	.0202	.0203	49.50	49.30
Saudi Arabia (Riyal)	.3005	.3005	3.3285	3.3285
Singapore (Dollar)	.4598	.4571	2.1750	2.1875
South Africa (Rand)	.8013	1.2500	1.2480	.8000
South Korea (Won)	.0017	.0017	588.00	588.00
Spain (Peseta)	.0141	.0141	71.25	71.25
Sweden (Krona)	.2356	.2353	4.2450	4.2500
Switzerland (Franc)	.6021	.5887	1.6610	1.6920
30-Day Futures	.6058	.5954	1.6507	1.6795
90-Day Futures	.6124	.6031	1.6330	1.6580
180-Day Futures	.6211	.6127	1.6100	1.6320
Taiwan (Dollar)	.0278	.0278	36.00	36.00
Thailand (Baht)	.05	.05	20.00	20.00
Uruguay (New Peso)				
Financial	.1160	.1160	8.62	8.62
Venezuela (Bolivar)	.2329	.2329	4.2930	4.2930
West Germany (Mark)	.5568	.5490	1.7960	1.8215
30-Day Futures	.5582	.5510	1.7915	1.8149
90-Day Futures	.5608	.5546	1.7832	1.8030
180-Day Futures	.5637	.5591	1.7740	1.7885

$$= [(2.2710 - 2.2810) \div 2.2810] \times 100$$

$$= -0.438 \text{ percent}$$

The per period forward premium is 0.438 percent. The annual rate is 5.26 percent $[(360/30) \times 0.438$ percent$]$.

The annual rate for 90-day futures is

$$\text{Forward discount} = \frac{360 \text{ days}}{90 \text{ days}} \times \frac{2.2605 - 2.2810}{2.2810} \times 100$$

$$= 4 \times 0.00899 \times 100$$

$$= 3.59 \text{ percent, i.e., } 3.59 \text{ percent premium}$$

And the annual 180-day forward rate is

$$\text{Forward discount} = \frac{360}{180} \times \frac{2.2485 - 2.2810}{2.2810} \times 100$$

$$= 2.85 \text{ percent, i.e., } 2.85$$

The comparable rates for the other currencies are set forth in Table 31-1.

Problem 2

As the financial manager of What-Not, Inc., you have $10 million to invest for 1 year and are considering United States or British loans. Say the United States interest rate on 1-year loans of this size is 10.75 percent, the current spot rate on the British pound is that shown in Figure 31-1, and the rate of interest on 1-year investments in Britain is 13 percent. What forward rate of exchange is needed to make you indifferent between investing in United States and British 1-year loans?

Solution

To solve this problem, the schematic which depicts the interrelationships among differences in interest rates, expected differences in inflation rates, the expected change in spot rates, and difference between forward and spot rates is necessary. The formulas are as follows:

$$\text{Difference in interest rates} = \frac{r_\$ - r_£}{1 + r_£} \tag{1}$$

$$\text{Expected differences in inflation rates} = \frac{E(i_\$ - i_£)}{1 + i_£} \tag{2}$$

$$\text{Expected changes in spot rates} = \frac{E(s'_{\$/£}) - s_{\$/£}}{s_{\$/£}} \tag{3}$$

$$\text{Differences between forward and spot rates} = \frac{f_{\$/£} - s_{\$/£}}{s_{\$/£}} \tag{4}$$

Because everything depends on everything, and more strongly, everything *equals* everything, each equation may be set equal to any other, so that

Table 31-1 Forward discounts (premiums), percent		30-day	90-day	180-day
	British pound	−5.36	−3.59	−2.85
	Canadian dollar	−3.28	−2.67	−1.64
	French franc	−0.50	−0.34	−0.59
	Japanese yen	1.71	0.66	0.66
	Swiss franc	7.37	6.84	6.31
	West German mark	3.02	2.87	2.48

Differences in interest rates = expected differences in inflation rates = expected changes in spot rates = differences between forward and spot rates

In this case you are interested in equations (1) and (4), because you are dealing with differences in interest rates, equation (1), and differences between forward and spot rates, equation (4). Right? Right! So we have

Differences in interest rates = differences between forward and spot rates

$$\frac{r_\$ - r_£}{1 + r} = \frac{f_{\$/£} - s_{\$/£}}{s_{\$/£}}$$

Filling in the available data, we have

$$\frac{0.1075 - 0.13}{1 + 0.13} = \frac{f_{\$/£} - 2.281}{2.281}$$

$$-0.0199115 = \frac{f_{\$/£} - 2.281}{2.281}$$

$$-0.054181 = f_{\$/£} - 2.281$$

$$f_{\$/£} = 2.2356$$

The equilibrium 1-year forward rate on British pounds is 2.2356.

Problem 3

If the West German expected inflation rate is 4 percent, that of the United States is 9 percent, and 1-year West German loans return 5 percent, what is the implied rate of return on United States 1-year loans?

Solution

From the set of equations set forth in the solution to problem 2 we find that the equations (1) and (2) are to be used to solve this problem. The setup follows:

Difference in interest rates = expected differences in inflation rates

$$\frac{r_\$ - r_{DM}}{1 + r_{DM}} = \frac{E(i_\$ - i_{DM})}{1 + i_{DM}}$$

$$\frac{r_\$ - 0.05}{1.05} = \frac{0.09 - 0.04}{1.04}$$

$$= 0.0480769$$

$$r_\$ - 0.05 = 0.0504808$$

$$r_\$ = 0.1004808 = 10.05 \text{ percent}$$

Problem 4

Using the data in Figure 31-1 for the spot rate, assuming the 1-year forward Swiss franc rate is 0.6402, and assuming an expected 1-year inflation rate in Switzerland of 3 percent, what is the implied United States inflation rate for the coming year?

Solution

Equations (2) and (4) are used to solve this problem.

Expected differences in inflation rates = differences between forward and spot rates

$$\frac{E(i_\$ - i_{SF})}{1 + i_{SF}} = \frac{f_{\$/SF} - s_{\$/SF}}{s_{\$/SF}}$$

$$\frac{i_\$ - 0.03}{1.03} = \frac{0.6402 - 0.6021}{0.6021}$$

$$i_s = 9.52 \text{ percent}$$

Problem 5

What-Not, Inc., has two operating subsidiaries in two mythical countries, Myth 1 and Myth 2. What-Not's United States corporate tax rate is 46 percent and those for Myth 1 and Myth 2 are 35 and 50 percent. Both Myths have a double-tax agreement with the United States. If What-Not earns $1 million before taxes in both countries, what taxes are paid in the United States and overseas, if all net income is remitted in the form of cash dividends?

Solution

		Myth 1 (tax = 35%)		Myth 2 (tax = 50%)
Profits before tax		$1,000,000		$1,000,000
Overseas tax		350,000		500,000
Net profits		$ 650,000		$ 500,000
Received in United States		650,000		500,000
United States company tax	$460,000		$460,000	
Less double-tax relief				
(maximum $460,000)	350,000		500,000	
United States tax payable		110,000		0
Available for dividends		$ 540,000		$ 500,000

Summary

Financial managers dealing with foreign countries face some peculiar problems because of differences in currencies, interest rates, and rates of inflation between and among the countries. Although the principles of financial decision making studied to this point do not change, they must be modified to accommodate these peculiarities which purely domestic companies do not need to reflect. Even choosing a discount rate by which to determine the net present value of an investment is clouded by international currency risk. And it is certain that when investments are considered in an international context, the financing and investing decisions cannot be separated.

List of Terms

Eurobonds
Eurocurrency market
Eurodollars

European composite units
European currency unit
European unit of account

Exchange agio
Expectations theory of
   exchange rates
Floating rates
Forward market

Interest agio
Interest rate parity theory
Law of one price
Spot rate of exchange

Exercises

Fill-in Questions

1. An American company importing from Japan (buys, sells) _____ yen, whereas a Mexican company buying American goods (buys, sells) _____ pesos.

2. Exchange-rate quotations for the price of a currency for immediate delivery is known as _____.

3. Financial managers who buy and sell currency for future delivery do it in the _____ market for foreign currencies.

4. If a financial manager loses interest when making a loan in terms of sterling but gains because she can sell sterling forward at a higher price than she paid for it, the interest rate differential is called _____ ; the annual forward discount under these conditions is called _____ ; and the _____ theory says that the two must be equal.

5. The _____ theory of exchange rates says that the percentage difference between forward exchange rates and spot exchange rates is equal to the _____ change in the _____ rate.

6. When the price of a foreign currency is always equal to the ratio of foreign and domestic prices of goods, the _____ _____ is at work.

7. The law of one price suggests that changes in the spot rate of exchange may be approximated by estimated differences in relative _____ rates.

8. The theory that states that the sterling rate of interest covered for exchange risk should be the same as the dollar rate is called the _____ theory.

9. The European international market for short-term loans that are virtually free of government regulation is called the _____ market.

10. The expectations theory of forward rates says that on average the _____ rate is equal to the _____ spot rate.

11. Eurodollars are _____ in banks outside the United States.

12. The European international market for long-term debt is called the _____ market.

Problems

1. Using the data contained in Figure 31-1, calculate the Friday forward discount or premium for each of the following currencies: British pound; Canadian dollar; French franc; Japanese yen; Swiss franc; and West German mark. Compare your calculations with those in worked problem 1. What differences do you observe? Are they what you expected? Why or why not? Explain fully.

2. Using the data below, complete the answers that are left blank. Show all calculations.

	A	B	C
$r_\$$, percent	10	10	9
$r_£$, percent	12		9
$E(i_\$)$, percent	7	7	
$E(i_£)$, percent			7
$E(s'_{\$/£})$		2.300	
$s_{\$/£}$	2.219	2.200	
$f_{\$/£}$			2.400

3. What-Not, Inc.'s two foreign operating subsidiaries face 32 and 52 percent corporate tax rates, whereas the domestic company is confronted with a 42 percent United States corporate tax rate. Double-tax agreements are in effect. The financial manager wants you to determine the estimated dividends available for shareholders, if the $100,000 that each subsidiary earns is repatriated as cash dividends. What would you say to her? Show whatever calculations you may make.

Essay Questions

1. How does international financial management differ from domestic financial management?

2. The Brealey-Myers text identifies four problems with which financial managers must contend when dealing in foreign countries. What are they? Give a one-paragraph explanation of each. Also provide a one-paragraph discussion of how a financial manager should comport the financial affairs of his enterprise when confronted with each of these conditions.

3. How are money rates of interest in each country related to their respective real rates of interest? Additionally, how are money rates of interest among countries related to the real rates of interest among the same set of countries? What implications do your answers have for efficient financial management?

4. What rationale can you give for the idea that fixed assets are likely to keep their dollar value in the event of a foreign currency devaluation? Why does this concept not apply equally well to financial assets, such as bonds, short-term investments, and foreign currencies? What implications do your answers have for the methods of financing foreign operations?

5. What does it mean to repatriate funds and what potential problems might financial managers encounter when dealing with foreign countries?

6. When making international investment decisions, what analytical framework must a financial manager employ to determine the correct discount rate? Explain fully.

Answers to Exercises

Fill-in Questions

1. buys; sells
2. spot rate of exchange
3. forward
4. interest agio; exchange agio; interest rate parity theorem
5. expectations; expected; spot
6. law of one price
7. inflation
8. interest rate parity
9. eurocurrency
10. forward; expected future
11. dollar deposits
12. eurobond

Problems

1.

Annual forward discounts (premiums), percent	30-day	90-day	180-day
British pound	−4.25	−2.74	−1.99
Canadian dollar	−3.01	−1.34	−0.72
French franc	3.57	1.53	0.85
Japanese yen	2.30	1.15	1.68
Swiss franc	13.66	9.78	8.15
West German mark	4.37	4.08	3.68

2. Col. A: $E\ (i_\pounds) = 8.95$ percent; $E\ (s'_{\$/\pounds}) = 2.1796$; $f_{\$/\pounds} = 2.1794$
   Col. B: $r_\pounds = 5.22$ percent; $E\ (i_\pounds) = 2.35$ percent; $f_{\$/\pounds} = 2.30$
   Col. C: $E(i_\$) = 7.00$ percent; $E\ (s'_{\$/\pounds}) = 2.40$; $s_{\$/\pounds} = 2.40$

3. Subsidiary with 32 percent tax: $58,000; subsidiary with 52 percent tax: $48,000

32 *Pension plans*

Introduction

Because private pension plans are so very important to society and assume greater and greater financial importance to most corporations, financial managers must understand them. The obligation to provide retirement income for employees is abiding because private pensions are likely to form the major source of retirement income for most employees, social security notwithstanding.

What to Look For in Chapter 32

Most pension schemes are defined benefit plans in which specified sums of money are paid to eligible employees when they retire. The dollar amount of a person's pension is based on either a career-average or a final-average formula, the latter becoming more and more prevalent with the advent of recent high levels of inflation. The Employee Retirement Income Security Act (ERISA) is the federal legislation which provides, among other things, for eventual full vesting of pension benefits and which established the Pension Benefit Guarantee Corporation which guarantees the payment of fully vested but unfunded pension liabilities.

Pension Liabilities   Pension plan liabilities arise from past as well as future services of employees. The present value of the pension plan consists of the fund's value today and the present value of future contributions. The present value of expected benefits for past services and the expected present value of future services are added to obtain the total pension liabilities. If the present value of the fund assets is less than the present value of accrued benefits, as measured by the benefit security ratio, an unfunded accrued benefit, which must be met in subsequent years out of a company's operating income, arises. Changes in the value of pension fund securities, employee turnover, increased pension benefits, and changes in assumed actuarial discount rates all influence the total amount of pension benefits that must be met out of corporate income.

Pension Fund Management   Pension funds are managed either by insurance companies or through a trust, which in turn hires professional money managers. Through simulations, a pension fund's total risk and expected rate of return may be estimated.

Pension Fund Performance   Financial managers must know the elements of pension fund performance measurements, because that performance may significantly influence the amount of future pension fund liabilities. Although the internal rate of return, sometimes called the dollar-weighted rate of return, is often used to measure performance, the time-weighted rate of return is preferred because it gives equal weight to each unit of time as well as to the cash flows into and out of the pension fund. When evaluating pension fund performance, two dimensions are looked at: what the pension fund would have earned were it a benchmark portfolio, the benchmark being determined by the beta of the portfolio times the risk premium on a completely unmanaged, or market portfolio; and the portfolio manager's ability to pick stocks. The evidence suggests that trying to pick stocks has not been a fruitful endeavor.

Worked Examples

Problem 1

If the present value (PV) of What-Not, Inc.'s pension fund is $4.5 million, the PV of contributions for future services is estimated at $3.5 million, the PV of expected benefits from past service is $6.5 million, and the PV of expected future service cost is $7.5 million, estimate the deficit of pension plan assets. Also indicate what you, as the firm's financial manager, should allocate to the fund if you wish to amortize the deficit over the next 15 years, assuming that you obtain a 9 percent annual compound return on your investments.

Solution

To estimate the deficit today, take the difference between the sum of the present value of the pension fund and the contributions the firm anticipates making during the next 15 years and the sum of the present values of the expected benefits, from both past service and future service.

$$\text{Deficit} = (\text{PV pension fund} + \text{PV of future contributions}) - (\text{PV of benefits from past service} + \text{PV of expected future service costs})$$

$$= (\$4.5 \text{ million} + \$3.5 \text{ million}) - (\$6.5 \text{ million} + \$7.5 \text{ million})$$

$$= \$8.0 \text{ million} - \$14 \text{ million}$$

$$= -\$6 \text{ million}$$

To amortize this deficit in present value by the end of the fifteenth year, use the annuity method to determine how much should be set aside in each year, assuming the rate of return on the contributed monies is 9 percent compounded annually. Using a hand-held calculator, the answer is $744,353, or $744,000 a year for convenience. Using Appendix Table 3, the answer is $6 million ÷ 8.061 = $744,325 annually.

Problem 2

What-Not, Inc.'s financial manager is a trustee of the company's pension plan which is managed by Make Money & Co., investment counselors. To prepare for a meeting with the portfolio manager, she is reviewing the following information of the equity portion of the fund. What analysis should the financial manager make, so that she may ask intelligent questions?

	Returns, %	
	What-Not, Inc.'s pension fund	Standard and Poor's 500 Composite
1969	−11.9	−8.5
1970	9.3	4.0
1971	9.9	14.3
1972	18.5	19.0
1973	−13.3	−14.7
1974	−23.8	−26.5
1975	45.0	37.3
1976	23.0	24.0
1977	−12.9	−7.2
1978	2.8	6.4
Average return	4.66	4.81
Standard deviation of return	20.88	19.44
Beta	1.05	1.00
Average Treasury bill rate, 1969–1978: 5.98%		

Solution

The first step is to determine the fund risk premium.

Fund risk premium = average fund return − average rate of interest

= 4.66 percent − 5.98 percent

= −1.32 percent

It is already apparent that being in equities during this time was not too keen, because simply holding Treasury bills would have garnered an average rate of return of 1.32 percent more than the equity return. Yet we must go on, for there may be more surprises she must be aware of.

The second step is to determine the rate of return obtainable on a benchmark portfolio; she wants to know the return "any dummy could have obtained if he had merely bought and held the market portfolio as represented by the Standard and Poor's 500 Composite Stock Index," to put it in her words. The benchmark portfolio is obtained by multiplying the risk premium on the market portfolio by the beta of What-Not's equity portfolio.

Benchmark portfolio's risk premium = beta of fund × risk premium on the market

= 1.05 × (4.81 percent − 5.98 percent)

= 1.05 × (−1.17 percent)

= −1.23 percent

It's still not all peaches and cream, but the dummy, or benchmark, portfolio would have been a better performer than the managed portfolio.

Next let's calculate the alpha of the pension fund to find out how good the portfolio manager was at picking stocks; after all, this period for which she is being evaluated was one of the most turbulent in stock market history, what with the oil embargo of 1973, a recession second in magnitude only to the deep depression of the thirties, quadrupling of per barrel oil prices, and unusually high inflation. Stock picking is picked up by the concept of alpha.

$$\text{Alpha} = \text{gain from picking stocks}$$

$$= \text{fund risk premium} - \text{benchmark portfolio's risk premium}$$

$$= (r - r_f) - \beta(r_m - r_f)$$

$$= (4.66 \text{ percent} - 5.98 \text{ percent}) - 1.05(4.81 \text{ percent} - 5.98 \text{ percent})$$

$$= -1.32 \text{ percent} - 1.05(-1.17 \text{ percent})$$

$$= -1.32 \text{ percent} + 1.23 \text{ percent}$$

$$= -0.09 \text{ percent}$$

A small loss in the portfolio return arose from the manager's ability to pick stocks. Even this small loss, however, indicates that the risk of the fund portfolio is greater than the risk of the Standard and Poor 500. If it were not, the alpha would be zero because there is no stock picking in the benchmark portfolio is greater than the risk of the Standard and Poor's 500. If it were not, the alpha would be zero because there is no stock picking in the benchmark portfolio. To illustrate this, construct a second benchmark portfolio which has both the same risk as the market portfolio and some unique risk. By taking the ratio of the standard deviation of the portfolio to the standard deviation of the market portfolio, and then multiplying by the market risk premium, a benchmark portfolio, which has the same riskiness as the market and some unique risk too, is constructed. Armed with that information we can obtain the clues we need to tell us about the manager's skills in picking stocks. Set it up this way.

$$\text{Net gain from picking stocks} = \text{fund risk premium} - \text{risk premium on second benchmark portfolio}$$

$$= (r - r_f) - \sigma/\sigma_m(r_m - r_f)$$

$$= (4.66 \text{ percent} - 5.98 \text{ percent}) - [20.88/19.44 \\ (4.81 \text{ percent} - 5.98 \text{ percent})]$$

$$= -1.32 \text{ percent} - 1.07(-1.17 \text{ percent})$$

$$= -1.32 \text{ percent} + 1.25$$

$$= -0.07 \text{ percent}$$

By constructing the portfolio she did, the portfolio manager actually lost a small fraction of a return from picking stocks. Notwithstanding, the larger issue, unaddressed here, is whether she should have been in stocks at all. If she had no choice, as so many equity portfolio managers do not, she did well. If she had a choice, she was either unlucky or unskillful at picking the times to be in stocks and the times to be in Treasury bills. As a matter of fact, managing pension funds is far more complex than this little example demonstrates. Nonetheless, our financial manager is now equipped with some insights regarding the manager's abilities during this period. Whether they will persist remains to be seen, and continues to be one of her many responsibilities. Let's see how this analysis works out in the next problem.

Problem 3

Recognizing that the period of analysis is short, what analysis should be made of What-Not, Inc.'s pension fund portfolio manager during the last 4 years for which there are data?

Solution

The setup is the same as it is in problem 2. The average return on the Standard and Poor's 500 was 15.125 percent; the average return on the pension fund was 14.475 percent; the average return on Treasury bills was 5.85 percent; and the standard deviations of the index and the fund were 19.54 and 25.10 percent. During this period the fund's beta was 1.28. The calculations are as follows.

1. Fund risk premium = 14.475 percent − 5.85 percent = 8.625 percent
2. Benchmark portfolio's risk premium = 1.28 × (15.125 percent − 5.85 percent) = 11.872 percent
3. Alpha = 8.625 percent − 11.872 percent = −3.247 percent
4. Net gain from picking stocks = 8.625 percent − (25.10/19.54)(9.275 percent) = −3.29 percent

During this time period the portfolio manager was not particularly skillful at picking stocks. Indeed, she penalized the portfolio because of her stock selection activities, because the actual return is substantially below the "dummy," or benchmark, portfolio. In her defense, however, we hasten to add that the results are just barely significant.

Summary

Pensions are growing rapidly and thus are becoming important liabilities of corporations, both profit and nonprofit ones. Current and past pension liabilities may or may not be fully funded. Financial managers must make provisions for full payment of pension claims. Usually, this is accomplished by setting up an investment fund into which funds are placed each year. Gauging the performance of pension funds is important for financial managers, because the better the performance the less the corporation has to pay into the fund, and vice versa, of course.

List of Terms

Accrued benefit cost method	Normal cost
Alpha	Pension Benefit Guarantee
Benefit security ratio	Corporation
Defined benefit plan	Risk premium
Dollar-weighted rate	Supplemental liability
of return	Time-weighted rate
Employee Retirement Income	of return
Security Act	Unmanaged portfolio
Experience losses	Vesting

Exercises

Fill-in Questions

1. The federal legislation which governs pension funds is called

   _____.

2. A retirement plan which offers employees a firm promise of so many dollars a month from age 65 or a specified proportion of their final salary is called a _____.

3. The two plans most commonly employed to determine the amount of pension benefits are _____ and _____. The _____ plan pays a pension equal to a specified percentage of the employees' compensation in each year that they were members of the plan, whereas the _____ plan bases its pension payments on the average of the last given set years of service. The _____ pension compensation scheme is a better hedge against inflation than the _____ compensation scheme.

4. The _____ part of the retirement plan entitles members to part or all of their pension benefits, no matter what.

5. The two principal liabilities of a pension plan arise from _____ and _____ services, and are expected to be covered from _____ and _____.

6. The greater the rate of return on the pension fund, the (greater, less) _____ future contributions will be, and the (greater, less) _____ will be reported earnings.

7. If the benefit security ratio is 0.8, the present value of unfunded accrued benefits is _____ for every dollar of present value accrued benefits.

8. The stream of contributions to cover pension costs is called

   _____.

9. Pension fund losses resulting from a difference between expectations and experience are called _____, whereas losses in the present value of a pension fund arising from such items as increased pension benefits are called _____.

10. The internal rate of return, when applied to measuring pension fund performance, is called the _____ rate of return, although the _____ rate of return is preferred to it because it gives _____ to each unit of _____.

11. The premium that a pension fund receives for assuming risk is equal to the difference between the fund's return and the _____.

12. Positive risk premiums result because of either _____ equity markets or _____ stock selection.

13. The risk premium on a pension fund may be broken down into two components: _____ and _____.

14. If the risk premium on the market portfolio is 10 percent and the beta of an unmanaged portfolio is 1.2, the benchmark portfolio's risk premium is _____.

15. The gain from stock selection is called _____ and is measured as the difference between _____ and _____.

16. If you desire a portfolio beta of 0.93, you may achieve this goal by placing _____ percent of your money in the market portfolio and the remainder in _____.

Problems

1. The present value of Book Ends, Inc.'s pension fund is $32.5 million; the present value of expected future service costs is $64.0 million; the present value of contributions for future services is estimated at $59.8 million; and the present value of expected benefits from past service is $42.2 million. Estimate the deficit of pension plan assets. What sums of money should the financial manager allocate annually, if she wishes to amortize the deficit over the next 10 years? 15 years? 20 years? Assume that the financial manager expects to obtain an 11 percent compound annual rate of return on all invested funds.

2. The financial manager of Book Ends, Inc., is also a trustee of the company's pension fund. She is attending the quarterly trustees' meeting at which, among other things, the investment counselor that runs the trusteed money, We, Can, Pickum & Co., Inc., is presenting its yearly review of pension fund performance. She is presented with the information found at the top of the next page, and immediately proceeds to analyze it (using her hand-held calculator, of course). What quantitative measures should she use as a first pass at the data? Show all calculations.

3. How did the firm of We, Can, Pickum & Co., Inc., perform during the first 5 years for which there are data? During the last 6 years? Assume the Treasury bill rate for the past 6 years averaged 7.0 percent a year and that for the first 5 years it was 5.77 percent.

	Returns, %	
	Book Ends, Inc.'s pension fund	Standard and Poor's 500
1969	−8.8	−8.5
1970	5.2	.4.0
1971	15.4	14.3
1972	18.9	19.0
1973	−12.2	−14.7
1974	−27.7	−26.5
1975	35.3	37.3
1976	26.6	24.0
1977	−14.0	−7.2
1978	7.3	6.4
1979	2.3	0.3

Average Treasury bill rate, 1969–1979: 6.44%

Essay Questions

1. Why is the study of pension funds important to financial managers?
2. What are the sources for pension liabilities, how are these liabilities financed, and how might they affect the company's income statement? The value of the firm? To what extent should the financial manager worry about these factors? Why?
3. What are the implications of poor investment performance of a pension fund for a company's pension liabilities?
4. If the actuary does not allow for wage inflation in calculations of required contributions to a pension fund, and subsequent labor negotiations insist on wage adjustments, how might the firm's financial plans be affected?
5. The typical pension fund is sponsored by a corporation. Organizationally, a set of trustees is appointed to administer the trust established by the plan sponsor, the corporation. Under the 1974 Employee Retirement Income Security Act (ERISA), the trustees are charged with the responsibility to act as a prudent investor would act under similar circumstances. If the financial manager is one of the trustees, as they invariably are, what does this say about the knowledgeability and information set that a financial manager must now acquire?
6. What does a financial manager need to know about pension fund performance and its implications for efficient financial management of a firm?
7. Why is the internal rate of return inappropriate for measuring pension fund performance? Is your answer in any way similar to the inappropriateness of using yield maturity to evaluate a bond?
8. Outline the steps financial managers should take to evaluate the performance of their company-sponsored pension funds. Indicate why you chose the steps you did.

9. "Any dummy can obtain the rate of return on the market portfolio. In order to induce me to hire a professional money manager to oversee my pension fund, he must demonstrate his ability to achieve rates of return in excess of that of the market rate of return." This statement was made at a recent board of directors meeting of What-Not, Inc. How would you respond to this financial manager's comment? Explain fully.

Answers to Exercises

Fill-in Questions

1. 1974 Employee Retirement Income Security Act (ERISA)
2. defined benefit plan
3. career-average; final-average; career-average; final-average; final-average; career-average
4. vested
5. past; future; the present value of the pension fund; the present value of future contributions
6. greater; less; greater
7. 20 cents
8. normal costs
9. experience losses; supplemental liability
10. dollar-weighted; time-weighted; equal weight; time
11. risk-free interest rate
12. rising; successful
13. premium on an unmanaged fund; reward for stock selection
14. 12 percent
15. alpha; fund risk premium; the benchmark portfolio's risk premium
16. 93; Treasury bills

Problems

1. Deficit: $13.9 million; 10 years: $2,360,240; 15 years: $1,933,007; 20 years: $1,745,501

2.

	Pension fund	Standard and Poor's 500
Average return, %	4.39	4.40
Standard deviation of return, %	19.00	18.49
Beta	1.02	1.00
Correlation with market	0.99	1.00

Fund risk premium: −2.05%
Benchmark portfolio risk premium: −2.08%
Alpha: 0.0308%
Net gain from picking stocks: 0.0463%

3.

	Pension fund	Standard and Poor's 500
First 5 years:		
Average return, %	3.70	2.82
Standard deviation of return, %	13.96	14.41
Beta	1.02	1.00
Correlation with market	0.98	1.00
Last 6 years:		
Average return, %	4.97	5.72
Standard deviation of return, %	23.78	22.66
Beta	1.04	1.00
Correlation with market	0.99	1.00

	First 5 years	Last 6 years
Fund risk premium, %	−2.07	−2.03
Benchmark portfolio's risk premium, %	−3.0090	−1.3312
Alpha, %	0.9390	−0.6988
Net gain from picking stocks, %	0.7879	−0.6867

33 *Conclusion: What we do and do not know about finance*

Introduction

So, here we are at the end of what must have seemed a long journey. You have traversed the entire landscape of financial decision making within corporations. It is now time to bring together the bits and pieces so as to determine how financial managers should behave. In order to do that, we must isolate the set of things that we know for certain and some of the important things that are still up in the air.

What to Look For in Chapter 33

What can one say that is intelligent when one has traversed over 700 pages of text? One can say several things, that's what. Most of all, what you must ask yourself, and should have been asking yourself all along is: How does a financial manager make rational decisions in light of what we know and, more importantly in some respects, in light of what we do not know? This chapter summarizes the blood and guts issues confronting all financial managers, regardless of the size of their firms.

What We Know   Here is the shopping list of things we know:

1. Net present value is the only proper way by which to evaluate assets.
2. We know that an asset's risk is composed of a market-related component and one indigenous to the firm.
3. We know that firm-related risk may be diversified; so we may conclude that only market-related risk counts when making financial decisions.
4. Following therefrom, we know that mergers and acquisitions do not add value unless the combined firm produces greater cash flows than either firm produced when they were independent of each other.
5. We know that security prices react quickly to almost all available information (reflecting fully what is known), and hence present prices are the best estimate of true value.
6. Financial managers, therefore, should make their decisions on the assumption that capital markets are efficient.
7. We know that the discount rate used to evaluate investment projects is an opportunity cost, a rate of return, and is measured by returns on investments of comparable risk.
8. We know that the assets of comparable risk are found in security markets.
9. We know that the risk of comparable assets is measured by beta, which captures the nondiversifiable risk facing investors.
10. We know option theory will loom large in financial decision making, because all decisions represents options—claims—on some specific event, a series of cash flows or an option to default on the debt, for example.

11. Because of the value-additivity principle, we know that the particular way in which the income of a firm is split between its creditors and owners does not influence the total value of the firm, and Modigliani and Miller, bless their souls, continue to hold forth.

Is It All Peaches and Cream?   The above litany of things we know gives the illusion that financial decision making is an open-and-shut case. You should have a healthy skepticism for such a simplistic view of the finance world. This list of things we do not know is, and always will be, far larger than the list of things we do know. (Quick, which Brealey and Myers' law is that?) And if that were not enough, we will learn new and better ways to cope with what we already know, the capital asset pricing model being a case in point.

What We Do Not Know   "Well then," you are probably saying, "what are the things we do not know, or about which we have some serious questions." Here we go:

1. We know that financial managers make financial decisions, but we do not know precisely how they make them. We know how they should make them; but the process they actually use eludes us, especially when it comes to strategic financial planning.
2. We know that net present value is the only proper way to evaluate investment opportunities, but we do not have many insights about how to discover investments that add more value to the firm than they take away.
3. We know that the expected return on comparable-risk assets should be used to evaluate investment opportunities, but we do not know how to estimate, with the degree of assurance we would like, the beta of a firm's investments opportunity set.
4. We can all fall in love with the capital asset pricing model, at least at first blush. But such amorous feelings may well wane after we find out that it is hard to prove or disprove; that statistical tests may be flawed; that results do not seem to square with the model; that, heaven forbid, investors seem to be concerned with diversifiable risk; and that not all investors have the same outlook for their financial rewards.
5. The evidence is fairly convincing that the markets for financial assets, at the minimum, are fairly efficient, but a disquieting tad of evidence has emerged in recent years that suggests that they may not be nearly as efficient as we once thought.
6. We know that option pricing theory tells us a great deal about options traded in financial markets, but that it is only a glimmer in every financial theorist's eye when placed in the complex context of financing business enterprises.
7. We know that financial managers prefer not to use rights issues, even though the evidence says that they are cheaper than other methods. Do they know something we don't? And why are they not telling us about it!
8. We cannot say for certain whether capital structure decisions are important. We constantly observe different capital structures for firms of the same risk

321

CONCLUSION:
WHAT WE DO
AND DO NOT
KNOW ABOUT
FINANCE

class. Are financial managers telling (signaling a candidate for being the buzzword of the day, much as a beta is) us something we should know?

9. And dividend policy controversies are likely to go on and on. We know the theory says that dividend policy does not count, for the value of the firm is unaffected by them. Yet so many different dividend policies exist, policies inexplicable by taxes and such, that we must ponder this knotty problem even more than before.

10. And what of liquidity? We do not have too many intelligent things to say about working capital management because we do not have a complete and rigorous theory of liquidity as applied to financial managers of business firms.

11. Even mergers are not explicable by what we know. The value-additivity principle tells us that no new values are created from mergers unless the cash flows of the combined firms exceed the sum of the cash flows of the two firms when viewed separately. Why then are there so many mergers?

Summary

"Yikes," you may say, "that's really discouraging. I wish I had read this chapter first. It would have saved me tons of time studying all the other stuff that preceded it." Take heart, have faith, be stout, and forge ahead, knowing that to chronicle the problem areas confronting financial managers is merely to recognize that no field of study has all the answers, not even finance. Use what we know as an engine for discovery. Know also that so much of our theory, as neat as it is, translates into the art of financial management. Most of all, this is not the end of your studies; it is merely the beginning of your understanding of the world of corporate finance. Such is the nature of education. Such is life. One would be surprised were it otherwise.